D1170821

SINCE RECORDS BEGAN

EMI

The first 100 years

SINCE RECORDS BEGAN

EMI

The first 100 years

PETER MARTLAND

CONSULTANT EDITOR: RUTH EDGE

Amadeus Press • Portland, Oregon

Unless specifically credited, all photographs and
illustrations have been drawn from the EMI Archives.
The author would like to thank all those anonymous
photographers whose work has brought so
much life to this book.

Front cover microphones (left to right):
Blumlein 1993 stereo (binaural) model;
Neumann M50, 1951; Neumann TLM 50, 1991.

First published in Great Britain 1997

© EMI Group plc 1997

A CIP record for this book is available
from the Library of Congress.

ISBN 1-57467-033-6

Printed in Hong Kong

First published in North America
in 1997 by Amadeus Press
(an imprint of Timber Press, Inc.)
The Haseltine Building
133 S.W. Second Avenue, Suite 450
Portland, Oregon 97204, U.S.A.

Contents

PREFACE AND ACKNOWLEDGEMENTS

Writing this history has been a truly monumental task. The complex and at times confusing nature of the business proved a major problem. However, focusing on the British company and dividing the work both chronologically and according to subject matter have mitigated many of these difficulties. I have divided the book into three main chronological blocks, each of which consists of three chapters. The first starts with the birth of the recording industry and ends with the formation of Electric and Musical Industries (EMI). Chapter 1 covers the earliest years, whilst Chapters 2 and 3 are devoted to the respective histories of the Columbia Graphophone and Gramophone Companies and their artists. The second begins with the rigours of the Great Depression and ends with the start of the Beatles era. Chapter 4 covers the corporate history of EMI during these years, Chapter 5 is concerned with the Company's classical music recordings, whilst Chapter 6 is devoted to EMI's popular music recordings. The final block charts the emergence of EMI as a world leader in popular music recording, to match its pre-eminence in the classical field, and ends with the celebration of its centenary. Chapter 7 is concerned with the corporate history of the business, whilst Chapters 8 and 9 cover the classical and popular recording programmes respectively.

This book is not meant to be exhaustive: with more than eight million documents and over three quarters of a million recordings in EMI's Archive, that would have been an impossible task. Instead my purpose has been to highlight the important events, both corporate and creative, which have defined EMI's history. I hope that this book will add to the pleasure recorded music provides, and that it will stand as both a testament to the past and a beacon for the future of a great British company and its employees and artists past and present.

Many people at EMI helped to make this book. It would be impossible to list them all by name, but special thanks are due to Ruth Edge at the EMI Archive and Tony Locantro of EMI Classics for their many contributions to the text and their enthusiasm for the project; to David Hughes for commissioning the work; and to Claire Enders for acting as editor and constructive critic. Let me also acknowledge the invaluable assistance of Richard Abram of EMI Records, Mike Allen (now retired from EMI Music), Suzanne Lewis and Janet Lord of the EMI Music Archive, and Ken Townsend MBE, formerly head of Abbey Road Studios.

Thanks must also go to Anthony Pollard of *Gramophone* magazine, and Samuel S. Brylawski of the Library of Congress in Washington, D.C., who was instrumental in providing research materials on the birth of the record industry and early recording technology. I have also benefited greatly from the guidance of academic colleagues at Cambridge University and elsewhere, including Peter Adamson, Professor Christopher Andrew, Liam Denning, Professor Charlotte Erickson, Dr Nicholas Hiley, Dr Nigel Howarth, Tom Stephenson, Professor Barry Supple, Dr Jay Winter and Dr Patrick Zutshi. I am deeply indebted to Nick Goodfellow and Barney Southin for their research, particularly into the arcane world of popular music, and for their contributions to the text. Hundreds of Cambridge students past and present have participated in some way in the writing of this book; they have done more than they will ever know to make it a better book. Finally, from B. T. Batsford Publishers I would like to thank Gerard McLaughlin and Victoria Harvey.

Dr Peter Martland

FOREWORD

If I had my time over again, I would wish it to be only with EMI.

Apart from war service in the RAF, I spent all my working life with this company and I am delighted that its fascinating story is finally told.

This is the history of a remarkable industry, from its beginnings in the 19th century to the challenges of the 21st. The Gramophone and Columbia Graphophone Companies which merged to form EMI in 1931 were responsible for many of the technical and creative breakthroughs which carried the industry through its difficult early years.

It is a history of highs and lows. Many of the highs were creative ones. Fred Gaisberg, the company's first A & R (Artist & Repertoire) manager, signed Enrico Caruso in Italy and made the art of recording respectable. Caruso was followed by many other operatic legends. Gaisberg went on to become one of the pillars of the Company, and following his retirement in 1939 remained a consultant until his death ten years later.

The Depression of the Thirties marked the lowest of the lows, but the Company survived this period because it kept faith with the power of music. During the Second World War, EMI made a significant contribution through its pioneering work on radar and by turning its factories to munitions. Throughout these difficult times, the Company was able to release music which lightened the gloom and which, even today, evokes Britain's darkest days.

In the mid-1950s EMI suffered a major blow, the loss of its licensing arrangements with the American companies RCA Victor and American Columbia. In anticipation of that loss, the company acquired Capitol Records in the United States, and with it the rights to many historic recordings. It also formed an in-house team of producers who found and recorded the emerging pop talent in the Sixties, and the many innovative recordings of that period are still selling today.

As this book demonstrates, EMI has continued to build on its past successes, coping with an ever increasing demand from the customer and taking full advantage of the changes from the vinyl to compact disc.

The record industry today seems more complicated and faster moving than ever. But it is no less exciting or enjoyable. EMI continues to play a leading part worldwide – it is and always will be a great company.

L. G. Wood CBE
(Managing Director, EMI Records 1959–1966)

Introduction

If I had not become an EMI artist I probably would never have been an artist at all. My first experience of a record company was with Decca, who turned me down, as they did more famously later the Beatles. I am, therefore, immensely grateful for EMI's support over all these years and proud to still be with them during their centenary.

I feel I have worked for EMI all my life. Before my recording days, my first job was at Atlas Lamps, later part of Thorn. You can imagine how strange it felt when Thorn and EMI combined forces in 1979.

If I were to choose one person who contributed most during my years at EMI it would have to be the Columbia A & R manager, Norrie Paramor. Norrie was my first real contact with any record company. He took me under his wing to a point where he would be at a TV show ensuring the arrangements were correct; he would conduct the orchestra if I did a cabaret date; and he was always on the lookout for good songs. Norrie gave me 15 years of almost uninterrupted Top 20 hits and I will be forever grateful to him.

'Move it' was written on the bus on our way to an audition with Norrie which my agent, George Ganjou, had arranged. We got to the offices in Great Castle Street and just plugged our 16 watt

Selmer amp into the wall of his office and played it. The next thing I knew we were recording it on real tape at Abbey Road's Number Two Studio.

By one of life's coincidences, Norrie's assistant in those days, the young man who noted our comments on the songs that were being suggested for us to record, was Tim Rice. Over 35 years later, it was Tim Rice who took my ideas for a musical based on *Wuthering Heights* and helped make them a reality.

Over the years EMI and I have had a pretty damn good time of it really. I'm still the most 'known unknown' artist in America, but I have never seriously thought of taking my recording career anywhere else.

Sir Cliff Richard

Emile Berliner and Charles Sumner Tainter, Washington, D.C., 1919
Emile Berliner, who invented the gramophone and became a founder of The Gramophone Company, with
Charles Sumner Tainter, the inventor of the graphophone and a founder of the ventures that became The
Columbia Graphophone Company. (Picture courtesy of the Smithsonian Institution, Washington, D.C.)

CHAPTER I

A Hot Time in the Old Town

Graphophones and Gramophones

INVENTING AN INDUSTRY, 1881–1897

Prominent singers, speakers, or performers, may derive an income from royalties on the sale of their phonautograms and valuable plates may be printed and registered to protect against unauthorised publication. Collections of phonautograms may become very valuable and whole evenings will be spent at home going through a long list of interesting performances. [Emile Berliner, inventor of the gramophone, 1888]

Graphophones and Gramophones

INVENTING AN INDUSTRY, 1881–1897

EMILE BERLINER
(1851–1929)
★

Emile Berliner was born in Hannover, Germany, but emigrated to the United States in 1870. In 1878 his improvements to microphone technology were sold to Bell Telephone, and in 1884 Berliner turned his attention to problems relating to sound recording. His disc record and gramophone were demonstrated in 1888 at the Franklin Institute. Berliner's vision of spreading art and culture through the gramophone spurred him to develop his invention and train many of the first generation of recording and production engineers, and several of the industry's business leaders. Berliner was responsible for establishing the disc record business in the United States and Canada and, in 1897, he sent William Barry Owen to London to establish a European gramophone trade. However, the business problems he faced in the United States revealed Berliner as an inventor first and a businessman second; subsequent release from the business side allowed him to return to his creative skills. Whilst always active in the field he had created, Berliner developed other wide-ranging interests in aeronautics and acoustic tiles, among other things. For his achievements in the field of recording, the Franklin Institute awarded Berliner the prestigious John Scott and Elliott Cresson medals. Berliner also devoted his life to the promotion of child health and the eradication of preventable diseases. For instance, his Society for the Prevention of Sickness helped educate the public about the dangers of unpasteurised milk. When asked about his success, he replied, "the key to victory is never-ending application". This is evident in Roger Burlingame's assertion that, by his tireless efforts, Berliner was able "to lift himself into recognition as one of the foremost inventors of his time".

The inventor Emile Berliner in his laboratory during the 1920s.

Today, EMI is one of the world's largest record companies, with important catalogues of records catering for tastes as diverse as medieval music and the latest pop. Its origins go back through The Gramophone Company Ltd and The Columbia Graphophone Company Ltd – both of which were formed in 1897 and which merged in 1931 to form Electric and Musical Industries Ltd (EMI) – to the inventors of sound recording and to the very beginnings of the record industry in the United States. This remarkable genealogy gives EMI an extraordinary continuity among modern record companies, linking it directly to the 19th-century American founders of the record industry, and specifically with the work of the gramophone's inventor, Emile Berliner (see box), and the inventors of the graphophone, Alexander Graham Bell, Chichester A. Bell and Charles Sumner Tainter (see box, page 13).

Rocked in the Cradle of the Deep
THE INVENTION OF SOUND RECORDING

Emile Berliner invented the first commercial process of sound recording, although he was by no means the first in the field. Nor did the invention of sound recording take place in a scientific vacuum. By the middle of the 19th century, important scientific discoveries concerning the nature and properties of sound, by Lord

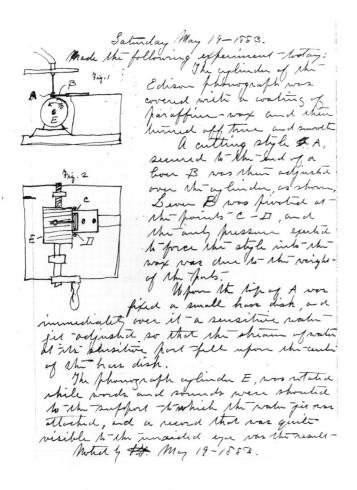

Saturday May 19—1883.

(handwritten notebook page)

CHARLES SUMNER TAINTER (1854–1940)

★

A precision engineer, Tainter worked with Alexander Graham Bell in 1879 to develop the radiophone, an instrument for transmitting sound waves using light-sensitive selenium cells. The following year, he became one of the three Volta Associates. Over the next five years, the three pursued many avenues of research, with Tainter concentrating on the development of sound recording, which he believed would prove to be "something that would pay". Recognizing the deficiencies of Edison's tin-foil phonograph, he redesigned it, creating a new form of talking machine: the graphophone. Reviewed in *Harper's Weekly* in July 1886, the instrument was called "a marvel of perfection in accuracy of the movements of all its parts". Tainter was also responsible for developing a means of creating a permanent sound record by cutting a signal into a wax-coated paper cylinder. This patent was so important that, during its lifetime, it became the focus of much litigation. In 1886, the six Bell and Tainter patents were sold for $200,000. Tainter later formed his own laboratory in Washington, D.C.

He was a man of ideas, as is revealed by the detailed notebooks he kept until his death in 1940. Fred Gaisberg, who was an early Tainter pupil, described him in his memoirs as "a scientist as well as a mechanical genius".

Above Extract from Charles Sumner Tainter's 1883 Volta Laboratory "Home" notebook, describing sound recording experiments using paraffin wax as a recording medium.

Léon Scott's phonautograph

RECORDING WITHOUT MICROPHONES, 1885–1925

★

Until the arrival of a reliable system of electrical recording in the 1920s, records were made simply by reversing the mechanical process of an old-fashioned horn gramophone. The sound vibrations in the air were collected and "funnelled" via a conical horn on to a diaphragm. This activated the recording stylus to produce a direct analogue of the sound in the wavy groove of a revolving disc or cylinder. The earliest gramophone recording-machines were hand-powered but, by 1898, electric power was used and, later, a more reliable falling-weight mechanism.

Because of the low sensitivity of the diaphragm and directionality of the horn, it was a real challenge to ensure that a solo singer or instrumentalist could be heard clearly, at the same time as the accompaniment, without overloading the recording. This required great skill and, sometimes, considerable tact if a diva more used to projecting into a vast expanse of opera house required a strict instruction to stand back or turn aside at a loud high note. Nevertheless, many early vocal recordings show quite clearly the experience and taste of the singers in adjusting their position and vocal production to the requirements in hand: there still exists a test recording of Melba where she repeats the same snatch of song at several different distances from the recording horn.

In the case of larger ensembles, such as orchestras, the players were positioned carefully to balance the tonal and directional characteristics of the instruments. In practice, this meant crowding everyone as close as possible to the recording horn – except for the loud brass, which were relegated to the back of the group. Early photographs show players uncomfortably piled together in a hot and noisy encounter, with some perched on wooden stands and the conductor tucked in next to the recording horn. These pictures also confirm what is plainly audible on the recordings themselves: an orchestra drastically cut in size, with lower strings often reinforced or even replaced by cruder but more effective bassoons and tubas, and violins frequently

transmogrified into strange devices with tiny horns instead of proper bodies – these "Stroh fiddles" were heavier and scrawnier-sounding, but at least they were *loud*.

After some strange-sounding experiments in late 1900, "orchestral" accompaniments to Gramophone Company artists were replaced for several years by the less ambitious, but more effective, piano. But even that caused problems. The recorded bass was limited by the length of the horn and the overall range by mechanical resonances of horn and diaphragm. Early pictures show recording-horns wrapped with tape to give support and reduce resonances. There was rapid progress in the art of selecting the right horn for different recording purposes: horns were made longer or narrower; some were square, or of wood instead of metal; sometimes, multiple horns were used. In practice, the overall tonal balance was organised to favour the human voice, so it is sometimes claimed that the frequency range was very precisely narrow (such as "198-2000 Hertz"), and that double basses and bass drums (for instance) never entered the recording studio. But several recordings belie this: Toscanini's

1920 Victor recording of Berlioz' "Rákóczy March" (HMV 3-0648) has a clear bass drum at 50 Hertz; Holst's own recording of his *St Paul's Suite* (Columbia L 1648-9) manages beautifully with string basses; and cymbals, sibilants and really high violin notes do get through occasionally. In fact, musical instruments recorded mechanically up to 1925 were actually much more varied than is generally supposed, and included such Western *esoterica* as the harpsichord and viola d'amore, the *kantele* and the Bronze Age *lur*, as well as a fair representation of Middle and Far Eastern instruments. Only the genuine church organ did not have a chance – it was replaced by a "grand" chamber organ (or worse).

Occasionally, the recording of a relatively large body of performers was attempted: a good example is the "Hallelujah Chorus" from Handel's *Messiah* (G & T 04761), proudly presented by "60 selected voices from the Leeds Festival Choir 1907". This record, while giving a good impression of a large choir set well back, does suffer from a distant and muffled sound because of room reverberation and the directional recording horn.

Harry Lauder recording at The Gramophone Company's City Road recording studio in 1905. Note the presence of Stroh violins and the music stands suspended from the ceiling.

Rayleigh in Britain and Hermann Helmholtz in Germany, were already being put to practical use to solve problems of communication by means of electricity. The invention of sound recording was an unexpected by-product of this research.

The phonautograph, a device that made sound waves visible, was one of sound recording's most important precursors. Invented in 1857 by the Frenchman Léon Scott, the apparatus consisted of a sheet of paper blackened with soot and mounted on a revolving drum. A pig's bristle stylus, connected to a diaphragm and a cone-shaped funnel, touched the paper. When the drum revolved, the stylus traced a straight line. However, speaking into the funnel made the diaphragm vibrate, causing the stylus to trace the voice's sound waves in the form of a zigzag pattern. At the time, the device was seen as an interesting novelty of little practical value. Its limitations were obvious: although the sound waves could be seen they could not be reproduced. Nonetheless, the phonautograph embodied many basic principles of sound recording, and in spite of its limitations, inventors and innovators engaged in developing the art of sound recording repeatedly returned to Scott's phonautograph as a model for their own work. Furthermore, until 1925, Scott's concept of focusing sounds on to a diaphragm by means of a cone-shaped funnel was a crucial part of the record-making process (see *Recording without microphones, 1885–1925*, page 14).

An important contributor to the invention of sound recording was another Frenchman, Charles Cros. In 1877 Cros wrote a paper in which he described how disc records could be made utilizing Scott's idea of tracing sound waves laterally. By using existing photo-engraving technology, he argued, it would be possible to create a sound record which could be played back. Although Cros failed to test this, Emile Berliner, who eventually created a working system incorporating some of Cros' ideas, always acknowledged the Frenchman's precedence.

The breakthrough came in the same year, when the great American inventor Thomas Alva Edison conceived the idea of a machine capable of storing and reproducing sound as a spin-off from experiments he was conducting into the possibilities of long-distance telephone communications. This – a mechanism he called the Phonograph, or Speaking Machine – became his most original invention. Edison incorporated into his phonograph many of the features of Scott's phonautograph; for soot-covered paper he substituted tinfoil as the recording medium; as a stylus, he used a steel point capable of impressing a sound signal into the tinfoil. Edison's 1878 phonograph patents were so original that they came to form the basis of sound recording. Although this first phonograph was little more than a crude laboratory

Thomas Alva Edison (1847–1931)
This 1889 portrait by Abraham Archibald Anderson shows Edison with his improved phonograph (National Portrait Gallery, Washington, D.C.)

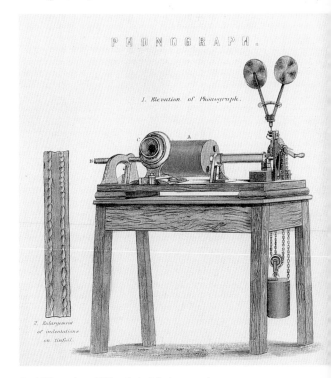

An 1878 version of Edison's tin-foil phonograph fitted with a gravity motor, together with a magnified illustration of the sound track from a tin-foil recording.

instrument, it caused a sensation. Some years later, Edison said of this phonograph:

No-one but an expert could get anything back from it; the record made by the little steel point upon a sheet of tinfoil lasted only a few times after it had been put through the phonograph. [*New York World*, 6 November 1887]

Curiously, after the early excitement had died down, Edison failed to develop this remarkable invention, and, after a year or so, he abandoned phonograph research altogether. As a direct result, others entered the field, and it was the fruits of their research, rather than of Edison's, that created the first commercial sound-recording technology. In the mid-1880s, spurred by such competition, Edison returned to sound recording and became a major force in the development of recording technology and in the creation of the record industry on both sides of the Atlantic.

The Laughing Song

ALEXANDER GRAHAM BELL AND THE GRAPHOPHONE

The first substantive thread linking the invention of sound recording to EMI can be traced to Edison's great rival, Alexander Graham Bell, the inventor of the telephone. Bell's interest in the science of sound derived from his work as a teacher of the deaf. However, his introduction to sound recording was not the happiest. In early 1878, on learning of Edison's invention, an angry and frustrated Bell wrote to his father-in-law:

It is a most astonishing thing to me to have let this invention slip through my fingers when I consider how my thoughts have been directed to this subject for many years. [Alexander Graham Bell to Gardner Hubbard, 18 March 1878. Bell Papers, Library of Congress, Washington, D.C.]

Graphophone 1888

In 1880, the year after Thomas Edison gave up his research into sound recording, Alexander Graham Bell created the Volta Laboratory in Washington, D.C. as a research facility to develop a range of ideas relating to the science of sound.

The graphophone was originally conceived as an office dictation machine and operated by treadle-power.

Between 1881 and 1885, Bell and two partners (known as Associates) – Chichester A. Bell, a British chemist who was Alexander's cousin, and Charles Sumner Tainter, a precision engineer – undertook important scientific research into the problems of sound recording. The Associates' research led to many far-sighted experiments using a range of different recording formats, including photo-engraved discs and magnetic tape. However, technical limitations forced them to abandon what subsequently became highly successful sound-carrying formats: the disc record, the tape recorder and the optical film soundtrack. By 1885, the Volta Associates had developed a range of innovations that transformed Edison's 1877 tinfoil experimental phonograph into a potentially commercial proposition.

Tainter's crucial innovation was the invention of a means of making permanent sound records. Reflecting on his search for material capable of forming a permanent record, Tainter later wrote: "In looking for a softer and more easily engraved material in which to form the record, it occurred to me to try beeswax." [Tainter, The Talking Machine, Some Little Known Facts, unpublished MS, Tainter Papers. Archives Center, Smithsonian Institution, Washington, D.C.]. To obtain a permanent record, he cut a sound signal into a paper cylinder coated with this uniquely pliable material. To reproduce it the Associates designed a mechanism they called the "graphophone". With these and other innovations, the Volta Associates created the modern art of record-making, and thus laid the technical foundations of the

Edward D. Easton (1856–1915)
The founder and president of The Columbia Phonograph Company General and The American Graphophone Company. A recording industry pioneer and entrepreneur, he had the acumen to realize the commercial potential of sound recording as a means of home entertainment.

record industry for the next 100 years.

In 1887, the six master Bell-Tainter patents were sold to the American Graphophone Company, a company formed to manufacture graphophones; the following year, commercial exploitation of the graphophone began. The head of American Graphophone was Edward D. Easton, a former Congressional and court stenographer. He thought the graphophone's potential was as a piece of office dictating equipment; the machine would take its place in the business revolution that had already made the telegraph, telephone, typewriter and ticker-tape machine standard equipment in the modern American office. In 1889, Easton and American Graphophone created The Columbia Phonograph Company as a selling agent in the Washington, D.C. area. From these small beginnings, The Columbia Graphophone Company Ltd, the British record company that merged in 1931 with The Gramophone Company to form EMI, traces its origins.

In 1889, because of the vast expense involved, neither American Graphophone nor Thomas Edison were able to market their products in the United States. Instead, they sold their merchandising rights to Jesse Lippincott, a venture capitalist, who formed the North American Phonograph Company. North American did not market the graphophone or phonograph itself. Instead, it franchised leasing and later selling rights to local sales agencies. Although North American failed in 1893, it was of crucial importance, since it attracted into the infant industry several of the key businessmen, managers and sound engineers who later formed and developed The Gramophone and Columbia Graphophone Companies and subsequently EMI. It was by this means that Alfred Clark (see box, page 24), EMI's founding chairman, came into the business he was to dominate for 40 years.

During North American's time, the first commercially made music records were produced and the first record catalogues published. Many early records were made and sold by former North American local sales agencies – some of which outlasted the 1893 failure – for use as coin-in-the-slot bar-room entertainment. Others were sold to travelling showmen, who charged the public five cents each to listen to a record on machines equipped with multiple listening tubes. Fred Gaisberg (see box, page 21), a pioneering record-maker who became The Gramophone Company's most celebrated recording engineer, and later EMI's first artistic director, wrote of this new business:

It was ludicrous in the extreme to see ten people grouped about a phonograph, each with a tube leading from his ears, grinning and laughing at what he had heard. [F. W. Gaisberg, *Music on Record* (London 1946), p.11]

Record consumers in the early 1890s
During the early 1890s, cylinder records began to feature at fairs and travelling shows, and be exploited by travelling hucksters across the United States. Although a donkey was an unusual means of bringing sound recordings to rural America, years later The Gramophone Company employed the same method in Russia.

Left Duplicating cylinder records in the 1890s.

Until 1902, when a cheap moulding process for duplicating original cylinders was introduced, manufacturers were unable to develop a mass market for records. Nonetheless, throughout the 1890s, there developed a small but important market for cylinder records. The Columbia Phonograph Company, American Graphophone's selling agency and a survivor of the 1893 crash,

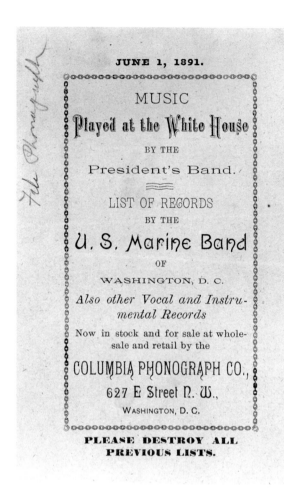

JUNE 1, 1891.

MUSIC
Played at the White House
BY THE

President's Band.

LIST OF RECORDS

BY THE

U. S. Marine Band
OF

WASHINGTON, D. C.

*Also other Vocal and Instru-
mental Records*

Now in stock and for sale at wholesale and retail by the

COLUMBIA PHONOGRAPH CO.,

627 E Street N. W.,

WASHINGTON, D. C.

**PLEASE DESTROY ALL
PREVIOUS LISTS.**

One of Columbia's earliest printed record
catalogues. In addition to recordings by singers,
comics, whistlers and others, it featured cornet
and banjo players and military bands. (Bell Papers,
Manuscript Division, Library of Congress,
Washington, D.C.)

was at this time one of the leading record companies.

The teenage Gaisberg received his first training as a recording engineer from Charles Sumner Tainter, the graphophone's inventor, and Thomas H. MacDonald, the engineer in charge of the American Graphophone factory at Bridgeport, Connecticut. Gaisberg recalled how – surrounded by three graphophones – he and John York Atlee (a recording artist described in early Columbia catalogues as the "Famous Artistic Whistler") spent their evenings turning out "countless records of performances of 'Whistling Coon', 'Mocking Bird' and 'The Laughing Song'". The inability to duplicate records and the limitations of recording technology imposed severe restrictions on the kind of recordings that could be made. Columbia's 1891 catalogue consisted of records by the U.S. Marine Band, the 3rd Artillery Band, U.S.A., the inevitable John York Atlee, cornet pieces and comic novelties, together with unidentified singers performing gems such as "You'll never miss your mother till she's gone", and "I had $15 in my inside pocket". In his unpublished memoirs, Alfred Clark described the problems experienced in those pioneering days of record-making:

The companies were unable to supply records at a popular price and at the same time by reasonably good artistes … Obviously artistes willing to accept such fees and put up with the tiresome experience of singing the same song over again, could hardly be classified as 'stars'. On the contrary, they were selected less for their artistic ability than for the strength of their voice, for the recording machines were not very sensitive and the best records were made by the singers who could make the most noise. [Alfred Clark, "His Master's Voice", unpublished MS, EMI Music Archive]

In 1895, Edward Easton reconstructed the American Graphophone Company from the wreckage of North American Phonograph. Subsequently, American Graphophone, jointly with the Columbia Phonograph Company, established the Columbia Phonograph Company General as a national and international selling agent. Furthermore, in 1896, Thomas H. MacDonald created a new graphophone in the form of a $10 machine, the Eagle, on which to play Columbia's new and much improved cylinder recordings. Armed with these new products, Columbia began to develop what to this day remains EMI's primary market – the home. In 1897, Columbia Phonograph Company General expanded its operations by opening its first European branch in Paris. (The fortunes of the Columbia Company's European venture are chronicled in Chapter 3.)

Columbia's Eagle graphophone

FREDERICK WILLIAM GAISBERG (1873–1951)

★

The legendary sound engineer and impresario Fred Gaisberg was born in Washington, D.C., the son of German immigrants. His association with the recording industry began in 1889, when he played piano accompaniment for cylinder records for The Columbia Phonograph Co. In 1894, he met Emile Berliner, and became "spell-bound by the beautiful tone of the flat gramophone disc". Gaisberg joined Berliner, who trained him in the art of disc record-making. In 1898, Gaisberg moved to London, where he established a recording studio to make the first European disc records. The following year, he went on the first of his many European tours, making records for the various distinctive local markets. As the Company's principal recording engineer, he then travelled further afield, capturing on record the music of artists in Russia, India and the Far East. However, Gaisberg's most important contribution to

The Gramophone Company's success came in 1902, when he recorded the Italian tenor Enrico Caruso in Milan. When Gaisberg made his first recording of Feodor Chaliapin, the great Russian bass, he began a life-long friendship which was

to see him help Chaliapin escape Russia following the Bolshevik revolution. In the decades after the first Caruso recordings, Gaisberg built up HMV's classical catalogue, signing and recording important international performers such as Beniamino Gigli, Nellie Melba, John McCormack and Fritz Kreisler. In the 1920s and 1930s, as artistic director, and especially after the introduction of electrical recording in 1925, he greatly expanded the range of music available. Gaisberg retired in 1939, allowing the men he had trained – Walter Legge and David Bicknell – to pick up the baton. He remained a consultant to EMI for the rest of his life, and continued to have an important influence on the recording industry as a whole. In particular, in the late 1940s, he argued in favour of the LP and stereophonic recording. He was highly respected in the industry, his natural sincerity, wisdom and shrewdness combining with candour and tact to solve problems in the studio and the committee room. David Bicknell said of him: "He was the master of his art, and he had a genius for the industry. He never missed out on a new artist."

Above Fred Gaisberg and William Sinkler Darby in Russia in 1899.
Below Fred Gaisberg with the Italian tenor Beniamino Gigli, London 1947.

JOURNAL

OF THE

FRANKLIN INSTITUTE

OF THE STATE OF PENNSYLVANIA.

FOR THE PROMOTION OF THE MECHANIC ARTS.

VOL. CXXV.   JUNE, 1888.   No. 6.

The FRANKLIN INSTITUTE is not responsible for the statements and opinions advanced by contributors to the JOURNAL.

THE GRAMOPHONE: ETCHING THE HUMAN VOICE.

BY EMILE B RLINER.

[*A paper read at the Stated Meeting of the* FRANKLIN INSTITUTE, *May 16, 1888.*]

JOS. M. WILSON, President, in the chair.
THE PRESIDENT introduced Mr. BRELINER, who spoke as follows:

MEMBERS OF THE FRANKLIN INSTITUTE, LADIES AND GENTLE-MEN:—The last year in the first century of the history of the United States was a remarkable one in the history of science.

There appeared about that period something in the drift of scientific discussions, which, even to the mind of an observant amateur, foretold the coming of important events.

The dispute of Religion *versus* Science was once more at its height; prominent daily papers commenced to issue weekly discussions on scientific topics; series of scientific books in attractive popular form were eagerly bought by the cultured classes; popular lectures on scientific subjects were sure of commanding WHOLE No. VOL. CXXV.—(THIRD SERIES, Vol. XCV.)   29

Emile Berliner's paper introducing his invention was published in the June 1888 edition of the *Journal of the Franklin Institute*

Down went McGinty to the bottom of the sea

EMILE BERLINER AND THE GRAMOPHONE

The most significant genealogical thread leading to the formation of EMI can be traced to the towering figure of Emile Berliner, the gramophone's inventor. He was the initiator of the British venture that became The Gramophone Company Ltd, which later formed one-half of EMI. Berliner was a founding director of The Gramophone Company Ltd, and his British and European patents played a crucial role in the Company's early development. Furthermore, Berliner taught the art of disc record-making to the Company's first generation of recording engineers, and launched a number of key executives on their record industry careers.

A largely self-educated German-born American, Emile Berliner also came to study the problems of sound recording through his work on the telephone. In 1877, he developed the microphone that turned Alexander Graham Bell's telephone into a commercially viable proposition. He received $50,000 from The Bell Telephone Company for this invention. In 1884, he turned his mind to the problem of sound recording.

Emile Berliner began his research by reassessing the fundamentals of sound recording. He reasoned that the Edison principle of indenting a sound signal into tinfoil, and the Bell Tainter process of cutting a sound signal into the floor of a wax cylinder (the hill-and-dale cut), were fundamentally flawed, and caused serious distortion in the sound reproduced from cylinder records. In an attempt to resolve this problem, he adapted Scott's principle of a zigzag sound wave, to which he added a record groove strong enough to carry a reproducing stylus across its surface. This important innovation (in sharp contrast to the graphophone and the phonograph) did away with the need for a feedscrew in his reproducing machine. Instead of a cylinder, Berliner used a flat disc, and by using the existing art of electrotyping to make metal negatives (matrices), he was able to make multiple copies of the original recording. Unfortunately, the fundamental Bell Tainter patent for cutting sound signals into wax prevented Berliner from using that substance as a recording medium. Instead, after trying unsuccessfully to generate recordings using a photo-engraving process, he created an ingenious method of making disc records by acid-etching sound signals into zinc plates. Berliner called the machine which played his discs the gramophone.

In June 1888, Berliner introduced the gramophone and his recording process to the public at a meeting of the Franklin

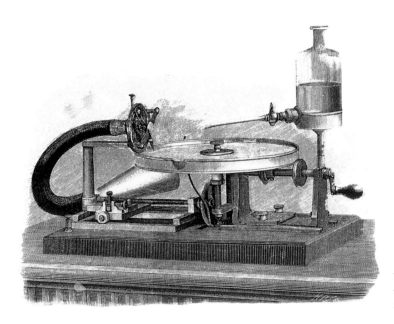

The recording machine Berliner used when he introduced his gramophone at the Franklin Institute.

Institute, a Philadelphia-based scientific society. In the course of this demonstration, Berliner explained the principles underlying his invention and the methods he had employed to develop the technology. Berliner also described and demonstrated the process whereby etched records were made. He took a polished zinc plate, which he coated in a compound of wax and benzene to create an etching ground. The sound recording was scratched into the wax coating, revealing the zinc plate beneath. The disc was then immersed in chromic acid, of which he said "the lines will be eaten in and the result will be a groove of even depth, such as is required for reproduction". The etching process was quick and, within 15 minutes of cutting the disc, Berliner had played the record to an astonished audience. He concluded his paper with a series of uncannily accurate predictions as to the gramophone record's future course, forecasting the creation of copyright protection for records, royalty payments to recording artists, and the centrality of the gramophone record in domestic leisure activities.

After his success at the Franklin Institute, Berliner experienced a decade of slow and often frustrating developmental work. Eventually, with the help of others, he transformed his basic concept into a new and commercially viable form. In 1889, by way of a beginning, he returned to his native Germany. There, he demonstrated his invention to the applause of German men of science, but little by way of investment capital came his way. He did, however, contract Kämmer und Reinhardt, a

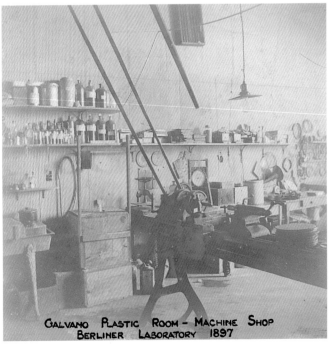

Berliner's laboratory in 1897. The following year, it was destroyed in a disastrous fire.

23

ALFRED CLARK
(1873–1950)

★

Born into an affluent New York family, Alfred Clark began his record industry career in 1889 with North American Phonograph. However, for a while in the early 1890s, he also worked for Edison's kinetoscope organization, where he produced *Mary Queen of Scots*, Edison's first scripted film. He returned to the record industry in 1895, and eventually joined Emile Berliner as a sales manager at The Berliner Gramophone Company's store in Philadelphia. At this time, he also became engaged in experimental work, helping Eldridge Johnson redesign the gramophone soundbox, which they patented. In 1899, Clark went to France as agent for Thomas Edison and Emile Berliner. There, in a joint venture with The Gramophone Company, he established the Compagnie Française du Gramophone. He sold his holding in 1904 but continued to run the business until 1908. His retirement lasted less than a year, and in 1909, aged 36, he became The Gramophone Company's managing director, a position he held until 1930, when he became The Gramophone Company's chairman. He was a central if reluctant player in the negotiations that led to the formation of Electric and Musical Industries Ltd, of which he was the first chairman. Clark finally retired in 1946, taking the honorific post of EMI president. However, within six months, after a bitter boardroom row, he resigned from the firm he had done so much to build up. Clark once wrote: "it has been a drab, plugging career, nothing spectacular, a business of laying one brick upon another", a humble assessment by a man who was probably the most important figure in the development of the recording industry outside the United States. Fred Gaisberg described him as "the fine thread running through the very fabric of HMV history".

Above A 1944 portrait of Alfred Clark, EMI's first chairman and record industry pioneer. He is holding the Clark-Johnson soundbox.

Right In 1899, just before Alfred Clark came to Europe, Thomas Alva Edison gave him this testimonial letter to introduce him to dealers as his accredited agent.

> Orange N.J. January 17 1899
>
> To whom it may concern—
>
> Mr Alfred Clark of New York, the bearer of this letter, is making a visit to Europe for the purpose of introducing the apparatus and specialities, manufactured by this Company of which I am the sole proprietor. Any information afforded him will be much appreciated by me
>
> Thomas A. Edison

firm of toymakers in Walterhausen, to manufacture and distribute toy gramophones, complete with 5-inch records pressed from Berliner-made matrices. In this way, the invention that transformed musical appreciation throughout the world first reached Britain as a plaything in the nurseries of wealthy families.

In 1891, beset with technical problems and lacking research capital, Berliner returned to the United States. In the years that followed, his efforts began to bear fruit. He solved many problems concerning the manufacture of high-quality metal negatives from his original discs. At that time, Berliner records were pressed from celluloid and rubber-based compounds. In experiments, he found that shellac compounds (a resin derived from the Lac beetle) gave a greatly improved sound. Berliner wrote of this important innovation:

Rubber records were imperfectly pressed and showed flat places ... I remembered an attempt by the Bell Telephone Company in 1877 ... to substitute a shellac composition for the hard rubber of which hand telephones were made. [Emile Berliner, "The Development of the Talking Machine", *Journal of The Franklin Institute*, August 1913, pp. 189–99]

In order to test the new material, Berliner sent a nickel-plated copper matrix of a record to a manufacturer of shellac compounds. When played on a gramophone, the pressings he received were louder and sounded more lifelike. Berliner noted that the new compound "proved at once a great success, and ever since shellac composition has been used for making disc records". The shellac compounds used by Berliner to manufacture his records eventually became the industry standard. They were used in the manufacture of 78-rpm records until the advent of modern vinyl plastics in the middle of the present century. Other problems were not so easily solved. In 1891, Berliner, desperate for additional development capital, offered his invention to North American Phonograph. Fortunately for him, his proposals were rejected. In 1892, he formed The American Gramophone Company, though this company appears never to have traded. In 1893, he formed The United States Gramophone Company to hold his valuable patents and, in 1895, after giving a further Franklin Institute paper, he persuaded some Philadelphia merchants to invest in The Berliner Gramophone Company, which he formed to manufacture Berliner records and gramophones.

In 1894, Fred Gaisberg came to work at Berliner's Washington, D.C. laboratory. Within a short time, he was joined by his brother William and by a school friend, William Sinkler Darby (see box, page 26). Berliner imparted the secrets of disc record-making to these young men. Within a few years, all three had moved to Europe, where, as recording engineers,

LIST OF PLATES.

JANUARY 1895.

BAND MUSIC.

118 Dude's March
130 Black and Tan
111 Marching Through Georgia
(with cheers)
111 The same Patrol
2 La Serenata
115 Star Spangled Banner
8 Coxey's Army
11 Salvation Army
9 Semper Fidelis (with drums)
139 After the Ball
126 Bocaccio March
144 Liberty Bell March
140 Washington Post March
142 Admirals Favorite March
4 Friedensklange
105 National Fencibles
13 Gladiator March
19 Schottische, Nancy Hanks
15 Loin du bal
17 Waltz, Aphrodite
20 Mendelsohn's Wedding March

INSTRUMENTAL QUARTETTE.

807 Die Kapelle
808 Circus Band
806 March, King John
800 Ein neues Blatt

BARYTONE.

163 When Summer Comes Again
182 Sweetheart Nell, and I
175 Old Kentucky Home
191 Black Knight Templars
185 Throw Him Down McCloskey
183 Oh, Promise Me
176 Love Me Little, Love Me Long
150 Oh, Fair Art Thou
155 Anchored
170 Mamie Come Kiss your Honey Boy
166 Then You'll Remember Me
160 The Maiden and the Lamb
165 Red, White and Blue
169 The Coon That Got the Shake
157 Tramp, Tramp, Tramp
158 Sweet Marie
196 The Whistling Coon
189 Phœbe
193 Back among the old folks
198 Swim out O'Grady
902 Sword of Bunker Hill

CLARIONET.

300 Allegro (Verdi)

CORNET.

200 Polka, Elegant
205 Call Me Thy Own
206 Emily Polka
202 U. S. Military Signals
203 Welcome, Pretty Primrose

Cornet Continued.

211 Cloverleaf Polka

CORNET DUETTS.

242 Alpine Polka
248 Swiss Boy
243 La Paloma

DRUM AND FIFE.

700 Biddy Oates
706 American Medley
702 St. Patrick's day
705 The Spirit of '76
(very dramatic)

TROMBONE.

75 In The Deep Cellar

PIANO.

256 Geisterfunken
253 March, Jolly Minstrels

INDIAN SONGS.

51 Three Melodies from the Ghost Dance
52 Three Melodies from the Ghost Dance
50 Three Melodies from the Ghost Dance

ANIMALS.

53 Morning on the farm

Hebrew Melodies.

400 Parshe Zav

SOPRANO.

359 Oh, Promise Me
352 Oh, How Delightful
355 Star Spangled Banner
353 I've something sweet to tell you
363 Tell her I love her so
362 Some Day
350 Past and Future
365 Punchinello
354 In the gloaming
356 Loves Sorrow

CONTRALTO.

550 Beauties Eyes
551 Drink to me only
552 Oh, Promise me

RECITATION.

We have for this important department secured the co-operation of the eminent versatile elocutionist, **Mr. David C. Bangs.**
602 Marc Anthony's Curse
A Lesson in Elocution
600 The Village Blacksmith
(Many others in preparation.)

VOCAL QUARTETTE.

851 Blind Tom (negro shout)
853 Grandfather's Birthday
855 Negroes' holiday

It is expected that between 25 and 50 New Pieces will be added every month.
THE UNITED STATES GRAMOPHONE CO.,
1410 Pennsylvania Ave., N. W.,
Washington, D. C.

Berliner's United States Gramophone Company, and later The Berliner Gramophone Company, published monthly lists of new recordings.

WILLIAM SINKLER DARBY
(1878–1950)

★

William Sinkler Darby joined the staff at Emile
Berliner's laboratory in 1895, and learned the
art of record making. Early in 1899, Berliner
sent Darby, then aged 20, to Europe, where he
made the first disc recordings in Russia. Later,
he joined Fred Gaisberg in London and
thereafter he was soon plunged into the hectic,
peripatetic life of a recording engineer,
travelling all over the world making records.
His surviving photographs, letters and diaries
convey both the frustration and the excitement
of the job. A brilliant engineer, he was held in
the highest regard by Emile Berliner, Eldridge
Johnson and his Gramophone Company
colleagues. He left the Company in 1920,
although he remained associated with the
record industry on both sides of the Atlantic.
At the onset of the Depression, he retired
from active life.

William Sinkler Darby
The above photograph shows William Sinkler
Darby, aged 20, shortly after his arrival in Europe
in 1899. Within a few years, Darby was recording
some of the most influential Gramophone
Company artists, including Chaliapin and Caruso.

Right An 1896 advertisement for The
Berliner Gramophone Company.

they became the most important figures on The Gramophone
Company's staff. Berliner also employed his nephew Joseph
Sanders at the laboratory. He was trained in the twin arts of
making metal negatives and in the manufacture of record
material. In 1898, he too went to Europe, where he
manufactured The Gramophone Company's first British-made
records (see Chapter 2).

Initially, Fred Gaisberg's value to Berliner lay in his ability
to assemble a variety of performers with recordable voices. By
1895, The Berliner Gramophone Company had published a
record catalogue containing around one hundred 7-inch records.
In his memoirs, Gaisberg recalled the musical quality of these
recordings, and the standing of the artists who made them:

Professional phonograph vocalists of established reputation like George J. Gaskin, the Irish tenor, Johnny Meyers, the baritone, and Dan Quinn, the comedian, were expensive, but they had loud clear voices and provided us with effective records of "Down went McGinty to the bottom of the sea", "Anchored", "Sweet Marie", "Comrades" and so forth. [Gaisberg, ibid., p.17]

Another Berliner recording artist recruited by Gaisberg was George Graham. He was described as:

A character of Washington life, a type of happy-go-lucky vagabond met with in the saloons, dodging the eyes of the bartender and cadging for drinks … George recorded his lecture on "Drink". In this he hammered home his point … "Drink is an evil habit; all my life I've devoted to putting drink down, and I'm still putting it down." [Gaisberg, ibid., p.17]

Although the bulk of recordings from the Berliner record studios were of popular music and comic items, there were also some early forays into classical music. In 1896, the Italian tenor Ferruccio Giannini recorded a number of arias, including "La donna è mobile" (Berliner 967) and "Questa o quella" (Berliner 983), from Verdi's opera *Rigoletto*. These were the primitive beginnings of EMI's current classical catalogue. Among other early records were pieces rendered by the inventor himself, one particular favourite being *The Lord's Prayer*, which Berliner used in early demonstrations of his process. This seemed to have been chosen less for spiritual edification than because the still primitive nature of gramophone records made it advisable to record items everyone knew by heart.

William Conrad Gaisberg (1877–1918)
Fred Gaisberg's younger brother Will joined him in 1902 after a period as recording engineer with The Berliner Gram-O-phone Company of Canada. In 1910, he became manager of the Recording Department, providing a vital link between the head office and its overseas territories.

Mocking Bird

FRANK SEAMAN, WILLIAM BARRY OWEN AND ELDRIDGE R. JOHNSON

In 1896, The Berliner Gramophone Company hired Alfred Clark to manage its Philadelphia retail shop. His business experience with Edison and North American Phonograph readily commended itself to what was a poorly managed company. The same year, The Berliner Company concluded a marketing agreement with Frank Seaman, a New York advertising executive. This contract gave Seaman exclusive rights to sell Berliner products throughout America. In a move that proved central to the later formation of The Gramophone

Company, Seaman hired William Barry Owen (see box, page 36), an experienced salesman, as his general manager. Owen's ambition, and his infectious enthusiasm for the gramophone, aided the speedy development of an American marketing network, and marked out Owen as the man to spearhead the future European venture.

Eldridge Johnson's original machine shop in Camden, New Jersey. It was here that Johnson developed the "trademark" gramophone.

Unfortunately for Owen and Seaman, Berliner's gramophone products were still very primitive. The gramophone was crude and hand-propelled, whilst its soundbox lacked the necessary sensitivity to reproduce Berliner records satisfactorily. Furthermore, there were serious shortcomings in the zinc recording process, because the chromic acid used to eat into the etching ground would spread into the adjoining wax-covered surface. This flaw often resulted in poor sound quality. By 1896, more than a decade on from Berliner's first experiments, it was evident that neither the inventor nor his associates possessed the necessary engineering or chemical skills to transform the brilliant concept into a marketable product capable of competing with the piano as the centre of domestic leisure activities. To overcome these problems, The Berliner Company was forced to look elsewhere.

In his memoirs, Fred Gaisberg related how he spotted an advertisement in a Philadelphia newspaper which offered to supply spring motors for sewing machines. On visiting the inventor of this device with a view to using such motors on gramophones, Gaisberg was dismayed to find a hugely impractical machine weighing a couple of hundredweight. Although the advertisement failed to produce the hoped-for breakthrough, the inventor did put The Berliner Company in touch with the man who was to transform the fortunes of the infant disc record industry – Eldridge R. Johnson (see box). At the time, Johnson ran a business as a highly skilled but small-time machinist in Camden, New Jersey, just across the river from the city of Philadelphia. Despite such humble beginnings, within a few years he had come to dominate the rapidly growing disc record industry. By 1921, Johnson's contribution to the industry included 72 sound-recording patents, and the giant Victor Talking Machine Company. Johnson, like Berliner, was also a central figure in the formation of The Gramophone Company, which he later joined as a director (see Chapter 2). Alfred Clark remembered his first meeting with Johnson:

On that summer day in 1896, accompanied by William Barry Owen, then head of the National Gramophone Company of New York … I crossed the ferry to Camden and called at the Johnson workshop. It was a very small place … [Johnson] displayed a keen interest in the hand-worked gramophone and said that he had no doubt that he could design and build a spring motor capable of running it satisfactorily and at a price which would be reasonable. [Clark, "His Master's Voice", ibid.]

According to Clark, Owen and he left Camden "with a distinct feeling of confidence" in Eldridge Johnson; that confidence proved to be more than justified over the next 30 years. Much later, Johnson recalled his first encounter with the gramophone:

The little instrument was badly designed. It sounded much like a partially educated parrot with a sore throat and a cold in the head. But the wheezy instrument caught my attention and held it fast and hard. I became interested in it as I had never been interested in anything before. [E. R. Fennimore Johnson, *His Master's Voice Was Eldridge R. Johnson* (Dover, Delaware, 1974), p.36]

The machine Johnson designed and manufactured at his workshop created the springboard for the gramophone's success on both sides of the Atlantic. Furthermore, when it

**ELDRIDGE R. JOHNSON
(1867–1945)**

Eldridge Johnson was born in Dover, Delaware, and was trained as a mechanical engineer. His association with the recording industry began in 1896, when he was approached by The Berliner Gramophone Company to design a motor for its machine. Within a few months, he had produced a redesigned gramophone, complete with his patented spring-driven motor, and secured a contract to supply the machine to Berliner's company. Johnson's curiosity with the machine did not stop there, and he next developed and patented (with Alfred Clark) a better soundbox and other improvements. His most significant innovation was a new process for recording directly on to wax discs.

The patent conflicts of the late 1890s persuaded Johnson of the need to consolidate Berliner's gramophone patents with his own. This was achieved in 1901, when he founded and became president of The Victor Talking Machine Company. Johnson had an acute business sense and Victor quickly became the leader of the American record industry. He never forgot the importance of technical quality, but combined it with a carefully structured repertoire, a comprehensive sales network and effective advertising. In 1920, when Victor acquired almost half of The Gramophone Company's shares, Johnson took a seat on the board. He accounted for Victor's success by saying: "Our greatest secret process is this – seek to improve everything we do every day". A reluctant captain of industry, Johnson, beset by illness, sold Victor to a group of bankers in 1926 and retired.

FRANCIS BARRAUD (1856–1924)

★

Francis James Barraud was born into a family of artists in London. He studied art at the Royal Academy School and in Antwerp. An accomplished technician, he was a frequent exhibitor at the Royal Academy and elsewhere. One of his early works, *An Encore Too Many*, is displayed in the Liverpool Walker Art Gallery, and the painting *His Master's Voice* brought him worldwide fame. Barraud was never to recapture that success, however, and by 1913 was in financial straits. When he learned of this situation, Alfred Clark commissioned Barraud to paint a copy of *His Master's Voice* for The Victor Company. Thereafter, Barraud painted a total of 24 copies of his most famous work. In recognition of these services, the Gramophone and Victor Companies paid Barraud a pension. *His Master's Voice* remains one of the world's best-known trademarks: many would agree with Clark's sentiment when he wrote: "The whole world saw it and succumbed to its charm."

Opposite page Francis Barraud in the studio.

Below The trademark gramophone.

was featured in the picture painted by Francis Barraud, *His Master's Voice*, it gained an undreamed-of immortality (see *Nipper*, page 32). Other design features attracted Johnson's attention. With Alfred Clark, he built a superior and more sensitive soundbox, which greatly improved the sound quality of Berliner's records. And, from an early stage in his association with The Berliner Gramophone Company, Johnson (realizing that the Bell-Tainter wax recording patent was nearing the end of its term) began to experiment with a new recording process using wax discs. By 1900, Johnson had brought his wax recording process to the point of commercial use. In the following year, The Gramophone Company paid him £2,000 for his patents and trade secrets. In return, he built the Company its first 10-inch wax disc-cutting machine, and trained the Company's recording engineers in the new process. The improvement in sound quality brought about by Johnson's wax-cut records, together with other technical developments (specifically the increase in record size from 7-inch to 10-inch and later 12-inch, which took playing time from two to four minutes), enabled The Gramophone Company to build its catalogue of popular and celebrity records.

Unfortunately, the relationship between the Seaman and Berliner businesses deteriorated. There was a series of bruising legal actions that threatened to engulf both Owen and Johnson. Had not Berliner and Johnson maintained supplies of goods to The Gramophone

NIPPER

★

The painting of a fox terrier listening to an early gramophone remains one of the oldest and certainly the best-known of trademarks and record logos. It was a brilliantly conceived piece of commercial art, with a clear simple message that has retained its universal appeal for almost one hundred years.

Nipper was a stray dog found by Francis Barraud's brother, Mark, in 1884. When Mark died three years later, the dog came into Francis's possession. He painted the picture some time before 1899, although in its original form, the dog was listening to a phonograph (a cylinder machine). Barraud submitted this version of the painting for copyright with the title *Dog Looking at and Listening to a Phonograph*. Reflecting on how he came to paint the picture, Barraud wrote : "It is difficult to say how the idea came to me beyond the fact that it suddenly occurred to me that to have my dog listening to the phonograph, with an intelligent and rather puzzled expression, and call it *His Master's Voice* would make an excellent subject. We had a phonograph and I often noticed how puzzled he was to make out where the voice came

from. It was certainly the happiest thought I ever had."

Barraud tried to sell the finished painting to several publishers and to a phonograph manufacturer, but without success. After it had languished for a time, a friend suggested that Barraud make the picture more attractive by replacing the black horn with a brass one. At that time Berliner gramophones

were sold with brass horns, so Barraud called at the offices of The Gramophone Company in Maiden Lane to borrow one. On seeing a photograph of the painting, William Barry Owen expressed an interest in acquiring the original, though he asked Barraud to replace the phonograph with their own machine, the gramophone. Although Nipper was already dead by this time, the artist completed the revision, which was delivered to The Gramophone Company.

The purchase price for the picture took the form of two payments, each of £50. The first gave the Company sole reproduction rights, whilst the second ceded Barraud's copyright. In 1900, Emile Berliner copyrighted the painting for use as a trademark in the United States and Canada. The following year, the copyright passed to The Victor Talking Machine Company, who extended copyright to Central and South America, the Far East and Japan. This division of trademark ownership persists to the present.

Company, (see Chapter 2), it is possible that all three companies would have collapsed. However, in the summer of 1901, Seaman was decisively beaten in the American courts. Realizing their opportunity, the Johnson and Berliner enterprises merged in October 1901 to form The Victor Talking Machine Company. Johnson became company president, whilst Berliner took shares for his patents and other interests. This combination guaranteed the success of the American business, and brought the new Company into an even closer relationship with the British Gramophone Company.

Above Francis Barraud's painting, which was submitted for copyright registration in 1899. (Crown copyright: Public Record Office, Kew).

Left The revised picture that became the HMV trademark.

A Charm
entirely their own

"His Master's Voice"
RECORDS

CHAPTER 2

Roamin' in the Gloamin'

THE GRAMOPHONE COMPANY, 1897–1931

Well, so long! Bon Voyage and success! I hope you'll have a jolly time all around.
[Emile Berliner to William Barry Owen, 13 July 1897]

My Pilot o'er Life's Sea

COMPANY FORMATION, 1897–1901

WILLIAM BARRY OWEN (1860–1914)

★

The founder of The Gramophone Company, William Barry Owen, was born in 1860, the son of a whaling captain at Vineyard Haven, Massachusetts. He discovered his true *métier* as a salesman whilst studying law at Amherst College. A gambler who enjoyed a high lifestyle, he saw in the exploitation of Berliner's foreign patents a unique opportunity to make a great deal of money. As his interest in the original partnership, Owen was allotted a large block of Gramophone Company shares; however, his personal financial obligations forced him to sell them. Owen strove to bring about the merger of the Berliner and Johnson interests with those of The Gramophone Company. When these efforts failed, as did his ill-fated typewriter venture, he seemed to lose interest in the business. His wish to be paid a portion of the Company's profits led to his departure. However, he retained his seat on the board until 1906. On leaving the Company, Owen quit Britain for good. He returned to the United States, where he established several unsuccessful agricultural ventures. By 1910, he had lost his fortune and was beset by debt. He lived for the remainder of his life on a pension paid to him jointly by the Gramophone and Victor Talking Machine Companies.

William Barry Owen in London with his two sons Kent and Paul.

In July 1897, William Barry Owen resigned his post with The National Gramophone Company and sailed for Britain. The cheerful message Emile Berliner sent him as he was leaving New York highlights the feelings of unbounded confidence, optimism and trust Berliner placed in his European agent, and in the prospects for the new business. The inventor was correct in his assessment: one hundred years after Owen arrived in London, the record business he created is still trading today as EMI Records, the principal British company of EMI.

When Owen arrived in London, he began to put into effect Berliner's instructions: to establish a British market in gramophone goods and to find British venture capitalists willing to invest in the new enterprise. By early August 1897, Owen had installed himself at the Hotel Cecil in the Strand and begun trading as an unincorporated business with the self-styled title of The Gramophone Company. He purchased gramophones from

Eldridge Johnson's American factory and records from The Berliner Gramophone Company, via its American marketing agent, The National Gramophone Company of New York. Initially, he used National Gramophone's own record catalogues which included recordings of Sousa's band and trombone solos by Arthur Pryor, supplemented by cornet solos, comic songs by Dan W. Quinn and tenor solos by George J. Gaskin.

To develop the business, Owen recruited an experienced British salesman, Theodore B. Birnbaum (see box), who toured Britain during the autumn of 1897, demonstrating and selling gramophones and records, and creating dealerships. The British gramophone venture expanded at such a rate that serious supply problems developed, which resulted in irate letters from dealers. One complained:

When can we get the 125 machines ordered from you some time ago? I am really afraid to meet my customers, as I have put them off so long … Also let me have the records (1,500) as per list given you, as soon as possible, and don't forget the extra needles.
[Formation Papers, 1897, EMI Music Archive]

Furthermore, records made in America – reflecting American rather than British musical tastes – were often not appreciated. As early as September 1897, a Scottish dealer observed:

Negro Funerals, Advertising and that class of Record do not take with us, neither do German or Italian songs. What we want are well known airs and songs from modern and popular operas.
[Formation Papers, 1897, EMI Music Archive]

Although Owen's gramophone business was an immediate success, it proved less easy to find investors. After several failures, Owen met Trevor Williams (see box, page 38), a wealthy British solicitor who became interested in his proposals. In February 1898, Williams and Owen travelled to the United States, where they met Berliner, Johnson and Frank Seaman. During the course of that visit, Williams concluded an agreement with Berliner which made him and Owen Berliner's British licensees. In return, Williams agreed to invest up to £5,000 in Owen's venture. Williams also took an option to purchase

THEODORE B. BIRNBAUM (1865–1921)

Born into a family of businessmen in London, Theodore Birnbaum was already an experienced salesman when he met William Barry Owen in August 1897. Over the next seven years, Owen's expectations of Birnbaum were more than justified. Whether as marketing manager in London, or as manager of the Company's Central European branch, Birnbaum's flair led to financial success. He was a cultured and educated man, and knew many of the performers who later made records for the Company. This knowledge and patronage of the arts was furthered by his father-in-law, the eminent lawyer Sir George Lewis, who, in addition to his duties as solicitor to the King and high society, was also legal advisor to many great artists. This professional relationship proved to be of enormous significance to Birnbaum when he was negotiating with figures like Adelina Patti, whose record contract Lewis wrote. According to his successor, Alfred Clark, Birnbaum was a tireless worker who paid the penalty, suffering a severe breakdown in his health during 1908. Fred Gaisberg said of his subsequent resignation: "I don't know what the Gramophone Company is coming to now that all of the old men are out of it." Birnbaum remained a director until 1910, when he left the record business altogether.

TREVOR WILLIAMS
(1859–1946)

Edmund Trevor Lloyd Williams was born into a wealthy Welsh land-owning family and trained as a lawyer. He was consulted by William Barry Owen in 1897 concerning proposals to develop his small gramophone business. Williams counselled against the deal, but expressed a personal interest in the venture. When Williams incorporated the business in 1899, he also acquired a controlling interest in Deutsche Grammophon (the German record factory) and purchased Berliner's British and European patents. He was also the Company's largest single shareholder and chairman of the board. In 1900, he and Owen formed The Gramophone and Typewriter Ltd to acquire the old company and other assets. He became chairman of this venture, a position he held until his retirement in 1930. Initially, he was content to leave the commercial and technical aspects of the business to others. However, over the years, he acquired a comprehensive knowledge of the trade. Williams had important outside business interests which included the Roneo office equipment company, of which he was a founding director, and an ill-fated film company, The British Mutoscope and Biograph Ltd. In 1931, Williams became a founding director of EMI. He remained an active board member until his death in 1946.

Right The Gramophone Company's Maiden Lane offices.

Berliner's valuable British and European gramophone patents. On his return to London, Williams, together with Edgar Storey (a Lancashire businessman and colliery owner) and Owen, took over Owen's venture as an informal business partnership. Owen remained manager of the concern, whilst Williams and Storey obtained the necessary bank guarantees required to expand the business. Offices were procured at 31 Maiden Lane, off the Strand. These moves were the start of Trevor Williams's association with The Gramophone Company (and subsequently EMI), an association that ended only with his death in 1946.

With access to additional working capital, The Gramophone Company grew rapidly. However, in June 1898, the business began to be adversely affected by the American disputes between Emile Berliner and Frank Seaman (see Chapter 1). Seaman, who supplied Owen with all his records, tried to take over the British gramophone trade for himself. He cut supplies of records to London in an attempt to kill off The Gramophone Company, and encouraged the Edison-Bell Company, which had just begun to market its own British-made records using the cylinder format, to sue The Gramophone Company and its dealers for patent infringement. To withstand this totally unexpected crisis, Berliner, Owen, Williams and Storey were forced to make quick decisions. Their impact transformed the small marketing organization from

what could have become merely a transient novelty trade into an established manufacturing and selling business, with a secure long-term future.

The Gramophone Company had to break Seaman's embargo, and to avoid the possibility of such problems arising in the future, set up its own European-based recording and manufacturing facilities. To accomplish the former, Johnson surreptitiously bought quantities of records and shipped them to Britain: as Johnson's factory was manufacturing large quantities of gramophones for Owen and Williams, it was in his interests to see that the business stayed afloat. To achieve the latter, Emile Berliner contacted his brother Joseph, who managed the family-owned telephone factory at Hannover in Germany, and they agreed to establish record-pressing facilities at the factory.

In July 1898, Emile Berliner dispatched to Europe two key figures from his American laboratory. One was his nephew Joseph Sanders, an expert both in matrix-making and record-pressing. The other was Fred Gaisberg, the recording engineer. Whilst Sanders went to Hannover to set up the record factory, Gaisberg came to London. In the basement of The Gramophone Company's Maiden Lane offices, he established a makeshift recording studio and prepared to make the first European disc records. On 6 August 1898, Owen wrote to Johnson: "Gaisberg

Above Fred Gaisberg's London recording studio. In early August 1898 Gaisberg set up this makeshift recording studio in the basement of The Gramophone Company's Maiden Lane offices, where he made the first European disc records.

Above, top Fred Gaisberg (left) and Joseph Sanders (centre) crossing the Atlantic on the SS *Umbria* en-route to Liverpool in July, 1898.

THE GRAMOPHONE COMPANY'S FIRST DISC RECORDS

★

On 23 July 1898, Fred Gaisberg and Joe Sanders sailed for Europe on the fast transatlantic Cunard liner *Umbria*. They reached Liverpool on Sunday 31 July, and journeyed by train to London. Whilst Joe travelled on to Hannover to help Joseph Berliner establish the record-pressing plant, Fred set about getting the new London recording studio ready for action. He had brought with him only "a complete recording outfit plus a twenty-five dollar bicycle with pneumatic tyres, and a notebook stuffed with [recipes], addresses, and advice in Berliner's own handwriting", and so he had to buy all the working materials – chemicals for preparing and etching, electrical equipment and sheet zinc for the master record plates.

The Gramophone Company had rented offices in the Cockburn Hotel in Henrietta Street, taking as their address the back entrance in Maiden Lane, and Gaisberg set up the recording machinery "in the old smoking-room." His own photographs of the early studio show a room of heavy wallpaper and bare floorboards; the recording machinery and electric motor were mounted on a wooden structure, with a cluster of small conical horns to collect the sound, arranged at the height of a singer's mouth. To ensure that the accompanying piano was equitably recorded, it had been hoisted – along with the pianist – on to a suitable platform to bring it level with the horns.

Within a few days, Gaisberg was able to commence recording: each zinc plate, exposed by the action of the recording stylus, had the title, date and other information inscribed by hand through the wax covering, with a stamped heading proclaiming Berliner's patent. All this appeared along with the recording groove in the zinc when it was etched; the "plate" was then sent to Hannover, where a catalogue number was embossed. An electrotype negative then stamped out positive replicas complete with "label" information – which soon included the new Recording Angel trademark. The earliest discs issued are dated "8-8-98", though this is thrown into doubt by the evident inaccuracy of dates in Gaisberg's notebook entries: 9 August is more likely.

Gaisberg's first London recordings were along the same lines as their American counterparts: cornet, piano and "clarionet" solos, comic recitations and popular songs of the day. Early visitors to the studio included members of the Moore and Burgess Minstrels, the banjo duo Mays and Hunter, and orchestras from the Hotel Cecil and Trocadero Grill; both Irish and Scottish bagpipes appeared amongst these early recordings, and even a viola solo (Miss F. M. Brooke-Alder) and a boy soprano (Master John Buffery). On 19 August, the well-known Savoyard H. Scott Russell made the first of several recordings, "Jack's the Boy" from the musical comedy *The Geisha* (Berliner E 2005). By the end of 1898, the Gramophone had captured other famous names from the world of entertainment, including Maurice Farkoa, Cissy Loftus and Albert Chevalier, and the actor Charles Wyndham.

The early 7-inch discs were not only crude in appearance and sound but played for a mere two minutes, allowing only snippets to be recorded from more substantial works. Despite this, as fresh records were added, the catalogue showed that not only popular entertainment was to be catered for: the infant Gramophone Company also had serious aspirations. During October 1898, discs were made by Albert Fransella's brand new flute quartet and the young cellist W. H. Squire; the contralto Edith Clegg recorded Schubert's "Ave Maria" (Berliner E 3023) and G. H. Snazelle essayed "Revenge Timotheus cries!" from Handel's *Alexander's Feast* (Berliner E 2109), paving the way for recordings of art songs and operatic arias; even the crude orchestral recordings soon included such delights as a glimpse of the Introduction to Act III of *Lohengrin* (Berliner 585).

Left The first London recording studio in 1898.

The Hannover record factory in 1899, featuring (left to right) the plating plant, charging the dies with shellac compound and (partly hidden) the hand-presses.

will commence to take records tomorrow". One of the first records to be released from that August session was "My Pilot o'er Life's Sea" (Berliner E 5016), a cornet solo by C. Burgess. Other records quickly followed and, by the end of 1898, a substantial list of British-made recordings was available to dealers (see *The Gramophone Company's First Disc Records*, page 40). Although Berliner and Owen had intended Gaisberg's stay in London to last only a few months, he stayed for the rest of his life, during the course of which he became the industry's greatest recording engineer, and, in 1920, The Gramophone Company's first artistic director.

By the end of 1898, Sanders, operating from the Berliner record factory in Germany, was supplying London with most of its manufacturing needs. To protect their new investment, the Berliner brothers formed a small German company, Deutsche Grammophon Gesellschaft, whose main asset was the record factory. Taken together, these moves foiled Seaman's attempt to kill off The Gramophone Company. The supply crisis, and the creation of a British recording studio and German manufacturing facilities, were of cardinal importance in causing a change in public perceptions of the gramophone. Once The Gramophone Company began to make its own records using British artists performing British popular music, the commercial value of the disc record was transformed.

In 1899, the partners incorporated the business as The Gramophone Company Ltd. Trevor Williams became company chairman and Owen managing director, with Storey, Birnbaum and Berliner as directors. At the same time, the Company began its expansion into Europe. It acquired a controlling interest in the Berliner pressing facility in Germany, Deutsche Grammophon,

The first British record catalogues
Thanks to the work of Gaisberg in London and Sanders in Hannover, by the autumn of 1898, as this earliest surviving list of London made recordings shows, the recording programme had started to bear fruit.

41

The Gramophone Company expanded rapidly and, in 1901, moved to premises in the City Road. The bustle of the business is vividly captured in these 1905 images of the gramophone assembly plant, the office of manager William Morrison and the record stockroom.

purchased Emile Berliner's and Eldridge Johnson's British and European gramophone patents, formed sub-companies in France and Italy, and created markets in Central Europe and Russia. The same year, the new company purchased from the artist Francis Barraud its most famous trademark, the painting *His Master's Voice*. This endearing picture, together with the Company's original trademark – the Recording Angel (designed in 1898 by Theodore Birnbaum) – subsequently became two of the Company's, and later EMI's, most important logos.

To exploit the Company's new markets in Europe and Russia, it proved necessary to create a strong organization in Central Europe. Owen's associate, Theodore Birnbaum, was put in charge of this expansion. In November 1899, he established an office in Berlin, a city at the crossroads of Europe. From that unique vantage point, he created what became the hub of the Company's key European and Russian selling and distribution network. In order to meet local musical needs in these highly diverse European and Russian markets, Birnbaum created catalogues of locally recorded music. To achieve this, he took Fred Gaisberg and William Sinkler Darby – now the Company's two recording experts – on the first of their many overseas recording tours (see *The Experts' Travels, 1899–1914*, page 44). The records made between 1899 and 1914, together with the agencies and dealerships Birnbaum established, were key elements in the Company's broader success, so much so that, by 1904, the Central European and Russian markets generated more than half the Company's profits.

In December 1900, The Gramophone and Typewriter Ltd was formed in London to acquire The Gramophone Company Ltd (and its European operating companies); the rights to manufacture and sell the Lambert typewriter; and the remaining

The Lambert typewriter
As a hedge against the failure of the gramophone, Owen introduced the Lambert typewriter as a second product. Unfortunately, the machine lacked a standard keyboard and failed to attract buyers.

THE EXPERTS' TRAVELS, 1899–1914

★

The Gramophone Company's worldwide growth was reliant on the efforts of its young travelling recording engineers (known also as "Experts"), whose relish for foreign challenges fuelled the ever-expanding repertoire needed to meet new markets and replenish old ones. Regarded as the elite, those employed as recording experts led a demanding lifestyle, a typical year seeing three to four postings to Europe's extremities or the Far East. The Gramophone Company's recording engineers were well rewarded for their efforts. In comparison to skilled mechanical engineers in other industries, who could earn around £100 a year before 1914, the Company's junior recording engineers could earn up to £300. Gaisberg and Darby, the chief recording engineers, were in a position to earn up to a staggering £1,500 a year. Keen to record not only the music but also their impressions of the areas visited, "the Boys", as they were affectionately known within the Company, experienced their own kind of Grand Tour at the height of European imperialism. During those journeys, they captured in wax the music and culture of societies that, in some cases, were consumed by this century's wars. Fortunately for posterity, much of their extraordinary work survives today in EMI's unique archive.

The pioneering standard which the experts had to follow was set by Fred Gaisberg, whose early expeditions prompted feelings which all could later relate to. Leaving Tilbury Docks bound for the Far East in 1902, he wrote: "As we steamed down the channel into the unknown I felt like Marco Polo starting out on his journeys." This sense of excitement and adventure would remain with him, for, as he recalled in his memoirs, "I was like a drug addict, ever longing hungrily for newer and stranger fields of travel". Recording trips to the world's more remote areas included Turkey's interior, China and the

principalities of Central Asia, the simplicity of life experienced making any notion of holiday superfluous. The Experts were hard-working and highly skilled professionals who had to endure technical and artistic difficulties whilst coping with what Gaisberg described as "the anxiety of making records that must keep a branch going for a year". Since sound recording as an art was still in its infancy, the conditions faced by the travelling engineer ensured that improvisation and quick thinking were essential skills. In a letter written in 1911 to

the managing directors, William Gaisberg, head of the London Recording Department, observed that "the recording expert of today is a first-class tool maker", and the Experts' correspondence was full of technical sketches and "tinkering" improvements, often hit upon in response to the supply shortages they faced. In addition, travelling with a large amount of suspicious-looking baggage often led to problems, especially at borders: in his diaries, Darby recounts how he managed to get his illegal benzene into Sweden by passing it off as "a Special Brand of Oil which I used for lubricating my Philosophical Apparatus".

The general practice was to set up a makeshift recording studio in a hotel room and, through experimentation create the best acoustic conditions possible. The interest generated by the arrival of what

many of the local people regarded as "some kind of magician" (Darby) was immense, packed lobbies and lengthy queues generating an atmosphere like that of a show. Rarely did this accord with the wishes of the hotel's other residents and, with most of the recording taking place in the evenings (owing to cooler conditions), astute financial bargaining was often necessary to placate the proprietor.

When they arrived in new areas, the Experts were often called upon to act as talent scouts and musical advisers. In Moscow, Darby would go out to the city's bars and theatres at night "looking for artists until 2 and 3 o'clock in the morning", judging recording potential and the artistic merit of an alien culture. In Turkey, he observed that a particular "love song sounded like two cats fighting on a backfence". Fred Gaisberg felt a similar sentiment when recording Tartar music in Kazan: so bad was an accordion player that "we asked him to stop if we paid him 5 Roubles, and bring in someone who could sing. He agreed".

The constant demands of their pioneering work could produce disillusionment. Even the enthusiastic William Gaisberg wrote to his brother Fred in 1909 that "I have seen quite enough of this Bohemian life". Gruelling travel arrangements often led to exasperation: on one occasion, Darby found that his train in Hungary "stopped at every house and when it came it to a double house it stopped twice". However, cynicism was a rare trait among the Experts and throughout their foreign experiences, one can discern a touching innocence. Eye-opening incidents abound, ranging from Darby's astonishment at his piano in India being "transported around the cities by eight men, carrying it on their heads!" to William Gaisberg's observation that it was only in Hyderabad that "we realized how many different degrees of smells there are in the world".

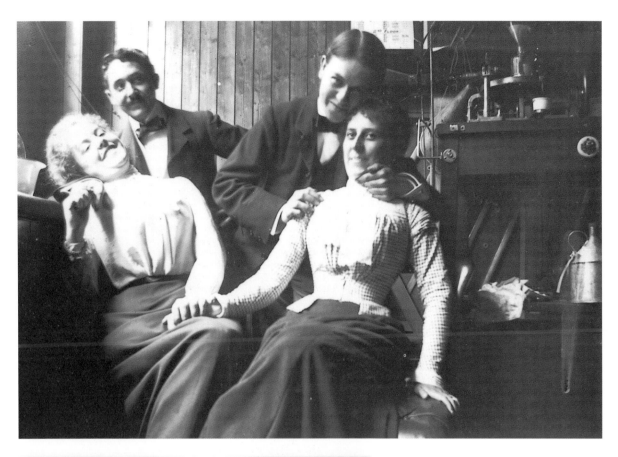

Above and left Life during recording sessions was not all hard work for "the boys".

***Opposite page* The Experts' travels**: Darby en route to Spain in 1899.

These beautiful record catalogues were produced by The Gramophone Company's branches in India and Cairo before the First World War.

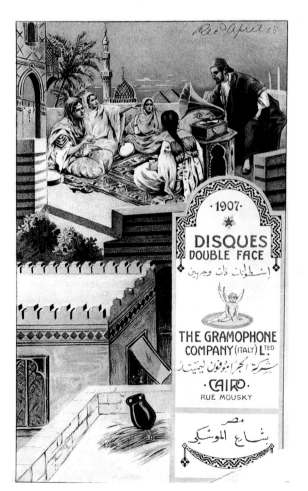

shares in Deutsche Grammophon. The typewriter was seen by Owen as an insurance against the gramophone's failure, but it subsequently proved to be an unsuccessful venture and, by 1904, it had been dropped. (In 1907, the Company changed its name back to The Gramophone Company Ltd.) The Company entered the new century with a profitable and expanding British and European organization, large and important catalogues of recorded music, and a continuing international recording programme. The scale of the Company's activities was now such that it had to move to new premises at 21 City Road, in the City of London.

The Gramophone Company faced a number of serious problems trading in overseas territories. One of the most costly to overcome was the imposition of increasingly punitive tariff barriers by European states anxious to protect their own infant recording industries. In response to these pressures, and at the same time to create strategically located manufacturing facilities to meet the needs of the growing trading network, the Company built record factories in Germany, Spain, France, Russia and India.

The Company enjoyed several years of impressive, effectively monopoly profits before competitors challenged its position in the British, European and Russian disc record markets. However, rather than pay large and, in the long term, unsustainable dividends, and anticipating the emergence of competition, the board wisely retained much of the early profits. Nonetheless, despite this prudent policy, Gramophone Company shares were a very attractive investment before 1914. After the first hesitant years, dividend payments (with the exception of one year) never fell below a nominal 10 per cent, and, on one occasion, rose to 30 per cent of the issue price. In 1904, the Company gained a listing on the London Stock Exchange, and in the decade that followed, the price of the one pound ordinary shares remained high, on one occasion reaching almost four pounds.

At the centre of the Company's business strategy was a close relationship with the American gramophone businesses of Emile Berliner and Eldridge Johnson. In 1901, this link was further strengthened when Berliner and Johnson merged their interests in a new business, The Victor Talking Machine Company. The two companies became so close that, early in the century, a number of proposals were made to

PLANÇON

The French bass Pol Plançon (1854–1914) was one of the first established celebrity artists to record for the Company.

THE HAYES FACTORIES

Until quite recently, much of EMI's British manufacturing was focused on a large industrial site at Hayes, near London. It was first occupied by The Gramophone Company in 1907, when a record factory was built to process original wax discs, and to manufacture and distribute records. As The Gramophone Company itself grew, so did the Hayes site. In 1912, a new head office, a suite of recording studios and further manufacturing facilities were added. A light engineering factory (known as the machine factory) was also built to make clockwork motors and other metal parts for gramophones. Further developments included a research facility built in the late 1920s that later became the Central Research Laboratories (known as the CRL).

By 1929, the whole site covered an area in excess of 58 acres, and more than 7,500 people were employed there, most of whom worked on an eight-hour round-the-clock shift system. During the Depression, all of EMI's British manufacturing was concentrated at Hayes, and production began of a new range of products, including radios, televisions, refrigerators and other domestic appliances. In 1952, the record factory started to manufacture LP and 45-rpm vinyl records. In the late 1950s, domestic appliance manufacture ended at Hayes and, by 1960, much of the site had been disposed of or closed. In 1973, pressure on remaining space at Hayes, combined with the requirements of music cassette tape manufacture and a need to build a new distribution centre, forced EMI to move record production and distribution to a new site in Uxbridge Road, Hayes.

The commencement of CD manufacture in Swindon in the mid-1980s, and the general growth in that sector of the record market, resulted in the rapid decline of vinyl manufacture at Hayes. The establishment of a new distribution centre at Leamington further undermined the viability of the Hayes plant. However, to the surprise of many, demand for LP and 45-rpm record manufacture remained unexpectedly buoyant, and has continued to be a profitable venture. As a result almost 90 years from the commencement of production, record and tape manufacturing continues at Hayes.

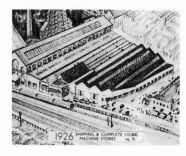

merge the businesses into a single multinational enterprise. Unfortunately, until 1920, nothing came of them. The relationship between the Gramophone and Victor companies was mediated by a number of important inter-company trading agreements. At the core of these was a division of the world into two non-competing trading areas. Victor took the Americas and the Far East (after 1907 this included Japan), whilst The Gramophone Company took the rest of the world. Other factors included The Gramophone Company's dependence, until the end of the First World War in 1918, on Victor for supplies of gramophones, and a licensing agreement giving both companies rights to each other's recordings. During the early years of this agreement, Victor gained rights to recordings of European-made celebrity records and, later, The Gramophone Company was able to exploit the extraordinary catalogue of popular as well as celebrity recordings made by Victor's galaxy of stars from the Metropolitan Opera House, New York, and elsewhere. This licensing agreement became the foundation of the relationship and lasted for more than 50 years.

In 1904, William Barry Owen resigned his post and returned to the United States. Fundamentally, he was a speculator, and not the man to lead the Company beyond its pioneering phase. Although highly respected – both personally and as a businessman – he was, as Fred Gaisberg remarked, "an opportunist … and a bold gambler". Owen's successor as managing director was Theodore Birnbaum, the creator of the Central European and Russian branches. It fell to him to transform the Company from a pioneering record business into Europe's leading record manufacturing and competitive selling organization.

To cope with demand, the Company built a new record factory at Hayes in Middlesex. The first sod of the Hayes development was cut in 1907 by Edward Lloyd, the British tenor and Gramophone Company artist, using a silver spade. Lloyd had recorded a series of 10-inch records, among which was a favourite concert piece of the time, "I'll sing thee songs of Araby" (G&T GC2-2024). A photograph taken during the sod-cutting ceremony shows the Company's Chairman, Trevor Williams – the model of a prosperous up-to-date Edwardian – swathed in motoring clothes, complete with goggles. As building progressed, Nellie (later Dame Nellie) Melba, (see box, page 79), then the Company's greatest recording star, was persuaded to lay the foundation stone. The Hayes factory reduced the cost of manufacturing records dramatically, and

1935 SUPPLIES & TRAFFIC 60,500 sq. ft.

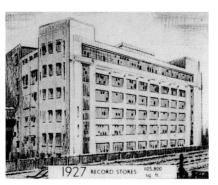

1927 RECORD STORES 105,800 sq. ft.

1911 CABINET FACTORY 218,300 sq. ft.

1929 ASSEMBLY FACTORY 122,500 sq. ft.

1937 DAWLEY WORKS 299,600 sq. ft.

The Hayes factory in 1931.

The Hayes Site
In 1907, the singer Edward Lloyd cut the first sod on the Hayes site, using a silver spade now preserved at the EMI Music Archive.

the Company was able to cut record prices by 20 per cent. The record factory was just the beginning of large-scale investment at Hayes by The Gramophone Company, and later by EMI.

In June 1912, one of the Company's most important celebrity artists, the Russian bass Feodor Chaliapin (see box, page 71), formally opened new purpose-built recording studios at Hayes. These quickly became a centre for recording some of the world's greatest performing artists. Among the earliest star names to make records at the new studios were the singers Louise Kirkby Lunn, Mario Sammarco and Peter Dawson (see box, page 53), the Polish virtuoso pianist Ignacy Jan Paderewski (see box, page 54), and the Scottish entertainer

PETER DAWSON
(1882–1961)

★

The Australian bass-baritone Peter Dawson was the Company's most prolific recording artist during the 78-rpm era. He came to Britain in 1902 to study singing, and made his first records in 1904; engineers soon discovered that his voice was easy to record. Dawson also had the temperament and flexibility to perform whatever was required, from imitations of Harry Lauder to opera in English. He recorded under many pseudonyms, including Will Danby, Will Strong, Hector Grant and J. P. McColl. Dawson's repertoire was in keeping with his times, and he recorded countless songs of Empire, including "Waltzing Matilda" (HMV B 8771) and his own setting of Kipling's poem "Boots" (HMV B 3072). One of his greatest successes was his 1917 recording of "The Cobbler's Song" from *Chu Chin Chow* (HMV C 756), which he made after scanning the music just once. He also made records of serious music. Among the most successful of these were "O ruddier than the cherry" from Handel's *Acis and Galatea*, coupled with "Honour and Arms" from *Samson* (HMV C 1500), which are still admired by lovers of Handel's music. During his long career, Dawson made many tours of the British Empire and the Far East, before he finally retired to Australia in 1956. Fred Gaisberg said of him: "The velvety quality of his well-produced voice, his ability to throw pathos, tears, laughter and drama into it, his quickness at reading, musicianship and contagious good humour, made him a recorder's dream come true."

Peter Dawson (right) in the Hayes recording studio in the early 1920s.

Harry (later Sir Harry) Lauder (see box, page 67). A new headquarters was also built at the Hayes factory site and, when the First World War broke out in 1914, the rest of the business moved there.

Birnbaum remained as managing director until 1909, when poor health forced his resignation. His successor was Alfred Clark, who between 1909 and 1912 shared the post with Sydney Dixon (see box, page 64), previously the British branch manager. Clark, whose association with the record industry went back to 1889 (see Chapter 1), had come to Europe in 1899 and established what became the French branch of The Gramophone Company.

IGNACY PADEREWSKI
(1860–1941)

The great romantic pianist Ignacy Jan Paderewski was born in Podolia, Poland. He studied at the Warsaw Conservatoire, where he graduated in 1878 and immediately became a teacher. He later went to Vienna as Leschetizky's pupil, and subsequently made sensational debuts there and elsewhere. His slight build, pale artistic features and shock of reddish-gold hair aroused great public admiration; Saint-Saëns famously remarked: "He is a genius who also plays the piano." Paderewski's first recording session for HMV took place at his Swiss home during the summer of 1911, when he recorded several works by Chopin, including the Waltz in C sharp minor (HMV 045529) and his own Minuet in G (HMV 045530). He later recorded in Paris and London. When war was declared in 1914, Paderewski retired from performing to devote himself to the affairs of Poland, which finally emerged as an independent republic under his premiership. Despite his innate qualities of dignity and wisdom, his political career was not entirely successful and he returned triumphantly to the concert platform in 1922: he had lost none of his charisma or musical ability. Primarily a great performer of Chopin, he also achieved some success as a composer, although his output was small. In 1940, he joined the Polish government in exile. He died in New York in 1941.

The Absent-Minded Beggar

RECORDING ARTISTS

At first, established classical performers were dismissive of the gramophone. As Fred Gaisberg wrote: "Our recorded repertoire consisted only of ballads, comic songs and band records. When we approached the greatest artists, they just laughed at us and replied that the gramophone was just a toy." [Gaisberg, *Music on Record*, p.42] In order to build a catalogue of British records, Gaisberg had to entice performing artists into his Maiden Lane recording studio from nearby music halls and theatres. As the Company's first offices and recording studio were adjacent to Rules Restaurant, at the time a haunt of music hall and theatrical artists, many early recording artists were persuaded to make records after a good meal. Among those whose records appeared in The Gramophone Company's earliest catalogues were music hall stars such as Dan Leno, Eugene Stratton, Gus Elen, Ada Reeve and Albert Chevalier (the last of whom negotiated the first royalty payment, of 1 shilling (5 pence) per dozen records sold).

These music hall artists were joined by singers such as Ion Colquhoun, called without exaggeration the "Iron-Voiced Baritone". His powerful voice proved a great asset in Gaisberg's primitive studios. Colquhoun sang patriotic songs made popular in the late 1890s during the Anglo-Boer War, then at its height. He recorded almost 40 songs for The Gramophone Company, including Leslie Stuart's "Soldiers of the Queen" (Berliner 2716). However, Colquhoun's most important recordings, released in December 1899, were two special records of "The Absent-Minded Beggar". Commissioned by the *Daily Mail*, the great Victorian composer Sir Arthur Sullivan had written a musical setting of Kipling's original verse. Unfortunately, the song was too long to fit on one 7-inch disc, and Gaisberg was forced to record it over two separate discs (and, even then, two of the four choruses were omitted). The records sold for 5 shillings (25 pence) per set, and the funds generated by their sale went to the *Daily Mail's* war fund. To mark this important association with a national newspaper, The Gramophone Company placed its first ever advertisement, in the *Daily Mail* in December 1899. It featured the release of the "Absent-Minded Beggar" records and gave the Company much-needed Christmas publicity.

Between 1900 and 1906, significant improvements in the art of sound recording, together with the later innovation of a disc with a recording pressed into both sides, further popularized the appeal of the gramophone record. With these advances, The Gramophone Company set about changing the attitudes of established artists. To this end, two successful young musicians

"The Absent-Minded Beggar."

With the kind permission of the "Daily Mail,"

IAN COLQUHOUN has generously sung for us Sir A. SULLIVAN'S Musical Setting of RUDYARD KIPLING'S Celebrated Poem. IT IS CLEAR, LOUD, AND DISTINCTLY ENUNCIATED. The song required two discs for the reproduction, and is sold in complete sets only. The total receipts from the sale of these records at the full price, 5s., are to be forwarded by us to the "Daily Mail" War Fund. We fill all orders for these records through our Agents only. We will in all cases direct purchasers to our nearest Local Agent. Our Agents will all act for us in this matter from purely patriotic feeling.

GRAMOPHONE CO., LTD.,
31, MAIDEN-LANE, STRAND.

The great Dan Leno, doyen of British music hall and an early Gramophone Company artist.

Left The first advertisement for The Gramophone Company Ltd appeared in the Daily Mail, on 21 December 1899 complete with misspelling of the artist's name.

Telegraphic Cable address Jabberment, London.

Telephone No. 2836. Gerrard.

o/w.

The Gramophone Company.

General Manager: Wm. Barry Owen.

31, Maiden Lane, London. W.C.

15th October, 1898.

Albert Chevalier Esq.
  c/o Mr. Burt,
  6, Arlington Street, W.

Dear Sir,

In consideration of your singing and furnishing us with records for the Gramophone, we hereby agree to pay you a royalty at the rate of 1/- per dozen upon all records sold from the plates with which you supply us, and to make a full accounting quarterly, such accounting to be subject to verification by your authorised agent, who shall have ample opportunity to inspect our books for such verification.

Trusting that you will find this entirely satisfactory, -
We are, dear Sir,

Yours truly,

The Gramophone Company.

The music hall performer Albert Chevalier was the first British recording artist to negotiate a royalty-based recording contract (left), which was signed in October 1898.

Sir Landon Ronald (1873–1938) was The Gramophone Company's first British musical director. His position in the British musical establishment as an eminent musician and principal of the Guildhall School of Music helped the Company achieve recognition for the cultural and educational value of its records. His influence and standing with important artists persuaded many of them to make records.

were hired as musical advisors: Carlo Sabajno in Italy, and Landon (later Sir Landon) Ronald in London. In his memoirs, Landon Ronald recalled that his first task was to overcome "the tremendous prejudice that existed in the minds of all artists against what was considered by them an outrage on their art". [Landon Ronald, *Variations on a Personal Theme* (London 1922), p.97]

The breakthrough came in April 1902, when The Gramophone Company made the first recordings of the Italian tenor Enrico Caruso (see box, page 57). Fred Gaisberg, who made the records, regarded them as being of seminal importance in the development of the industry. Caruso's power and influence as a performer, combined with the quality of the records he made, were central to bringing artistic respectability to the gramophone, and they also demonstrated what was to become the record's greatest strength: its ability to spread art and culture around the world. Surviving evidence suggests that Caruso's meteoric rise to fame in the early 1900s was in part due to his recordings, which were already on sale in Britain when he made his Covent Garden debut later in the spring of 1902. Caruso's voice was thus already well known to those opera lovers who owned a gramophone and had the means to buy his records. Furthermore, the availability of Caruso's 1902 Gramophone Company recordings in the United States appears to have been decisive in negotiations that led to the artist's 1903 New York debut at the Metropolitan Opera House. Finally, after Caruso's sensational 1904 debut in Berlin, a local newspaper highlighted just how important his records had been in making the debut a success, remarking on "Caruso, who has become famous in other countries through his voice and his art and whose name has become a household word in Germany through the gramophone". [Caruso Artist File, EMI Music Archive]

In 1924 – three years after the singer's death – Compton Mackenzie, founder of the *Gramophone* magazine, wrote:

If you are anxious to test the measure of Caruso's vitality, consider what he meant to the gramophone. He made it what it is … He impressed his personality through the medium of his recorded voice on kings and peasants. ["Gramophone Celebrities: Enrico Caruso", *Gramophone*, Vol.2, July 1924]

Once Caruso had shown how important his records were as a medium for spreading his art, others – including many established performers – followed. They were lured into the recording studio by lucrative royalty-based contracts and advances, potential world audiences, and what no other

ENRICO CARUSO
(1873–1921)

★

Enrico Caruso, generally acknowledged to be the greatest tenor of the 20th century, was born in poverty in Naples, Italy. When he made his first Gramophone Company recordings in 1902, he was already a rising opera star. Caruso's son, who attended one of his father's later recording sessions, wrote of his father's affinity for recording: "It struck me that father was not merely delivering a tune but was living each song. His face was animated, and he acted out the words as he would on the concert stage, so that I not only heard but also 'saw' the song." Caruso first sang at the Metropolitan Opera in New York in 1903 and remained there as one of its greatest stars for 18 consecutive seasons, until his untimely death at the age of 48. After 1904, all his recordings were made for Victor in the United States; The Gramophone Company obtained access to them through its Victor licensing deal. The Company released a total of 240 Caruso recordings, the most popular being his 1907 version of "Vesti la giubba" from Leoncavallo's opera *Pagliacci* (HMV 052159). Fred Gaisberg later wrote of the singer: "He was the answer to a recording man's dream … He had the interpretative art of a born singer and a sense of pitch that nothing could shift."

Left The first separate catalogue of celebrity records was released in 1902. Among the stars whose records featured was the celebrated French mezzo-soprano Emma Calvé.

SIR EDWARD ELGAR (1857–1934)

Sir Edward Elgar was already secure in his position as Britain's leading composer when he began his exclusive association with The Gramophone Company in 1914. His first recording of his short orchestral piece *Carissima* (HMV 0967) was followed by others of his own music, including his wartime composition *Carillon* (HMV 2-0522–3), and his most popular work, the *Pomp and Circumstance* March No.1 ("Land of Hope and Glory") (HMV 2-0511). As David Bicknell noted: "Elgar was extremely fond of recording and was never troubled by it … he was the grand Old Man of English music and a pioneer of recording." During the final decade of his life, a unique partnership developed between The Gramophone Company and Elgar, and he recorded virtually all his orchestral compositions. With this venture, Elgar became the first major composer to create a definitive recorded canon of his own works. Notable records included excerpts from *The Dream of Gerontius* (HMV D 1242–3) with the Royal Choral Society in 1927, the "Enigma" Variations (HMV D 1154–57) with the Royal Albert Hall Orchestra; the Violin Concerto with Yehudi Menuhin (HMV DB 1751–6), the Cello Concerto with Beatrice Harrison (HMV D 1507–9), both the symphonies (HMV D 1944–9 and D 1230–35) and *Falstaff* (HMV DB 1621–4), the last of which inaugurated Abbey Road's Number One Studio on 11 November 1931. Shortly after Elgar died, Fred Gaisberg wrote: "the greatest English composer has, for the first time in history, left to posterity his own interpretations of his works."

Above, right Sir Edward Elgar at a 1915 Hayes recording session attended by Princess Alice (Countess of Athlone), the Crown Prince of Romania, and the Earl of Athlone. Note the high chairs which raise the instrumentalists to the level of the recording horn.

Right This pre-1914 supplement associates His Master's Voice records with sophisticated music-making among the leisured classes.

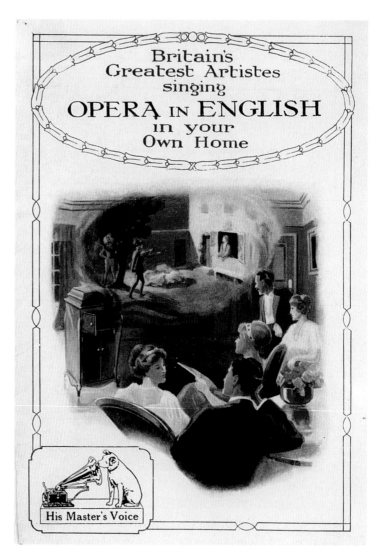

generation of performing artists had ever dreamed of: artistic immortality. In the years immediately before the outbreak of war in 1914, Caruso was the industry's most successful artist. He earned anything up to £20,000 a year from world sales of his records, and his immediate post-war earnings may have been as high as £200,000. A few artists earned fabulous fortunes from their recording activities, whilst the Gramophone Company in return gained kudos from its association with them. Fred Gaisberg wrote of the Company's early relationship with the composer Sir Edward Elgar (see box, page 58), who did not make a fortune from his recording activities: "Elgar's association with my Company before 1925 was chiefly decorative, his name carrying the prestige of England's greatest composer." [Gaisberg, ibid., p.233]

The two most important established performers The Gramophone Company wanted to record were the sopranos Adelina Patti and Nellie Melba (see box, page 79). In 1905, Patti, who was living at the time in semi-retirement at her massive South Wales castle, finally agreed to make records. All the arrangements were handled by her solicitor, Sir George Lewis (who was Theodore Birnbaum's father-in-law). Fred Gaisberg and his brother William (who had joined the Company in 1902) took their equipment to Patti's home. There, they captured on wax the voice and art of a singer who had dominated the artistic world for more than 40 years. On hearing her finished recordings, Patti wrote:

The gramophone of today, I find, is such an improved instrument for recording the human voice that my hitherto objection to allow the thousands who cannot hear me sing personally to listen to the reproduction of my voice through the instrumentality of your gramophone is now quite removed, and the records you have lately made for me I think are natural reproductions of my voice.
[Patti Artist File, EMI Music Archive]

In a 1904 letter, Theodore Birnbaum told Sydney Dixon (then manager of the Company's British branch): "If we can secure Melba, we shall have done something far beyond what we have up to now achieved". [Melba Artist File, EMI Music Archive] Melba was an astute businesswoman and aware of her value to The Gramophone Company. As a result, she played hard to

Adelina Patti (1843–1919)
In the magnificence of her South Wales castle the great Victorian soprano Adelina Patti recorded her voice for the gramophone.

Despite the price, 2,000 copies of Melba's records were sold in Britain within a month of their release.

Francesco Tamagno (1851–1905)
The Italian tenor Francesco Tamagno in the role of Otello, the part Verdi wrote for him. In 1903, Tamagno made a handful of recordings for The Gramophone Company including, several extracts from *Otello*. These are among the Company's first recordings of an artist in a role he created.

get. She was relentlessly pursued by Dixon and Landon Ronald, who went to extraordinary lengths, including making a series of private recordings of her voice at her London home for relatives in Australia – but still she refused to make recordings. In desperation, they turned for assistance to her then lover, the Australian writer Haddon Chambers. His intervention appears to have clinched the deal. However, Melba's first contract was exacting. She received an advance of £1,000, and the 12-inch records – each bearing a special mauve label and a facsimile of her signature – were sold for one guinea (£1.05) each. After recovery of the advance, Melba received a royalty of five shillings (25 pence) per record sold. The success of the first Melba recordings led to further sessions in Britain and the United States. Melba even permitted her name to be associated with a top-of-the-range gramophone.

Artists at the beginning of their careers were much more pliable and were happy to accept the fees paid by The Gramophone Company. During the early years of the century, the most important of these new artists was the Irish tenor John McCormack (see box, page 61). By 1910, he had signed a long-term record contract with Victor. Although McCormack recorded many fine operatic arias, it was ballads such as "I hear you calling me" (HMV 4-2076), and Irish songs like "Believe me if all those endearing young charms" (HMV 4-2141) that were among his best sellers, and remained so until he made his last records during the Second World War (see Chapter 5). Although these and many other McCormack records were made in the United States, they became available to music lovers throughout the world thanks to the Victor Gramophone Company licensing agreement.

By 1914, most major international performing artists featured in the Company's celebrity catalogue. They included some of the greatest performers of their generation. One such was Francesco Tamagno, for whom Verdi wrote the title role in *Otello*. In 1903, he recorded arias from that opera, including "Esultate!" (G&T 052101), together with arias from other operas. These were later released, with great fanfare, at the impressive price of £1 each. After her spectacular 1907 Covent Garden debut as Violetta in Verdi's opera *La traviata*, Luisa Tetrazzini (see box, page 62) began making records for The Gramophone Company and later for Victor. None was better received than her two-record set of "Ah! fors'è lui" (G&T 053147 and G&T 053196) from *La traviata*. Other great

JOHN McCORMACK (1884–1945)

John McCormack, one of the greatest lyric tenors of his generation, was born in Athlone, Ireland. In 1903 he won the gold medal at the Dublin Feis Coeil (music festival). The following year, he began his long Gramophone Company career, recording a number of Irish songs for a fee of 25 guineas (£26.25), plus a gramophone and two dozen records. In 1905, McCormack went to Milan to study singing, and two years later he made his Covent Garden debut in Mascagni's opera *Cavalleria rusticana*. Over the following years his operatic career blossomed, but he eventually decided that he was more at home on the concert platform. In 1910, he signed a contract with Victor, and he recorded exclusively for Victor and HMV until 1942. McCormack's records ranged from Lieder and opera to popular ballads and Irish songs, all of which he sang with great refinement. His 1916 recording of "Il mio tesoro" (HMV 2-052110) from Mozart's opera *Don Giovanni* is regarded by many as his finest disc. McCormack loved recording: in 1930, after a particularly pleasing session, he wrote to Fred Gaisberg: "Please tell the boys at the recording department that I have never enjoyed a session of recording as much as this last and I am grateful for their kindness and whole-hearted co-operation." In 1927, in recognition of his generosity to Catholic causes, McCormack was created a Papal Count. When he died in 1945, Gerald Moore, his last accompanist, said: "This great minstrel will never be forgotten. He is enshrined in the hearts of his people for his singing lifted them up and showed them beauty and romance."

A pupil of Leschetizky, the pianist Mark Hambourg was, for more than a quarter of a century, a prolific Gramophone Company artist.

LUISA TETRAZZINI
(1871–1940)

★

The Italian soprano Luisa Tetrazzini, whose discs were among the most popular of all pre–1914 celebrity recordings, was born in Florence. By the time of her sensational 1907 Covent Garden debut, she was already an international star. She made her first Gramophone Company recordings shortly after her London debut, and thereafter recorded regularly for HMV and Victor. By the standards of the time, her records were best-sellers, with British sales between 1908 and 1914 exceeding 63,000 copies, earning her royalties of £16,000. Her most successful records were "Caro nome" from Verdi's *Rigoletto* (HMV 2-053050) and "Una voce poco fa" from Rossini's *Barbiere di Siviglia* (HMV 2-053056). She became a regular and popular visitor to the Company's Hayes factory site, and laid the corner stone for the cabinet factory in 1911. Although she lived mainly in Italy during the First World War, she did visit Britain and gave several wartime concerts for war workers at Hayes, and in September 1919 she returned for what became a highly successful series of concert tours. Her voice was remarkable for its effortless agility and great range. The German soprano Frieda Hempel said of Tetrazzini: "There was something in the way she sang that swept you off your feet – an élan that sent chills running up and down your spine."

performers in HMV's catalogue of Celebrity Records by International Artistes included the singers Emma Eames, Mattia Battistini, Emma Calvé and Fernando de Lucia, the virtuoso violinists Pablo de Sarasate, Joseph Joachim, Mischa Elman, Fritz Kreisler (see box, page 63), Jan Kubelík and Joseph Szigeti, the pianists Ignacy Jan Paderewski and Mark Hambourg, and the composer Camille Saint-Saëns. Even though the making of orchestral recordings was beset by difficulties – not least how to fit an orchestra into a small recording studio – several orchestral recordings were made before 1914. The most important was a complete recording of Beethoven's Fifth Symphony (HMV 040784–91), with the Berlin Philharmonic Orchestra conducted

Left The Italian baritone Titta Ruffo (1873–1953) leaving The Gramophone Company's City Road office in 1907. Note the window display of his recordings.

by Arthur Nikisch. The cultural riches created by this first flowering of the art of sound recording gave The Gramophone Company a unique standing as a new force that could preserve forever that most ephemeral of all arts, performance.

Although celebrities and celebrity records were a central feature of the Company's marketing strategy, they were not central to its profits. As Theodore Birnbaum remarked in 1907: "This class of business is very difficult to handle, and it is questionable whether it can be regarded on any other basis than high-class advertising". [Report to the Board, The Gramophone Company Ltd, Board Papers, 1907, EMI Music Archive] As an example, less than one per cent of the Company's unit sales in 1913 were Celebrity records.

FRITZ KREISLER
(1875–1962)

★

Fritz Kreisler, whose effortless technique and sweet tone made him one of the century's greatest violinists, was born in Vienna. He was the youngest pupil ever accepted by the Vienna Conservatory. His first big success came in December 1899 at his debut with the Berlin Philharmonic under Nikisch, and the grace and charm of his faultless playing soon established him internationally as a celebrity. From 1924 to 1934 he lived in Berlin, where he made some of his acclaimed early concerto recordings with the Berlin State Opera Orchestra conducted by Leo Blech; these included the violin concertos of Beethoven (HMV DB 990–94), Brahms (HMV DB 1120–24) and Mendelssohn (HMV DB 997–1000). Kreisler was also a talented composer: in addition to several substantial works, he wrote and recorded a number of delightful short salon pieces which are perfect examples of their kind, including "Schön Rosmarin" (HMV DA 1044) and "Caprice viennois" (HMV DB 1091). He also made "arrangements" of pieces by various minor 18th-century composers which he later admitted were in fact his own compositions. Kreisler continued playing until the end of the 1940s. His outstanding talents and the "Viennese" qualities in his music-making were admired by many other violinists and musicians. He was also an early idol of Walter Legge's, who said of him that "the nobility and warmth of Kreisler's tone gave me a new and unimagined concept of sound."

Right The Spanish virtuoso violinist and composer Pablo de Sarasate made a series of recordings of his own and others' works.

SYDNEY DIXON, OBE
(1868–1922)

Sidney Wentworth Dixon joined The Gramophone Company in 1902 after service in the Anglo-Boer War. Initially he acted as William Barry Owen's assistant, often managing the entire business during Owen's frequent periods of absence in the United States. However, after Owen's departure in 1904, he became manager of the then newly created British sales branch. In 1909, he and Alfred Clark became joint managing directors and, in 1912, he became sales director. It was largely through his mass advertising campaigns that the HMV trademark became the most readily identifiable of all record company trademarks. Dixon also created new record labels to match those of his competitors, and he turned the British record market into the Company's single most important source of sales and profits. When war broke out in 1914, Dixon rejoined his regiment. Although he returned to the Company in 1919, the war had shattered his health. He succeeded Will Gaisberg as head of the Recording Department, which he reorganized, creating the International Artistes Department. He threw himself enthusiastically into this job until his sudden death, aged 54, in 1922.

Right This Gramophone Company advertisement shows the gramophone as an essential part of the every day leisure and domestic activities of the wealthy educated middle classes.

Opposite page HMV vied with Columbia in recording the best music from London revues.

I Love a Lassie

THE BRITISH BRANCH, 1904–1914

Until William Barry Owen left the Company in 1904, the British end of the business was handled by what was essentially the Company's London head office. One of Theodore Birnbaum's first acts as managing director was to create a separate British branch, with Sydney Dixon as manager. At the time, unit sales of records in Britain were around 600,000 units a year; by 1914, the figure had risen to nearly 4 million.

In the early years of the century, the British record market was dominated not by The Gramophone Company's disc records, but by the rival trade in cylinder records. As Dixon told the board in 1905: "In Great Britain the phonograph [cylinder] trade is gigantic and the disc trade is very small".

Reproduced by permission of The Haycock Cadle Co.

Hippodrome Revue
'HULLO TANGO!' RECORDS
vocal · instrumental · ragtime

Special Record
of two of the finest descriptive num-
bers ever issued in record form on
ZONOPHONE
No. 1050
By STANLEY KIRKBY.

"'TIS A STORY THAT SHALL
LIVE FOR EVER"
and (descriptive of the Capt. Scott disaster)

"BE BRITISH" (a realistic account of the
wreck of the "Titanic")

10-inch 2/6   *Pelham & Wright.*
                  Published by Lawrence Wright Co.

Startling Development, *see page 4.*

1909.
SEPTEMBER
ZONOPHONE RECORDS.

The Zonophone soaring higher than ever.

NEW
GRAMOPHONE
RECORDS

"HIS MASTERS VOICE"

Above In 1909, the French pilot Louis Blériot flew across the English Channel. The attention his flight received in the British press made everyone aware of this latest wonder of the age. Zonophone publicists were quick to capitalize on this, as can be seen from this fanciful record supplement.

Above, top The twin tragedies of Captain Scott's ill-fated polar expedition and the sinking of the SS *Titanic* were both the subject of commemorative recordings.

Right Gramophone record catalogue, 1905, featuring the HMV trademark, the three sizes of record then in use and needle tins.

[Monthly Epitomes, The Gramophone Company Ltd Board Papers 1905, EMI Music Archive] However, as Britain was then Europe's wealthiest nation, the potential existed for the Company to create a large market. To do this, it began to advertise extensively: displayed prominently in these advertisements were its royal warrants, granted by various British and foreign royal households. Valuable publicity was gained when the Company sent a gramophone and records with Captain Scott to the Antarctic. However, the tragedy of

SIR HARRY LAUDER (1870–1950)

Harry Lauder, the great Scottish entertainer, was born in Portobello, near Edinburgh. A background of grinding poverty forced him to work in local coalmines from the age of 13. He made his London debut in 1900 at Gatti's music hall. Thereafter, he developed his remarkable talents as an international entertainer, creating the Scots persona which became his hallmark, complete with a pastiche of highland dress, broad accent and a canny eye on his money. He soon extended his activities, undertaking arduous though highly successful tours of the English-speaking world. From 1902, Lauder recorded extensively for The Gramophone Company, and by the outbreak of war in 1914, much of his repertoire was on both HMV and Zonophone. Lauder was an ardent Imperialist and an uncritical supporter of the war. The death of his only son on the Somme in 1916 prompted him to visit soldiers on the Western Front. On his return to London, he made a record appealing for £1 million (HMV D 1) to help disabled Scottish servicemen, and gave numerous concerts at home and abroad. At the war's end he was knighted for services to the Empire. In 1924, he recorded what became one of his most famous songs, "Keep right on to the end of the road" (HMV D 1085 and Zono GO 64), a ballad of stoicism and fortitude. After the introduction of electrical recording, Lauder remade much of his earlier repertoire for HMV, Zonophone and Victor.

Left The Scottish entertainer made recordings for both the HMV and Zonophone labels.

that failed expedition overshadowed the gesture (the machine was returned to London and is in the Company's Archive to this day). Respectability was further bestowed by the roster of celebrity artists, who were also featured in advertising, as also by the Company name, the trademark *His Master's Voice* and its familiar form as the initials HMV.

Music hall performers, such as the Scottish entertainer Harry Lauder, also featured in the Company's advertising and in monthly releases of new records. Lauder was one of the new generation of performers who saw record-making as a natural extension of existing music hall activities. Lauder's records sold throughout the English-speaking world in large numbers (90,000 in Britain alone during 1908). Even so, before 1920 Lauder did not make a great deal of money from his recording activities. His earliest contracts stipulated the payment of a retaining fee and of a fixed sum for every record

The season of giving as illustrated in this Christmas 1912 Deutsche Grammophon trade card.

he made. Nonetheless, during this period, Lauder recorded some of his most enduring songs, including "I love a lassie" (G&T GC3-2322), first recorded in 1905, and "Roamin' in the gloamin'" (HMV 02320), recorded in 1911.

In 1904, apart from records by classical and music hall performers, The Gramophone Company's record catalogues were filled with brass and military band music and popular songs. These, and all new recordings of this type, were re-released on the Zonophone label. Zonophone records were distributed through the wholesale trade and retailed by hardware shops, sports stores, tobacconists, bicycle dealers and general stores. In the decade before 1914, 9 million Zonophone records were sold – initially for 3 shillings and 6 pence (17.5 pence), subsequently reduced to 2 shillings and 6 pence (12.5 pence) – demonstrating that, even in those early years, there existed a strong market for budget records.

Seizing on the success of the Zonophone label, The Gramophone Company launched other budget labels, including the Twin, priced at 2 shillings and 6 pence (12.5 pence), and the Cinch, priced at 1 shilling and 1 pence (5.1 pence). Nearly 2 million Twin records were sold before the marque was integrated with Zonophone in 1911, and 2.5 million Cinch records were sold in the first year of their existence. The aim of these ventures was to capture the mass market and to interest new audiences in the pleasures of disc records in the home. In 1908, Dixon reported on the size of this sector: "It is a common occurrence for a small talking-machine dealer to sell one thousand records between 2 o'clock on Saturday afternoon and closing time" [Monthly Epitomes, The Gramophone Company Ltd Board Papers 1908, EMI Music Archive] Other developments in the market were keenly followed. As a result, in 1912, the Company introduced a fresh concept, the mid-price plum-label record. The success of this label was such that it retained a place in the Company's record catalogues until the end of 78-rpm records, and was carried through into the LP era with the CLP and DLP series.

By the outbreak of war, the British branch had become the Company's single most important subsidiary, with sales up from £116,000 in 1904 to £300,000 in 1914. Profits, which stood at a mere 16 per cent of the Company's total in 1905, had risen to an impressive 44 per cent by 1914. By that year, the disc record had brought about major changes in British leisure habits: one third of all households possessed some kind of gramophone and 13 million disc records had been sold in Britain. Of these, one in four was a product of

The Gramophone Company. Thanks to the pioneering efforts of The Gramophone Company's British branch, what had initially been regarded by many in Britain as a foolish toy had become an integral part of British musical life.

How the King went to war

RUSSIA, 1900–1918

With a population of 150 million, Russia was potentially The Gramophone Company's biggest market. However, contrasts of unbelievable wealth and dire poverty, together with chronic political and business corruption, made trading there a high-risk venture. Yet for much of its life, The Gramophone Company enjoyed a highly successful Russian trade which at one stage

A Letter – Agreement with the Grammophone Co. Ltd. of London.

———————

Herewith I agree to sing ten songs ~~enumerated below~~ (10) in any language other than Russian for a remuneration of one rouble (R. 1.) per each "record" (plate, disc etc.) ~~of the ten songs enumerated below~~ sold outside the boundaries of Russia, which ten songs are to be done during the month of October 1911 and not later than January 1912.

I agree to accept fifteen thousand roubles (15.000 Rbl!) by way of an advance on account of the above mentioned remuneration, which advance must be paid to me immediately after the said songs have been sung by me.

Herewith I further agree that the present letter shall be regarded as a part of my agreement with you and shall form one of its clauses.

The three words "ten songs enumerated below" struck out in the original I request to be regarded as non-written.

(signed) Th. Schaliapin.

Also the word

"enumerated" is struck out

and considered as non-existant.

(signed) Th. Schaliapin.

The Imperial Russian Consulate herewith certifies the identy of the above signature of Theodor Schaliapin.

Nice, 10/20. March 1911.

Consul.

(signed) E. Kanshin.

L.S.

Charges Frs. 8.-- Rbl. 3.--

paid.

Chaliapin's 1911 contract
For this contract to make ten records in languages other than Russian, Chaliapin received an advance of £1,500.

The Gramophone Company's Russian headquarters in St Petersburg.

accounted for more than half the Company's profits. Unfortunately, it was prey to dishonesty from both traders and Russian employees. This dishonesty took many forms, including the illegal copying of records, and resulted in a rapid withering of profits; so much so that in 1908 The Gramophone Company's usually handsome profits were reduced to almost nothing.

The Russian trade began in earnest in 1900 with an early recording trip. In 1900, Norbert Rodkinson was appointed the first Russian branch manager. Not without irony, Gaisberg described this extraordinary man:

Rodkinson was the well-educated son of a Russian–American Rabbi. He was handsome and ruthless in business and love, his two absorbing habits … The combination of Russian and American business methods, introduced by him, showed a versatility that amazed even the hardened Polish and Russian Jewish dealers of the old Russian Empire. [Gaisberg, ibid., p.30]

Demand for records became so great that, in 1903, it became necessary to open a record factory in the Latvian capital of Riga (then part of Imperial Russia).

F. P. Raphoff, a merchant associated with the Company from its earliest days, told Gaisberg that, in order to flourish in Russia, it was essential to obtain recordings of the great artists from the Imperial Opera, including Feodor Chaliapin and Nicolai Figner: "If they could snare such birds as these they would be worthy of red labels." Making records of artists such as Chaliapin was not easy. Gaisberg described, how on one occasion, Chaliapin simply took control of everything: "His chest stripped and bare like a prize-fighter he starts his recording. As on the stage and everything else he takes full direction of orchestra and laboratory". [Gaisberg, "Recording Chaliapin in Moscow, May 1913", Typescript] By 1914, despite these nerve-racking experiences, The Gramophone Company had recorded a representative sample of Chaliapin's art. Among the most popular was the ballad "How the King went to war" (HMV 022093). Raphoff made a most important contribution to marketing strategy with his idea of placing red labels (a sign of quality in Russia) on the Celebrity recordings.

The Gramophone Company's agents also began selling in the Russian hinterland. To develop these markets, new records reflecting the local ethnic and cultural diversity were required. Fred Gaisberg recalled making records in Kazan for the Tartar market: "So to the working-men's cafés and to the low-class brothels we went, since they were the only places where we could get the Tartar songs we wished to record." [Gaisberg, ibid., p.38]

Frederick Tyler, the Company's manager in Tblisi (then called Tiflis) in Georgia, took charge of the vast Central Asian territory. He wrote to London in 1911:

Perhaps the greatest increase can be looked for in the trans-Caspian territory which is a comparatively new field for the gramophone business and where there are yet to be tapped several large and more or less populous districts lying wide of the railway line. To open up these districts I have made arrangements with our representative in Tashkent to send out his native assistant with a supply of motors [gramophones] and records carried on horses or donkeys. He is instructed to give a concert in each town or village and afterwards to sell his stock as may be possible or take orders … I have great hopes that this will lead to a considerable addition to the business as there is a wide field lying beyond Tashkent to the borders of Western China which has so far been practically untouched. [Frederick Tyler to Sydney Dixon; 9 Sepember 1911, Russian File, EMI Music Archive]

During the First World War, Tyler and other British managers stayed in their posts; they witnessed years of disruption,

FEODOR CHALIAPIN (1873–1938)

Feodor Ivanovitch Chaliapin, the Russian bass, was born in 1873 at Kazan, Russia, a town on the Volga river. As a youth, he played on its banks and watched the workers haul the barges upstream; they sang a traditional monotonous chant which, years later, became one of Chaliapin's most successful records – "The Song of the Volga Boatmen" (HMV 2-022016). Chaliapin was already the idol of musical Russia when he made his first records in Moscow in 1901. His fame quickly spread and by 1914 he had appeared in all the major European and American opera houses. He sang most of the principal bass parts, including the Mefistofeles of both Gounod and Boito, and was especially fêted for his dramatic performances of the title roles in Moussorgsky's *Boris Godunov*, Rimsky-Korsakov's *Ivan the Terrible* and Rubinstein's *Demon*. The Great War and the Russian Revolution were disastrous for Chaliapin, but with the help of The Gramophone Company, he was brought to safety and spent the final phase of his life in Paris. He continued to make records until 1936; all capture something of his magnetic personality and commanding vocal presence. When he died in 1938, the Daily Telegraph said of him: "He was the one singer with whom one gave no special thought to the voice … to see him come on stage was to forget everything but the opera … everything was somehow lifted – songs, instruments and drama …."

shortages, war and revolution until, in 1918, the Bolshevik regime expelled them.

Take me back to dear old Blighty

THE GREAT WAR, 1914–1918

In August 1914 – quite unexpectedly – the first general European war for one hundred years broke out. No individual or business remained unaffected, least of all multinational businesses like The Gramophone Company. At the very moment war was declared, the Company had been planning its activities for the next selling season, whilst the previous month, the first Branch Managers' Convention had been held at Hayes. At its conclusion, the general feeling had been one of growing success in all sectors.

The Gramophone Company released its first war supplement in October 1914. Among the records featured were the national anthems of the Allied nations, and the then top-selling "It's a long way to Tipperary".

However, instead of the anticipated boom, the 1914–15 season almost destroyed The Gramophone Company.

As a major British-based multinational business with a domestic British market accounting for less than half of turnover or profits, The Gramophone Company proved very vulnerable to war-induced disruption. Nothing highlighted this vulnerability better than the war-time actions of the German and Russian governments. These governments seized the Company's local branches, which it permanently lost, with the consequent reduction of one-third of its assets. A critical loss was the German factory at Hannover, the pre-war supplier of the Company's main European markets, and the storage centre of the priceless collection of metal matrices (including those made by celebrities) built up since the foundation of the business. After the war, it took years of frustrating negotiation and legal action before the matrices were returned and compensation paid.

Initially, the reaction of Europe's populations to the war was, as Alfred Clark wrote: "an immediate cessation of all buying. The public, stunned by the unexpected crisis, decided to save rather than spend". [Clark, *His Master's Voice*] The combined loss of control of cash-earning branches and of income from sales led to an immediate cash-flow crisis. With extraordinary bad luck, the declaration of war coincided with the long-planned commencement of gramophone manufacture at the Company's new £120,000 Hayes factory. In the circumstances, the Company had little option but to shelve its manufacturing plans for the duration. To ensure the Company's survival, staff wages were cut by half. Recognizing the need to keep the factory staff together (in order to commence gramophone manufacture as soon as the war ended), Clark and his staff obtained war-related munitions contracts. The demand for war matériel increased as hostilities continued. As a direct consequence, employment at Hayes increased four-fold and, by the war's end, a total of £6 million worth of business had been generated. Without this work, the Company would not have survived.

The immediate collapse in sales of records and machines in the autumn of 1914 proved short-lived. However, during the crisis, the Company's branches tried to stimulate sales by producing special record supplements of patriotic records (see also Chapter 3). Alfred Clark said of this phenomenon: "In

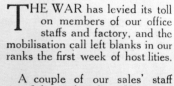

"His Master's Voice" AND THE WAR

THE WAR has levied its toll on members of our office staffs and factory, and the mobilisation call left blanks in our ranks the first week of hostilities.

A couple of our sales' staff are fighting for their King and Country, and one of them, Lieut. Jack Gibbons, is already with his unit abroad with the Expeditionary Force. May they return with a glorious record !

TURNING to another aspect of the war, many of the Hospitals are being equipped with the world's greatest entertainer, "His Master's Voice" Gramophone, to cheer the wounded. What could be better? Public-spirited givers are freely presenting gramophones to the hospitals. The following letter is of interest :—

3rd London General Hospital.
R.A.M.C.T.F.
Royal Victoria Patriotic School,
Wandsworth, S.W.
Aug. 17, 1914.
I am requested by the Commanding Officer, Lieut. Colonel Bruce-Porter, to express his most sincere thanks for the three "His Master's Voice" Gramophones with Records for the Hospital Wards

THE WATCH DOGS

16

Women provided a large part of the workforce engaged in the manufacture of munitions at the Hayes factory during the First World War.

Berlin, St Petersburg and London … there is a brisk little trade in special new patriotic records, but of course the total of this turnover is but a drop in the bucket." [Clark to Eldridge R. Johnson, November 1914. Clark Papers, Eldridge R. Johnson Museum, Dover, Delaware]

Throughout the war, the British record industry experienced a period of significant growth, with sales of Gramophone Company records rising from 3.3 million units in 1913 to nearly 5 million in 1919. In part, this growth was caused by the unavailability of German-manufactured records, which by 1914 had captured half the British market. However, the biggest boost came from the circumstances of the war itself: the strains of war caused those on the home front and in the trenches to turn to gramophone records as a means of release, despite the shortage of gramophones.

By far the most successful record from the early war years

The Italian opera star Luisa Tetrazzini, one of a number of HMV artists to give lunchtime concerts for war workers at the Hayes factories.

was "It's a long way to Tipperary". Not actually a new song, "Tipperary" had first been released by The Gramophone Company in 1913 with the Cecilian Quartette (HMV 2-4206) and Harry Fay (Zono 1070), and had proved a modest if undistinguished success. However, in the opening weeks of the war, a *Daily Mail* reporter heard some troops of the British Expeditionary Force singing it as they disembarked in France. Within a few days, every newspaper had printed the words of the chorus, and the record industry experienced its greatest hit to date. For many, "Tipperary" became synonymous with that awful conflict.

The musical output of the war's middle years was dominated by two great soldiers songs, neither of which had a hint of the earlier patriotic froth. The British composer Ivor Novello wrote "Till the boys come home" (popularly known as "Keep the home fires burning") in 1915; The Gramophone Company's record of the song was performed by the contralto Renee Mayer (HMV B 624). Early in 1916, the American song "There's a long, long trail" appeared; the Company's best-known recording of this song was made for Zonophone Records in 1916 by Ernest Pike, its

house tenor (Zonophone X 3-42569). Musically, the final phase of the war was characterized by a mood of romanticism, yearning for home and an end to the war, as reflected in songs such as "Take me back to dear old Blighty" (HMV B 760), recorded in 1917 by Eric Courtland and Walter Jeffries (pseudonyms for George Baker and Ernest Pike), and, most evocatively, in "Roses of Picardy" (HMV C 793), recorded in 1918 by Pike.

Apart from rapid movements of armies in France and Flanders during the opening and closing phases of the war, the Western Front was essentially static. In these circumstances, there were opportunities for gramophones and records to find their way into rest areas, support lines and even into the front-line trenches themselves. Accounts of life in the trenches make frequent references to gramophones and records. As a result, men who had never taken the gramophone seriously became firm believers. One example of the soldier turned record buyer was Arthur (later Sir Arthur) Bliss, the composer and EMI artist, who later became Master of the Queen's Musick. In early 1916, he wrote from the Western Front: "I have suddenly found solace in the gramophone. Kennard [his brother, killed later in 1916] who I believe has ordered all Berlioz for that touching instrument says they sound divine." [Arthur Bliss to E. J. Dent. Add. MS 7973/B/29, Cambridge University Library] In the 1970s, EMI recorded Bliss's symphony *Morning Heroes* (HMV-Angel SAN 365), a work dedicated to the dead of the First World War, and particularly to the memory of Kennard Bliss, with the Royal Liverpool Philharmonic Orchestra conducted by Sir Charles Groves. Gramophone enthusiasts like

Bliss had a significant impact: they supported Compton Mackenzie's magazine the *Gramophone* when it appeared in 1923; and they helped create a market for recordings of complete instrumental, chamber and orchestral works (see below and Chapter 5). As a result, important classical works were recorded for the gramophone, and this helped expand and develop the range of recorded music released by The Gramophone Company, and later by EMI.

In October 1918, a month before the Armistice was signed, The Gramophone Company became engaged in a somewhat bizarre venture: an attempt to record the sounds of war. Many people believed that the Great War would be, as the writer H. G. Wells put it, "The war to end all war". It was argued quite logically that if there was to be no more war then, for the benefit of posterity, it was essential to record the sounds of battle. To this end, the Company sent William Gaisberg, the head of the London recording studio, to the Western Front. There, in front of the French city of Lille, he recorded the Royal Garrison Artillery firing off a gas barrage. By the time this historic record was released (HMV 09308), the war was over. Tragically, William Gaisberg, who had been slightly gassed during the expedition, fell victim to the flu pandemic then raging and died at the end of November 1918.

The Japanese Sandman
THE GOLDEN YEARS, 1919–1931

The war had left the world economy in disarray: debased currencies fluctuated wildly and, in Britain and the rest of Europe, there was unprecedented price inflation. Like the devastated continent, The Gramophone Company was financially exhausted. It faced the task of rebuilding its worldwide trading and manufacturing organization almost from scratch. In early 1919, The Gramophone Company ceased government work and the long-delayed manufacture of gramophones began at Hayes. For the first time in its history, the Company made all its own products. This coincided with a major consumer boom: in that year, the British branch sold a record 60,000 gramophones and over 6 million records. Unfortunately, a severe recession followed in the years 1920-22. Company profits collapsed from £150,000 to £26,000. The need to raise fresh capital, more than any other consideration, led to a new partnership deal with the American Victor Company. In 1920, Victor gave The Gramophone Company a massive capital injection in exchange for 50 per cent of

Gilbert and Sullivan
Although the 1920s are usually associated with jazz and dance band music, recordings of older musical forms were also best-sellers. None enjoyed greater sales in Britain than the series of Gilbert and Sullivan complete opera recordings which HMV made after 1919. This special *Pirates of Penzance* supplement featured a Pirate King bearing a remarkable resemblance to the former German Kaiser, Wilhelm II. The early HMV Gilbert and Sullivan series were recorded under the supervision of Rupert D'Oyly Carte, with members of the D'Oyly Carte opera company, including Sir Henry Lytton, augmented by Gramophone Company artists such as Peter Dawson and George Baker.

the Company's ordinary shares. In addition, two Victor executives, one of whom was Eldridge Johnson (Victor's founding president), joined the board. With this reinforcement, the long-planned expansion of the Company could begin.

To develop an international recording programme, the Company reorganized the existing Recording Department, and, in 1920, created the International Artistes Department. This timely reorganization provided the Company with the facilities and the strategy to compete for talent in the world market. The main purpose of the International Artistes Department was to recruit artists with international rather than national reputations. The costs of recording such artists were too great to be borne by a single branch of the Company, so this department made their recordings and arranged for them to be marketed on a worldwide basis. The first manager of the International Artistes Department was the former sales director, Sydney Dixon, whilst Fred Gaisberg became its first artistic director. Over the previous two decades, Gaisberg had developed a remarkable talent for handling performing artists in the often fraught atmosphere of the recording studio. He now created for himself a new and special role as the friend and confidant of a whole generation of performing artists, many of whom saw in him the personification of His Master's Voice. Gaisberg remained artistic director until he retired in 1939, and was a consultant to the Company until his death in 1951.

In 1921, prefiguring EMI's later expansion of its retailing activities, the Company opened its flagship store in Oxford Street, London (see Chapter 7). The opening was considered so important that Elgar, then HMV's most prestigious English artist, was persuaded to perform the ceremony.

In 1926, Trevor Osmond Williams (the nephew of the Company's founding chairman) became manager of the International Artistes Department. Over the next four years, until his sudden death in 1930, he and Gaisberg achieved great things, creating recording programmes that became the foundation of the Company's unique worldwide reputation as makers of recordings of the highest quality. Among his other achievements, it was through Williams's vision and persistence that the Abbey Road recording studios were built (see below). Furthermore, through his connections with the wider musical world, Williams established important links between HMV, Covent Garden and the London Symphony Orchestra.

Trevor Osmond Williams managed HMV's International Artistes Department between 1926 and 1930. This was a time of great opportunity, with sales of classical music expanding and the new electrical recording process creating important new avenues for recording.

DAME NELLIE MELBA
(1861–1931)

★

The soprano Dame Nellie Melba was the most important of The Gramophone Company's early celebrity artists. Born Helen Porter Mitchell in Melbourne, Australia, by 1904, when she finally agreed to make records, she was the most celebrated opera singer in the world. She imposed stringent conditions, demanding that the recordings be made in her London home and that she be accompanied by an orchestra instead of a piano as was usual at that time. Fred Gaisberg later recalled Melba's overbearing manner at the first sessions: "When she addressed one, she made no attempt to clothe her speech with sweetened words. She was a woman who had risen to the top of her profession by sheer driving force." Among the titles Melba recorded in that first year were Tosti's "Mattinata" (G&T 03015), part of the Mad Scene from Donizetti's *Lucia di Lammermoor* (G&T 03020), and the Bach–Gounod "Ave Maria" with violin obbligato played by Jan Kubelík (G&T 03033). Although she had a limpid, clear voice and an impeccable singing technique, the beauty of tone for which Melba was renowned was not easily captured by the mechanical recording process. But the early records were a commercial success and she continued to record throughout the rest of her career. Once the public accepted her as a recording artist, she became wholly committed to the new medium, and in 1907 she laid the foundation stone for The Gramophone Company's new Hayes record factory. In June 1926, aged 67, she gave an emotional farewell performance at Covent Garden, where she had reigned supreme for almost four decades, and retired to Australia.

Dear Mr Dixon – When
my royalties are
due will you kindly
send them to me
direct this time –
instead of original
agreement –
I am writing to

This letter from Melba shows that the diva had both a firm hand and a clear head for business.

Mr Haygate –
Yrs sincerely
Nellie Melba

HMV's mobile recording van
The introduction of the electrical process made on-the-spot recordings a realistic possibility. To exploit this opportunity, HMV built a mobile recording van, shown here in 1927 outside Hereford Cathedral recording excerpts from the Three Choirs Festival.

Right Medleys and "vocal gems" from top London shows featured prominently in HMV's catalogues.

O, for the wings of a dove

ELECTRICAL RECORDING

By the early 1920s, records made by the mechanical process of sound recording were sounding increasingly antiquated. The advent of radio broadcasting, together with demands for high-quality recordings of complete works performed by full orchestras and of dance music, forced the record industry to examine ways in which microphones and electrical amplifiers could be used to make records. In 1923, The Gramophone Company created its own research and development facilities at Hayes. Work was immediately begun on the development of electrical recording and reproducing systems and, significantly, on television. The Western Electric Company in the United States was the first to develop an effective system of electrical recording. The Gramophone Company began using this system in 1925, paying a royalty of one penny for every record sold (see Chapter 4). Fred Gaisberg recalled:

Acoustically recorded sound had reached the limit of progress. The top frequencies were triple high C, 2,088 vibrations per second, and the low remained at E, 164 vibrations per second. Voices and stringed instruments, were confined rigidly within these boundaries, although the average human ear perceives from 30 to 15,000 vibrations per second and musical sounds range from 60 to 8,000 vibrations. Electrical recording encompassed this and more. A whisper fifty feet away, reflected sound, and even the atmosphere of a concert hall could be recorded – things hitherto unbelievable. [Gaisberg, ibid., p.81]

The introduction of electrical recording resulted in several other important changes. To accommodate the new technology, mechanical engineers were replaced in the recording studios by electrical engineers skilled in the new art of electrical recording. For the old mechanical engineers, it became a question of "adapt or leave". Almost overnight, their skills had become obsolete. The Company's existing recording facilities at Hayes had been designed to meet the needs of the old technology and were unsuited to the new. Other venues, such as the Small Queen's Hall and the Kingsway Hall in London, were pressed into service. However, Trevor Osmond Williams recognized the Company's need to develop state-of-the-art recording studios and eventually persuaded The Gramophone Company to make the necessary investment. A large house at 3 Abbey Road, St John's Wood, London, was acquired, extended and converted into recording studios. In November 1931, Abbey Road Studios were opened by Sir Edward Elgar. To mark the occasion, a recording was made of Elgar conducting the London Symphony Orchestra in his "symphonic study" *Falstaff*.

The introduction of electrical recording also made the possibility of making "live" recordings of operatic performances a reality. In June 1926, The Gramophone Company demonstrated the effectiveness of the new process by recording the Covent Garden farewell of one of HMV's pioneering performers, the soprano Dame Nellie Melba. Portions of this historic occasion were recorded, and two recordings were released: "Donde lieta uscì" from *La bohème*, coupled with Dame Nellie's "Farewell Speech" (HMV DB 943). In 1931, as a tribute to Melba after her death, the aria

During the 1920s and 1930s HMV continued to record the works of Gilbert and Sullivan.

from *La bohème* was re-released, this time coupled with another excerpt from her farewell performance, "Piangea cantando" from *Otello* (HMV DB 1500). These gramophone records became unique souvenirs of an artist whose contribution to recorded art had been decisive. The Melba records, together with live recordings of Feodor Chaliapin in Boito's *Mefistofele* (HMV DB 942), also recorded in 1926, and in Mussorgsky's *Boris Godunov* (HMV DB 3464), recorded in 1928, revealed the potential of the gramophone as a preserver of live performance.

In 1926, The Gramophone Company began using a mobile recording van for location recordings. An early example provided the Company with its first, and possibly its most unusual, million-selling record. The 14-year-old Ernest Lough, a choirboy at the Temple Church, London, recorded Mendelssohn's *Hear my Prayer*, which included the treble solo "O, for the wings of a dove" (HMV C 1329). This record achieved an unprecedented popularity: in Britain alone, 650,000 copies were sold within six months of its release. In the wake of his unexpected stardom, many strange

Ernest Lough, chorister and treble soloist of the Temple Church, London, achieved worldwide fame aged 14 with his recording of Mendelssohn's *Hear My Prayer*. A modest boy, he found this adulation mildly annoying, especially when his father insisted he answer the fan mail which rolled in from all corners of the world. In 1963, EMI presented Ernest Lough with a gold disc to mark what had become HMV's best-selling record of the 78-rpm period.

The Most Sublime Record
Ever Made

Boy Soloist and Choir of the
Temple Church
London
EXCLUSIVELY ON
"His Master's Voice"
ELECTRICAL   RECORDING

rumours circulated about Ernest Lough; one in particular suggested that he had died as he completed his last soaring notes.

Just before the introduction of electrical recording, HMV had begun to issue discs with recordings pressed on both sides. This innovation halved the purchase price of such recordings. Together with the major improvement in sound reproduction brought about by electrical recording, it caused a tremendous boom in demand for classical records. As a result, Fred Gaisberg and Osmond Williams developed a large-scale recording programme.

Casals, Thibaud and Cortot recording in the late 1920s.

For example, between 1925 and 1931, piano trios by the greatest classical composers were recorded by the virtuoso performers Alfred Cortot, Jacques Thibaud and Pablo Casals. As The Gramophone Company was a multinational business serving many national markets, these records were able to make good sales: British sales alone during the five years before 1930 exceeded 100,000 sets. Recordings appeared of core repertoire by great orchestras such as the Berlin Philharmonic and the Vienna Philharmonic.

At the Jazz Band Ball

THE JAZZ AGE

The Company's first jazz records, derived from Victor matrices shipped to Britain as part of the licensing agreement, were released on the HMV label in November 1919. They consisted of records by the Original Dixieland Jazz Band, then the performing sensation of the first post-war London season: "At the Jazz Band Ball" coupled with "Ostrich Walk" (HMV B 1021) and "Bluin' the Blues" and "Sensation Rag" (HMV B 1022). The records and the Original Dixieland Jazz Band's stage performance scandalized many because of their abandonment of established western musical conventions.

Above The Original Dixieland Jazz Band
at the time of their London debut in 1919.

Right Despite the 1921 Depression,
HMV continued its programme of dance
record releases.

Nonetheless, these records enjoyed a huge success: the band performed to full houses and even entertained the Royal Family. More importantly, this helped bring about a revolution in popular music; that revolution gained momentum in the 1920s, and its impact remains with us today.

In the early 1920s, orchestrated versions of "jazz", developed in the United States by performers such as Paul Whiteman and his Orchestra, tamed and harmonized the new art form, making it acceptable for mass audiences. In 1921, Whiteman released the first of his many hit records, "The Japanese Sandman", coupled with "Whispering" (HMV B 1160). It was the beginning of a major new popular music craze that boosted the record industry throughout the decade. British dance bands quickly followed the American lead. The earliest HMV dance bands were William Debroy Somers's Savoy Orpheans, whose best-selling record "Student Prince", coupled with "Valencia" (HMV B 2272), achieved sales in excess of 275,000, and Reginald Batten's smaller Savoy Havana Band, which in the ten years 1923–32 achieved cumulative sales of more than 3 million copies. These bands proved to be the precursors of other British dance bands, led by figures such as Bert Ambrose and Jack Hylton. In the heady days of the late 1920s, these performers enjoyed a huge following through their personal appearances, their many recordings for HMV and their broadcasts for the BBC. Nearly 7 million copies of Hylton's records were sold between 1923 and 1933. As late as the summer of 1930, when the effects of the Depression were already making serious inroads on record sales, his popular hit "The Stein Song" (HMV B 5844) nonetheless sold 175,000 copies.

JACK HYLTON
(1892–1965)

The dance band leader Jack Hylton, the best-selling HMV artist of the 78-rpm period, was born in Bolton, Lancashire. Captivated by the syncopated sounds produced by the American Paul Whiteman and his Orchestra in the early 1920s, he learned to imitate them, and, crucially, to create his own orchestrations. In 1924, after a spell with the Queen's Dance Orchestra, during the course of which he made and directed his first HMV recordings, Hylton formed his own orchestra and began a brilliant career which defined popular music for a generation. He was HMV's star artist, developing increasingly sophisticated musical arrangements and a unique and instantly recognizable "Jack Hylton" sound. The more than 300 records he made for HMV before 1931 formed the core of its popular dance catalogue, with several achieving sales in excess of 100,000 copies. These best-sellers included "In sunny Havana" (HMV B 2146), "Shepherd of the Hills" (HMV B 5207), "Varsity Drag" (HMV B 5506), "Loveable and Sweet" (HMV B 5704), and his Depression hit "Happy days are here again" (HMV B 5771). In 1931, in the midst of the Depression, Hylton left HMV. Although he returned in 1935, to make what by the standards of the time were successful records, the glory days of the 1920s were over and the record business a shadow of its former self. Nonetheless, Hylton continued recording, touring in Britain and overseas, broadcasting, film-making and other activities until 1940, when he made his last records – two hits from Walt Disney's feature cartoon, *Pinocchio*: "Give a Little Whistle", coupled with "Little Wooden Head" (HMV BD 5570) – and disbanded his orchestra. He subsequently enjoyed a highly successful career as an impresario.

Above Jack Hylton and his orchestra rehearsing for a recording session, c.1931.

Tiptoe through the Tulips

THE BUSINESS, 1919–1931

From the mid-1920s, The Gramophone Company sought to expand its overseas activities. Abroad, the hopeless task of trying to reclaim the pre-war German branch was abandoned and in 1925, the Company, trading as Electrola GmbH, re-entered the German market. To meet the needs of the new branch, a large factory was purchased near Potsdam, together with offices, recording facilities and a Berlin-based sales outlet. The new venture soon established itself and, by 1929, the new German branch had sold more than 2 million Electrola records and 35,000 gramophones. Other important overseas developments in the 1920s included the replacement of overseas agencies with new wholly or partly owned operating companies in Holland, Italy, Australia and New Zealand, and the building of a large factory (together with recording facilities) at Erskinville, near Sydney, Australia, together with new factories at Dum-Dum, near Calcutta in India, at Nogent in France, and in Italy and Turkey.

In 1929, as if to emphasize The Gramophone Company's transition from a business engaged in essentially light engineering to one at the cutting edge of electrical engineering, the Company acquired Marconiphone, then a major British radio manufacturer, together with its interest in the Osram Valve Company. Thus, by the time Electric and Musical Industries Ltd was formed in 1931, The Gramophone Company had transformed itself into one of Britain's leading radio manufacturers.

Until 1930 and the onset of the Depression, the Company and the wider record industry boomed as it had never done before. At its 1929 peak, nearly 12 million HMV and Zonophone records were sold in Britain, and annual record production at Hayes (for domestic and overseas markets), reached an incredible 25 million records. In order to meet all these orders, the Hayes factories worked around the clock and employment doubled. The 1920s boom saw the Company's profits reach new heights. In 1928, they exceeded £1 million for the first time; this was surpassed the following year when they reached £1.2 million. By that stage, the Company's assets stood at an

By 1923, dance band records were HMV's best-selling line.

impressive £5.3 million. In Britain, The Gramophone Company became not just a purely commercial enterprise but also a national institution. Its central role in developing national and international music-making was rivalled only by its competitor, The Columbia Graphophone Company, and by that other national institution created during the 1920s – the BBC. In 1923, The Gramophone Company received the ultimate seal of approval when King George V and Queen Mary recorded "A Message to the Children of the Empire" (HMV RE 284). Other royal records followed, and in 1927 the King and Queen made their first tour of the Hayes factories.

In 1930, Trevor Williams, the Company's founding chairman and sole survivor of the original 1898 partnership, retired from the chair. Although he remained a director until his death in 1946, this move ended his active participation in the affairs of the Company he had done so much to develop. His successor was the man who had guided the Company through the war emergency and the good years of the 1920s: the managing director, Alfred Clark.

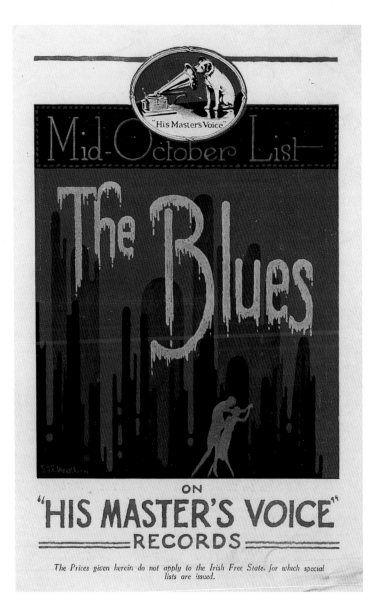

Throughout the 1920s, HMV's range of jazz and blues records was published in special record supplements.

Clark assumed the chair at the very start of the Depression. Amidst collapsing orders and profits, Clark had to ensure the very survival of the business. To guarantee this, it became necessary to rationalize the international record industry of which The Gramophone Company was such an important part. This was achieved in 1931, with the formation of Electric and Musical Industries Ltd (EMI), the result of a merger between The Gramophone Company and its major competitor, The Columbia Graphophone Company.

HMV advertising reflected the dramatic change from a sedate pre-war world to the jazz age.

CHAPTER 3

It had to be you

COLUMBIA IN EUROPE, 1897–1931

Your Company is now in the position of holding a premier place in almost every market so that with its widely spread interests … the prospects of steady expansion are excellent.
[Sir George Croydon Marks, chairman of The Columbia Graphophone Company, 1928]

My Flo from Pimlico

BEGINNINGS, 1897–1909

**FRANK DORIAN
(1870–1940)**

Like so many notable record industry pioneers, Frank Dorian was born and educated in Washington, D.C. A stenographer and reporter by training, he joined the Columbia Phonograph Company as general manager in 1889. After the failure of North American Phonograph, Dorian became a key figure in the rebuilding of the business, and eventually became general manager of The Columbia Phonograph Company General. When Dorian returned to the United States in 1909, he became sales manager for the dictaphone, Columbia's office dictating machine. Like his competitor William Barry Owen, Frank Dorian had the vision to see the record business as more than a transient novelty. He said in 1904: "There is no reason why it [the record player] should not become as familiar an article in the home, as, say, the sewing machine."

Opposite page By 1900, Columbia had produced a hand-cranked toy graphophone that played disc records – the precursors of the disc records Columbia released after 1902. In Britain, this machine sold for 8 shillings (40 pence).

In August 1897, soon after William Barry Owen arrived in London to start his European gramophone venture, Frank Dorian, a sales executive with The Columbia Phonograph Company General, was dispatched to Europe to establish a trade in American-made Columbia cylinder records and graphophones.

Dorian arrived armed with the Company's new range of graphophones and greatly improved cylinder records. In contrast to Owen, Dorian did not seek out venture capitalists to invest in his business; instead, he traded as The Columbia Phonograph Company General, the foreign branch of an American corporation (except in Germany, where local laws forced him to form a small trading company). This situation remained unchanged until 1917, when a British-registered business, The Columbia Graphophone Company Ltd, was formed. Even then, Columbia traded as a wholly owned sub-company of its American parent. The dependence on the American business proved to be Columbia's greatest weakness, and recurrent financial difficulties in the American concern quickly affected the European branch.

Until 1900, British patent restrictions prevented Columbia trading directly in what eventually became its most successful market. As a result, Frank Dorian made his headquarters in Paris, where he opened a sales office on the Boulevard des Italiens. He was soon trading in competition with Pathé Frères, a local French company (subsequently acquired by Columbia in 1928) which had established a modest market with its own cylinder machines and records. Dorian relied on American supplies of graphophones and cylinder records. Early orders of records were shipped by the barrel-load, each barrel containing 125 assorted records. A storage depot was acquired at the free-port of Antwerp to stimulate a wider European trade and to circumvent prohibitively high French customs duties. In 1899 Dorian was joined by Charles Gregory (see box, page 93), an experienced Columbia-trained recording engineer who had gained his early training in Washington, D.C. with Fred Gaisberg. To compete with Pathé, Gregory produced locally made records of the latest French popular songs and music, and so Columbia began its first overseas recording programme. A writer on the American trade journal *The Phonoscope* described the Paris operation:

I called at the office of the Columbia Phonograph Company, Boulevard des Italiens and found a large and well equipped establishment. Mr Frank Dorian, its well-known manager, was away, but I had the pleasure of meeting Mr Wake, his assistant. Their force is large and in keeping with the size of the plant. They are manufacturing a good grade of French records which is necessary in order to compete for the French trade. [F. M. Prescott, *The Phonoscope*, March 1899]

In May 1899, Dorian opened a permanent office in Germany, which permitted Columbia to expand its business into Germany, Austria-Hungary, Poland and Russia. In a 1903 interview, Dorian described Columbia's European organization:

Our Paris office supplies the whole of France, Holland and Switzerland, Spain, Portugal, Italy, Servia and Egypt, with agents in all those countries. From our Berlin headquarters, our trade is directed throughout Germany, Austria, Hungary, Russia, Denmark, Sweden and Norway, with representatives in each country. [*Talking Machine News*, Vol. 1, June 1903]

To meet the needs of these highly individual markets, Columbia developed extensive European recording programmes. Furthermore, to secure the long-term future of its central European and Russian businesses, Columbia created its own wholesale and retail outlets, and forged important trans-European and other links with merchants and agents.

In May 1900, when the British patent restrictions expired, Dorian relocated Columbia's European headquarters to London, initially in Wells Street, then in Oxford Street. In 1901,

CHARLES GREGORY
(1880–1946)

Gregory began working for the Columbia Phonograph Company in 1894, where he trained as a recording engineer. In 1899, he moved to Europe, where he engineered Columbia's first European recordings. In 1900 he arrived in London and built Columbia's London recording studios. He was one of the very few recording engineers who successfully made the transition from mechanical to electrical recording. Gregory engineered much of Columbia's, and later EMI's, classical catalogue, recording Sir Thomas Beecham, Sir Henry Wood, Felix Weingartner and Bruno Walter, and an impressive list of complete opera recordings. In July 1939, on what proved to be his last European tour, he went to Rome to engineer the recording of Verdi's *Requiem* with Caniglia, Gigli, Pinza and Stignani. During the Second World War, Gregory became head of recording at Abbey Road Studios. When he died, Fred Gaisberg wrote: "Artists liked him to handle their recordings because he never fussed, and when listening to play-backs, he could quickly grasp defects and if the artists were at fault, candidly tell them how to remedy flaws."

CORONATION MUSIC.

EVERYONE who uses a Graphophone or Phonograph wants suitable Coronation Music for his machine. Our Special List includes many appropriate selections, including the PRIZE CORONATION MARCH.

London Military Band.

200574—**Prize Coronation March** (Percy Godfrey's Celebrated Composition).

Great Britain's Reception of the Nations at the Coronation of Their Majesties Edward VII. and Queen Alexandra. Being a series of records embracing the national airs of the principal nations that will be represented at the Coronation.

200564—America (Hail Columbia, Yankee Doodle, Star Spangled Banner).
200565—Austria and Italy.
200566—Denmark and Greece.
200567—France and Russia.
200568—Germany and Turkey.
200569—Spain and Portugal.
200570—Egypt and Persia.
200571—Japan (the new Ally).
200572—Colonies and Empire (National Airs of the two principal colonies, Australia and Canada, and "Rule Britannia").

200573—Hallelujah Chorus from the Messiah.
200575—Coronation March from the Prophet.
200576—Tschaikowsky's Coronation March (written for the coronation of Czar Nicholas II.).
200577—Pomp and Circumstance March, No. I.
200578—Pomp and Circumstance March No. II.
200287—King and President March ("God Save the King" and "Star Spangled Banner").

Gilmore's Band.

1603—God Save the King.
31558—King Edward VII. March.

Baritone Songs by Henry Bailey.

200302—Here's a Health unto His Majesty.
200344—Soldiers of the King.

Furnished in "P" and "G" Records.
"P" Style, 1/6 each. "G" Style, 5/- each. Postage Extra.

COLUMBIA PHONOGRAPH Co. GEN'L,

122, OXFORD STREET, LONDON, W.

Columbia British trade circulars
To keep dealers informed of the latest Columbia records and advertising campaigns, the Company made regular mailings of trade circulars. These 1902 circulars highlight two of the year's most important events: the signing of a peace treaty ending the Anglo-Boer War, and the coronation of King Edward VII.

GOD SAVE THE KING.

In recognition of the Peace just concluded, we announce the following special records. Suitable for all Graphophones and Phonographs. Made in "P" and "G" styles only.

London Military Band.

200604 **Field Call Galop,** introducing the Bugle Calls used in South Africa.

200605 **Patrol of the Boers,** introducing their National Hymn.

200606 **The Warriors' Return,** as played for the return of the troops from South Africa.

200607 **When the Boys Come Home Once More.** A welcome to the fighting heroes.

200442 **Rose, Shamrock and Thistle.** Sousa's Patrol founded on Melodies of the British Empire.

200596 **New Colonial March.**

200597 **Our Favourite Regiment March.**

200598 **Rule Britannia** and God Save the King.

Gilmore's Band.

1603 **God Save the King.** This record can be furnished in the XP (high speed, extra loud) variety. Price **2/-** each.

"P" Records 1/6 each. "G" Records 5/- each.
Postage extra—3d. each for "P" Records.
6d. each for "G" Records.

Columbia Phonograph Company Gen'l,

122, OXFORD STREET, LONDON, W.

Columbia's British branch produced its first graphophone and record catalogues. Since Columbia's new range of graphophones and cylinder recordings had carried off the Grand Prix at the recent Paris Exposition, the machine catalogue claimed that the graphophone was "the most advanced type of the talking machine". At that time, an important consideration for any would-be purchasers of Columbia music records was the cost of a Columbia cylinder graphophone. They ranged from as little as one pound and 5 shillings (£1.25) for the cheapest model to £30 for the top-of-the-range Graphophone Grand, which played massive five-inch diameter cylinders. For the average pocket, there was the Eagle model, which retailed at one pound and

15 shillings (£1.75), and the Columbia Graphophone, which retailed at five pounds and 10 shillings (£5.50). There was also, as a harbinger of things to come, a toy model which sold for 8 shillings (40 pence), and which played discs rather than cylinder records.

In 1902, Columbia introduced an inexpensive method of moulding cylinder records. Before then, all the Company's cylinder records were derived either from original recordings, or copied from originals. Such production limitations seriously inhibited Columbia's potential for growth, and made the process of cylinder record-making a tedious job for both recorder and performer. Unfortunately, no accounts survive of Charles Gregory's early attempts at record-making in London. However, Joseph Batten, a British recording engineer who joined Columbia as musical director in the 1920s, wrote in his memoirs of a recording session he attended at the turn of the century which had been organized by Dan Smoot, an American recording engineer. Batten described how an upright grand piano – with its back and front removed, so that maximum sound could be obtained – had been hoisted on to a platform so that it was level with the recording horn:

There was no music stand, the music being held up by anybody who had nothing else to do at the time. I had to climb four high wooden steps to reach the piano, which brought my head to within a few inches of the ceiling. The singer, an arm resting on the piano, stood within a few inches of a recording horn which measured five inches in diameter, in such a position that I could not see him. In this fantastic setting and throughout the sultry heat of the day A. H. Gee and Montague Borwell, baritone and tenor alternated in singing "Come into the garden, Maud", "The Diver" and "The Soldiers of the Queen". Precariously perched on a stool on the rostrum, coat discarded, perspiring profusely, I hammered out the accompaniments. Dan Smoot had demanded of me to make the tone "double forte" and double forte it was. From time to time the singers whispered appeals to "keep it down". If, appalled myself at the din I was making, I did so, Dan Smoot would clamber up the rostrum with the agility of a monkey and fiercely command: "Take no notice. Keep it loud. You're doing fine." I could not judge. My brain, usually cool, detached and critical of what my hands were doing rattled off the accompaniments like an automaton. At the end of the day I was paid fifteen shillings for my six hours work. I was asked to come again the next day, so the presumption was that I had given satisfaction.
[Joseph Batten, *Joe Batten's Book, the Story of Sound Recording* (London 1956), p.33]

95

W. H. Berry was an early Columbia recording star. He specialized in making cover versions of popular songs made famous by other performers.

Before 1908, the majority of records sold by Columbia were in the cylinder format. This 1906–1907 catalogue cover illustrates Columbia's dependence on recordings from the American parent to supplement the output from the British subsidiary.

With the introduction of moulded cylinder records, Columbia's European record business was transformed. The new process permitted a significant reduction in the price of cylinder records, from two shillings (10 pence) to one shilling and six pence (7.5 pence), and later to one shilling (5 pence). Mass production and the reduction of cylinder record prices increased Columbia record sales generally, creating an important British market for cylinder records. In 1905, industry-wide sales of cylinder records in Britain exceeded 5 million. Edward Easton, president of Columbia Phonograph Company General, commented on the popularity of Columbia's moulded cylinder records in Britain in 1903:

In the United States, the disc record is undoubtedly [more popular] but that is probably because there are more disc than cylinder machines in existence. Our experience over here is quite contrary, why, for each disc record we sell here three wax [cylinder] ones. [*Talking Machine News*, Vol.1, August 1903]

In a move that, in the long term, was crucial to the business's survival, Columbia introduced a new product range alongside moulded cylinder records: 7-inch and 10-inch disc records. Initially, Columbia's disc records sold for two shilling (10 pence) and four shillings (20 pence) each. Later, prices were reduced and, in order to play these records, two types of disc machine were produced, one retailing at four pounds and 4 shillings (£4.20), and the other at eight pounds and 8 shillings (£8.40).

Whether in disc or cylinder form, almost all the records in the early British Columbia catalogues were derived from the Company's American recordings. They were made up largely of instrumental, brass and military-band selections, by ensembles like Gilmore's Band, who were described in the 1901 catalogue as having "a reputation second to none". Their list of records included instrumental arrangements of operatic tunes, marches, patriotic and religious music, and solos. Many artists appearing in these early catalogues also appeared in the catalogues of other American record companies, including those of The Berliner Gramophone Company and (later) Victor. Gregory's British recordings were made up almost exclusively of comic songs and turns, together with ballads and other songs. This new range of cheaper products presented Columbia's British and European branches with fresh opportunities and in a 1903 interview, Frank Dorian outlined the new situation:

We are turning out here [in London] about 50,000 [cylinder] records a month, all of them the work of British Artists. We make records too, of course in Paris and Berlin, whilst we sell over here immense quantities of American, in addition to British records. The American records we sell, are, by-the-way, chiefly instrumental. We are even sending out Chinese records at the present time. [*Talking Machine News*, Vol.1, May 1903]

Reflecting these additions, Columbia's 1903 British record catalogue was significantly larger than previous editions (108 pages listing 5,000 different titles). The cylinder record section contained 25 pages of British-made records, compared to 36 pages of American-made records. The most prolific of Columbia's British recording artists was the singer and comic actor W. H. Berry. Berry specialized in patter songs, and his list

SIR GEORGE ROBEY
(1869–1954)

George Robey, the 'Prime Minister of Mirth', was one of the greatest stars of British music hall and revue. Born George Edward Wade in London, Robey began working professionally in music halls in 1891. Although his songs were full of social comment, his patter could be suggestive, and he adopted an attitude of pained indignation when his audience became carried away with his humour, admonishing them that he hadn't come there to be laughed at. In 1916, he appeared in his first revue, the phenomenally successful *The Bing Boys Are Here*, in which he sang "If you were the only girl in the world" (Columbia L 1035) which became a hit. A number of other equally successful shows followed, including *Zig-Zag*, *The Bing Boys on Broadway* and his own revue, *Bits and Pieces*. Robey performed in several films, including *Don Quixote* opposite Feodor Chaliapin. In 1935, he achieved possibly the greatest success of his career, as Falstaff in Shakespeare's *Henry IV Part I*, a part he repeated in Laurence Olivier's 1944 film of *Henry V*. He was knighted in 1954, the year of his death. Throughout his long career Robey made many records for Columbia and HMV, including music hall numbers such as "Archibald! certainly not" (HMV C 546) and "The Mayor of Mudcumdyke" (HMV C 551), but he is best remembered today for "If you were the only girl in the world".

Record-buying has always taken place primarily during the period from October to March. To entice customers to buy new records, during this season, manufacturers such as Columbia produced brightly coloured monthly record-supplements with covers reflecting – no matter how tenuously – a link between the season and buying records.

of 112 cylinder records included such gems as: "English as she is spoken" (Columbia XP 200490), and "My Flo from Pimlico" (Columbia XP 200700), described in the catalogue as "This Season's Pantomime Success". It was be no means uncommon to see songs and patter made famous by one music hall performer recorded by another. Berry was no exception to this rule. Listed at the side of his records are the names of the more famous artists – such as Dan Leno and George (later Sir George) Robey (see box, page 97) – who had originally performed and popularized them. Berry was one of the earliest recording artists. In 1903, he explained how his association with Columbia began and how he thought his records had advanced his career:

It was not until the Autumn of 1901 that I commenced singing into the Graphophone of the Columbia Phonograph Co. I need hardly say I have never regretted my debut as a record maker; as, not only does it keep a singer in constant practice, but also the wider circulation of his efforts is an excellent advertisement for a professional man.
[*Talking Machine News*, Vol. 1, May 1903]

The list of disc records was the most significant addition to the catalogue. Although this initial list was exclusively of American-made recordings, by 1906 the bulk of the 1,800 Columbia disc record titles available had been recorded either in Britain or Europe, and included recordings of famous operatic and instrumental performers. The first Columbia celebrity recording tour was undertaken by Frank Capps, a senior American engineer, who went to Russia in 1903, where he recorded the great Russian tenor Andrei Labinski. As Edward Easton noted with undeniable pride:

We have just completed a catalogue of Russian disc records, made up by the principal Russian vocalists and instrumentalists, including the Czar's own band, his favourite operatic singers, some of whom had never before made a record for the talking machine.
[*Talking Machine News*, Vol. 1, September 1903]

Lillian Nordica

After completing his Russian recording programme, Capps went on to make the first Columbia disc records in Berlin, Vienna, Milan and other European cities. On his return to the United States, he began to record the first series of Columbia Grand Opera records. These records, under Columbia's system of exchanging matrices between the American and European branches of the business, appeared in Britain and elsewhere. Among the opera singers Capps recorded were several stellar names, including Edouard de Reszke, Emmy Destinn, Ernestine Schumann-Heink, Antonio Scotti, Marcella Sembrich and Suzanne Adams. A major selling point of these Grand Opera records was their price, which was the same as that of ordinary 10-inch Columbia discs.

To assist in engaging American celebrities, Columbia recruited as its musical advisor the noted music critic and teacher Herman Klein. Through his good offices, the distinguished American dramatic soprano Lillian Nordica, an old friend of Klein's, was

ALBERT W. KETÈLBEY
(1875–1959)

Albert William Ketèlbey was born in Birmingham. After studying music in London, he worked as an organist before taking up conducting. He toured extensively with a light opera company and was appointed musical director of the Vaudeville Theatre at the age of 22. In 1906, he joined The Columbia Graphophone Company as musical director and house conductor. In 1912 his cello composition *The Phantom Melody*, won several prizes, and in 1915 he wrote the first and most famous of his descriptive orchestral works: *In a Monastery Garden* (Columbia 564). This was followed by a number of successful compositions in a similar style, including *In a Persian Market* (Columbia 9404), Bells *Across the Meadow* (Columbia 9410) and *Sanctuary of the Heart* (Columbia 9405). Further recordings of Ketèlbey conducting his own works were issued in 1929, including the *Cockney Suite* (Columbia 9860-2) and *In a Camp of Ancient Britons* (Columbia 9866).

persuaded to record. Years later, he recalled the circumstances:

It occurred to me to ask her if she had ever made a gramophone record. She had not. I asked her why? "I can hardly tell you," she replied, "unless it is that the idea of it has given me a nervous feeling, as though I should never be able to put my real voice into that dreadful horn. You have to sing into a horn, have you not? Well, I am sure I should never make a success of it." [Herman Klein, "The Gramophone and the Singer", *Gramophone*, Vol.2, June 1924]

Nordica's own assessment was correct. As Klein later conceded, the records she made failed to do justice to her art: the voice sounded thin and pinched, and, for the period, the recordings were distant and muffled. Nonetheless, Columbia considered the Nordica records, together with those made by the Italian tenor Alessandro Bonci, sufficiently prestigious to be sold at the premium price of twelve shillings and six pence (62.5 pence). Herman Klein was able to persuade several other American-based celebrity performers to record for Columbia and, luckily, the quality of their records was much more satisfactory. They included Anton van Rooy, Lillian Blauvelt and Ruth Vincent. The modest sales appeal of these and other Columbia celebrity records was heavily outweighed by the boost they gave to the Company and to the wider record industry. From that point, Columbia was seen – and saw itself – not as a provider of musical novelty, but as an important diffuser of musical culture.

In the early years of the century, Columbia's British and continental business experienced prodigious growth. In 1904, Barnett Samuel and Son Ltd, the large London musical wholesalers, reported that they:

first started business with the Columbia Company [in 1900]. Those were the days of small orders … From orders for 5,000 records they quickly jumped to orders for 50,000; from hundreds of machines to thousands. [When they first appeared] they did an extraordinary trade with Columbia disc machines. [*Talking Machine News*, Vol.2, June 1924]

This growth placed an intolerable strain on Columbia's European and American record factories, which were often unable to deliver orders for records (particularly American-made disc records). This in turn imperilled Columbia's highly profitable but volatile trade in ephemeral popular music. Delays of a week, or even of a few days, in this sector of the market resulted in lost sales. In 1904, to ensure that the needs of its domestic market were met, and to serve all Columbia's

Images of Columbia's
London factory.

Columbia's Oxford Street, London offices and showrooms.

European, Russian and overseas markets the Company built a large record factory in London. In late 1905, with an initial daily manufacturing capacity of 10,000 records, the factory began cylinder record production. The following year, disc record production, initially of 5,000 discs per day, began.

In 1906, Charles Gregory initiated Columbia's first British disc recording programme. This move lessened the company's reliance on its American parent and created a catalogue of British-made disc recordings. Albert W. Ketèlbey (see box, page 100), the composer and conductor, joined the Company at this time and enjoyed a long and fruitful collaboration with Columbia. Records of his compositions graced the pages of the Columbia record catalogues for several decades.

By 1907, the European branch of Columbia Phonograph General Company seemed a prosperous and secure business with substantial record catalogues – in the twin formats of cylinder and disc – filled with opera stars, concert artists, music hall performers, brass and military bands and instrumentalists. It also had a British-based record factory and an important retail and wholesale British, European, Russian and Imperial trade. Yet, within two short years, important changes in buying habits, a major depression, and the intrinsic financial instability of the American parent, ruined the business and almost succeeded in pushing Columbia out of the marketplace altogether. A major cause of this disastrous collapse was the switch from the manufacture of cylinder to disc players (which were cheaper and easier to make) by German and Swiss machine makers. As a result, German disc record manufacturers, who undercut Columbia's cylinder prices, became much more powerful. Compounding this was a major recession between 1907 and 1909 which resulted in the bankruptcy of several British and European cylinder manufacturers. As a consequence, creditors of these businesses dumped large stocks of cylinders at rock-bottom prices on an already depressed market. Taken together, these factors destroyed the British and European market in cylinder records.

By the end of 1908, the Columbia Phonograph Company General, the American parent company, was virtually bankrupt. The business Frank Dorian had begun in 1897 was almost consumed by this debacle. To keep the American company afloat, the European business had been steadily milked, leaving Dorian without the necessary capital to keep the existing operation going through the recession. As a consequence, he was forced to close all Columbia's British retail branches and dismiss his travelling salesmen and many other employees. In 1909, Dorian resigned as Columbia's European general manager to return to the United States to assist Edward Easton in the reconstruction of the American business. Dorian's successor was John A. B. Cromelin, the manager of Columbia's Central European branch. Among Cromelin's immediate tasks was to end cylinder production at the British factory. From that point on, the British and European branches of Columbia became manufacturers of disc records (and later disc machines), with the business of selling conducted entirely through the wholesale trade and, later, through dealerships. In November 1909, in one of John Cromelin's and Columbia's most astute acts ever, Louis (later Sir Louis) Sterling (see box, page 104) was appointed as British sales manager. Sterling became Columbia's white knight, rescuing it and restoring its fortunes.

In 1910, Arthur H. Brooks (see box, page 119), an experienced disc record engineer, was recruited by the British branch to expand Columbia's British disc recording programme. For Brooks, it was the beginning of 20 years' affiliation with the Company, first as a recording engineer, then as an artist and repertoire manager.

Everybody's doing it now
RECONSTRUCTION, 1909–1914

Louis Sterling had already had some success in the disc record industry. In 1908, he had formed The Rena Manufacturing Company Ltd to manufacture and sell disc records and machines. To create a catalogue of records, he turned to the British branch of Columbia, which provided him with record-pressing facilities and recordings from the existing Columbia catalogue. This proved to be a sensible move for both parties, as the work of pressing Rena Records saved Columbia's European manufacturing and recording facilities from bankruptcy and gave Sterling, with no capital costs on his part, access to Columbia's recordings. The first list of fifty 10-inch Rena Records, with a recording pressed into both sides of the discs, appeared in December 1908. They were priced at two shillings and six pence (12.5 pence), sixpence cheaper than Columbia's price for similar records. Rena Records were carefully chosen from Columbia's list of popular songs recorded by well-known performers, who included the music hall artists Harry Fay, Harry Bluff, Vesta Victoria, George Lashwood, G. H. Elliott, Whit Cunliffe and Harry Fragson. In the rising market of 1909, an advertising campaign promoted Rena Records in the trade press, and in newspapers and magazines read by its core consumers, the

BRANSBY WILLIAMS (1870–1961)

Bransby Williams, known as the 'Hamlet of the Halls', was an actor and music hall star who specialized in dramatic monologues and character studies. He originally intended to be a missionary, but made his professional debut in 1896 at a music hall in Shoreditch. Billed as the 'Actor Mimic', he started out impersonating famous actors and music hall comics of the day but soon developed his own presentations of speeches from Shakespeare and character sketches from Dickens. Highly skilled at quick changes, he made the most of his acting ability to create a host of different characters, from Sydney Carton and Little Nell to Dr Jekyll and Mr Hyde. In 1908, he began recording for The Gramophone Company with scenes from Dickens. He then moved to Columbia, where in 1913 he first recorded "The Green Eye of the Little Yellow God" (Columbia 388), a monologue which became so popular that it was often imitated and burlesqued by other performers, including Billy Bennett, who recorded his own version as "The Green Tie on the Little Yellow Dog" (Columbia 4004). Williams made his last theatrical tour in 1946 in the play *The Shop at Sly Corner*, more than 50 years after his first appearance on the stage. Peter Gammond, in *Your Own, Your Very Own!*, shrewdly summed up Williams thus: "If he was only a great 'ham' actor in the end, he struck a vein of powerful exaggeration that really had the audience gripped with its magic even though they knew they were being had."

SIR LOUIS STERLING
(1879–1958)

Louis Saul Sterling was the managing director of The Columbia Graphophone Company Ltd, and later of EMI. He was also an entrepreneur, banker and philanthropist. Sterling was born in New York, the son of an accountant. Employment with import-export agents brought him into contact with William Barry Owen, who, in 1904, offered him employment with The Gramophone Company. However, once in Britain, Sterling went into business on his own account. He joined Columbia in 1910 and, by 1923, had master-minded a management buy-out of the business. Sterling came into close contact with European and American bankers, who controlled the bulk of Columbia's shares, and it was at the behest of one, Thomas Lamont of J. P. Morgan, that Sterling reluctantly agreed to merge his interests with The Gramophone Company's. Through his association with Edward de Stein, Sterling developed important business interests outside the record industry. He was a principal shareholder of the music publishers Chappell, and became a founding partner of the merchant bank S. G. Warburg. After his departure from EMI, he became chairman of A. C. Cosser, the electrical engineers and early computer manufacturer. For decades, Sterling and his wife made their home in Regent's Park a meeting place for artists, bankers and men of letters, and their Sunday afternoon soirées became an important feature of London's artistic life. Sir Louis Sterling (he was knighted in 1937) was known for his generosity: he gave away over £1,500,000 during his lifetime, including £100,000 to Columbia employees on his 50th birthday. During the 1930s, he personally helped and supported many of the Company's displaced Jewish employees. He presented his fine personal library of rare early books to the University of London in 1956, saying, "I have made most of my money in London. I think it fitting that my books should be used for relaxation and knowledge by coming generations."

Sir Louis Sterling from the portrait by David Jagger.

skilled working classes. In sharp contrast to Columbia's failure, the sales generated were such that, later in 1909, John Cromelin bought the business and persuaded Sterling to join Columbia. Henceforth, until 1915, all Columbia discs produced bore the label 'Columbia-Rena Records'.

Louis Sterling's first Columbia employment contract reveals much about the state of that company's finances and Sterling's confidence in his own abilities: he received no salary, and was paid entirely on commission. By 1911, Sterling had achieved a dramatic turnaround in Columbia's fortunes, as the British trade journal *Talking Machine News* noted:

Since Louis Sterling took over the British Managership the rapidity with which the Columbia Company has forged ahead is indeed remarkable and is evidence of what can be done, even in these days of keen competition. [*Talking Machine News*, Vol.9, August 1911]

Between 1909 and 1914, Sterling re-established Columbia as a major British record company, and in so doing demonstrated the flair, imagination and ability that, in 1931, made him the obvious choice as EMI's first managing director. He overcame the set-back of a disastrous fire in 1912 which destroyed the London factory and all the stock (but fortunately not the all-important metal matrices used

Amadeus Press

To receive a free list of our other fine titles, just complete and return this card.

Name (please print)
_____

Address
_____

City _____ State _____ Zip _____

We'd also welcome your comments on this book.

_____

Title of Book: _____

BUSINESS REPLY MAIL

FIRST CLASS MAIL PERMIT NO. 717 PORTLAND, OR

POSTAGE WILL BE PAID BY ADDRESSEE

AMADEUS PRESS

The Haseltine Building

133 S.W. Second Avenue, Suite 450

Portland, OR 97204-9743

to press the records), and he rebuilt and developed the record catalogue, attracting new and important artists to record exclusively for Columbia. Among the new names were music hall performers such as Harry Champion, George Bastow and Bransby Williams (see box, page 103). Williams's monologues of Victorian classics became a mainstay of the Columbia spoken-word catalogue for several decades. Another music hall performer to make his first Columbia records at this time was Harry Tate. The recording he made of his famous sketch "Motoring" (Columbia 320) was premiered at the first Royal Variety Performance in 1912. New records by exclusive Columbia Celebrity artists (some from the American parent and some signed by Sterling) also appeared in the British catalogues. Recordings were made by instrumentalists such as the violinist Eugène Ysaÿe and the pianist Josef Hofmann, and the singers Olive Fremstad, Mary Garden, Leo Slezak and Giovanni Zenatello.

Columbia's managers were also quick to seize on new developments in popular music. In May 1912, for example, a Columbia advertisement of new releases announced: "Ragtime Rage. Here are all the latest Ragtime Hits". The list included two of the young Irving Berlin's greatest hits, "Alexander's Ragtime Band" (Columbia 1907), and "Everybody's doing it now" (Columbia 1908).

In the years before 1914, the range and quality of American-made Columbia disc machines (known as Grafonolas) improved dramatically. However, sales were low because high-priced American machines could not compete with imports of cheap German machines. The British market in disc records was also transformed by increasing competition from German manufacturers. There were nearly 40 different record labels, selling at prices ranging from one shilling and six pence (7.5 pence) to one pound and 10 shillings (£1.50). To meet such diverse competition, Sterling introduced two new budget record labels: the Phoenix, priced at one shilling and one penny (5.5 pence), to

Mary Garden (1877–1967)
The soprano Mary Garden created Mélisande in Debussy's opera *Pelléas et Mélisande* in 1902. In 1904, with Debussy as accompanist, she recorded a fragment of her part – "Mes longs cheveux" (G&T 33447) – and four *Ariettes oubliées* which the composer had dedicated to her (G&T 33448–51). Unfortunately, she loathed the sound of her recorded voice and her art can only be judged by the handful of records she made.

compete with The Gramophone Company's Cinch Record
(see Chapter 2); and, in 1914, the two shillings and six pence
(12.5 pence) Regal, designed to compete with The Gramophone
Company's Zonophone label. All Phoenix recordings were
garnered from the Columbia-Rena back-catalogue. In addition to
using recordings from this source, the Regal label quickly built up
its own recording programme and soon gained a reputation as a
label able to deliver the latest songs and up-to-the-minute musical
selections, performed by popular artists, quality brass and military
bands, and instrumentalists. Ten-inch Regal Records, priced at one
shilling and six pence (7.5 pence), compared favourably with the
two shillings and six pence (12.5 pence) Columbia-Rena 10-inch
records, and were aimed at and priced within the reach of the
skilled working classes. Records in the more
expensive Columbia-Rena catalogues
were marketed and priced with the
more musically sophisticated
middle-class customer
in mind.

Columbia offices
Columbia's advertising department with the latest
advertising material. Note the manager using a
Columbia dictaphone.

In 1914, the Company
issued the whole, albeit
in truncated form, of
Tchaikovsky's Fifth
Symphony (Columbia
487–8). The recording
was made with 50
members of the Milan
Symphony Orchestra,
conducted by Maestro
Romani. To accommodate an
orchestra of that size in the cramped
conditions of a recording studio, get the
balance right and, using the mechanical recording
process, make an acceptable recording was at that time quite an
accomplishment. That year, Columbia also released an almost
complete recording of Verdi's opera *Aida* (Columbia D
5558–74), on 17 records, costing £3, including libretto.

Louis Sterling and his staff were adept at advertising and selling
their product. They gained an intimate knowledge of the British
newspapers and magazine trade, and used this medium of mass
advertising to promote individual Columbia releases in the national
and regional press. By this means, Columbia claimed that it could
reach 15 million potential customers (the combined readership of
the papers carrying its advertisements). Columbia's British
corporate identity was further strengthened by the introduction of

the "Magic Notes" trademark on all its products. In 1913, the cumbersome name Columbia Phonograph Company General was dropped in favour of The Columbia Graphophone Company.

In the same year, the Company moved its European headquarters and British sales branch to new premises – complete with well-equipped recording studios – at Clerkenwell Road, in the City of London. However, despite Sterling's great success in rebuilding Columbia from the wreckage of 1908, nothing could have prepared him or the business for the coming of war in 1914.

DAME MAGGIE TEYTE (1888–1976)

Born Margaret Tate in Wolverhampton, the soprano Maggie Teyte trained at the Royal College of Music in London and later with Jean de Reszke in Paris. She sang in a number of roles at the Opéra-Comique in Paris, where she changed the spelling of her surname so that it would be pronounced correctly by the French. Her biggest success came in 1908, when Debussy chose her to succeed Mary Garden as Mélisande in his opera *Pelléas et Mélisande*. Debussy also coached and accompanied her in recitals of his songs. Her European operatic career flourished and she was a celebrated member of the Chicago and Boston Opera Companies. Between the wars, she sang with the British National Opera Company at Covent Garden. She recorded substantial extracts from Messager's *Monsieur Beaucaire* in 1919 (Columbia L 1310–16) and items from several other operettas. She was then neglected by the record companies until 1936, when she was invited to record a number of Debussy's songs with Alfred Cortot at the piano (HMV DA 1471–7). These records were an immediate success and, over the next decade, she made many more. Maggie Teyte also gave a series of outstanding recitals of this repertoire in London. In 1945, she returned to the United States to give broadcasts and concerts, and she performed Mélisande with the New York Opera Company in 1948. She was made a Dame of the British Empire in 1958. Writing of her in the *New Grove Dictionary*, Desmond Shawe-Taylor concluded: "Her voice recorded ideally, and her records of the French repertory have set a standard."

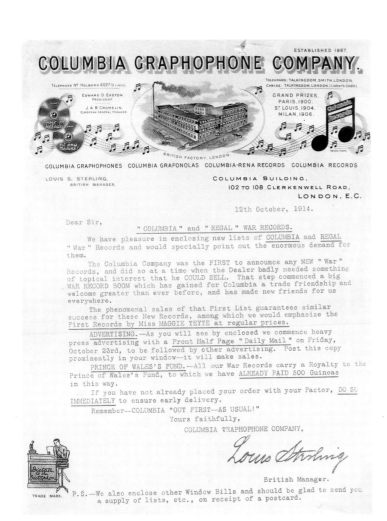

First World War

In the wake of the sudden and unexpected declaration of war in 1914, the public stopped buying luxuries such as records. To counter this, Louis Sterling issued a series of Columbia and Regal war records. This trade circular from October 1914 reveals the success this series had already achieved, and the lengths to which Sterling went to ensure that his message was brought to the attention of the record-buying public.

Columbia war records
The despatch room in the autumn of 1914 bears witness to the success of Sterling's strategy of issuing special war supplements.

If you were the only girl in the world

THE FIRST WORLD WAR, 1914–1918

The start of the war had a devastating impact on the record industry (see Chapter 2), which came to a shuddering halt as wholesalers refused to distribute printed matter and retailers stopped ordering fresh supplies of records. In June 1937, W. S. Meadmore recalled these events and Sterling's role:

A lot of hard thinking was done in the Clerkenwell Road [offices of Columbia] in those dark days, and it was Louis Sterling who saved the situation. He called all the managers together, told them to rake up all the patriotic records they could find, and to find out if any composers had written new songs. "Rush them all out as war records", he said. Within ten days they were issued. The confidence thus expressed reacted on the trade generally, other manufacturers quickly followed this lead, soon records were everywhere expressing the then war-like sentiments of the nation. [W. S. Meadmore, "Sir Louis Sterling", *Gramophone*, Vol.15, June 1937]

FVRNIVALL

Columbia
Records
March 1917

Supplement No. 30

MAGIC NOTES
TRADE-MARK

Looking to a peaceful future. A Columbia wartime monthly supplement.

On 27 August 1914, the first of seven Regal War Supplements – each containing twelve records – was released. Every record carried a label promising to pay a special royalty on each copy sold to the Prince of Wales's Fund, which had been established at the outbreak of hostilities to alleviate wartime hardship. By February 1915, Columbia had subscribed more than £1,500 to this fund. Among the war records Sterling released were two by the British soprano Maggie (later Dame Maggie) Teyte (see box, page 107). These records, "Your King and country want you" and "The homes they leave behind" (Columbia 2467), were intended to reflect the patriotic rather than the artistic qualities of the performer, but they also demonstrated why this extraordinary artist graced the pages of the Columbia, HMV and then EMI catalogues for so long.

Sir Thomas Beecham at the time of his first Columbia recordings.

One immediate result of the war was the recall to the United States of several European-based Columbia executives. Among those to leave was the European general manager, John A. B. Cromelin. His successor, Louis Sterling, spent the war years in Britain, building Columbia into a formidable force in the British record industry. During the war, Sterling gave a series of interviews to the trade press on both sides of the Atlantic. In them, he chronicled the growth and the changing nature of Columbia's British trade. In 1916, he remarked that: "Nineteen hundred and fifteen was the best year of the Great Britain division of the Columbia Graphophone Co … We not only closed last year in point of sales volume, but also the best in profits." [*Talking Machine World*, January 1916]

The 1915 accounts bear out Sterling's optimism. British sales of records and grafonolas amounted to £182,698, whilst profits stood at £36,932 (an impressive 20 per cent of turnover). In 1918, Sterling noted: "Our sales during 1917 showed a gain of 25 per cent over 1916, making this year the best in our history." [*Talking Machine World*, April 1918] With a keen eye for changing social trends, Sterling explained the boom thus:

The British people as a whole are in no mood to enjoy visits to the theatre and other public places. They have loved ones at the front who are ever foremost in their minds, and they prefer to spend their spare time in their own homes. As they are all working harder than ever before, they need some form of amusement, and turn to the talking machine as best suited to entertain the whole family.
[*Talking Machine World*, April 1918]

In 1917, in order to better preserve the growing assets of the business, a British-registered joint stock company – The Columbia Graphophone Company Ltd – was formed. All the assets and the £200,000 share capital of this business remained the property of the American parent. The formation of the British company meant that, for the first time in its 20 years of trading, Columbia had its own legal identity in Britain and a local board of directors. Sterling became managing director, whilst the chairman was Sir George Croydon Marks MP (later Lord Marks of Woolwich), formerly Thomas Edison's British patent agent and an ex-chairman of his British record business. Both Sterling and Marks were later to become founding members of the EMI board. Also in 1917, Columbia Graphophone purchased the British assets, which included The Hertford Record Co. Ltd, of Carl Lindström, an important German manufacturer. Hertford brought to Columbia a large

Madame CLARA BUTT sings "THE ROSARY"

DAME CLARA BUTT
(1872–1936)

★

Born in Sussex, the contralto Clara Butt made her London debut in 1892. Her career was spent almost entirely in the concert hall, and she became famous for the ballad concerts she gave throughout the British Empire, and for her appearances at the great British music festivals. A number of works were written for her, including Liddle's "Abide with Me" (HMV 03179) and Elgar's *Sea Pictures*, from which she recorded "Where corals lie" (HMV 03299). In 1899, accompanied by her future husband Kennerley Rumford, she made her first Gramophone Company recordings, including "Night Hymn at Sea" (Berliner E 4054). Clara Butt and her husband returned to The Gramophone Company's studio in 1909, where they recorded some 42 titles. Her records carried an exclusive rich dark-blue label and the legend "The Voice of the Century". Butt and Rumford transferred their allegiance to Columbia in 1915, where, for the remainder of her life, this greatly loved singer reigned supreme as the Company's British super-celebrity. In 1920, she was appointed a Dame of the British Empire. Her powerful voice had no trouble filling the vast spaces of the Albert Hall and the Crystal Palace, occasioning Sir Thomas Beecham to remark once that on a clear day one could hear Dame Clara Butt across the English Channel.

Columbia ♫

and modern record factory and an important catalogue of records. For a while in 1918, Hertford took over pressing from the Columbia factory when it was destroyed yet again by fire. This acquisition was a harbinger of the firm's post-war expansion.

During the war, Columbia was able to attract many established British classical artists. Its greatest coup was an exclusive contract with the woman whose voice and repertoire, more than anyone else's, epitomized Britain and the Empire: the contralto Clara (later Dame Clara) Butt. Her recording of Elgar's "Land of Hope and Glory" (Columbia 7156) may have appalled the composer, but it resonated with the feelings of many at the time. In sharp contrast, Clara Butt recorded "Have you news of my boy Jack?" (Columbia 7145) in 1915 with an orchestra conducted by Sir Thomas Beecham (see box, page 173). The song, a sober and reflective piece more in keeping with the times, was a setting by Edward German of the melancholy poem Rudyard Kipling wrote in despair after learning that his only son, a British army officer, was missing in action, presumed killed on the Western Front.

PABLO CASALS
(1876–1973)

Born in Spain, the cellist Pablo Casals began his international career in 1899. His playing was characterized by intellectual strength as well as technical mastery, and his artistry engendered an increased appreciation of the cello and its music. Around 1907, Casals formed a chamber music trio with the pianist Alfred Cortot and the violinist Jacques Thibaud, but the conflicting pressures of their individual solo careers meant that it lasted only a few years. In 1915, he made his first recordings for Columbia: encore pieces, which included the Bourrée from Bach's Suite in C (Columbia 7132) and the "Air on the G String" (Columbia 7138). In 1926, Fred Gaisberg persuaded Casals, Cortot and Thibaud to re-form their trio and record for HMV. The recordings they made, beginning with Schubert's B flat Piano Trio (HMV DB 947–50), set new standards in the field. Casals was the first person in modern times to play Bach's solo cello suites in their entirety, and his recording of them in the late 1930s remains one of the glories of EMI's classical catalogue. Casals was also a conductor. In 1919, he founded in Barcelona the Pau Casals Orchestra, which he patiently developed until the Spanish Civil War curtailed his activities. An implacable opponent of Franco's regime, he moved to Prades, where he organized and took part in a chamber music festival. In 1956, he finally settled in Puerto Rico, where he also organized an annual festival.

After 1915, the number and quality of Columbia's orchestral recordings began to improve. By modern standards, these recordings often sound pitifully thin and brassy. However, the efforts of Columbia's engineers gave results that were remarkably fine for the time, and demonstrated just how far the art of sound recording had come since engineers began recording in London at the end of the 19th century. Henry (later Sir Henry) Wood (see box, page 113) said of his latest recordings in 1915:

In my opinion they surpass anything yet attempted in orchestral recording, because the characteristics of each orchestral instrument make their due effect. There is also plenty of light and shade, and one realizes that it is a full modern orchestra that is playing, and not a brass band. [Columbia Advertisement, 1915]

Other exclusive Columbia artists recording at this time were the soprano Elsa Stralia, and the tenor Gervase Elwes, who, in 1917, made an important recording of Vaughan Williams's Housman cycle *On Wenlock Edge* (Columbia 7146–50). Others included the pianist Vladimir de Pachmann and the great Spanish cellist Pablo Casals (see box). However, the most far-sighted signings were of the conductors Sir Henry Wood and Sir Thomas Beecham. Beecham's Columbia (and later EMI) career as a recording artist lasted until his death nearly 50 years later (see Chapter 5).

During the First World War, meeting the musical needs of soldiers and sailors became an important part of the making and selling of Columbia and Regal records. Sterling recognized this and, in an American interview, told reporters:

We are shipping many thousands of records per month to the boys at the front, and the orders for these records almost invariably call for 50 per cent popular music, and the remainder good standard selections and operatic numbers. The demand for the so-called patriotic popular number has practically passed into oblivion, the boys at the front calling for the straight popular selections. [*Talking Machine World*, April 1918]

In October 1916, Columbia published its first-ever list of best-selling records. This included three versions of "Down home in Tennessee", including one by Prince's Grand Concert Band (Columbia 618); "Kentucky Home", by the Unity Quartette (Columbia 2707); and "If you were the only girl in the world", sung by George Robey – at the time Columbia's most popular performer in revue and musical shows – and Violet Loraine (Columbia L 1035). Other titles in the list included "Pack up your troubles", coupled with "There's a long, long trail", by the Unity

SIR HENRY WOOD
(1869–1944)

★

The conductor Sir Henry Wood is best known for founding the annual Promenade Concerts now held by the BBC at the Royal Albert Hall in London. He was born in London, where, after studying at the Royal Academy of Music, he worked as a conductor. In 1895, shortly after the opening of the new Queen's Hall in London, he was invited to put on a trial season of nightly Promenade Concerts with tickets at affordable prices. The concept proved such a success that Wood continued to lead the Proms (as they affectionately came to be known) for 50 consecutive seasons until shortly before his death. Apart from organizing the Proms, Sir Henry devoted much effort to improving the standards of orchestral playing in Britain, and from 1923 he taught conducting at the Royal Academy of Music. He was one of the first major conductors to make records, beginning with a group of sessions for Columbia in 1915. These produced Wagner's *Lohengrin* Act III Prelude coupled with Wood's own orchestral arrangement of Rachmaninov's Prelude in C sharp minor (Columbia L 1005), and the Scherzo from Tchaikovsky's Fourth Symphony coupled with Grainger's *Shepherd's Hey* (Columbia L 1006). Wood's very positive influence on British orchestras was widely appreciated, as was his unbounded enthusiasm for his beloved Proms. Sir Adrian Boult said of him: "Sir Henry was the greatest popular conductor (in the finest sense of the adjective) that the world has ever seen."

Sir Henry Wood listening to a selection of his early Columbia records in the garden of his home.

Quartette (Columbia 2708); "My Mother's Rosary" also by the Unity Quartette (Columbia 2709); and three versions of "A Broken Doll", including one by Clarice Mayne (Columbia L 1041). Six different recordings of "Every Little While" from the London show *Some* were listed, including one by Lee White (Columbia L 1058), who created the song. The records were without exception slow, highly romantic, escapist songs, the kind of music capable of taking soldiers driven to the end of endurance out of themselves for a few minutes.

Wartime London revues and musicals were an important source of popular songs. Sterling realized that the soldiers, who flocked to see these shows in London whilst on leave, would want to take back to the trenches records of the songs and music performed by the original casts, many of whom either were or became exclusive Columbia recording artists. To help organize all this, Columbia hired an impresario to engage suitable artists from the original casts. *Business as Usual*, a revue that opened in November 1914, was among the first to have its hits recorded. They included Harry Tate and Violet Loraine's sketch "Fortifying the Home Front" (Columbia 504); Ambrose Thorn's and Violet Loraine's duet "When we've wound up the watch on the Rhine"

Violet Loraine, Harry Tate and Morris Harvey at the Columbia studios recording excerpts from *Business as Usual*. Note the wooden wall-cladding used to add resonance to the sound.

(Columbia 2484); and Violet Loraine's "Three cheers for little Belgium" (Columbia 2488).

Other wartime London musical shows whose hits were recorded by Columbia included *Rosy Rapture* (records of which were made and in the shops within ten days of the show's opening), *Bubbly* and *Zig-Zag*. Christopher Stone, who became the first London editor of the *Gramophone* magazine in 1923, wrote to his wife about the extraordinary conditions under which he had heard the records from *Zig-Zag*:

We are sitting in the mess with the gramophone playing a selection of *Zig-Zag*, quite a domestic pleasure: but every crevice of every entrance is blanketed and has been for two hours as we are being bombarded with gas shells this evening. [Eds. G. D. Sheffield and G. I. S. Inglis, *From Vimy Ridge to the Rhine*: Great War Letters of Christopher Stone (The Crowood Press, Marlborough 1989, P.117)]

The war finally ended in 1918, with Columbia in a strong position to take advantage of the new world of peacetime trading. Louis Sterling noted that year, "There is a very bright future indeed for the talking machine in England". [*Talking Machine World*, April, 1918] Between 1919 and 1931, no record company enjoyed a brighter future than The Columbia Graphophone Company.

Recording London shows

The Bing Boys are Here was the most popular of all London shows during the First World War. The excerpts Columbia recorded featured members of the original cast.

Advertising London shows

Throughout the First World War Columbia's recording engineers captured on wax the best of London entertainment. This 1917 advertisement illustrates the extent of Columbia's penetration of this important market.

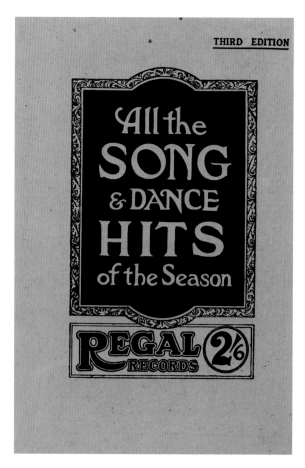

***Above* Columbia's Record Supplements**
The coming of electrical recording and a rising market for classical records presented Columbia with new opportunities for recording scenes from opera.

***Right* Regal Records**
During its heyday in the 1920s, Columbia's Regal label had a reputation for releases of up-to-the-minute records of popular music at budget prices.

It had to be you

THE RISE AND RISE OF COLUMBIA, 1919–1931

The years immediately after the end of the First World War saw the end of the link between The Columbia Graphophone Company Ltd and its American parent company. At the war's end, the American parent was once again in serious financial trouble. It was again reconstructed, emerging as The Columbia Graphophone Manufacturing Co. In 1922, that company went into receivership, which permitted the British board, financed by Edward (later Sir Edward) de Stein, to buy the American-held shares in The Columbia Graphophone Company Ltd. Once this was achieved, the board of the London company was reconstructed. The new board included Sir George Croydon Marks, MP (chairman), Louis Sterling (managing director), Michael Herbert (a partner in Morgan Stanley, then the British branch of the American investment bank J. P. Morgan) and Edward de Stein.

In 1923, with control over its destiny, Columbia became a

public limited company, issuing its £200,000 capital to the public as 400,000 ten-shilling shares. The Company also introduced a staff pension scheme for its British employees, funded partly from profits. In turn, the Columbia employees delivered the goods. Output at the British factory increased from 6.7 million records in 1923 to 15.5 million records in 1930. Production of grafonolas also rose from 18,000 in 1923 to 70,000 in 1927. Although much of this production was destined for Columbia's large overseas markets, many were also sold in the booming British market. Sterling noted in 1926 that, in the peak month of December 1925, the Company sold 1.75 million records in Britain. In the same month of the following year, he boasted of figures of more than 2 million.

Columbia's profits rose throughout the 1920s, peaking in 1929 at £500,000. Between 1925 and 1930, dividends to Columbia shareholders held steady at an impressive 40 per cent of the issue price of the shares, with an additional 20 per cent bonus paid in 1928. The shares were traded at huge premiums, rising at one stage to £15. Even though its shares were also listed in New York, The Columbia Graphophone Company Ltd remained a British-registered firm. However, by the end of the decade, the bulk of its shares were owned or controlled by J. P. Morgan.

The Company's most significant business achievement during the 1920s was to consolidate the world record industry. The first stage in this process was the acquisition of its former American parent company, yet again reconstructed from bankruptcy, this time as The Columbia Phonograph Co, Inc. In 1925, Columbia took a 60 per cent stake in the business, and by 1927, the London company owned practically all its shares. With gusto, Sterling – who became chairman of its New York board – set about turning around this loss-making leviathan, reorganizing the business and its manufacturing facilities and creating fresh recording programmes. As part of this process, Columbia Phonograph bought the American record business of Okeh. This important move gave Columbia access to the booming market in popular, jazz, dance and other distinctly American forms of music. In 1926, Columbia Phonograph reported its first profits in seven years. By 1928, profits had risen to an impressive $760,000. After a decade of disastrous losses, bankruptcy and reconstructions, the entrepreneurial skills of Louis Sterling had rescued Columbia Phonograph. In 1927, the American business invested $163,000 in United Independent Broadcasters, a small New York-based radio network. In return, the network broadcast Columbia records and changed its name to Columbia Broadcasting System (CBS); this was the origin of one of America's largest television networks. The investment lasted for

During the 1920s, the Christmas selling season was the occasion for distributing high quality advertising material to dealers and consumers. This 1930 Columbia supplement illustrates a conventional Christmas scene, with the records left to sell themselves.

OSCAR PREUSS
(1889–1958)

★

London-born Carl Oscar Preuss's first experience of the recording studio came when, as a child, he accompanied his sister's husband (the baritone Ion Colquhoun) to a recording session. Fascinated by what he saw, he joined the Odeon Company in 1904 and trained as a sound engineer. Between 1909 and 1914 he worked for the German International Talking Machine Company and recorded many of their most important classical artists, including Emmy Destinn, Jan Kubelík, John McCormack and Mario Sammarco, as well as popular music hall performers such as George Formby senior and Billy Williams. In 1923, he became Artist and Repertoire manager for Parlophone, a post he held until his retirement. During the decade after the war, Preuss rebuilt Parlophone's catalogue and was responsible for recording many of the label's principal British artists. In 1950, he helped create the London Baroque Ensemble under the conductor Karl Haas, and together they recorded much rarely heard 17th- and 18th-century music. Oscar Preuss retired in 1955, handing the Parlophone business over to his assistant George Martin. He died in London three years later, aged 60. George Martin described him as "my own dear mentor who had taught me so much."

Right As record sales dipped in the summer season, Columbia made great efforts to link gramophones and records with summer activities. This July 1929 supplement was produced at a time when annual sales of records were at an all-time high, a position not repeated until the late 1950s.

Supplement No. 160

only one year, but it provided Columbia Phonograph with unrivalled advertising for its products.

The Columbia Graphophone Company Ltd also purchased a controlling interest in Carl Lindström, at that time the largest German multinational record manufacturer, and its Dutch subsidiary Transoceanic Trading, which controlled Lindström's overseas manufacturing activities. As part of the Lindström\Transoceanic deal, Columbia acquired Lindström's London recording studios, and with them the services of Oscar Preuss (see box), who later became one of EMI's most distinguished Artist and Repertoire managers. As a result of this acquisition, the Company acquired the Parlophone and Odeon labels.

In order to manage its growing overseas holdings – with factories across Europe, the United States, Brazil and the Argentine, plus a worldwide distribution and selling network – Columbia created a holding company in 1925, Columbia (International) Ltd, with an initial share capital of £845,000. In 1927, to overcome protective tariffs and supply its growing Antipodean markets, Columbia opened a £100,000 Australian factory at Homebush, near Sydney, which was considered at the time to be the most up-to-date of its kind. In 1927, to penetrate the burgeoning Far Eastern market – especially Japan – Columbia acquired The Nipponophone Company, then Japan's most important record manufacturer, whilst in 1928 the assets of two small German businesses, Homophon GmbH and Nigrolit Werke GmbH, were purchased and were transferred to the Carl Lindström group. Columbia's last major acquisition, the recording division of the old French Pathé company, was made in 1928. Together with Columbia's own French branch, and Lindström's Odeon label, the acquisition of Pathé consolidated the company's position as the leading French record producer.

Parlez-moi d'amour

COLUMBIA'S ELECTRICAL RECORDINGS IN THE 1920S

In 1920, anticipating the technological leaps of the next decade, Columbia released recordings made on 11 November 1920 during the burial service of the Unknown Warrior in Westminster Abbey. This first ever sound recording of a major public event was achieved by the use of a microphone, which – with a primitive electrical amplifier – actuated a cutting tool. In 1923, Columbia created its own Research and Development Department. The team introduced the New Process laminated record. Records pressed using this process had the advantage of significantly reduced surface noise and a greatly enhanced quality of reproduction. In 1924, Louis Sterling – in an inspired long-term move – brought to Columbia the electrical engineer Isaac (later Sir Isaac) Shoenberg (see box, page 144). He reorganized Columbia's existing research facilities, whose efforts had been largely focused on methods of improving the existing mechanical recording process.

By the mid-1920s, Columbia's Research Department was working on a number of projects that had, by the end of the decade, transformed the business into a large manufacturer of electrical products, particularly radios, radio-gramophones and

ARTHUR H. BROOKS
(1875–1950)

★

Arthur Brooks began his professional career as an actor, touring Britain in musical comedies and Shakespeare. He had his first experience of the record business in 1903, when he was engaged by Nicole Frères in Holborn, London, to hire artists and record them. He joined The Columbia Graphophone Company in 1910 and eventually became recording manager of the Columbia Studios and artistic director. Brooks was closely involved with many of Columbia's most important classical projects, including Gervase Elwes's recording of Vaughan Williams's *On Wenlock Edge* and the Wagner recordings made at Bayreuth between 1927 and 1930. Christopher Stone once described him as "surely one of the best-known and best-loved men in the gramophone world". (*Gramophone*, December 1929)

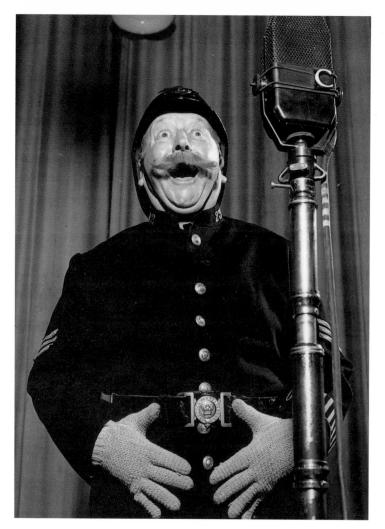

Above Stanley Holloway
The comic singer Stanley Holloway in a publicity shot for his early 1930s hit "With her head tucked underneath her arm".

Right Charles Penrose
Charles Penrose's name is forever linked with his 1926 recording of "The Laughing Policeman", one of the Company's most successful novelty recordings.

electrical record-players. Shoenberg's great strength was his ability to gather round him the finest available talent in the field of electrical engineering. In 1928, for instance, he recruited to the Columbia team Alan Dower Blumlein (see box, page 137), the greatest electrical engineer of his generation.

In 1925, the Western Electric system of electrical recording was introduced to the Columbia studios. Electrical engineers took over the actual disc-cutting functions, while the old mechanical disc-cutters – like Charles Gregory, Arthur Brooks and Oscar Preuss – either learned the new electrical engineering skills, or became studio managers, or artist and repertoire managers, posts formalized with the introduction of electrical recording. One of Columbia's earliest electrical recordings, released in Britain during 1925, was of the 850 voices of the Associated Glee Clubs of America, together with their audience of 4,000, singing "John Peel" (Columbia 9048). It proved a resounding success with the public, and became the springboard for a major British and European electrical recording programme. However, to make the most of the enhanced sound quality of these new records, it proved necessary to design new grafonolas. Within a year, Columbia was marketing its Viva-Tonal range of

Left **Will Fyffe**
The Scottish comic Will Fyffe with an effigy
of the character he created for his song
"I'm 94 today".

Below **The Handel Festival at London's
Crystal Palace**
In 1927, the Crystal Palace hosted the final Handel
Festival, with Sir Henry Wood conducting the
festival orchestra and massed choirs with a huge
illuminated baton. Portions of this extraordinary
gathering were captured for posterity by
Columbia recording engineers.

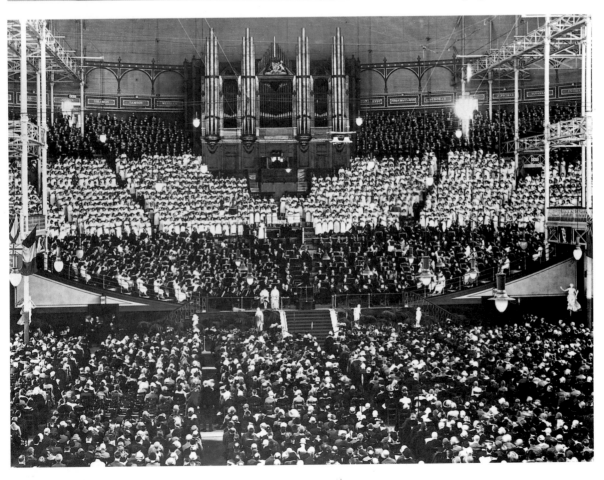

**RICHARD TAUBER
(1891–1948)**

★

Born in Linz, Austria, the tenor Richard Tauber
made his operatic debut in 1913 at Chemnitz
as Tamino in Mozart's *Zauberflöte*. In 1919, he
joined the Berlin State Opera and soon
became famous throughout Europe. In 1924,
he met the operetta composer Franz Lehár,
who wrote several roles for him, including
parts in *Paganini, Frederike, Die Zarewitsch* and
The Land of Smiles, the last-named providing
him with "Dein ist mein ganzes Herz" (You are
my heart's delight) (Parlophone-Odeon RO
20107), which became his signature tune. In
1931, Tauber made his London debut at Drury
Lane in *The Land of Smiles*, and thereafter he
undertook several successful tours of America.
He also appeared in films; in these he
epitomized the image of the romantic tenor,
immaculately dressed in top hat, opera cloak
and monocle. His Jewish background forced
him to leave Germany and Austria, and he
settled in London, where he continued to
record, scoring a big popular hit with "Pedro
the Fisherman" (Parlophone RO 20545). He
also had success with an operetta he wrote and
produced himself called *Old Chelsea*, from
which came "My Heart and I" (Parlophone
RO 20522). These excursions into popular
repertoire led to some criticism of his singing
of more serious music, but when the Vienna
State Opera visited Covent Garden in the
autumn of 1947, Tauber, though seriously ill,
sang a memorable Don Ottavio in Mozart's
Don Giovanni which confounded the critics and
delighted his devoted admirers. He died soon
after. Elisabeth Schwarzkopf, who was with the
Vienna company in 1947, wrote that Tauber was
"the greatest tenor I had the fortune to hear".

machines, and it later introduced the first all-electric grafonolas.

In April 1926, Charles Penrose remade his extraordinary manic record "The Laughing Policeman" (Columbia 4014); by 1931 it had achieved sales in excess of 130,000. As another instance, in 1929 the Scottish music hall performer Will Fyffe made a fresh recording of his most successful comic songs, "I belong to Glasgow" and "I'm 94 today" (Columbia 9928). The new catalogue reflected new and existing tastes in popular music, while many current Columbia artists remade their old recordings. It was during this period that the comedy artist Stanley Holloway began to record his many monologues for Columbia, the first being the famous "Pick up tha' musket" (Columbia DX 168).

Among Columbia's best-known choral recordings from this time was Humperdinck's *Hansel and Gretel* "Dance Duet" in a setting the composer could never have envisaged, coupled with Purcell's "Nymphs and Shepherds" (Columbia DB 9909). The record featured the Manchester School Children's Choir, under the direction of the redoubtable Miss Gertrude Riall, and the Hallé Orchestra conducted by Sir Hamilton Harty. Another Columbia record of choral singing in the mid-1920s contained two excerpts from Handel's *Messiah*, "And the Glory of the Lord" with "Behold the Lamb of God" (Columbia L 1768). This 1926 record captured the final gasp of what had been a venerable Victorian institution, the Handel Festival held at the Crystal Palace, London, with Sir Henry Wood conducting a chorus of 3,000 voices and a 500-piece orchestra. So considerable were the costs and organizational demands that never again were such musical resources gathered under one roof.

The Parlophone and Odeon labels brought a roster of important European classical artists, such as the tenor Josef Schmidt, the sopranos Lotte Lehmann (see box, page 167), Emmy Bettendorf and Jarmila Novotná, and the outstanding mezzo-soprano Conchita Supervia. Her recording of the principal arias and duets from Bizet's opera *Carmen* (Parlophone R 201127, R 20278, PXO 1017, PXO 1019 and Odeon 123774) marked her out as an outstanding Carmen, and hers remains one of the finest interpretations on record of this elusive part. Parlophone's most important classical artist was the Austrian-born tenor Richard Tauber (see box). Tauber made records of every kind of music, ranging from Mozart, Richard Strauss and Lehár to the popular music of his day. Among the many Tauber Parlophone-Odeon records available in the late 1920s and early 1930s was a fine recording of the finale from the second act of Johann Strauss's operetta *Die Fledermaus* (Parlophone R 20085), with Lotte Lehmann, Karin Branzell, Greta Merrem-Nikisch,

Josef Schmidt
The diminutive Romanian tenor Josef Schmidt (1904–1942) achieved worldwide popularity in the 1930s through his concerts and films. He recorded mainly for Parlophone, usually in German, but he also made English versions of his biggest hits, including "My song goes round the world" and "A star falls from heaven".

Conchita Supervia
The Spanish mezzo-soprano Conchita Supervia was renowned for her spirited interpretations of Rossini's comic heroines as well as Bizet's Carmen.

Waldemar Staegemann and the Berlin State Orchestra conducted by Frieder Weissmann. More than any other, this record conveyed Tauber's warmth, natural conviviality and good humour in the company of beautiful women. Other Tauber records from this period include three that remain closely associated with his name: "Oh! maiden, my maiden" (Parlophone R 20101), from Lehár's *Frederika*; "You are my heart's delight" (Parlophone RO 20107), from Lehár's *Land of Smiles*; and Siecynski's "Vienna, City of My Dreams" (Parlophone R 20121).

Important classical instrumentalists were also featured in the Parlophone catalogue. One of the most significant was the great pianist and pupil of Liszt, Moriz Rosenthal (see box, page 125). His Parlophone recordings included the first ever complete recording of Chopin's Piano Concerto No.1 (Parlophone R 902-4 and E 11113-14), with an orchestra conducted by Frieder Weissmann.

Parlophone and Odeon were not just vehicles for classical music. Sterling filled their lists with the latest popular music and selections from the extensive American Okeh catalogue. The records of several great American jazz artists, such as Louis Armstrong and the Dorsey Brothers, appeared for the first time in Britain on Parlophone. This strong tradition of using Parlophone-Odeon as a popular music label continued into the long-playing record period and on to the present era of the compact disc. In 1962, for instance, The Beatles (see box, page 313), EMI's greatest ever pop music success, made their first appearance as EMI artists on the Parlophone label (see Chapter 9).

In December 1924, the American jazz musicians Turner Layton and Clarence Johnstone (see box, page 126), released as a piano and singing duo 'Hard hearted Hannah' coupled with 'It had to be you' (Columbia 3511), the first of their many Columbia hit records. Over the next decade, these hugely talented black Americans became immensely popular, made many hundreds of recordings and sold more than 8 million records. Layton and Johnstone's attraction lay in their appeal to the great bulk of British record buyers, none of whom regarded themselves as musically sophisticated, or, in the terms of the times, "highbrow". In the same vein, Columbia artists such as the violinist Albert Sandler, and Flotsam and Jetsam (B. C. Hilliam and Malcolm McEachern), whose formula for success was based on a Victorian tenor and bass duet style which twitted contemporary British life, were enormously successful.

Columbia had been amongst the first record companies to recognize the potential of records by dance orchestras and jazz bands. Throughout the 1920s, every monthly supplement of new records revealed the latest hits, several of which sold more than 100,000 copies. Columbia's list of bands included Billy Cotton, Fletcher Henderson, Guy Lombardo, Jack Payne and the BBC Dance Orchestra, Bert Ralton and His Havana Band, and many more.

Columbia also continued to produce recordings of hits from London musical shows, performed by the original casts. With electrical recording, Columbia was able to record the hit *Desert Song* (Columbia 9211), and many others, directly from the stage at Drury Lane. In 1926, George Gershwin's *Lady, Be Good!* opened in London, starring the brother and sister team of Fred and Adele Astaire. The show's great songs were recorded with Gershwin himself at the piano. They included "Lady, Be Good!" (Columbia 3980), "Fascinating Rhythm" and "The Half of it, Dearie, Blues" (Columbia 3969). During the recording of "The Half of it, Dearie, Blues", Fred Astaire sang, danced and joked with Gershwin,

Fred Astaire and George Gershwin
The singer and dancer Fred Astaire and the composer George Gershwin, who made
a series of Columbia recordings in London during the mid-1920s.

revealing a relaxed sophistication that became the hallmark o/f
these two high priests of the jazz age.

As a by-product of its Pathé acquisition, the Company gained
access to the recordings of important French popular singers. As
exclusive Columbia artists their records were given an international
platform and distributed throughout the world. Among these was
cabaret singer Lucienne Boyer whose 1930 recording of "Parlez-moi
d'amour" (Columbia DB 673) was one of the first to win the Grand
Prix du Disque, France's most prestigious record award. Others
included Edith Piaf, Jean Sablon and Charles Trenet.

During the late 1920s, Columbia gained a reputation as a
promoter of contemporary classical music. Among the composers
recording their own works at this time were Maurice Ravel,
Francis Poulenc, Béla Bartók, Manuel de Falla and Ernst von
Dohnányi. Instrumentalists recording for Columbia in the 1920s
included the international virtuoso violinist Joseph Szigeti, amongst

MORIZ ROSENTHAL
(1862–1946)

The piano virtuoso Moriz Rosenthal left a small
but precious legacy of gramophone recordings
of great historical importance. In 1877, he met
Franz Liszt and became his protégé. He
remained under Liszt's supervision until the old
man died nine years later, by which time
Rosenthal was a mature artist of astonishing
virtuosity and accomplishment. He enjoyed a
brilliant and extremely long international career,
receiving unstinting praise from many leading
musical figures, including the critic Eduard
Hanslick and the composers Tchaikovsky,
Brahms, Johann Strauss II and Hugo Wolf. He
eventually settled in the United States, where
he founded a piano school. He made his first
record in 1928, when he was 65, an
arrangement of *The Blue Danube* (HMV EJ
329). After the record was released on the
HMV black label, Rosenthal had second
thoughts and wanted to remake it for HMV's
international celebrity red label. In 1934, after
much correspondence and negotiation with
Fred Gaisberg, Rosenthal began a series of
mainly Chopin recordings, including the Waltz
No.5 in A flat Op.42 coupled with the Preludes
Op.28 Nos.3, 6 & 7 (HMV DB 2772) and the
Mazurkas Nos.25 & 31 (HMV DB 2773). In
1935, the critic Neville Cardus wrote of
Rosenthal: "The exquisite melancholy of his
Chopin is nostalgic. We feel the presence of a
man left over from a proud, glamorous
civilization, meditating on the 'pathos of
distance', glancing back, not sentimentally but
as a connoisseur in rare emotions."

TURNER LAYTON
(1894–1978) &
CLARENCE JOHNSTONE
(1885–1953)

★

Turner Layton and Clarence Johnstone were
Columbia's best-selling artists in the 78-rpm
era. Layton had already written such hits as
"After you've gone" and "Way down yonder in
New Orleans" in collaboration with his original
partner Henry Creamer when he met
Clarence "Tandy" Johnstone. In 1923, having
failed to find work as a singing duo in New
York, they came to London, where they were
soon successful in cabaret at the Café de Paris.
The night before they were due to make a test
recording for HMV, Columbia's Raymond
Langley heard their act and immediately
offered them a contract. He wrote out the
financial terms there and then, and the singers
signed. It was the beginning of one of the most
fruitful relationships ever between artists and a
record company. During their recording career,
they made a string of best-selling records and
earned large sums in royalties. Among the early
hits were "Bye Bye Blackbird" (Columbia DB
4304) and "My Blue Heaven" (Columbia DB
4694). In 1935, following a scandal, Johnstone
returned to New York, where he vanished into
obscurity. Layton continued to work in Britain
for a further 20 years, singing and recording
mainly romantic ballads like "Smoke gets in
your eyes" (Columbia DB 1574) and "These
foolish things" (Columbia FB 1300). Brian Rust
said of Layton and Johnstone: "Few artists
have ever been so adaptable, few gave less
trouble to the engineers at a session, and few
were as polished, sophisticated, yet warm to
their audiences."

**Layton & Johnstone's first recording
contract**
Layton & Johnstone's 1923 Columbia contract,
written after Columbia's Raymond Langley had
heard them at the Café de Paris.

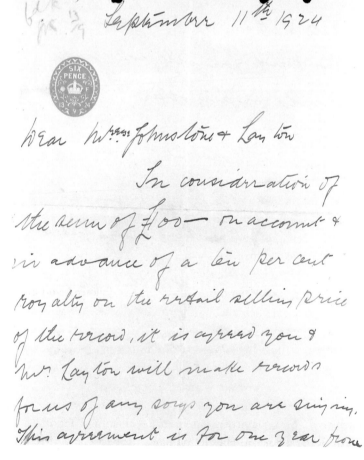

[handwritten letter]

date & it is further agreed during
this period you will not make
records for any other Talking machine
Company.

Very kind Yours

Raymond Langley

for the Columbia Graphophone
Co. Ltd.
102/8 Clerkenwell Rd.
E.C. 1

Read & agreed.

Signed.

Laytor & Johnstone

ISOBEL BAILLIE
(1895–1983)

★

Born in Scotland, Isobel Baillie grew up in Manchester. Encouraged by Sir Hamilton Harty, she studied singing in Italy and began her professional career in 1922. Her young voice showed a freshness which matured to warmth and charm. Isobel Baillie's preferred repertoire was Lieder and especially oratorio, in which her clear voice and musicianship were shown to particular advantage. She sang in countless performances of Handel's *Messiah* and her interpretation became a model for other singers. Although she made some test records for HMV in 1924, nothing came of them. From 1926 onwards, she was exclusive to Columbia, for whom her recordings included arias from the oratorios and operas of Purcell, Handel, Haydn, Mendelssohn and Elgar, as well as a number of songs. She also participated in a complete recording of *Messiah* (Columbia DX 1283–1301) made in 1946 with the Huddersfield Choral Society and the Liverpool Philharmonic Orchestra conducted by Malcolm Sargent. Her last recordings date from 1974, and she continued to teach and lecture until almost the end of her long life. On the occasion of her 80th birthday, her colleague Gerald Moore paid her this tribute: "She exemplified English singing at its best with her pure, silvery tone, her silken legato line and effortless unnervous approach that put the listener at smiling ease."

whose recordings were Bartók's Hungarian Folk Tunes (Columbia LX 31), and a dramatic interpretation of Brahms's Violin Concerto with the Hallé Orchestra conducted by Sir Hamilton Harty (Columbia L 2265–9). Columbia also made important recordings of chamber music with the Léner String Quartet, and also Albert Sammons, Lionel Tertis and William Murdoch. The Company at this time also began to make records of the British soprano Isobel Baillie (see box), then developing her reputation as an oratorio and concert soloist, and Eva (later Dame Eva) Turner, who was hailed internationally as a dramatic soprano of exceptional quality. In 1926, Eva Turner scored a major triumph when she first sang the title role in Puccini's opera *Turandot*, a part she made very much her own in the years that followed, and in 1928 she made a celebrated recording of Turandot's powerful aria "In questa reggia" (Columbia D 1631).

Gounod's opera *Faust* in English on 32 sides of 12-inch records was just one of Columbia's projects. The opera was recorded under the supervision of Joseph Batten, with Sir Thomas Beecham conducting the cream of British singers – all exclusive Columbia artists – as soloists, including Heddle Nash, Robert Easton, Harold Williams, Robert Carr, Miriam

Right The violinist Joseph Szigeti with conductor and composer Constant Lambert in the recording studio.

Below The British dramatic soprano Eva Turner as Puccini's Princess Turandot.

Licette, Muriel Brunskill and Doris
Vane, with the BBC Choir. Years later,
Batten recalled the perils of recording
with Beecham:

Sir Thomas took us through the opera at
such a pace that I renamed it Gounod's 'Fast'.
Sir Thomas said it was not speed, but rubato.
That may be, but he certainly played the very
devil with it. [Batten, ibid., p.114]

Between 1927 and 1930, following
arrangements with Siegfried Wagner
(the composer's son), a Columbia
recording team led by Arthur H.
Brooks and Charles Gregory made the
first ever recordings at the Bayreuth
Festival. In December 1927, extracts
from *Parsifal* (Columbia L 2007–13),
including the Transformation Scene
featuring the bells of Montsalvat,
especially designed to Wagner's
specifications and later destroyed in the
war, were released. Other recordings in
this series were excerpts from *Siegfried*
(Columbia L 2014–15), *Das Rheingold*
(Columbia L 2016) and *Die Walküre*
(Columbia L 2017). During the
recording sessions, the Festival
Orchestra was conducted variously by
Dr Karl Muck, Siegfried Wagner and
Franz von Hoesslin. This success prompted Columbia to send
Brooks and Gregory on further recording expeditions to
Bayreuth, where they recorded substantial portions of
Tannhäuser (Columbia LX 81-98) and *Tristan und Isolde*
(Columbia L 2187–206).

Gaisberg later wrote admiringly of the remarkable
standard of recording achieved by Gregory at Bayreuth, and
the demands the new electrical recording technology made on
engineers: "The outstanding quality of these records was due
in no small measure to the careful positioning of artists and
orchestra in relation to the microphone." [*The Voice*, February
1946] Working so far from base was not easy; however, the
problems encountered had their humorous side. Brooks, for
example, recalled how, on arrival at Bayreuth, he found the

NEW RECORDS   **DEC. 1927**

*The Ride of
the Valkyries.*

**BAYREUTH
WAGNER FESTIVAL**

*Astounding Electric Recordings taken
in the Bayreuth Wagner Theatre.*

ISSUED WITH THE APPROVAL
OF SIEGFRIED WAGNER —

EXCLUSIVE TO

Columbia

Supplement No. 131.

In 1927, Columbia engineers attended the
Bayreuth Festival, where, between performances
they recorded extracts from that year's
productions. This special supplement and trade
advertising (see overleaf) suggests the pride
Columbia executives felt at achieving what many
saw as a ground-breaking series of records.

BAYREUTH—the Mecca of All Opera-Lovers. The one Centre of the World where Wagner is played with a Cast and Orchestra and Scenically Produced in Absolute Perfection and Regardless of Cost!

IF ONLY such Performances could be recorded for the gramophone—what perfection in Records could be assured!

THE POSSIBILITY HAS COME TRUE—

COLUMBIA HAS RECORDED THE BAYREUTH FESTIVAL!

SIEGFRIED WAGNER approving and autographing for issue the Authorised COLUMBIA RECORDS of the BAYREUTH WAGNER FESTIVAL, 1927.

COLUMBIA enjoys the Exclusive Privilege of Recording the Bayreuth Festival!

THE Records were made in the wonderful Wagner Theatre, Bayreuth, where the Festival takes place. The acoustics of the Theatre are perfect, and this fact, combined with the unique Columbia electric process of recording in public halls and theatres, has resulted in RECORDS THAT EASILY TRANSCEND ANY PREVIOUS RECORDING ACHIEVEMENT

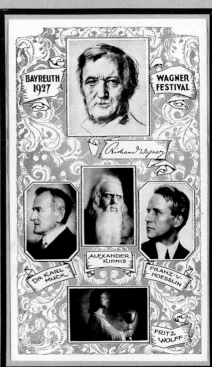

FOR LIST OF RECORDS SEE OVER

hundreds of wax blanks needed for the recording had failed to arrive. On enquiry to London, he discovered that, by mistake, they had been dispatched to Beirut (in the Lebanon).

In the late 1920s, one of Columbia's particular fortes was the recording of complete orchestral works by the world's leading orchestras under the batons of the greatest conductors of the age. Columbia conductors under exclusive contract at this time included Felix Weingartner, Dr Karl Muck, Bruno Walter, Willem Mengelberg, Sir Thomas Beecham, Ernest Ansermet, Sir Henry Wood, Sir Hamilton Harty and Walter Damrosch. Columbia also recorded the composers Igor Stravinsky, Dame Ethel Smyth, Gustav Holst and Alexander Glazunov conducting their own works. In 1926, Louis Sterling noted the interest in Britain and elsewhere in recordings of complete works:

An interesting development in the sale of Columbia records throughout Europe is the increased demand for records made by our big

orchestras, as exemplified by our Masterwork Series. These records have gained the approval of music lovers throughout the world, and, strange as it may seem, we have been shipping good-sized quantities of this type of record even to Japan. [*Talking Machine World*, October 1926]

Above The composer Gustav Holst recorded his *Planets* Suite for Columbia.

Left Dame Ethel Smyth was the composer of *The Wreckers* and made several recordings of her own works for Columbia.

Sales of these works were buoyant, but never matched those of popular music. In contrast to popular music, the investment required was high, and sometimes took several years to recoup. As Sir Louis Sterling cheerfully conceded in a 1957 interview, "'Boiled Beef and Carrots' subsidized Beethoven". [Interview with Sir Louis Sterling by David Bicknell, 1957]

By 1930, under the leadership of Louis Sterling, The Columbia Graphophone Company was a major engine of growth and innovation both in the highly competitive international recording industry and in the new British domestic electrical goods industry. By expanding its overseas markets, Columbia had become an important multinational, capable of meeting the diverse musical needs of consumers in every part of the world. However, in 1930, with the onset of the Great Depression, there occurred a dramatic collapse both in record sales and in the sale of other products. The collapse was so precipitous that in order to survive it became necessary to create an even bigger international business and rationalize manufacturing and marketing facilities. Pressed by the New York bankers J. P. Morgan – who by then controlled the bulk of Columbia's shares – Sterling and the Columbia board reluctantly agreed to merge their interests with those of their great British and international rival, The Gramophone Company. The merger took place in 1931, in the pit of the Depression, and the new business became known as Electric and Musical Industries Ltd (EMI). In approving the merger, the bankers made only one condition: that Louis Sterling be made the managing director of the new concern.

Supplement No. 167

The Hayes factory site in the 1930s

During the 1930s, the Hayes factory site boomed as the Company diversified into domestic electrical appliances such as radio, television and refrigerators.

CHAPTER 4

Move It

ELECTRIC AND MUSICAL INDUSTRIES, 1931–1961

Louis Sterling is said to have remarked that Decca was such an unconscionable time in dying [in the 1930s] that by the time the end came EMI themselves would be so weak they'd probably fall into the same grave. [Edward Lewis, *No CIC* (London 1956), p.38]

Brother, can you spare a dime

SURVIVING THE DEPRESSION, 1931–1939

1931 record supplement
In 1931 Louis Sterling tried to stem the collapse in record sales by instituting substantial cuts in the price of records.

In June 1931, in the midst of the Depression, the shareholders of The Columbia Graphophone Company and The Gramophone Company approved proposals to merge and form a new venture, Electric and Musical Industries Ltd (EMI). The first EMI board was drawn from senior directors of the merging companies with Alfred Clark as chairman and Louis Sterling as managing director. Non-executive directors included David Sarnoff, president of RCA Victor, and Trevor Williams (both formerly Gramophone Company directors), together with Lord Marks, Michael Herbert and Edward de Stein (all formerly Columbia Graphophone directors). They saw the new venture as a holding company which would manage the assets of the two existing businesses; it was hoped that they would continue to manufacture, trade and compete with each other as operating sub-companies. The sagacity of this strategy was questionable: during the two years before the merger, the combined profits of the two companies amounted to £1.7 million and £1.45 million. However in 1930–31, the final year of independent trading, combined profits had fallen to a mere £160,000. One of the new board's first acts was to dispose of its shares in the American Columbia Graphophone Company to avoid an anti-trust investigation of the merger by the Department of Justice in the United States.

EMI inherited cash and investments amounting to £2.75 million. Between 1931 and 1934, as the full weight of the Depression fell on EMI, sales halved and the Company experienced accumulated losses in excess of £1 million. During those dramatic years, finances were so bad that it proved impossible to pay shareholders even nominal dividends. To survive this collapse, the Company was forced to carry out a massive reorganization and rationalization of all aspects of its business. In 1933, with the world economy stabilizing, a reassessment was made of the Company's shattered capital base. As a result, the value of its share capital was reduced by one half. Taken together, these measures provided EMI with sufficient room for manoeuvre and enabled it to survive. In 1934, it turned in £500,000 in profits, the first since formation. With these profits, payments of the accumulated arrears in preference share dividends, and a 12.5 per cent dividend on the Company's ordinary shares, were made. Thereafter, apart from the first year of the Second World War and until the 1979 acquisition by Thorn Electrical Industries, it never

ALAN DOWER BLUMLEIN (1903–1942)

One of the 20th century's greatest electrical engineers, Alan Blumlein was a key figure in the development of telephony, sound recording, television and radar. He was born in London and educated at Highgate School. In 1921 he won a scholarship to study electrical engineering at Imperial College, where, on graduating, he joined the academic staff to work on problems connected with telephony and wireless telegraphy. Three years later, Blumlein joined the International Western Electric Corporation, where he helped improve long-distance telephone communications. In 1929 Isaac Shoenberg recruited him to Columbia, where he developed the moving-coil recording process; technically superior to the existing Western Electric system, it was eventually adopted by EMI's recording studios. In 1931, his patent on stereophony was published, establishing the present standard for cutting stereophonic sound signals into a single groove. That year, Blumlein joined EMI's Central Research Laboratories and became a major figure in Shoenberg's team working on television and, later, radar technology. After war was declared, Blumlein was seconded to the government, where he helped develop an interception radar system and the radio navigation aid known as H2S. In June 1942, Blumlein and two of his EMI colleagues were killed in an aviation accident whilst testing radar equipment. During his short working life, this extraordinary man produced no fewer than 128 patents, some of which were of seminal importance to the development of electrical engineering.

failed to declare a profit and to pay its shareholders dividends.

During the 1930s, nothing illustrated the crisis facing EMI more than the state of its record business, the Company's main cash-earning product before the Depression. In 1929 almost 30 million records were sold in Britain by the combined forces of the Columbia Graphophone and Gramophone Companies. In 1931, despite significant price cuts, the figure had fallen to 20 million. Record sales continued their free-fall until 1937, when they bottomed out at just under 5 million: an 85 per cent fall in sales since 1929. The scale of the collapse was so great that, during the entire period between 1931 and 1961, annual sales of records by EMI in Britain never recovered to the level achieved in 1929.

EMI was not the only record company to be affected. During the early 1930s, the entire industry suffered. By the outbreak of war in 1939, only two British record manufacturers, EMI and

Recording technology

Recording using Blumlein's moving-coil cutter at Abbey Road Studios in 1936.

Decca, were left in the field. The collapse was caused by three factors: the Depression, the rise of radio ownership, and the advent of talking pictures.

Paradoxically, at the very moment record sales were disintegrating, the technology of record-making took a massive leap forward. Just before the merger, Alan Blumlein had brought to fruition a much improved system of recording to replace the existing Western Electric recording system. Thus, the introduction of what became the new EMI process of recording improved the quality of the Company's recordings and, at the same time, provided the Company with significant and timely savings. The Western Electric royalty had been punitive: it had cost more than £500,000 in the decade after 1925.

Louis Sterling responded to the collapse by a rationalization of record making and selling. Within weeks of EMI's formation, prices had been cut across the range. Later, some record labels were integrated. In Britain, recording was concentrated at Abbey Road Studios. Similar moves followed in Germany, France and

Italy. Both in Britain and overseas, selling organizations were consolidated, which effectively eliminated the hoped-for competition between the various EMI brands. Where it proved impossible to sell EMI products profitably, agents were appointed to take over the business. An inevitable consequence of these changes was a reduction in record-making, with resultant redundancies among session musicians, performers, recording engineers and other staff involved in record production. Another feature of this rationalization was a record-pressing agreement negotiated between Louis Sterling and Edward Lewis at Decca. Under its terms, which greatly benefited EMI, the Company gained the exclusive right to press and distribute Decca recordings in South America, Australasia and the Far East. In return, Decca gained exclusive North American pressing and distribution rights to several EMI labels, including Parlophone and Odeon.

When EMI was formed in 1931, the Hayes record factory was still booming. However, within a few years this works was a shadow of its former self.

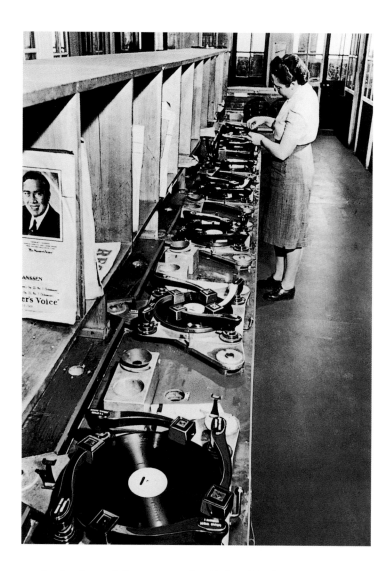

Wear test
EMI's Hayes record factory had its own quality control unit, where records were tested to destruction on special machines fitted with four tone arms.

At the time of the merger, the Columbia Graphophone and Gramophone Companies between them owned 50 factories in 19 countries: two were in Australia, three in South America, seven in Asia, and 38 in Europe. These factories either manufactured gramophone records, cabinets for gramophones, radios and radiograms and mechanical gramophones (a product made largely obsolete – with the exception of portable gramophones, which continued to be manufactured until 1961 – by changes in electrical technology and the coming of radio), or they assembled products from parts manufactured in Britain. In order to keep the factories supplied with orders and in profit, the Company relied on both the domestic market and a strong export trade. Unfortunately, during the Depression, there was a general collapse of exports. Alfred Clark told shareholders in 1933:

"HIS MASTER'S VOICE"

'POPULAR" AC RADIOGRAM IN WALNUT CABINET...MODEL 370

Here it is—the "H.M.V." radiogram *you* can afford! It reproduces your records electrically, and it also brings you in the British and Continental radio programmes, separate from one another, with true "H.M.V." tone at all volumes. Just look at the cabinet, too—a true "H.M.V." production with beautifully contrasted inlays—remember that it operates from A.C. electricity mains and no winding is necessary —and then, look at the price.

16 GNS.

Advertising

By the mid-1930s, EMI's most important product was the radio.
In an attempt to stimulate the ailing market for records, the
Company introduced a range of low-priced "radiograms", which
combined the advantages of a high-quality radio with a gramophone.

The export business from the English factories, as well as from foreign factories, was greatly diminished by embargoes, high tariff walls, quotas, fluctuating exchanges and restrictions on the movement of currencies. [Alfred Clark, *Chairman's Address*, General Meeting, 1933]

By 1933, more than half the factories had been closed. In Britain, manufacture of all EMI products was moved to The Gramophone Company's factories in Hayes, and both Columbia's London factory and the Marconiphone plant at Dagenham were closed. Overseas, a similar rationalization took place. In Australia, for example, The Gramophone Company's Erskinville factory was closed, and manufacture was centralized at Columbia's Homebush site. The EMI product range was also reassessed, and the Hayes factories began to manufacture a range of domestic electrical appliances (refrigerators, electric irons and electric heaters).

Goodnight Sweetheart
THE IMPACT OF RADIO, 1931–1939

In 1926, the year the BBC gained its Royal Charter, 25 per cent of households had a wireless. By 1931, that figure had risen to more than 35 per cent, and by the outbreak of war in 1939 it was over 80 per cent. This revolution in domestic leisure activities was realized thanks to radio manufacturers like EMI, who, during this period, achieved significant improvements in the quality and durability of radio receivers. In addition, throughout the 1930s, the retail cost of radios fell substantially, thanks to deflationary trends and fierce competition. The impact of radio on the British record industry was devastating. In essence, people turned away from gramophone records as a means of home entertainment and tuned into the BBC or to overseas stations. It was not that popular music records were no longer heard in the home: they were, but not on the gramophone.

At the time, the true relationship between radio and the record industry was widely misunderstood. In 1933, Christopher Stone, the London editor of the *Gramophone* magazine and an early BBC and European English-language radio presenter, wrote: "experience has shown that the judicious broadcasting of gramophone records is a direct stimulus to the sale of records" [Chistopher Stone, *Christopher Stone Speaking* (London 1933), p.116] Clearly, the reality was quite different. To add insult to injury, by comparison to the earnings of best-selling records in the 1920s, fees earned from the broadcasting of records were

derisory. In 1938, Alfred Clark confided to shareholders the unhappy situation into which the record business had fallen:

It is known to you that some years ago, as broadcasting developed, its effect upon records was felt very seriously. Previously the sales of records of the more popular type of music had in volume greatly exceeded those of classical and more expensive records, and it was, of course, the popular records which were hit by the radio. [Alfred Clark, Chairman's Address, General Meeting, 1938]

In 1938 Sterling unveiled one further attempt to tempt the public back into the popular record market by exploiting the huge appeal of radio: an electric record player which operated through a mains radio. With a selling price of 39 shillings and

For the less well-off EMI introduced a cheap record player which played records through the loudspeaker of a radio.

143

SIR ISAAC SHOENBERG (1880–1963)

Sir Isaac Shoenberg was the founder and long-serving director of what eventually became EMI's Central Research Laboratories (CRL). Shoenberg was born in Russia, where he became chief engineer of the Russian Wireless and Telegraph Company, but emigrated to Britain with his family in 1914. He was general manager of The British Wireless and Telegraph Company until 1924, when Louis Sterling's enticing offer of a generous research budget persuaded him to join Columbia as head of its Research Department. In 1929, Shoenberg recruited Alan Blumlein to develop a new system of electrical recording, and when EMI was formed in 1931, he became director of research at the Central Research Laboratories in Hayes. Under his leadership, the CRL became one of the world's leading research institutes, counting among its many achievements the development of the 405-line television system used by the BBC after 1936. His work on television gained Shoenberg many awards, including a knighthood and the prestigious Faraday Medal. In 1955, he became a director of EMI. Shoenberg's incomparable talent lay in his combination of scientific vision with personnel-management skills. Although a diffident man, he took justified pride in Rutherford's excitement that the CRL was doing almost pure laboratory physics and then applying it directly to industrial use. He recognized the importance of television and reflected: "I was saying to my boys that we are lighting a candle that will not be put out."

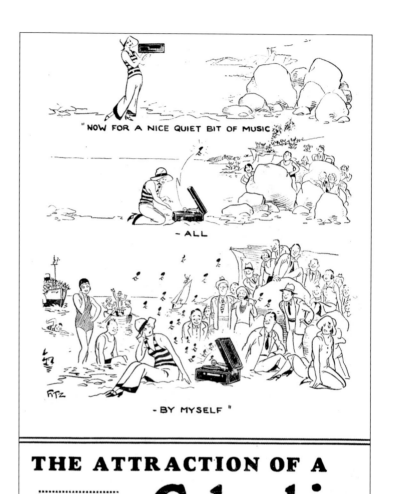

1932 gramophone advertisement
This 1932 advertisement shows that even in the depths of the Depression, EMI continued to market its portable gramophones as one of life's necessities.

6 pence (£1.97), the player was sold without profit, but in significant enough quantities to stimulate record sales. Alas for Sterling, the war ended any potential for developing the record market either in Britain or abroad.

During the 1930s, growth in radio manufacture was spectacular, but Sterling realized that demand for this product would inevitably decline as the domestic market reached saturation. New products would be required to fill this gap and the product he came up with was television. The Gramophone Company had had a television research programme since the mid-1920s. In the early 1930s, the

The men who guided EMI's fortunes between 1931 and 1951. Left to right: W. H. Brown, Alfred Clark, Sir Louis Sterling, Sir Ernest Fisk and David Sarnoff.

Company's Central Research Laboratories began research in earnest. By 1935, after an investment in excess of £1 million, Shoenberg, Blumlein and the other members of the television research team had produced a working 405-line television system which was to form the basis of British television broadcasting until the 1960s. The following year, a public television service using the EMI system was started by the BBC – the first in the world and three years ahead of the United States. The Hayes factories began manufacturing television receiving sets and studio equipment, and it appeared that the Company had successfully anticipated a market potentially as large as that of radio. The war destroyed those plans, but the Company's highly secret work on the development of the parallel technology of radar was central to the very survival of Britain during the Second World War, and subsequently became the foundation of EMI's post-war defence business.

1938 record catalogue
In the late 1930s, HMV was still producing strong monthly release lists. However, there had been a radical reduction in advertising spend: in the late 1920s releases were advertised in expensive colour monthly supplements, whereas ten years on the supplements were in cheap monochrome.

Underneath the Arches

THE DRIFT TOWARDS WAR, 1933–1939

In the early 1930s, war clouds had begun to gather over Europe and the Far East. The rise of Japanese nationalism had highlighted grievances against foreign-owned businesses. At that time, EMI owned Nipponophone, then the largest record company in Japan. Nipponophone pressed and distributed records from the Columbia and Carl Lindström catalogues, as well as producing its own catalogues of locally made recordings. In 1935, fearful of the future of its subsidiary, EMI sold the business to local entrepreneurs for £482,000. Fortunately, until December 1941 and the outbreak of war in the Far East, links were maintained with Nipponophone through a licensing agreement under the terms of which Columbia and Carl Lindström recordings were still pressed in Japan.

EMI had inherited extensive business interests in Germany. Its German companies, Electrola, Columbia and Carl Lindström, were major record and electronics manufacturers in the domestic

Television

Alfred Clark speaking at the opening of the world's first regular television service by the BBC at Alexandra Palace, London, in 1936. The television cameras were manufactured by EMI under the brand name Emitron.

market and enjoyed an important overseas trade, particularly in South America. Although much of Germany's domestic trade had collapsed, some business was done, and, until the outbreak of the Second World War in 1939, recording programmes with the many great German performing artists and orchestras under contract continued.

After Hitler came to power in 1933, circumstances for EMI employees in Germany became increasingly difficult. For example, in 1933, several Carl Lindström managers were arrested for pressing so-called "subversive" records by a Jewish singer. Although the managers were quickly released, the incident was a harbinger of things to come. Anti-Jewish laws forced many old and trusted figures from positions of responsibility in EMI's German businesses. Papers held at the EMI Music Archive indicate that the Company, together with individuals like Alfred Clark and Louis Sterling, made strenuous efforts to secure the release of their many Jewish colleagues and associates suffering in the Nazi terror. Much of this work was, of necessity, undertaken in conditions of secrecy, and often used subterfuge. One such case concerned the soprano Elisabeth Curth van Endert, the widow of Leo Curth (formerly Cohen), who, before his death in 1932, had been general manager of Electrola, and before that of Deutsche Grammophon AG (The Gramophone Company's old German business). In 1938, Madame Curth van Endert wrote to Sterling from Czechoslovakia. In her letter, she requested his aid to secure her escape from Germany. She told Sterling that if he wrote offering her employment abroad, the Nazi authorities would allow her to leave. Emphasizing that she would not hold the Company to such an offer, Madame Curth van Endert received a letter offering her a job in the terms she had suggested. Her next letter on file at the EMI Music Archive was from New York. Alas, not all of EMI's colleagues and associates were so lucky, and many perished in the Holocaust.

I'll Walk Beside You
THE SECOND WORLD WAR, 1939–1945

In sharp contrast to the sudden crisis of July and August 1914 that had plunged Europe into the First World War, the outbreak of the Second World War in September 1939 had been widely expected. Nonetheless, it left EMI, a major multinational business with factories, businesses and markets scattered throughout the world, highly vulnerable to war losses. To make matters worse, just before the war, there had been a fierce boardroom struggle at EMI which

PLEASE! **DON'T HOARD OLD RECORDS** *They are* **URGENTLY REQUIRED** *for* **SALVAGE**

We know that there are hundreds of thousands of old records in and around the country which have long outlived their usefulness.

These records, if salvaged, can be reborn.

They can be ground up, mixed with a small percentage of virgin ingredient, and then find their way back to the public again via the dealer's shop, giving new pleasure and new cheer in the camps and canteens of the Forces, in war factories ('Music While You Work' and other B.B.C. programmes), in the home, in fact, everywhere that music can be enjoyed, instead of collecting dust and cluttering odd corners and cupboards.

Please take all those old records you don't want to your local gramophone dealer and so make it possible to maintain the supply of new ones.

Wartime salvage drives

One immediate consequence of the Second World War was an acute shortage of shellac, the basic ingredient of 78-rpm records. In order to maintain supplies of records, the industry organized salvage drives. Old records were ground up and the mixture re-used in the manufacture of new ones.

was subsequently seen as a watershed in the Company's history: after years of tense relations between Louis Sterling and Alfred Clark, Sterling resigned. His departure ushered in 15 years of mediocre management.

In Britain, the outbreak of war had one immediate, unexpected, consequence: a significant boost to EMI's record business. In the first year of hostilities, the number of records sold rose by 1 million units. In 1940, this change of fortune prompted Alfred Clark to tell shareholders that:

Output of gramophone records has been considerably larger than in the previous year. The demand is healthy and indications are that the record business will continue to expand in spite of the handicap of the Purchase Tax. The need of entertainment in the home, and the great difficulty in receiving broadcasting programmes of good quality during air raids will, we believe, counteract to some extent the bad effect of such a tax on our sales. [Alfred Clark, Chairman's Address, General Meeting, 1940]

Clark was being a trifle over-optimistic. The effect of the imposition of Purchase Tax on gramophone records and serious shortages of pressing material (despite salvage drives and the recycling of old records), together with the impact of conscription and the inevitable loss of many performers to war service, meant the Company's recording programmes of both popular and classical music were severely curtailed. Furthermore, after the fall of France in 1940, Britain was cut off from Europe. Unable to make or gain access to recordings from its usual continental sources, EMI's releases of new recordings slumped. The Company became increasingly reliant for new recordings on its American licensors, RCA Victor and Columbia Records, Inc. Nonetheless, by 1945, sales of EMI records had grown to 6.3 million units; still a fraction of the levels achieved in the late 1920s, but an improvement on the situation in 1939. In 1945, Sir Ernest Fisk, an electrical engineer and businessman, and former Chairman of the Australian Wireless Manufacturing Company, was appointed EMI's fourth managing director, with the difficult task of rebuilding the Company.

Sir Ernest Fisk was EMI's managing director between 1945 and 1951.

Oh Mein Papa

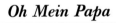

POST-WAR RECONSTRUCTION, 1945–1961

The end of the war found EMI exhausted, its financial resources and assets drained, its overseas interests and markets damaged or destroyed, and its core gramophone record business in the doldrums. By 1961, however, the Company had become extraordinarily successful. The dramatic change was brought about by a combination of slowly emerging changes within the Company and in the broader record and music industries. Other factors accelerated these changes, including innovations in recording technology, the worldwide post-war consumer boom and the creation of new markets based on the emerging youth culture (see Chapter 6).

Within the Company, the person most responsible for this transformation was Joseph (later Sir Joseph) Lockwood (see box, page 150), who became chairman and chief executive in 1955. During his 20-year chairmanship, Lockwood transformed the Company's fortunes from ailing giant to leading player in an increasingly international record market. However, when he joined

Sir Alexander Aikman was chairman between 1945 and 1954

SIR JOSEPH LOCKWOOD (1904–1991)

★

Sir Joseph Flawith Lockwood was chief executive of EMI from 1954 to 1970 and chairman from 1954 to 1974. A miller by trade, Lockwood knew nothing about the music business before 1954, when Sir Edward de Stein persuaded him to join the then troubled EMI board and take over as chairman. Lockwood succeeded in rebuilding and reorganizing the Company: he abandoned loss-making operations such as radio, television and record-player manufacture, and built up the rapidly expanding international record business. Lockwood retained an interest in scientific development and saw in the Company's Central Research Laboratories the vehicle for the technical innovation required to provide the next generation of products. Sir Joseph (he was knighted in 1960) stepped down as chief executive in 1970, and retired as chairman in 1974. He remained as a director until 1979, the year the Company was acquired by Thorn Electrical Industries. Lockwood was one of the most important figures in the Company's history. His ruthless reconstruction of the business in the 1950s undoubtedly saved EMI from bankruptcy and, in the 1960s, with the Beatles, he rode the crest of the British pop and rock revolution which transformed EMI's record business. An outstanding figure, he was an inspiring, single-minded, decisive, fiery character. When asked what his favourite records were, he replied, "the ones that sell".

the business, EMI's finances were in a parlous state, and Lockwood's first task as a board member was to raise a loan to keep the Company afloat.

EMI's difficulties had been created by Sir Ernest Fisk's post-war reconstruction of the business. In an effort to bring some order to EMI's disparate product range, Fisk had divided the Company into numerous wholly owned operating sub-companies. Unfortunately, this costly reorganization failed to work, and its imposition caused chaos, and practically split the Company. For example, the rapidly expanding record business found itself divided between EMI Studios Ltd, EMI Factories Ltd, EMI Sales and Service Ltd, and the old operating companies, The Columbia Graphophone and Gramophone Companies. Other problems included the Company's inability to manufacture televisions, radios and domestic appliances at a profit. Sir Ernest Fisk left the company in 1951 and was replaced by Leonard J. Brown, a former financial executive.

Dreamboat

TAPE, LONG-PLAYING AND 45-RPM RECORDS

In the late 1940s the art of recording was revolutionized when EMI introduced tape recording into Abbey Road Studios. Although the technology had been in limited use before the war, wartime developments in plastic tape coated with ferrous oxide made it a practical proposition as a recording medium. The use of tape changed not just the art of recording, but also the functions of the sound engineer and the record producer (see Chapters 5 and 6). Before its introduction, an artist was forced to make each 78-rpm side as many times as was necessary to produce a satisfactory record. With tape, it became possible for sound engineers to create a final recording by piecing together the best parts of various takes: the result was effectively a mosaic of sound. Although location recording of live performances had been undertaken from the earliest days of electrical recording, the introduction of tape made such recordings much easier.

The new technology opened up a wide range of new commercial opportunities for EMI. By the early 1950s, EMI was producing own-brand tape products, recording-studio and broadcast tape decks, and business and domestic tape recorders. Eventually, it produced reel-to-reel tapes of pre-recorded music. This new recording format prefigured the 1970s creation of a major new market in pre-recorded music on cassette. The reel-to-reel pre-recorded tape market failed to take off at this early juncture, partly because of the cost of early tape players, but also owing to the other revolution in recorded sound: the coming of $33\frac{1}{3}$-rpm long-playing ("LP") and 45-rpm ("single") records.

As a format, the 78-rpm record had changed very little since the earliest years of the century. Although the introduction of electrical recording in 1925 brought with it dramatic improvements in sound quality, the four-minute duration of each side of the record remained a serious – and for some an insurmountable – impediment to the enjoyment of longer pieces of music, particularly from the classical repertoire. During the war, EMI engineers began developmental research on a long-playing record. However, their ideas did not reach fruition. In June 1948, Columbia Records, Inc., EMI's American licensor, introduced its own long-playing record. Columbia's $33\frac{1}{3}$-rpm record could play for up to 20 minutes a side, as it used a microgroove cut of 220 turns to the inch (compared with the standard 100 turns to the inch on 78-rpm records). Furthermore, unlike British 78-rpm records, which were pressed from shellac-based compounds, the new records were pressed from vinyl

RECORDING TECHNIQUES: 1925–1961

★

The introduction of electrical recording by Western Electric in 1925 was a quantum leap in the quality of sound recording and revolutionized studio techniques. Acoustic recordings had a frequency range restricted to 164 to 2,000 cycles per second, whilst electrical recordings had a frequency range of 50 to 5,000. The new system produced stunning results, particularly in the bass and upper strings. At the same time, the introduction of microphones provided a new freedom to record in almost any venue. It was now possible to record almost anything, almost anywhere.

Louis Sterling was intent on using these innovations to ensure that Columbia kept pace with its rivals, but understandably less keen to pay the punitive royalties due to Western Electric. At the same time as planning began on the world's first recording studio complex at Abbey Road, Alan Dower Blumlein was perfecting his own system of electrical recording. The Blumlein system was installed at Abbey Road by the time Sir Edward Elgar opened the studios on 12 November 1931. Blumlein was also responsible for demonstrating the first stereo system in 1935, long before stereo recording became the standard for classical recordings.

In the same year, a German team at AEG demonstrated a prototype Magnetophone recording machine, which used plastic tape and was the precursor of tape-based recording equipment. This innovation substantially reduced the crackles and pops associated with disc recording. After the Second World War, a team of audio engineers from Britain and the United States visited Berlin to study this development. By 1947, 3M had introduced oxide tape, and Ampex began delivering tape recorders the following year. A development team assembled by EMI soon followed with the introduction of the BTR (short for British Tape Recorder), which was installed at Abbey Road in 1949. The BTRI subsequently became ubiquitous in British recording studios.

Tape recording had many advantages over disc recording and opened up endless possibilities for innovation. By using two tape machines a system known as "superimposition" was soon introduced. The track recorded on the first machine was sent back to the studio where additional instruments, sound effects or in extreme cases even the vocalist could be added without the original orchestra being present.

A consequence of the introduction of tape was the creation of a new range of so-called "post-production" facilities within the studio complex. For example, cutting rooms were fitted with the latest disc-cutting techniques which used aluminium discs coated with lacquer instead of the traditional wax discs. Disc-cutting became even more sophisticated. The disc-cutting engineer was able to influence what went on to the final disc; recording artists would often attend the "cut" to hear the lacquer before it went to the factory for processing.

At the same time that tape was introduced, the German manufacturer Neumann launched its celebrated range of condenser microphones. These incorporated gold-splattered capsules and built-in amplifiers, and were invaluable in achieving the optimum balance in

recordings. These microphones proved to be so good that they remain in daily use at Abbey Road and are much sought after.

Other developments in the 1950s at EMI included the "in line" console, with a capacity for mobile use, loudspeakers with a greatly increased frequency response, and, in 1954, stereosonic tapes, which were followed four years later by stereophonic discs. These and other innovations laid the foundations of present-day studio practice. Until then, the object of both classical and popular recording had been to reproduce as faithfully as possible the sound of the performers in the studio. Rock'n'roll producers wanted more than just a wide dynamic range; they insisted on a punchy sound that would come over loud and strident. To accommodate this and more, Abbey Road introduced a range of innovations, including limiters and compressors, the forerunners of what are now called "outboard gear", and a wide range of very sharp tone controls and "curve benders" which changed the sound dramatically. In the studio, separate miking of individual instruments or sections gave rise to multi-mike techniques, which in turn necessitated acoustic screens to prevent sound spillage. Vocalists were sometimes screened off and recorded "dry", often hearing the backing through headphones. Echo chambers added ambience not only to the voice but also to various instruments. Systems such as "Steed", "Fite" and "Tape Echo" were developed for delaying echo and tape looping. The increase in microphone use led to bigger and more complex mixing consoles and the enlargement of control rooms. Some of these innovations were also used in classical music recording.

Tape at Abbey Road
The introduction of tape revolutionized the recording process. This recording session shows the first EMI recording machine (BTR 1) in use at Abbey Road Studios.

Abbey Road control room, around 1960
Left to right: engineer Malcolm Addey, record producer Norman Newell and engineer Peter Bown in the Number Two Studio control room, Abbey Road. Note the increasing sophistication of recording technology.

plastic. This combination of the new recording technology and plastic material significantly reduced background noise and eventually led to improved sound quality. RCA Victor, Columbia's great American rival (and EMI's other licensor), responded by issuing its own 7-inch 45-rpm record, also pressed in vinyl plastic, which played for up to four minutes. The new record was smaller, lighter and more durable than the equivalent 78-rpm disc. Columbia and RCA Victor offered EMI both technologies, as each was anxious to see its particular format become the new industry standard.

The unexpected appearance of these major changes in format posed serious problems for EMI. The Company faced two choices: either it could ignore the changes, and rely on a buoyant market for its existing records, or it could build up a stock of the new records, and at the same time develop record players on which the new records could be played. Initially, the Company planned to introduce LPs and 45-rpm records, together with record players, in September 1949. However, Sir Ernest Fisk was highly sceptical of the LP's commercial potential and had seen the difficulties created in the United States by the introduction of

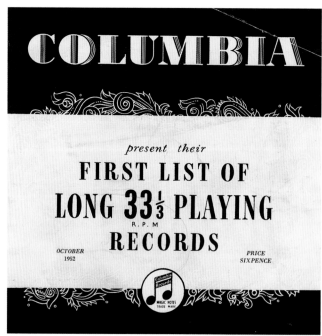

LP releases
In October 1952, EMI published its first lists of classical LPs. These images were used as record covers for the first releases of EMI's LPs.

***Opposite page* Columbia's June 1953 releases**
An early Columbia LP monthly release schedule showing a range of classical LPs issued to mark the coronation of Queen Elizabeth II.

two competing speeds. He decided that EMI could afford to wait before committing itself, and see which of the two speeds emerged as the industry standard. Furthermore, Fisk was also aware of the problems – in the days of post-war shortages and rationing – that the introduction of this new technology would pose to the British chemical industry, who would have to furnish the vinyl plastic resin needed to manufacture the new product. Announcing this – as it turned out – disastrous decision in a September 1950 press release, Fisk said:

The Record Companies of the EMI Group … will continue to produce standard [78-rpm] records in undiminished quantities to meet the needs of the millions of gramophones already in use throughout the world. The EMI Group associate themselves with the opinion expressed in the Press of various countries that it is in the public interest for the gramophone industry to continue to develop on the sound principle of a common turntable speed. [EMI Press Release, Mittell Papers, EMI Music Archive]

Shortly after releasing that statement, Fisk left the Company, and fresh plans were made to launch EMI's new LP and 45-rpm records and record players. In October 1952, the first EMI records in the new formats were released. However, by that time, Decca, EMI's chief British rival, had already established itself in this new field. By the mid-1950s, the LP and 45-rpm record had come to dominate both the classical and popular record market and, between 1956 and 1958, sales of 78-rpm records fell from 14.3 million to 6.7 million, whilst sales of LP records rose from 1.7 million to 2 million and sales of 45-rpm records increased from 1.3 million to 7 million. Between 1958 and 1960, sales of LP and 45-rpm records continued to grow rapidly and sales of 78-rpm discs collapsed. In 1961, production of 78-rpm records ceased at EMI's Hayes factory. Unfortunately, the difficulties surrounding the coming of the LP and the 45-rpm record were not the only problems facing EMI as it struggled to manage a record business growing at an extraordinary pace in the post-war boom.

True Love

EMI IN THE UNITED STATES: ANGEL AND CAPITOL RECORDS

After the end of the Second World War, sales of records took off throughout the world, and particularly in the United States, where record sales in 1946 reached an all-time high of $207 million, compared to the all-time low of $53 million in 1933. In this new environment, EMI's two American licensors, RCA Victor and Columbia Records, Inc., soon realized that their record businesses, formerly a marginal part of their overall business, had become major cash earners. In decisive moves that, in the end, led to the creation of the modern international record industry, RCA Victor and Columbia Records began to plan the development of the overseas part of their businesses, which were at the time entirely in the hands of EMI. Matters became more urgent when these companies came under increasing pressure from the United States Department of Justice to end the EMI licensing agreements, which it saw as monopolistic.

These moves could not have come at a worse time for EMI. Because of the war, its record catalogues had been seriously depleted of British and continental popular and classical recordings. As a result, in order to meet growing demand during the period of post-war reconstruction, the Company had become increasingly reliant on recordings from the United States. This dependence was such that, by 1950, recordings from America accounted for more than 70 per cent of all the records listed in the various EMI record catalogues. If its record business was to survive in the rapidly changing post-war world, the Company, in the short term, had to hang on to its crucial American licensing agreements for as long as possible, whilst creating its own worldwide record-making and marketing organization, in

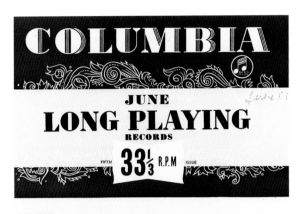

FRANK SINATRA
(BORN 1915)

★

Frank Sinatra inherited Bing Crosby's mantle as America's favourite singer, and has become one of the legends of the popular music business. Francis Albert Sinatra was born of Italian parents in Hoboken, New Jersey. With no formal musical training, he became a member of the Hoboken Four vocal and instrumental group. After the break-up of the quartet, he left Hoboken for New York, where he joined the Harry James Band in 1939 and later moved to the Tommy Dorsey Orchestra, singing with the Pied Pipers and Jo Stafford. Columbia Records signed Sinatra in 1942, and for several years he was a highly successful recording star. In February 1951, the English Columbia Company released a unique record which Sinatra shared with the Duke of Edinburgh (LB 104); it was sold on behalf of the National Playing Fields Association. In 1953, Capitol Records offered Sinatra a contract which immediately produced a string of hits, including "Three coins in the fountain" (Capitol CL 14120), "Learnin' the blues" (Capitol CL 14296) and "The Tender Trap" (Capitol CL 14511), as well as a collection of classic albums, such as *Songs for Swingin' Lovers* (Capitol LCT 6106) and *Come Dance with Me* (Capitol LCT 6179). In 1960, Sinatra achieved a long-held aim with the launch of his own record company, Reprise. His first celebratory release for the new company was an album entitled *Ring-a-Ding Ding*. In 1971, the British writer Benny Green said of Sinatra: "He is not simply the best popular singer of his generation, but the culminating point in an evolutionary process which has redefined the art of interpreting words set to music."

particular in the United States. In 1952, Brenchley Mittell (then head of EMI's recording business) summed up the position in a letter to the board:

Whichever course the Company follows, the fact remains that the entire record business is in a phase of violent change the world over; we have, therefore, to take an entirely fresh view of it, and to recognize that there is great strength in the EMI organization, but that everywhere it needs to adapt itself with new energy and new products to its new circumstances. Its opportunities, taking into account the Western Hemisphere [North and South America], are greater than ever before. [Report to the Board, Mittell Papers, EMI Music Archive]

EMI had no option but to begin making records, signing artists and doing business directly in the United States.

In 1946, Sir Ernest Fisk, in an attempt to reduce EMI's reliance on its existing American licensors, began negotiations that eventually led to a licensing agreement with MGM, the American record and film company. Seen as provocative by EMI's existing American associates, the move outraged Alfred Clark, the whole of whose business career had centred on the maintenance of the transatlantic links with RCA Victor. Matters came to a head at a board meeting in late 1946, when Clark faced down Fisk. In the ensuing row, Clark flung his papers across the table and stalked out of the meeting and the Company. He never returned. It was an unhappy end to a career that had started in 1889 with the very beginnings of the recording industry.

In 1952, Columbia Records finally ended its licensing agreement with EMI. It was a bitter blow. In the final year of its existence, this valuable contract accounted for nearly one quarter of EMI's record sales throughout the world. Relations with RCA Victor also began to unravel. The process had begun in 1944 when David Sarnoff, the president of RCA, and one of EMI's founding directors, had resigned from the EMI board. Although Sarnoff had rarely attended board meetings, his presence as a board member provided an assurance that the exchange of record matrices, technology and know-how with RCA would continue. As it turned out, his departure proved to be the beginning of the end of corporate links between the two companies. In 1952, Mittell renegotiated what became the final EMI/RCA Victor licensing agreement. In that year, records sourced from RCA Victor accounted for 50 per cent of EMI's total sales. This contract lasted until 1957, and contained a clause providing for the deletion of all RCA Victor records from EMI catalogues the following year.

In 1952, the Company formed Electric and Musical Industries (US) Ltd to market EMI's rapidly expanding classical catalogue in the United States. Because of an earlier division of assets, such as trademarks, by The Gramophone Company and the Victor Talking Machine Company, EMI did not have the right to use the His Master's Voice trademark in certain countries, including the United States and Canada. The new American catalogue was therefore launched under the Angel Records trademark. The Recording Angel had been The Gramophone Company's original trademark, and had been used until it was superseded by the

NAT "KING" COLE
(1917–1965)

★

Nat "King" Cole's relaxed singing style made him a major star of American popular music for over 20 years. Nathaniel Adams Cole was born in Montgomery, Alabama. He began as a jazz pianist but by the time the newly formed Capitol Records signed him in 1943 he had begun to sing as well. His very first Capitol record, "Straighten up and fly right" (American Capitol 154), with the drumless King Cole Trio, was an instant hit on the strength of Nat's vocals rather than the trio's playing. As his career blossomed he began to record with orchestral backing and soon emerged as a potent middle-of-the-road singer. His first hit with orchestra was the haunting "Nature Boy" (Capitol CL 13010) in 1947. Throughout the 1950s, Cole consolidated his position as a leading vocalist with a succession of hit singles and albums featuring mainly romantic ballads but also some up-tempo numbers like "Orange Coloured Sky" (Capitol CL 13392) and "Walkin' my baby back home" (Capitol CL 13774). He made occasional appearances in films and performed regularly in nightclubs, where he continued to display his elegant jazz piano playing as well as his singing; but it was as a recording artist that he made his greatest impact. Cole's popularity was not affected by the coming of rock'n'roll or the advent of bands. *The Guinness Who's Who of Fifties Music* says: "Nat Cole's voice, which floats butter-won't-melt vowel sounds in an easy, dark drawl, is one of the great moments of black music, and no matter how sugary the arrangements he always managed to sing as if it mattered."

GLENN E. WALLICHS
(1910–1971)

★

In the autumn of 1941, Wallichs, a Los Angeles record retailer, suggested to Johnny Mercer, the singer and songwriter, and Buddy DeSylva, a songwriter and executive producer at Paramount Pictures, that they set up their own record company. Early the following year, Capitol Records was founded, with Wallichs as chief executive and Mercer and DeSylva providing much of the capital. Wallichs's success was such that, by 1955, the year EMI bought Capitol, the business had achieved an annual turnover of almost $20 million. In 1956, Wallichs opened the striking Capitol Tower in Hollywood, which boasted the most up-to-date recording studios in America. Under his leadership, Capitol became one of the largest and most profitable record companies in America.

HMV logo in the early years of the century. Angel Records achieved immediate success and, in its first year, captured 6 per cent of the American classical record market.

In 1955, EMI further strengthened its American position by acquiring Capitol Records, Inc. for $8.5 million. Founded in 1942, Capitol was, at the time of the acquisition, America's fourth largest record company. Capitol's principal business was in popular music, although the company did release some classical records on its own label and on the Cetra label. When EMI took over the business, Capitol was headed by Glenn Wallichs (see box), one of the company's founders, and the man responsible for much of its success. At the time, Capitol had an impressive roster of artists, including Frank Sinatra (see box, page 156), Nat "King" Cole (see box, page 157), Stan Kenton, Peggy Lee, Dean Martin, Les Paul, Kay Starr and Gene Vincent. Wallichs remained as chief executive and joined the EMI board. Capitol's success exceeded all expectations. In 1956, it achieved sales of more than $35 million (£12.5 million), itself an increase of 37 per cent on the previous year. In 1957, EMI consolidated the Company's American operations by merging EMI (US) Ltd with Capitol. As it turned out, the recordings and profits derived from EMI's North American operations more than made up for the loss of the Columbia and RCA Victor licenses. Furthermore, by 1961, EMI's aggressive post-war search for international talent (see Chapters 5 and 6) ensured that the Company had become a world leader in recorded music.

Roulette

REBUILDING THE OVERSEAS COMPANIES

In parallel with EMI's move into the United States market, the Company began the task of reorganizing its European businesses, still recovering from the twin calamities of the Depression and the Second World War. Many of these businesses had been hurriedly cobbled together during the Depression simply to keep a Company presence until better days came. In the midst of Europe's post-war boom, the good times had clearly arrived, and EMI set about rebuilding and reinvesting.

Contact had been made with EMI's German business as early as the summer of 1945. During the allied bombing campaign, Carl Lindström AG had continued to record and press records in its Potsdam factory, and it did so until the Russian occupation of Berlin. In January 1946, although badly damaged, the Lindström factory began making and pressing records on the

Odeon, Imperial, Electrola and Columbia labels. However, Berlin's devastation and privation was such that, during the first winter of peace, Lindström's employees appealed to their fellow workers in Britain for clothing and food. The response of the Hayes factory workers towards their former enemies was generous and, as a result, many lives were saved. In 1953, as part of EMI's reinvestment programme, the Company's German business was completely reorganized, and the two businesses, Electrola and Carl Lindström, were merged to form EMI Electrola AG. New management was engaged, and headquarters and manufacturing facilities were established in Cologne, where they remain to this day.

Before the fall of France in 1940, EMI's French subsidiary was Les Industries Musicales et Electriques Pathé Marconi SA, which had offices in Paris and factories at Chatou. These factories manufactured records, gramophones and radios and, although damaged by German bombing in 1940 (action which resulted in the deaths of several EMI employees), the factory and business organization remained intact during the Occupation. After the liberation of France in 1944, EMI reclaimed the business.

At the beginning of the war, EMI owned two Italian businesses, La Voce del Padrone-Columbia-Marconiphone SpA and S. I. di Fonotipia SpA. Both ventures manufactured, assembled and marketed a range of products. During the course of the war, these companies and their assets were seized by the fascist state, but following the cessation of hostilities they were restored to EMI. Thereafter, the Company merged the two businesses, installed new management and began to plan fresh recording programmes. EMI's prompt action in reclaiming and reorganizing its European subsidiaries gave these businesses the organization, structure, management and investment necessary to exploit its products.

In 1950, contact was made with the Japanese Nippon Columbia Company (the successor in business to the pre-war Nipponophone Company). As a consequence of this, the two Companies concluded a pressing agreement in 1951, under the terms of which The Nippon Columbia Company released EMI records in Japan. In 1953, EMI concluded a fresh contract with Toshiba whereby the two businesses would work together in order to exploit this important market more effectively. Eventually, this successful partnership took the form of Toshiba–EMI, a venture in which EMI currently holds a 55 per cent stake, and which today is one of Japan's largest record companies. Finally, during the 1940s and 1950s, EMI's South American, Australasian, South African and Indian record businesses were rationalized.

In 1957 C. H. Thomas became the first managing director of EMI Records Ltd.

L. G. WOOD, CBE
(BORN 1910)

★

Born in London, L. G. Wood joined The Gramophone Company as a salesman in 1929. After war service, he returned as British sales manager for several record labels. One of Wood's main achievements was the array of American licensing deals with a range of often quite small popular record companies. As a consequence, Wood became known as an experienced and tough-minded negotiator. As managing director of EMI Records he helped make the company the most profitable sector of EMI's record business. When the post of international records director was created, Wood was the obvious choice. Wood was also a moving force behind the formation of the record industry trade association, The British Phonographic Industry (BPI). He became its president, and an active member of the BPI Council. Furthermore, he played an important role in the workings of the International Federation of Phonographic Industries (IFPI), especially in the vexed field of piracy and illegal copying of records. He was appointed CBE for services to the record industry.

Climb Ev'ry Mountain
EMI IN BRITAIN

In 1957, EMI formed EMI Records to manage the Company's British recording, manufacturing and marketing activities. Of the two original operating companies, The Columbia Graphophone Company ceased to trade in Britain in that year, although records bearing the Columbia logo continued to be released for some years. The new Company's first managing director was Charles H. Thomas, a highly capable EMI manager with a lifetime of experience in popular and classical records. In 1959, the management of EMI Records underwent an important restructuring. New executives took over the business, bringing to the fore a new generation in tune with the latest developments in the popular and classical record markets. The new team was led by C. H. Thomas's former deputy, Leonard G. ("L. G.") Wood. In 1960, EMI Records moved to new headquarters in Manchester Square.

What do you want

THE SATISFACTION OF SUCCESS

In 1961, Sir Joseph was in a position to reflect with some satisfaction on the first seven years of his chairmanship and the transformation he had wrought in the fortunes of the Company. His vision had been to see the rising tide of EMI's record business as a major cash earner capable of saving the Company. Indeed, by 1961, EMI's international record business accounted for more than half the Company's sales and profits. The last time this had happened was in the heady days of the late 1920s. Thirty years after its creation, EMI was at last beginning to fulfil the promised benefits of the merger in 1931.

Nothing shows the transformation in the Company's fortunes better than a comparison of EMI's 1945–6 turnover and post-tax profits with those of 1961–2. In its 1945–6 financial year, turnover and profit amounted to £7 million and £165,000 respectively; by 1961–2, they had grown to an incredible £82.5 million and £7.4 million. The most important aspect of this change was the growth in EMI's sales of gramophone records. In 1945–6, they amounted to just two per cent of turnover, whereas by 1961–2 they exceeded 50 per cent.

EMI at Manchester Square
Manchester Square, London, the home of EMI Records between 1960 and 1995.

E.M.I. House, London.   R.T. Cowe

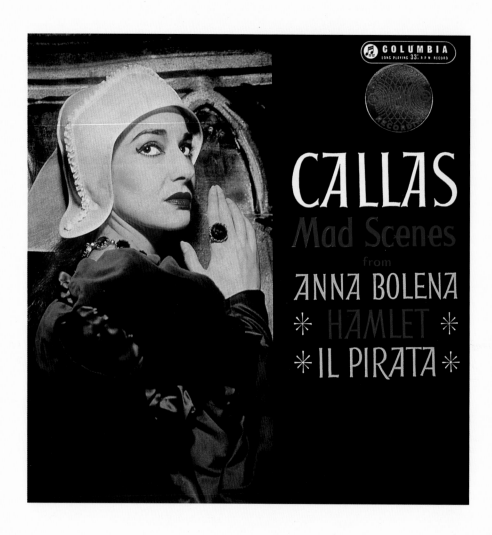

CHAPTER 5

Voi che sapete

EMI'S CLASSICAL MUSIC RECORDINGS, 1931–1961

I want to make records which will sound in the public's home exactly like what they would hear in the best seat in an acoustically perfect hall. [Walter Legge, EMI record producer, 1931–63]

"Unfinished" Symphony

1931–1939

Rex Palmer (1896–1972) was general manager of the International Artistes Department of The Gramophone Company (and later EMI) from 1930 to 1940. As a BBC presenter he was well known as "Uncle Rex" on the 2LO Children's Hour, and he was also an exclusive Columbia recording artist as both baritone and narrator.

After the creation of EMI in 1931, the classical recording organizations of the Gramophone and Columbia Graphophone Companies were merged into the International Artistes Department, which was headed by Rex Palmer. The department was responsible for the Company's international recording programmes, particularly in those countries with no branch organization; before the Second World War, this included the important Italian operatic recording programme. Its duties also included managing recording budgets, negotiating artists' contracts, the payment of royalties, arranging record release dates and the publication of the various label-based record catalogues. In addition, the International Artistes Department managed the Company's American licensing agreements with RCA Victor and Columbia Records, Inc. Although its functions were complex, the department itself remained quite small. The whole operation was controlled by a handful of artist and repertoire managers led, until 1939, by Fred Gaisberg.

Overall, EMI's record business experienced a traumatic collapse during the Depression of the 1930s and in the Second World War (see Chapter 4). Paradoxically, throughout that period, classical recording nonetheless remained a highly profitable business. Because of its export markets, the Company was in an unusually strong position to sell recordings around the world. These were so important that, during the 1930s, it was by no means unusual for the profits generated from overseas sales alone to cover artists' advances and recording and other costs. The International Artistes Department was therefore financially successful and, as a result, it was able to obtain the necessary capital to maintain existing recording programmes and to expand and develop the range of music available on records.

Nevertheless, during the Depression there was some rationalization of the catalogue and recording programmes for each of EMI's classical labels. In the early 1930s, an internal review of sales revealed that in Britain more than 80 per cent of EMI's classical record sales were generated by the HMV label, and sales on the Company's other classical labels were therefore very modest. As an illustration, there were two premium-priced versions of Schubert's "Unfinished" Symphony available in the British EMI record catalogues in 1932. The HMV recording – by the Philadelphia Orchestra conducted by Leopold Stokowski (HMV

Felix Weingartner (1863–1942) set the standards for modern-day orchestral performances of the German and Austrian classics. He made many notable records, including the first ever series of all Beethoven's symphonies. The conductor Wilhelm Furtwängler said of him, "What he did to maintain the dignity and purity of the classical style will, in the history of conducting, never be forgotten".

D 1779–81) – accounted for 5,000 sales, whilst the Columbia recording – with the Royal Opera House Orchestra conducted by Sir Henry Wood (Columbia DB 9513–15) – had sold less than 1,000 copies. As a result of this review, available resources were concentrated on the more commercially attractive HMV Red and Plum Label recordings, and many deletions were made from the Columbia classical catalogue. Important Columbia ensembles such as the Léner Quartet and the London Philharmonic Orchestra, and internationally famous conductors such as Bruno Walter (see box, page 177), Felix Weingartner and Sir Thomas Beecham were easily accommodated. However, older (and, by the 1930s, less commercially popular) Columbia ensembles, such as the London String Quartet, and the conductors Sir Hamilton Harty and Sir Henry Wood, all found their recording activities curtailed and their slow-selling records withdrawn.

DAVID BICKNELL
(1906–1988)

David Bicknell's fruitful career with EMI lasted 44 years, during which he was head of EMI's international classical recording activities from 1957 until 1969. James David Bicknell had intended to enter his father's firm in the City of London, but in 1927, at the age of 21, he took the advice of his father's friend, Trevor Williams, then chairman of The Gramophone Company, and joined the Company's International Artistes Department. Bicknell worked for 12 years as assistant to Fred Gaisberg and, as well as recording many famous artists of the time, he supervised the first commercial recordings of Mozart's operas *Le nozze di Figaro*, *Don Giovanni* and *Così fan tutte* at Glyndebourne, a recording project which began in 1934. When Gaisberg retired in 1939, Bicknell became the principal HMV classical producer until the outbreak of war, when he joined the Royal Engineers. After the war, he returned to the International Artistes Department as HMV manager and, alongside Walter Legge as Columbia manager, immediately set about re-establishing an artist roster, signing performers such as Beniamino Gigli, Victoria de los Angeles, Victor de Sabata, Tito Gobbi and Guido Cantelli. In 1957, he was appointed manager of the International Artistes Department, a position he handed over to Peter Andry in 1969 before he eventually retired completely in 1971. The accompanist Gerald Moore paid this tribute to David Bicknell at a lunch to mark his retirement: "I have never met a man who commanded such respect and who did his work with such enormous dignity and modesty".

Die Walküre

A WINDFALL

During this period, the International Artistes Department was able to assemble the finest collection of classical artists the industry had ever seen. In part, this feat was accomplished as a result of disastrous misjudgements by the two American classical titans, RCA Victor and Columbia. The Depression had hit the United States especially hard; combined with the impact of radio broadcasting, it almost completely destroyed the market for popular and classical records. After 1931, RCA Victor and Columbia, who had both assembled large broadcasting interests, erroneously concluded that the record business was finished. They dismissed their most experienced recording staff, who migrated towards jobs making talking pictures in Hollywood. More importantly for EMI, they dismantled their extraordinary rosters of artists, many of whom were immediately signed by EMI. David Bicknell (see box) recalled what he described as RCA Victor's loss of nerve, and its impact both on artists and EMI:

The Russian-born pianist Vladimir Horowitz (1904–1989) was one of the major artists HMV took under contract in the early 1930s after he was dropped by RCA Victor.

Arturo Toscanini (1867–1957) was a towering figure and is generally acknowledged to have been one of the greatest conductors of the 20th century.

I remember coming back to my office after lunch to find a cable reading "Dropping De Luca and Horowitz any interest – Victor". It seems unbelievable today that such cables were arriving daily. And not only cables – the artists started to arrive in person. Heifetz was one of the first. Fred [Gaisberg] invited him to lunch and the three of us met at the Berkeley [Hotel] where Heifetz started the conversation by saying "Well Fred, in this fearful slump there were some fortunate people who got out and some who were cleared out, and I belong to the latter category. I must get going again and what can you do to help." By the end of that luncheon we had signed him too. [David Bicknell, British Institute of Recorded Sound lecture, 19 May 1972]

The International Artistes Department seized the initiative and undertook major recording programmes. This period produced

LOTTE LEHMANN
(1888–1976)

★

The operatic soprano Lotte Lehmann was born in Perlsberg, Germany. Her musical training commenced in 1906, and she began her professional career in 1909. Her first major success was in 1911 as Elsa in Wagner's *Lohengrin* conducted by Otto Klemperer. Moving to Vienna in 1916, she scored a personal triumph in the role of the Composer in the revised version of Richard Strauss's *Ariadne auf Naxos*. She also had success at Covent Garden, where she sang in almost every season from 1924 to 1938. She made her first records for Deutsche Grammophon and Parlophone-Odeon, but later moved to HMV, where she recorded substantial portions of two of her most famous roles, namely the Marschallin in Richard Strauss's *Rosenkavalier* (HMV DB 2060–72), which also featured Maria Olczewska and Elisabeth Schumann with the Vienna Philharmonic Orchestra conducted by Robert Heger; and Sieglinde in a recording of the whole of the first act of Wagner's *Walküre* (HMV DB 2636–43), with Lauritz Melchior and the Vienna Philharmonic Orchestra conducted by Bruno Walter. Although she came to the United States late in her career, she achieved great fame there, and became a naturalized American citizen. After she died, Walter Legge wrote: "Lotte Lehmann will be as enduring a part of vocal history as Malibran and Patti. Her impact was, is, and, through her records, will remain irresistible and engulfing. Lotte sang and acted as if she were inviting, urging every member of her audiences to enjoy her generous heart and her very self."
[*Opera News*, 1976]

The abridged version of Richard Strauss's *Rosenkavalier* made in Vienna in 1933 captured performances that have become legendary. The principals (left to right) were Maria Olczewska (Octavian), Elisabeth Schumann (Sophie) and Lotte Lehmann (The Marshallin).

Edwin Fischer
The pianist Edwin Fischer (1886–1960) made many recordings for HMV, including the important society edition of the 48 Preludes and Fugues of J. S. Bach, recorded at Abbey Road between 1933 and 1936.

many of the Company's finest records, some of which are still listed in the current EMI catalogue. In particular, it assembled remarkable casts and ensembles for complete recordings of instrumental, orchestral and chamber works and operas.

In addition to American artists, the Company attracted into its studios important European musicians, not least the conductors Arturo Toscanini and Wilhelm Furtwängler (see box, page 197), and the singer Lotte Lehmann, all of whom became HMV artists. Because of the limitations of the 78-rpm format, Toscanini detested record-making at that stage of his career. However, during the 1930s, he was induced to make a number of recordings in Britain with the newly formed BBC Symphony Orchestra. Among these were three of Beethoven's symphonies, including the "Pastoral" (HMV DB 3333–7), and works by Brahms, Haydn, Rossini, Weber and Mozart. In November 1937, Wilhelm Furtwängler made his first HMV recording, of Beethoven's Fifth Symphony with the Berlin Philharmonic (HMV DB 3328–32). The recording marked the beginning of a long artistic association with EMI that was interrupted only by war and would continue until his death in 1954. Lotte Lehmann appeared on many HMV recordings during the 1930s, including an important recital of Lieder (HMV DA 1466–70).

In a 1971 interview in the *Gramophone*, Bicknell reflected on those pre-war years:

We always held to our belief in records and we achieved a virtual monopoly over the next … seven years. When people achieve a monopoly they're supposed to be very unenterprising; in actual fact, I think those were our most adventurous times. ["David Bicknell talks to Alan Blyth", *Gramophone*, Vol.49, September 1971]

Winterreise

THE SOCIETY SERIES

In 1931, Walter Legge (see box, page 169) introduced the first "society" series of subscription recordings by the finest available interpreters of given works. In an innovation that departed from established recording philosophy, the costs of each society release were guaranteed to be fully covered, as the recordings were made only after sufficient subscriptions had been received. In 1971, Bicknell, looking back enthusiastically on the series, said: "we covered a whole field of music we don't record today, particularly in the chamber-music field". ["David Bicknell talks to Alan Blyth", ibid.]

WALTER LEGGE (1906–1979)

★

After Fred Gaisberg, Walter Legge was the most important classical recording producer in EMI's history and a key figure in the record industry.

Harry Walter Legge was born in London, the son of a modestly successful tailor. Educated at Latymer School until he was 16, he excelled at languages and collected records as a hobby. Encouraged by his father, he regularly attended the Albert Hall Sunday concerts and taught himself to read music and German; but he did not receive a conventional musical training. The boy was expected to follow his father's trade but, determined to pursue a career in classical music, he secured a job in 1927 at the HMV record store in Oxford Street. Although the employment lasted only a few months, he soon got another job with HMV, this time as a a writer of sleeve-notes and also editor of *The Voice*, HMV's monthly magazine for retailers. In this capacity, he began attending recording sessions and quickly impressed Fred Gaisberg with his musical knowledge and discernment. Under Gaisberg's direction Legge soon started to take an active role in the recording studio, initially in the production of society editions and later recording artists such as Myra Hess, Benno Moiseiwitsch and Walter Goehr for the British HMV catalogue.

In 1934, Legge first met Sir Thomas Beecham, who was so impressed that he insisted the young man supervise all his recording sessions; a demand to which Fred Gaisberg readily acceded, since Beecham was one of the few artists with whom he did not get on well. Beecham also made Legge assistant artistic director of his opera company at Covent Garden, with the freedom to engage singers and conductors. Always critically appreciative of the talents of performers, he would rush to hear a promising new soprano "almost before she had hit top C" and he provided Beecham with a dazzling array of fine singers and conductors until the outbreak of war in 1939 put an end to opera at Covent Garden.

During the Second World War, Legge's poor eyesight exempted him from war service, but he worked for ENSA, organizing classical concerts for the armed forces and war workers, and he also continued to supervise EMI's classical recordings. When hostilities ceased, Legge returned to the International Artistes Department as Columbia manager and, together with David Bicknell as HMV manager, immediately began to restore EMI's artist roster, signing Herbert von Karajan, Wilhelm Furtwängler, Dinu Lipatti, Elisabeth Schwarzkopf, Walter Gieseking and many other artists. Legge also founded his own orchestra – the Philharmonia. He once remarked, "I did it for a hobby", but he felt the need for a virtuoso British symphony orchestra with which he could make recordings that would set new standards. Karajan became its principal conductor, and guests included Furtwängler, Toscanini, Cantelli, Giulini and many others. When Karajan left to succeed Furtwängler as principal conductor of the Berlin Philharmonic Orchestra, Legge appointed Otto Klemperer to take his place. The period from 1945 to 1964 was a golden age during which Legge's talents as both record producer and impresario reached their peak. Throughout these years, he continued to sign the greatest artists in the world, enriched London's musical life with his Philharmonia concerts and made a vast number of outstanding recordings that set the highest standards and which remain the core of EMI's classical catalogue. In March 1964, after a disagreement with Otto Klemperer over the recording of Mozart's *Zauberflöte*, Legge left; he produced no further recordings for EMI except those involving his second wife, the soprano Elisabeth Schwarzkopf.

In obituary tributes, *Records and Recordings* described Legge as "possibly the greatest classical producer the industry has known", whilst the *Observer* said: "In a country that makes a fetish of the second-rate Legge was a fanatic for quality, and therein lay the source of his achievements."

Whilst recording Donizetti's *Lucia di Lammermoor* in the Kingsway Hall, London, in 1959, the producer Walter Legge and the conductor Tullio Serafin realize that something is not right.

"We have a problem", muses Legge as Serafin wonders what to do.

"This is how it must be done", Legge demonstrates to a bemused Serafin.

ARTUR SCHNABEL
(1882–1951)

The Austrian pianist and teacher Artur Schnabel was perhaps this century's greatest exponent of Beethoven's piano music. Schnabel was born in Lipnik, and studied the piano in Vienna with Leschetizky, who guided him away from the showy music of composers like Liszt towards Schubert and Beethoven, saying: "You will never be a pianist; you are a musician." In his youth, he made a series of triumphant tours throughout Europe. After much intense study of the works, he played all 32 of Beethoven's piano sonatas in public in Berlin in 1927, astounding audiences and critics with the intellectual depth and expression of his performances. From 1931 to 1939, he undertook the monumental task of recording Beethoven's complete solo piano works for the HMV Beethoven Society, an undertaking which was fraught with difficulties. Edward Fowler, manager of Abbey Road Studios who worked with Schnabel on all his recordings, recalls: "When making the 'Diabelli Variations' I used 29 waxes on one particular side. He would keep stopping, kick the piano stool away, bang down the lid of the piano and walk around the studio saying 'This is impossible'. Eventually of course we made it successfully." The set was issued in 15 volumes, each containing six or seven 78 rpm discs. The 1994 *Penguin Guide to Compact Discs* says of Schnabel's Beethoven Piano Sonata set, now reissued on compact disc: "this is one of the towering classics of the gramophone." Schnabel also recorded all five of Beethoven's piano concertos with Malcolm Sargent, between 1932 and 1935.

The first set of society records cost one pound and ten shillings (£1.50), and consisted of a recital of Hugo Wolf songs by Elena Gerhardt (HMV DB 1615–20), with analytical notes by the music critic Ernest Newman. It was released as a limited edition of 500 sets, all of which were immediately sold. After the success of the Gerhardt recordings, many other singers made society records. Among them was the baritone Gerhard Hüsch, who recorded Schubert's song cycles *Winterreise* (HMV DB 2039–44 and DA 1344–6) and *Die schöne Müllerin* (HMV DB 2429–36). Other seminal performers who made records for the society series included the pianists Artur Schnabel (see box) and Edwin Fischer, the cellist Pablo Casals, the violinist Fritz Kreisler and the harpsichordist Wanda Landowska (see box, page 176), as well as many of the world's great orchestras and conductors.

The society series succeeded in placing before the public many significant recording firsts. Of these, none was more important than the complete recording of Beethoven's piano sonatas by Artur Schnabel, considered the greatest Beethoven exponent of his day. This major project continued throughout the 1930s, with fresh releases of records at regular intervals. The act of faith

required to complete such a monumental series as this, in the circumstances of the Depression and the deteriorating international situation, reflected the courage and leadership that was characteristic of the International Artistes Department in the 1930s.

Although society recordings were mainly released on the HMV label, Sir Thomas Beecham made a number of recordings of Delius's music on the Columbia label for the Delius Society. Beecham had been Delius's friend and patron, and, through the medium of these recordings – together with concert performances of his works – he was able to introduce this important British composer to worldwide audiences. The Parlophone label, too, was used as a vehicle for society series, with recordings for the Mozart and Haydn Chamber Music Societies. Recognizing the existence of small but important niche markets for this kind of classical music, the International Artistes Department introduced the "Connoisseur" and "Special" catalogues, which featured records only available through dealers by special order. These specialist classical record series made a very substantial body of first recordings available, and their success demonstrated that there was – in sharp contrast to the experience in the United States at this time – a market for high-quality, non-mainstream, classical music on record even in the difficult circumstances of the 1930s.

SIR ADRIAN BOULT
(1889–1983)

Sir Adrian Boult was the epitome of Edwardian dignity, and the embodiment of the spirit of British music. He was born in Chester and graduated in music from Christ Church, Oxford, in 1914. He joined the music staff at Covent Garden and, in 1918, Holst invited him to conduct the first performance of *The Planets* at Queen's Hall, London. During the 1920s, he worked with various opera companies and choral societies and was musical director of the City of Birmingham Symphony Orchestra until 1930. The turning point in Boult's career came in 1930, when the BBC engaged him to train and conduct the newly formed BBC Symphony Orchestra, which he quickly brought to a high level of excellence. He made a number of important recordings with this orchestra, including Elgar's Second Symphony (HMV DB 6190–95) in 1944 and Holst's *Planets* (HMV DB 6227–33) in 1945. In 1949, when Boult reached the age of 60, the BBC peremptorily retired him, whereupon he took over the London Philharmonic Orchestra with great success. He nominally retired in 1957 but continued to make guest conducting appearances and began a final fruitful association with EMI, recording all the symphonies of Vaughan Williams and Elgar as well as many other works in authoritative readings. He was knighted in 1937. In his biography, *Adrian Boult*, Michael Kennedy writes: "He was a man of wide and cultured tastes, but in the last analysis music was all that mattered to him. Like Richard Strauss, he conducted as if it was just a way of passing the time. But it was in deadly earnest."

The veteran British conductor Sir Adrian Boult with Christopher Bishop, who produced most of his recordings during the 1960s and 1970s.

Die Zauberflöte

EXPANDING THE CATALOGUE

EMI recordings in the 1930s brought to the fore the talents of a new generation of British conductors, such as Dr (later Sir) Malcolm Sargent (see box, page 185) and Dr (later Sir) Adrian Boult (see box, page 171). However, EMI's most important British conductor during the period was Sir Thomas Beecham. In 1932, with financial guarantees in the form of recording commitments from EMI, Beecham established the London Philharmonic Orchestra as a permanent ensemble. They embarked on an ambitious recording programme of works by major composers such as Handel, Rossini, Wagner, Haydn, Brahms, Beethoven and, especially, Mozart. Beecham's recordings of Mozart's late symphonies would remain a yardstick for many years to come.

In 1934, John Christie opened the first Glyndebourne Festival, under the direction of the conductor Fritz Busch. In the course of Glyndebourne's first three years, EMI recorded three Mozart operas, the first ever to be recorded complete. David Bicknell was in charge of these sessions, and his insights into 1930s recording methods and the problems faced are instructive. He said in 1988:

We generally reckoned that we ought to get four 78-rpm sides in a three-hour recording session. In fact, I think I almost did the record at Glyndebourne, when I recorded thirteen. As a result of that, the Musicians' Union, who were very quiet in those days, arrived on the scene and eventually made a limit of four sides: sixteen minutes of music [in a three-hour session]. [*Memoirs of a Musical Dog*, BBC Omnibus, 1988]

In 1937, Beecham – on loan to HMV – undertook the first complete recording of Mozart's *Zauberflöte* (HMV DB 3465–83). The sessions took place in Germany with the Berlin Philharmonic Orchestra; the cast included Tiana Lemnitz as Pamina, Gerhard Hüsch as Papageno and Erna Berger as the Queen of Night. As it turned out, this was EMI's final large-scale recording in Germany before the outbreak of war, and it was a *tour de force*. Elisabeth (later Dame Elisabeth) Schwarzkopf (see box, page 187), who later married Walter Legge, quoted his comments on this recording:

This was my first complete opera recording and I prepared it with particular care for every detail imaginable. I selected the members of the orchestra and even rehearsed the singers in Berlin, so that

SIR THOMAS BEECHAM, (1879–1961)

One of Britain's greatest conductors, Sir Thomas Beecham founded five symphony orchestras, lost a fortune supporting opera in Britain and was an indefatigable recording artist throughout his long career. Thomas Beecham was born in St Helens, Lancashire. He displayed early musical talents but received little training as he was expected to join and eventually inherit the family pharmaceutical business. Against his father's wishes, he left for London in 1902 to pursue a career as a conductor. His first job was with a small opera company touring the theatres of outer London but, after five weeks of playing to small and unresponsive audiences, the opera company and the job both came to an abrupt end. In 1906, he led the newly formed New Symphony Orchestra, and gave concerts at Queen's Hall. Two years later, he formed the Beecham Symphony Orchestra, which became the most adventurous orchestra in London, performing rarely heard works and establishing Beecham's reputation as a conductor of some substance. In 1910, with financial support from his father, Beecham gave his first opera season at Covent Garden and achieved a tremendous success with the British première of Richard Strauss's controversial new opera *Elektra*. In July 1910, he made his recording debut with The Gramophone Company in a group of operatic items involving members of the Beecham Opera Company and the Beecham Symphony Orchestra, the first of which was "The Doll's Song" from Offenbach's *Tales of Hoffmann* (HMV 03193) sung by the soprano Caroline Hatchard.

Over the next few years Beecham continued to present an extremely varied assortment of operas by Richard Strauss, Mozart and a number of French and Russian composers. During the First World War, he worked hard to keep classical music alive in Britain, giving concerts with the Hallé and the London Symphony Orchestras (to whom he also contributed financial support). In 1915, Beecham began his long association with the Columbia Company,

providing the first two 12-inch discs on the new Light Blue Celebrity Label: Mozart's *Zauberflöte* Overture (Columbia L 1001) and the "Polovtsian Dances" from Borodin's *Prince Igor* (Columbia L 1002) with the Beecham Symphony Orchestra. The following year, Beecham succeeded to his father's baronetcy. In 1919 and 1920, he

presented joint seasons of opera at Covent Garden with the Grand Opera Syndicate, but his family finances were in such a state that he was then forced to retire from musical life for several years to put them in order.

In 1932, dissatisfied with the existing orchestras in Britain, he established the

London Philharmonic Orchestra, with whom he continued to record for Columbia. Amongst the recordings he made during this period, a series of Mozart symphonies was particularly admired, as were his pioneering recordings of works by Sibelius and Delius, two contemporary composers with whom he was closely associated. Of the latter's music he once said: "I found it as alluring as a wayward woman and determined to tame it." Also in 1932, after an absence of some years, he returned to Covent Garden as artistic director. From 1935, he was in sole charge there, conducting several complete *Ring* cycles himself and presenting a series of outstanding opera performances with many distinguished singers and guest conductors.

In 1946 Beecham founded yet another orchestra, the Royal Philharmonic, and began to make records for RCA (issued on HMV in Britain), including several major works by Richard Strauss, whose music he continued to champion. One of these was *Ein Heldenleben* (DB 6620–24), considered by the clarinettist Jack Brymer to be "as good as we can hope for in this imperfect world". He also continued to make many recordings for EMI and, in his final highly productive period, he recorded two complete operas which are considered to be amongst the finest achievements of the gramophone: *La bohème* (HMV ALP 1409–10) and *Carmen* (HMV ALP 1762–4 & ASD 331–3), both featuring the soprano Victoria de los Angeles. After the advent of tape Beecham could make his recording sessions an exasperating experience for the engineers and producers; he would record sections from several different uncompleted projects during the same session. W. S. Meadmore recalled that many were "unable to decide whether Beecham was a heaven-sent genius or a flashy charlatan", but universal opinion felt his death in March 1961 as a great loss to the musical world. In a tribute in the *Daily Telegraph*, Martin Cooper wrote: "Beecham may well have done more for music in this country than any one man before."

when Beecham arrived the company was ready for him.
[Elisabeth Schwarzkopf, *On and Off the Record* (London 1982), p.60]

Throughout the 1930s, many of the premerger recording programmes continued under the new régime. The most important were the continuing HMV recordings of Sir Edward Elgar's works, principally with the London Symphony Orchestra, conducted by the composer himself. Elgar's personal commitment to the project is manifest in the numerous letters from him in the EMI Music Archive. In July 1932, with the recording of the Violin Concerto (HMV DB 1751–6), this remarkable collaboration between EMI and one of Britain's greatest composers reached its apogee. The soloist on that occasion was the 16-year-old Yehudi Menuhin (see box, page 175). David Bicknell, who had helped Fred Gaisberg arrange the recording, recalled: "Yehudi – like a sort of meteorite – burst on the musical scene. He played marvellously for Elgar, and Elgar was enchanted". [*Memoirs of a Musical Dog*, ibid.] Menuhin's own thoughts on that memorable recording were:

With the Elgar Violin Concerto my recording activities really centred on Abbey Road. It was a great occasion, with a really great man, Sir Edward Elgar, conducting this huge orchestra; the largest orchestra I had ever played with as soloist ... [It] was the great experience of that period, preparing for the Concerto: that was Fred Gaisberg's doing, and Elgar rather enjoyed it. [*Memoirs of a Musical Dog*, ibid.]

One the many letters from Sir Edward Elgar to Fred Gaisberg. He discusses his role in the Abbey Road opening ceremony.

Menuhin said of the result of that remarkable collaboration: "Fortunately, that recording was made with the romantic vision of searching for expression, for beauty of sound ... I was a very romantic boy, and the music suited me." [*Memoirs of a Musical Dog*, ibid.] The stature of this recording is such that, in the more than 60 years since its release, it has never been absent from the EMI classical catalogue.

LORD MENUHIN (BORN 1916)

★

From precocious childhood to active old-age, Lord Menuhin has continually distinguished himself as a musician of the highest calibre, as well as a noted humanitarian.

Yehudi Menuhin was born in New York of Russian-Jewish immigrant parents. When only four years old, he was already receiving violin training from Sigmund Anker in San Francisco, where the family had settled. Recalling his attitude to the violin in those early days, Menuhin later said: "I really needed it, to say things that would touch people, to express my very deep feelings, even anger." Lessons continued with Louis Persinger in 1923, and he made his debut, aged seven, on 29 February 1924 in Oakland, California, playing Bériot's "Scène de Ballet" with Persinger as accompanist. On 17 January 1926, he gave a recital in New York, and he made a sensational European debut in Paris on 6 February, 1927 with Paul Paray and the Lamoureux Orchestra. Whilst in Paris, he studied with the Romanian composer and violinist Georges Enescu, who proved to be an enduring influence on his musical development. Returning to New York, Menuhin gave a memorable account of Beethoven's Violin Concerto with the New York Symphony Orchestra conducted by Fritz Busch; it won him unanimous acclaim from both public and press and established him as an international celebrity.

Menuhin began his recording career with Victor in the United States in 1928, with a number of short encore pieces which were released by HMV in Europe. When the Menuhin family moved to Europe in 1929, Yehudi began to record for HMV and later EMI under a succession of contracts that have continued without a break – an achievement without parallel in the history of the record industry. In 1935, Menuhin completed his first world tour, performing in 73 cities in 13 countries, including Australia. During the Second World War, he tirelessly entertained American and Allied troops, giving

over 500 concerts in many theatres of the war. He continued to record extensively after the war, making new versions of his main concert repertoire, particularly the violin concertos of Brahms, Beethoven and Mendelssohn, which revealed new depths of interpretative power and musicianship.

In addition to his work as a soloist, Menuhin organized a number of music festivals at Bath, Windsor and Gstaad and also took on the role of conductor. His first conducting engagements were with the Bath Festival Orchestra and, in 1958, he founded his own chamber orchestra. Although seemingly untouched by the advancing years, Menuhin eventually relinquished the violin to concentrate on conducting. In this he achieved particular success with his interpretations of Elgar, as well as other composers, including Mozart and Vaughan Williams.

Menuhin has always been keen to encourage the development of young musicians, and in 1962 he founded a school for musically gifted children at Stoke d'Abernon in Surrey. He has enthusiastically supported the school ever

since, and it has turned out many fine players, the best-known of which are the violinist Nigel Kennedy and the keyboard player Melvyn Tan. In recognition of his great contribution to music and his outstanding qualities as a citizen of the world, Menuhin has been the recipient of many honours both in Britain and

elsewhere. Most notably, he became an honorary Knight Commander of the Order of the British Empire (KBE) in 1965; this was recognized as a formal knighthood in 1987. He was also appointed to the select Order of Merit (OM) and, in 1993, was elevated to the peerage as Lord Menuhin of Stoke d'Abernon.

On the occasion of Menuhin's 50th birthday, David Bicknell said: "Yehudi Menuhin is one of those rare musicians who seemed to leap fully equipped with every talent into the musical arena without losing any time in preliminaries and has stayed there ever since."

Paul Tortelier and Yehudi Menuhin
The French cellist Paul Tortelier discusses a musical point with Yehudi Menuhin while recording the Delius Double Concerto in 1976.

WANDA LANDOWSKA
(1879–1959)

The Polish keyboard virtuoso Wanda Landowska led the 20th-century revival of the harpsichord and its repertoire. Born in Warsaw, Landowska studied the piano at the conservatory there and in Berlin, before moving to Paris in 1900. She threw herself wholeheartedly into researching all aspects of 17th- and 18th-century keyboard music, and eventually decided that it could be fully appreciated only when performed on the harpsichord, an instrument which had become obsolete following the arrival of the modern piano in the early 19th century. Despite initial public resistance, Landowska championed the harpsichord vigorously, giving concerts throughout Europe and writing combative articles and a book about the instrument. In 1912, she commissioned a large two-manual harpsichord from Pleyel which she spectacularly introduced at the Breslau Bach Festival. Eleven years later she took four Pleyel harpsichords on tour to the United States, and to other countries, continually impressing her audiences with the brilliant articulation and vitality of her playing. In the 1930s, she made a number of important HMV Society recordings of music by J. S. Bach, François Couperin, Handel and Domenico Scarlatti. When the war forced her to leave France in 1940, she went to the United States, where she continued to perform and to teach. She was honoured by the governments of both Poland and France and universally acclaimed in musical circles for her pioneering work on early keyboard music and for establishing a modern harpsichord technique. The American composer and critic Virgil Thomson said of her: "Landowska plays the harpsichord better than anybody else plays anything." Landowska herself once famously said to a rival harpsichordist: "You play Bach your way; I'll play it his".

Right A typical example of the forthright letters Wanda Landowska wrote to the Company about her recordings.

'Goldberg' Variations

EARLY MUSIC

The reintroduction of early music into the mainstream repertoire began during the interwar years, and EMI was prominent in giving a platform to the pioneering exponents of this musical genre. In 1933 the harpsichordist Wanda Landowska made the first ever recording of Bach's "Goldberg" Variations (HMV DB 4908–13). A reviewer wrote that Landowska had "a striking intellectual and technical grasp of the music which gives all the brilliance called for in a work written primarily for entertainment." ["Music for Sleepless

Nights", *Gramophone*, Vol.12, 1934] The many letters from Landowska surviving at the EMI Music Archive reveal an intelligent and tenacious woman, prepared to debate with the International Artistes Department the merits of her recordings, the publication of her records, and the correct interpretation of the score; she usually won on all points.

In 1935, the Busch Chamber Players recorded Bach's Brandenburg Concertos (Columbia LX 436–49). Despite the use of a piano, their interpretation was more in tune with Bach's intentions than were such accepted interpretations as those recorded by Sir Henry Wood with an 80-piece orchestra (for example, Concertos Nos.3 and 6; Columbia LX 173 and LX 412). Other examples of early music followed and, in 1938, a set of madrigals recorded in France under the direction of Nadia Boulanger introduced the music of Claudio Monteverdi to the British HMV catalogue. Writing in the *Gramophone*, Richard Holt commented: "the records will enrich any collection, and introduce the possessor to one of the unfamiliar giants of music". [*Gramophone*, Vol.15, March 1938]

Addio, senza rancor

THE END OF AN ERA

Whilst the 1930s brought Bicknell and Legge to the fore, those same years also witnessed the final flowering of Fred Gaisberg, the man who had contributed more than anyone else to the development of the art of record-making. As artistic director of the International Artistes Department, he spent the 1930s recording both in London and in Europe. During this phase of his career, he made some astonishing recordings of complete operas, along with other important discs of orchestral, choral and instrumental music. In April 1937, despite the deteriorating political situation, he recorded Dvořák's Cello Concerto in Prague with Pablo Casals and the Czech Philharmonic Orchestra, conducted by George Szell (HMV DB 3288–92). He later wrote of this experience:

I feel it to be something precious and rare snatched from that seething cauldron of Europe before the storm broke … The records turned out to be an unqualified success, and as soon as they were published I sold the first set to a most appreciative music-lover and record collector, Jan Masaryk [the Czech statesman]. [Jerrold Northrop Moore, *A Voice to Remember* (London 1976), p.220]

BRUNO WALTER
(1876–1962)

Bruno Walter was a kind and gentle man whose warmly lyrical style of conducting was particularly suited to the music of Mozart, Bruckner and Mahler. Born Bruno Walter Schlesinger in Berlin, he dropped the family name early in his career. He worked in various German opera houses before becoming assistant to Gustar Mahler at the Court Opera in Vienna in 1901. Shortly after Mahler's death in 1911, Bruno Walter conducted the premiere of *Das Lied von der Erde* in Munich. He worked mainly in Germany until the rise to power of the Nazis in 1933 forced him to move to Vienna. There, in 1936, he made the first recording of *Das Lied von der Erde* (Columbia ROX 165–71), at a public concert commemorating the 25th anniversary of the composer's death. His landmark recording of Mahler's Ninth Symphony (HMV DB 3613–22) was also made live, in Vienna's Musikvereinssaal on 16 January 1938, just before Hitler's troops marched into Austria; the catastrophe forced Walter to leave and Mahler's music to be banned. In 1939, he emigrated to America, where he conducted the leading symphony orchestras in Los Angeles, Philadelphia and New York and worked at the Metropolitan Opera, New York. He gave his farewell performance in Vienna with the Vienna Philharmonic Orchestra in 1960. In his book *Conductors – A Record Collector's Guide*, John L. Holmes writes of Bruno Walter: "He was always conscious of the spiritual dimension of the great central European masters and ever sought to express it."

BENIAMINO GIGLI
(1890–1957)

★

Beniamino Gigli, who succeeded Enrico Caruso as the world's best-loved Italian tenor, was born into a poor family in Recanati, Italy. First prize at a singing contest in Parma led to his debut as Enzo Grimaldo in Ponchielli's *Gioconda* at Rovigo in October 1914. His debut at La Scala under Toscanini in a memorial performance of Boito's *Mefistofele* in 1918 brought Gigli to international prominence. His first performance at the Metropolitan Opera in New York on 26 November 1920, again in *Mefistofele*, earned him 34 curtain calls and a letter of congratulation from Caruso himself. After the premature death of Caruso in 1921, Gigli took over his lyric roles at the Metropolitan for a number of seasons (he left only because of a dispute over pay). He reigned supreme as the world's leading Italian tenor for over 30 years. Gigli began his recording career for The Gramophone Company in Milan on 4 October 1918 with "Dai campi, dai prati" from Boito's *Mefistofele* (HMV 7-52110) and continued to record prolifically until his retirement in 1955. He was the first important tenor to record most of his main operatic roles in their entirety, and he also made many successful records of ballads and popular songs, such as Leoncavallo's "Mattinata" (HMV DA 1454) and the Bach-Gounod "Ave Maria" (HMV DA 1488). Gigli's vocal mannerisms, especially the interpolated sobs and aspirates, were sometimes criticised, but his voice was always golden and he poured his heart and soul into everything he sang. His colleague Tito Gobbi, in his autobiography *My Life*, said: "When he opened that miraculous throat and sang no one needed any special training to know that one of God's greatest gifts was being spread before them."

In January 1938, Gaisberg made his final recordings in Vienna. The occasion was a live performance of Mahler's Ninth Symphony (HMV "Mahler Society" DB 3613–22) with the Vienna Philharmonic Orchestra conducted by Bruno Walter. The choices of orchestra (Mahler's own) and conductor (Mahler had dedicated this symphony to Walter) were felicitous. These treasured recordings, together with those made by Gaisberg of

Furtwängler and the Berlin Philharmonic Orchestra and of other great European performers, such as the pianist Artur Rubinstein, who recorded all Chopin's Nocturnes (HMV DB 3186–96) and Polonaises (HMV DB 2493–2500), appear in retrospect to have been a final blossoming of pre-war European culture before it was crushed by the Nazis.

At Abbey Road Studios in 1938, Gaisberg directed the last recordings of the great Polish pianist Ignacy Jan Paderewski. At this final session, Paderewski recorded seven sides but, as Gaisberg, who had made the great man's first recordings in 1912, sadly noted:

… he was beginning to show his seventy-eight years … In his playing I found a lack of virility. To help compensate there were fine flashes of poetry, and in the cadenzas he showed all his old-time bravura. [Gaisberg, ibid., p.178]

Fred Gaisberg took particular pride in the brilliant recordings of complete operas made with the greatest tenor of the time, Beniamino Gigli (see box, page 178). With his extraordinary eye for talent, Gaisberg had spotted Gigli's potential as a recording artist whilst recording in Italy during the First World War. In May 1918, he wrote from Milan to his brother William, then The Gramophone Company's chief London-based recording engineer:

I have heard him [Gigli] and today I made a test of his voice. I tell you he is wonderful … he is going to have a great career. You can describe him as a second Caruso except he has a greater vocal flexibility. It is a real lyric voice that rings out all over the place …
[Gigli Artist File, EMI Music Archive]

During the 1920s and early 1930s, Gigli established himself in the world's opera houses as the greatest tenor of his generation. However, it was his bad luck to come to maturity at a time when the popularity of single recordings of songs and arias was in decline. As a result of this change in fashion, Gigli never achieved the same sales (or royalties) as his distinguished predecessor, Caruso, whose record sales had remained buoyant well into the 1930s.

Gigli also featured in the company's ground-breaking recordings of Puccini's three great operas, *La bohème*, *Tosca* and *Madama Butterfly*. The 1938 recording of *La bohème* (HMV DB 3448–60), which featured Licia Albanese as Mimì and Afro Poli as Marcello, was issued to coincide with Gigli's 1938 Covent

The 1930s recordings of complete operas featuring the tenor Beniamino Gigli were central to the development of HMV's classical catalogue. The 1938 release of Puccini's *Tosca* was the highlight of that year's operatic issues.

"HIS MASTER'S VOICE"

MADAMA BUTTERFLY
with GIGLI and DAL MONTE

RECORDS FOR MARCH 1940

Supplement No. 4003

This March 1940 wartime release of Puccini's *Madama Butterfly*, featuring Beniamino Gigli and Toti dal Monte, was the last international recording undertaken by EMI before the war.

Garden season. Later that same year, Gaisberg recorded Tosca at the Teatro Reale in Rome (HMV DB 3562-75). As well as Gigli, the cast included Maria Caniglia and Armando Borgioli. During the course of the recording, Gaisberg wrote to Rex Palmer in London: "Gigli is like a boy, I have never heard him sing better. He has a great capacity for work that leaves one amazed." [Gigli Artist File, EMI Music Archive] The making of this recording was not, however, without its own high drama: the soprano originally cast to sing the role of Tosca was taken ill at the first recording session and prompt action was required, as Gaisberg noted in a further letter to Palmer:

Gigli was a trump – he and I went to Caniglia's [the replacement soprano] hotel, got her out of bed, put her in a taxi; and brought her around to the theatre where the Maestro [de Fabritiis] went through the first act duet at the piano. At four o'clock we started up again and before six o'clock we had made five excellent records with her and Gigli: we had only lost one hour of the orchestra. [Gigli Artist File, EMI Music Archive]

The ability to act decisively in a crisis was one of Gaisberg's greatest gifts. After the recording, Rex Palmer wrote admiringly to him:

You have certainly done wonders over the *Tosca* recording and nobody could have managed it better or half as well. It was a great stroke to get hold of Caniglia at the last moment and turn a potential defeat into a victory."
[Gigli Artist File, EMI Music Archive]

Just before war broke out in 1939, *Madama Butterfly* (HMV DB 3859–70), the final recording in the Puccini series, was made by the International Artistes Department, this time without the benefit of Gaisberg's expertise: in April 1939, at the age of 66, Fred Gaisberg had retired. To mark the event, a banquet was held in his honour at the Savoy Hotel. The whole industry – including many artists – turned out to salute this extraordinary figure. In his speech, Compton Mackenzie (the editor of the *Gramophone*) remarked: "Great artists from practically every nation are represented here tonight to do honour to this little man who has stood up over all those years and held up this great business." [*The Voice*, May 1939] Felix Weingartner, as if he were speaking for all the artists past and present who had known and worked with Fred Gaisberg, said to him: "I salute you, not only as an artist but as a friend, and for that friendship you have always extended to me." [Ibid.] With characteristic modesty, Gaisberg wrote of that event:

In a way the evening marked the close of an epoch. It was one of the last gatherings of musicians in London before the war set in. It almost seemed as though some premonition had brought about a rally of the clans before the storm burst. [*A Voice to Remember*, ibid., p.230]

Although Fred Gaisberg formally retired in 1939, he was retained by EMI as a consultant, a post he held until his death in 1951.

O my beloved father

WARTIME

The coming of war in 1939 effectively brought this remarkable and creative period to an end and severely curtailed EMI's classical recording programmes. Within a short time, David Bicknell and Rex Palmer had left the Company for military service. As the war progressed, Walter Legge became increasingly involved with ENSA activities, and less able to

Dame Joan Hammond
During the 1940s, Joan Hammond's recordings of operatic arias in English were amongst the most popular titles in EMI's British catalogues. Although her career was disrupted by the war, her unstinting efforts in giving countless civilian and military concerts throughout the country, as well as voluntary ambulance driving in London, earned her a special place in the affections of the British people.

Dame Myra Hess
Dame Myra Hess organized daily lunchtime concerts at the National Gallery in London throughout the war, and helped to raise the spirits of a nation deprived of other opportunities to hear live music.

The contralto Kathleen Ferrier (1912–1953) recorded a small number of arias and songs for HMV and Columbia in 1944 and 1945. Her death at the early age of 41 deprived the British musical world of one of its best-loved figures.

devote his energies to record-making. In Britain, recording activities were further disrupted by the conscription of both men and women to military and other war work; both classical and popular artists found themselves in uniform, often posted far from the London recording studios. All this inevitably caused the break-up of many major orchestras and ensembles, and also prevented the emergence of fresh talent.

As a result of Britain's isolation, EMI lost touch with its most valuable sources of artistic talent, and, of course, was unable to make recordings in Europe. To make matters worse, the Company lost many of its most important performing artists, a large number of whom left Europe permanently for the United States to avoid Nazi persecution and the privations of the war. In a reversal of the situation in the early 1930s, many of these artists were warmly welcomed by RCA Victor and Columbia Records, who had once again begun to make classical records. As a result, EMI lost its leadership of the classical record market, and, for the duration of the war and for a decade after, American record companies dominated the classical record market.

During the war, Purchase Tax on records was introduced, and the use of shellac based material restricted. The former curtailed the demand for records, and the latter limited their supply. Inevitably, as pre-war stocks of records dried up, there was a wholesale programme of deletions from the various EMI classical record catalogues. EMI's classical recording budget (including artists' advances and royalty payments), shrank from £55,000 in 1939 to a mere £27,000 in 1945. Through the entire war, only 48 sets of records were released on Columbia's premium 12-inch LX classical label. Although they included several Beecham recordings of Mozart symphonies made early in 1940, the rest were almost entirely made up of unissued pre-war recordings and records released before the outbreak of war. One of the most popular of these was Myra (later Dame Myra) Hess's piano arrangement of J. S. Bach's chorale setting "Jesu, Joy of Man's Desiring" (Columbia D 1635). This recording was originally issued in 1928, and in its day had been modestly successful. Myra Hess played the transcription regularly in wartime broadcasts and the lunch time recitals in the National Gallery that made her a household name. As a result, it became one of the Company's best-selling records – so much so that HMV remade it as HMV B 9035.

Despite wartime restrictions, new recordings also appeared on the 10-inch Columbia label, and several became popular successes. One of these records, by Joan (later Dame Joan) Hammond, then at the beginning of her recording career, was

SIR JOHN BARBIROLLI (1899–1970)

Sir John Barbirolli was born Giovanni Battista Barbirolli in London of an Italian father and a French mother. Following in the footsteps of his father and grandfather, he began his musical career as a cellist. He made his conducting debut in 1925 with his own Barbirolli Chamber Orchestra. Between 1926 and 1937, he also conducted opera at Covent Garden and elsewhere. In the concert hall, he worked with several British provincial orchestras, and in 1937 he was appointed to succeed Toscanini as permanent conductor of the New York Philharmonic. He remained in New York until 1943, when he returned to Britain and took over the Hallé Orchestra, which he eventually restored to the glory it had formerly enjoyed under Sir Hamilton Harty. From 1961 to 1967, he was also principal conductor of the Houston Symphony Orchestra in Texas. Barbirolli signed his first contract with The Gramophone Company in 1928 and made some recordings with his own chamber orchestra, but he proved more valuable as an accompanying conductor for leading artists like Gigli, Chaliapin, Heifetz, Rubinstein, Kreisler and Casals, with whom he frequently recorded throughout the 1930s. In 1962 he re-signed an exclusive contract with EMI, for whom he recorded three complete operas and a range of music (mainly by English composers) with the Hallé and several of the London orchestras, and symphonies by Mahler and Brahms (in Berlin and Vienna respectively). In spite of EMI's efforts to increase Barbirolli's role on the international scene, his heart remained firmly with his beloved Hallé Orchestra, with which he continued to work to the end of his life.

"O my beloved father" (Columbia DB 2052), from Puccini's opera *Gianni Schicchi*, recorded at Belle Vue Gardens, Manchester, with Leslie Heward conducting the Hallé Orchestra. This record was widely praised, became a huge seller, and helped establish Joan Hammond's reputation as a singer of opera in English. Britain's greatest post-war contralto, Kathleen Ferrier, made her first appearance on record in 1944 as a Columbia artist with recordings of Maurice Green's "I will lay me down in peace" and "O praise the Lord" (Columbia DB 2152).

Pre-war classical titles on the Parlophone-Odeon label were made up largely of European – mainly German – recordings. With the outbreak of war, this source came to an abrupt end. However, the tenor Richard Tauber, one of Parlophone's most prolific pre-war recording artists (see Chapter 3), was still available. An Austrian of Jewish

John McCormack and Gerald Moore
Fred Gaisberg took this photograph in September 1942 during what proved to be John McCormack's final recording session at Abbey Road. The accompanist is Gerald Moore.

The horn player Dennis Brain (1921–1957) and the pianist Denis Matthews (1919–1988) take time off from their duties with the armed forces to visit Number Three Studio at Abbey Road in April 1944 to record Beethoven's Horn Sonata.

descent, he had fled his native country when it was occupied by the Nazis in 1938. Tauber recorded popular and light classical music regularly for Parlophone-Odeon throughout the war; his most popular wartime recording was "My Heart and I" from his own operetta *Old Chelsea* (Parlophone RO 20522). Indeed, so many Tauber recordings were released on Parlophone during the war that, by 1945, the label had become known within the Company as 'Tauberphone'.

Columbia's wartime experience was largely mirrored by that of HMV. In the course of the war, only 150 new records were issued on HMV's 10-inch Red Label classical series. Of these, half were derived from American RCA Victor recordings, whilst the rest were nearly all London made. The artist responsible for nearly half these London recordings was the veteran singer John McCormack (see Chapter 2). Although McCormack had retired from the concert platform in 1938, he returned when war was declared to sing for HMV, the Red Cross, ENSA and the BBC. He was one of the few HMV international artists to remain in Britain, where, after the fall of France, he was joined by Maggie Teyte. McCormack continued to make records until 1942, when illness occasioned his final retirement to his native Ireland. His wartime recordings of such songs as "The Star of the County Down" and "I'll walk beside you" (HMV DA 1718) helped boost morale and kept the 10-inch HMV Red Label before the public. McCormack's contribution to EMI's war effort was not confined to the recording studios. In 1940, he inaugurated a highly successful series of celebrity lunchtime concerts for EMI employees and war workers at the Hayes factories.

During the war, the main thrust of EMI's classical recording was focused on its cheaper range of labels, the Columbia 12-inch DX Dark Blue label and the HMV 12-inch C series Plum label. Columbia releases included a recording by the young pianist Denis Matthews of Mozart's Piano Concerto No.23 (Columbia DX 1167–9), with the Liverpool Philharmonic Orchestra conducted by George Weldon. Among Matthews's other recordings were Beethoven's Clarinet Trio in B flat (Columbia DX 1164–6), with Reginald Kell (clarinet) and Anthony Pini (cello), and Beethoven's Sonata for Horn and Piano (Columbia

DX 1152), with Dennis Brain, the equally young and brilliant horn player. A number of wartime Plum label releases were funded by the British Council, a government body established to promote British culture overseas, and all were produced, despite the weight of his other commitments, by Walter Legge.

The Plum label recording programme consisted entirely of British repertoire, and represented mainly (although not entirely) the previously unrecorded work of contemporary composers. In 1940, excerpts from the Glyndebourne production of John Gay's famous ballad opera, *The Beggar's Opera* (HMV C 3159–64), at the Haymarket Theatre, London, were recorded; the star attraction of this set was Michael Redgrave as Macheath.

SIR MALCOLM SARGENT (1895–1967)

★

Sir Malcolm Sargent is best remembered for his work in maintaining British choral traditions and for conducting the Promenade Concerts for some 20 years. Harold Malcolm Watts Sargent was born in Ashford, Kent. He began his career as a church organist but was encouraged to take up conducting by Sir Henry Wood. It was in choral and vocal music that he felt most at home, and he was soon working with various choral societies and opera companies, including the D'Oyly Carte. From 1924, he conducted the Robert Mayer children's concerts, and, from 1929, the Courtauld–Sargent concerts, which enriched London musical life during the Depression years. He assisted Sir Thomas Beecham in 1932 in founding the London Philharmonic Orchestra, later touring with it during the Blitz, and was successively chief conductor of the Hallé Orchestra (1939–42) and the Liverpool Philharmonic (1943–49). He was chief conductor of the Promenade Concerts from 1948 until his death, and was in charge of the BBC Symphony Orchestra from 1950 to 1957. But he never neglected his interest in choral music, regularly conducting the Royal Choral Society and the Huddersfield Choral Society and making many fine choral recordings, including three of Handel's *Messiah*. He was knighted in 1947. Sargent's immaculate grooming and polished manner on the podium made him a popular figure with audiences. In his book *Conductors: A Record Collector's Guide*, John L. Holmes says of Sir Malcolm Sargent: "To the world he was the very model of the modern Englishman; to many Englishmen he was just 'Flash Harry'."

Solomon (1902–1988) was one of the finest pianists Britain ever produced. In 1956, while still at the peak of his powers, he suffered a stroke and was forced to retire completely.

HERBERT VON
KARAJAN (1908–1989)

Herbert von Karajan became the best-known conductor of his time. The son of a Salzburg doctor, Karajan was first engaged as a conductor by the Ulm opera house, where he remained for five years, learning all aspects of opera production. In 1934, he was appointed music director at Aachen, and in 1938 he joined the Berlin State Opera, where he worked until the house was destroyed by bombing in 1944. In 1946, Walter Legge signed Karajan to record for EMI with the Vienna Philharmonic Orchestra; shortly afterwards, he appointed him principal conductor of his newly formed Philharmonia Orchestra in London. In 1955, Karajan succeeded Furtwängler as principal conductor of the Berlin Philharmonic Orchestra and, by 1960, having gained control of the Vienna State Opera and the Salzburg Festival, as well as influence at La Scala, he had become the "musical director of Europe". With the Berlin Philharmonic, he made many recordings for both EMI and Polydor. Some critics found his predilection for beautiful sound vitiated the musical substance of his performances, but the public had no such doubts and his name became synonymous with the best in mainstream classical music. Karajan always took a keen interest in new technology, remaking his principal repertoire for each new recording format, and actively exploiting film, video and laserdisc. Walter Legge, quoted in *On and Off the Record*, said: "The enduring validity and, on listening to his records, the satisfaction that Karajan brought to music is his musical integrity."

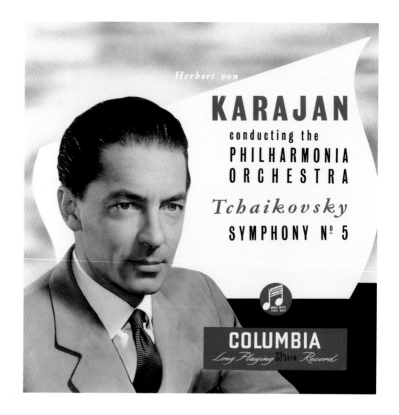

Other recordings included William Walton's *Belshazzar's Feast* (HMV C 3330–34), recorded in 1943 with Dennis Noble, the Huddersfield Choral Society, the Liverpool Philharmonic Orchestra and brass bands; Arthur Bliss's Piano Concerto in B flat (HMV C 3348–52), also recorded in 1943, with Solomon and the Liverpool Philharmonic Orchestra conducted by Adrian Boult; Arnold Bax's Third Symphony, recorded in 1944 by the Hallé Orchestra under its new conductor, John (later Sir John) Barbirolli (see box, page 183); Ralph Vaughan Williams's Fifth Symphony (HMV C 3388–92), recorded in 1944 by the Hallé Orchestra conducted by Barbirolli; and finally – released in 1945 just after VE Day – Elgar's *Dream of Gerontius* (HMV C 3435–46), with Heddle Nash, Gladys Ripley, Dennis Noble and Norman Walker and the Liverpool Philharmonic Orchestra conducted by Malcolm Sargent.

With these and other recordings, EMI helped keep culture alive during the darkest days of the war. With the advent of peace, the Company was in a strong position to pick up the threads of its pre-war activities and begin the mammoth task of rebuilding its record catalogues.

The Nuns' Chorus

1945–1961

By the end of 1945, the International Artistes Department and EMI's domestic British recording activities had been reconstituted. At the same time, Walter Legge and David Bicknell

DAME ELISABETH SCHWARZKOPF (BORN 1915)

★

Elisabeth Schwarzkopf stands as one of the greatest singers of Lieder and also one of the finest opera singers of the 20th century. Olga Maria Elisabeth Friederike Schwarzkopf, the highly intelligent daughter of a German classics teacher, studied at the Berlin Academy of Music. By 1938, she was a member of the Berlin Städtische Opera. She became a pupil of the soprano Maria Ivogün, and made her recital debut in Berlin in 1942, the same year in which she was invited by Karl Böhm to join the Vienna State Opera. When Walter Legge visited Vienna immediately after the war in search of new artists for EMI, Schwarzkopf was one of the singers he took under contract. In 1947, she joined the resident opera company at Covent Garden, where for five seasons she sang an amazingly wide range of parts from the French, Italian and German repertoire, all in English. Later, she preferred to restrict her operatic career to a handful of roles and appeared more frequently in concert halls, where her highly developed artistic sensibilities, combined with a voice of great expressiveness, illuminated the work of many composers, especially Schubert and Hugo Wolf. Throughout her career, she made many recordings, all of which were supervised by Walter Legge, whom she married in 1953; they have become benchmarks in the art of singing on record. After her retirement from singing in 1979, Schwarzkopf devoted herself to giving Master Classes. She was appointed a DBE in 1992. The pianist Gerald Moore, who regularly accompanied Schwarzkopf in concerts and on recordings, said of her in his memoirs *Am I too Loud?* "It seems to me quite unfair for anyone to look so ravishing and sing so beautifully."

Dinu Lipatti's small but precious catalogue of piano recordings preserves an outstanding talent that was denied its complete fulfilment by his premature death at the age of 33. This recording of Chopin's Third Piano Sonata was described in *The Record Guide* (1951) as one of the glories of the gramophone.

The Vienna Philharmonic Orchestra
By early 1947, the fruits of Walter Legge's recording expeditions to Central Europe began to appear in the Columbia catalogues. This was the first recording made in Vienna after the war.

returned to the Company. Their immediate task was to create a new classical catalogue. This was made more difficult as many of EMI's greatest performers – such as Paderewski and John McCormack – had died, whilst others had retired, or, like Kreisler and Tito Schipa, were coming to the end of their careers. Furthermore, there seemed little hope of tempting back the many EMI artists who had abandoned Europe for the United States in the 1930s. The team's priority was thus to visit continental Europe and there re-establish links with the Company's pre-war organizations, renew contacts with such artists as were left and test the quality of the new generation of artists.

Die Meistersinger

WALTER LEGGE

In January 1946, Legge made his first post-war visit to Austria and Germany. However, as wartime regulations prohibiting trade with enemies were at that time still in force, this first visit was fraught with practical difficulties. Legge managed to overcome most of them by attaching himself to Turicaphon, EMI's Swiss subsidiary, and by using Turicaphon's name in contracts with artists. Whilst Legge was in Switzerland preparing for his Austrian visit, he entered into fresh contracts with the pianists Edwin Fischer and Wilhelm Backhaus, and he met the brilliant Romanian pianist Dinu Lipatti, whose life and career were tragically cut short by leukaemia. Legge later wrote of his recording activities with Lipatti: "Our work together produced a small but perfect collection of records which are a permanent monument to this supreme artist". [*On and Off the Record*, ibid., p. 63] Surprisingly, large numbers of EMI's pre-war artists had survived amid the wreckage of Central Europe, and many were living in Vienna. Legge accordingly went to Vienna, where he met and signed exclusive contracts with many of the musicians who were to become the backbone of EMI's post-war classical catalogues: the Vienna Philharmonic Orchestra, Wilhelm

Furtwängler, Josef Krips, Hans Hotter and others. It was during this first visit that Legge began negotiations with the Austrian conductor Herbert von Karajan (see box, page 186). Karajan later signed an exclusive contract that marked the beginning of a long-term relationship with EMI, and which helped to launch him on his spectacular international career.

It was also during this first visit to Austria that Legge met and auditioned his future second wife, the soprano Elisabeth Schwarzkopf. He had spotted her in 1946, whilst she was singing Rosina in *Il barbiere de Siviglia*. In a subsequent audition, at which Karajan was present, Legge put her through her paces with a Hugo Wolf song, "Wer rief dich denn?" Schwarzkopf later wrote of the audition: "This stranger [Legge] had me sing the last phrase in untold different ways, colours and expressions until – after an hour – Karajan fled, mumbling, 'This is pure sadism'." [*On and Off the Record*, ibid., p.64] Schwarzkopf got the contract and, in 1953, she and Legge were married.

The process of post-war reconstruction was boosted when, in 1945, Legge created a new London-based orchestra, the Philharmonia. The amount of recording EMI had to offer the new orchestra enabled it to flourish during Legge's time with the Company. By selecting the best available musicians, Legge and the orchestra set new standards of British orchestral playing, and EMI made many important recordings with this ensemble, using conductors as diverse as Herbert von Karajan, Josef Krips, Sir Malcolm Sargent, Carlo Maria Giulini, Otto Klemperer (see box, page 200), Wilhelm Furtwängler, Warwick Braithwaite, Sir Arthur Bliss, Sir William Walton and others. In 1954, the orchestra made its first recordings under the baton of Otto Klemperer: they marked the beginning of an 18-year association between Klemperer, EMI and the orchestra. In *Putting the Record Straight* (London 1981), the record producer John Culshaw wrote of this relationship: "Klemperer's recordings for EMI with the Philharmonia Orchestra until his death in 1973 became not only legendary, they were best sellers as well."

In 1946, British musical life was further enhanced when Sir Thomas Beecham formed the Royal Philharmonic Orchestra. With his new orchestra, Beecham began a series of outstanding recordings for EMI, including several complete operas, in a schedule that continued until shortly before his death in 1961.

In September 1946, EMI began to make records once again in Central Europe. The venue for the first session was Vienna's Musikvereinssaal, which was to be the scene of many great recordings over the next decade. The first work was Beethoven's Eighth Symphony, with the Vienna Philharmonic Orchestra

The Spanish virtuoso Andrés Segovia (1893–1987) was responsible for re-establishing the guitar as a serious classical instrument. He recorded for HMV during the 1930s and returned to Abbey Road for the last time in 1949 to make recordings of Castelnuovo-Tedesco's First Guitar Concerto and a number of other works.

MARIA CALLAS (1923–1977)

★

Maria Callas is the best-known operatic soprano in living memory, representing to the world at large the quintessential *diva* – gifted, glamorous, temperamental and, ultimately, tragic. She was born Maria Anna Sophie Cecilia Kalogeropoulos in New York of Greek immigrant parents. When her parents separated in 1937 she returned to Greece with her mother. After studying at the Athens Conservatory, she sang with the Lyric Opera Company in Athens until 1945. She then returned to New York, determined to make a career in America, but achieved nothing until she secured an engagement to sing the lead in Ponchielli's opera *La Gioconda* in 1947 at the Arena in Verona. There she met the veteran conductor Tullio Serafin, and also the wealthy industrialist Giovanni Battista Meneghini, who soon became her manager and married her a few years later. During her early career in Italy she was offered only the heaviest dramatic parts, like Puccini's Turandot and Wagner's Isolde. Then, under the guidance of Serafin, she startled the musical world by singing the coloratura role of Elvira in *I puritani* by Bellini at La Fenice in Venice just a few days after undertaking her first Brünnhilde in Wagner's *Walküre*. This was the turning point in her career: she dropped the heavier parts to concentrate on reviving the long-neglected *bel canto* operas of Bellini, Donizetti and Rossini.

In 1951 Callas opened the season at La Scala, Milan, in *I vespri siciliani* by Verdi, scoring a notable success which firmly established her in the house that was to be the scene of her greatest triumphs for the next seven years. In 1952, after lengthy negotiations, Walter Legge persuaded Callas to sign an exclusive EMI recording contract, the first fruit of which was Donizetti's *Lucia di Lammermoor* (Columbia 33CX 1131–2), made in Florence. Soon afterwards she began to record the celebrated series of complete operas at La Scala which represent

her art at its finest. In 1954 Callas dramatically changed her appearance, reducing her weight by some 30 kilos and turning herself into a glamorous and svelte beauty. Her stage performances improved in terms of dramatic intensity under the guidance of directors like Luchino Visconti and Franco Zeffirelli, and she continued to record several complete operas and recitals

for EMI each year. In addition to La Scala, she appeared regularly at Covent Garden in London and also in the United States, first in Chicago and then at the Metropolitan in New York.

By the end of the 1950s Callas had reached the pinnacle of her profession, and she turned her attention to the international social set. She became attracted to the Greek shipping magnate Aristotle Onassis and started to neglect her career; during 1958 she was involved in a series of highly publicized disputes with the managements of the Rome Opera, La Scala and the New York Metropolitan, and terminated her relationships with all three. In 1959, she separated from Meneghini in order to live with Onassis and reduced her public appearance to a few concerts each year. In 1964, when her relationship with Onassis

was beginning to founder, she was persuaded by Zeffirelli to return to the stage in a triumphant new production of Puccini's *Tosca* at Covent Garden and, shortly afterwards, Bellini's *Norma* in Paris. In May 1965, suffering from problems of blood pressure, she was unable to finish her last *Norma* in Paris, and in London a few months later she sang her last ever performance on stage as Tosca.

When Onassis tired of her, Callas was devastated. She tried to find new interests, making an unsuccessful film of the play *Medea* by Euripides directed by Pasolini, and giving a series of master classes at the Juilliard School of Music in New York. She began a relationship with her old colleague Giuseppe di Stefano, who talked her into undertaking an extensive international recital tour with him. She sang for the last time in public in Sapporo, Japan on 11 November, 1974. The liaison with di Stefano ended and Callas finished her days as a sad, lonely recluse in her Paris flat, where she died on 16 September, 1977.

Her voice, frequently the subject of controversy, possessed an individuality, a variety of tone colour and an exceptional agility which made it ideal for a wide range of roles. Always a perfectionist, she *became* the part she impersonated on stage. She set standards by which others are now measured. Tito Gobbi, who partnered Callas in many recordings and stage performances, said of her in his autobiography *My Life*: "She shone for all too brief a while in the world of opera, like a vivid flame attracting the attention of the whole world, and she had a strange magic that was all her own."

The first Columbia 12" LP, 33CX 1001.

Left Bayreuth Festival, 1951
Walter Legge made the first ever complete recording of *Die Meistersinger*, which was conducted by Herbert von Karajan.

conducted by Herbert von Karajan (Columbia LX 988–90). This was followed immediately by other titles with the same orchestra and conductor and by recordings with Elisabeth Schwarzkopf, Irmgard Seefried and Hans Hotter. The following year, Legge returned to Vienna for a more extended period and recorded both Karajan and Furtwängler with the Vienna Philharmonic Orchestra; particularly noteworthy was Brahms's Requiem (Columbia LX 1055–64), with Elisabeth Schwarzkopf and Hans Hotter and the Vienna Philharmonic conducted by Karajan. With the latest recording technology, not least the introduction of tape, Legge was able to initiate a programme of milestone recordings of complete operas. These included *Le nozze di Figaro* (Columbia 33CX 1007–9) and *Die Zauberflöte* (Columbia 33CX 1013–15) by Mozart, both recorded in 1950, with casts featuring Elisabeth Schwarzkopf, Irmgard Seefried, Sena Jurinac and Erich Kunz; they were among EMI's earliest releases of long-playing records.

In 1951, Legge gained recording rights – on behalf of EMI – to the restored Bayreuth Wagner Festival. During that year's festival, Legge produced what became EMI's first LP version of Beethoven's Ninth Symphony (HMV ALP 1286–7). On that occasion, the Bayreuth Festival Orchestra and Chorus were conducted by Furtwängler; the soloists were Schwarzkopf, Hopf, Höngen and Edelmann. Despite the many intrigues and the jealousies between the Wagner family and the conductors Karajan and Furtwängler, Legge recorded *Die Meistersinger von Nürnberg*, later released in both 78-rpm and LP formats (Columbia LX 1465–98 and Columbia LP 33CX 1021–5), with Schwarzkopf, Kunz, Hopf, Unger, Edelmann and the Bayreuth Festival Chorus and Orchestra under Karajan. At 34 records, this was the longest work ever released on the 78-rpm format.

Of all EMI's post-war singers, Maria Callas (see box, page 190) was by common consent the greatest. It has been said that during the course of the 20th century three singers – Enrico Caruso, Feodor Chaliapin and Maria Callas – dominated and defined operatic performance in the opera house and on record. All three recorded for either The Gramophone Company or Columbia and had recordings released by EMI. During her career, Maria Callas recorded more than 20 complete operas and several recital discs, most of them for EMI. She made her first appearance in an EMI record catalogue in 1949, with a recording of "Casta Diva" from Bellini's opera *Norma* (Parlophone R 30041) issued under licence from the Italian record company Cetra. In the almost 50 years since the first appearance of that record, Callas has never been absent from EMI's classical catalogues. By the mid-1950s, she had recorded 10 complete operas, including Donizetti's *Lucia di Lammermoor*, with Giuseppe di Stefano and Tito Gobbi (Columbia 33CX 1131–2), and *I puritani* by Bellini with di Stefano and Rolando Panerai (Columbia 33CX 1058–9), *Norma*, with Mario Filippeschi and Ebe Stignani (Columbia 33CX 1179–81). Puccini's *Tosca*, with di Stefano and Gobbi (Columbia 33CX 1094–5). The mixing of rare perfectionist talents such as Callas and Legge in the circumstances of such demanding recording programmes did not always result in sweetness and harmony. However, respect between artists was at the core of their relationship, as was illustrated in March 1959, when Legge wrote to David Bicknell about the stereo re-make of *Lucia di Lammermoor:*

Lucia was completed in eleven sessions and unless I am very much mistaken will be a sensational success. Callas has never sung so well, and at the end of the ordeal all members of the cast were still on speaking terms. [Callas Artist File, EMI Music Archive]

Walter Legge earned for himself the reputation of a master craftsman able to bring together and inspire – or terrify – the finest musicians. However, as a precociously creative being within an organization like EMI, he was at times difficult to manage. An imperious nature and ferocious temperament were combined in a personality more in keeping with that of a triumphal renaissance prince than of a record company employee. Nevertheless, between 1945 and 1964 (the year he left EMI), and despite occasionally tense relationships with his colleagues and the Company's artists, Legge produced a series of consistently great recordings which set standards for others all over the world and remain the jewels of the current EMI classical catalogue.

Il barbiere di Siviglia

DAVID BICKNELL

Walter Legge was not alone in re-establishing EMI's credentials as the world's greatest classical record company after the war. David Bicknell was also engaged in the search for talent and recording opportunities in post-war Europe, specifically in Italy. On his first post-war visit in 1946, he found La Scala destroyed and Italy's musical centre temporarily removed to Rome. In a detailed report to EMI in London, Bicknell wrote of the poor standard of singer he found:

The best performances are being given largely by those singers who were famous before the war and who in some cases have been before the public for 20 years or more, i.e. Gigli, Lauri-Volpi, Caniglia, Stignani. Even such old artists as Tito Schipa (now 58 years of age) give occasional performances. There are few singers to replace these veterans and conditions are not likely to produce them. [David Bicknell, "Report on Artistes and the Musical Situation in Europe – Autumn 1946 – as affecting EMI Ltd". Board Papers, EMI Music Archive]

Bicknell noted that "Gigli [then 56] is still the finest Italian tenor". He thought that Ferruccio Tagliavini was "the most promising young tenor today and hailed erroneously as Gigli's successor. He is really a successor to Tito Schipa as his voice is lighter than Gigli's". He considered the soprano Maria Caniglia "a fine artist who is now at the height of her powers", whilst the young baritone Tito Gobbi was "very popular as opera singer and film star". Bicknell regarded the Orchestra of Santa Cecilia in Rome as the best orchestra in Italy: "I heard it give magnificent performances under de Sabata of the 8th and 9th Symphonies (Beethoven) and under Klemperer, 1st Symphony (Brahms)." In Bicknell's opinion, de Sabata was Italy's greatest Italian conductor

Tito Gobbi
Throughout the 1950s and early 1960s Tito Gobbi (1913–1984) was the principal baritone mainstay of EMI's Italian opera recording programmes on both the HMV and Columbia labels. In all, he appeared in more than 20 complete opera recordings.

The Czech conductor Rafael Kubelik (1914–1996) and the Italian violinist Gioconda de Vito (1907–1994) recording Mozart's Third Violin Concerto in the Kingsway Hall, London, 1959.

JUSSI BJÖRLING
(1911–1960)

Jussi Björling was acclaimed in his time as the operatic tenor *par excellence* in the Italian repertoire. Johan "Jussi" Jonaton Björling was born in Stora Tuna, Sweden, and began singing professionally whilst still a child with his father and two brothers in the Björling Male Voice Quartet. He made his operatic debut in 1930 as Don Ottavio in Mozart's *Don Giovanni* at the Royal Swedish Opera, Stockholm; his international career began in 1935, when he sang Radames in Verdi's *Aida* in Vienna. His reputation was further enhanced through the recordings he made for EMI, initially for the local Swedish branch (sung in Swedish) and later for the international market. On 24 November 1938 he made a spectacularly successful debut at the Metropolitan Opera in New York as Rodolfo in *La bohème*; he sang there during almost every season until 1959 (except for the years 1941–5, when he remained in Sweden). His Covent Garden debut took place in 1939, but he did not return there until March 1960, when despite heart trouble he triumphed again as Rodolfo, the part he had recorded so memorably for EMI a few years earlier (HMV ALP 1409–10). His health continued to deteriorate, and he sang for the last time at a concert in Stockholm on 20 August 1960, just a few weeks before he died. Björling was blessed with a voice of lyrical sweetness that could also ring out heroically when needed. The critic Irving Kolodin said of him: "There was a shine on his sound from the first, and he was musically exemplary in everything he did. He had a beautiful gift and he used it not only well but wisely."

after Toscanini and, with Tullio Serafin, the greatest operatic conductor. By the time he had left all the performers mentioned by Bicknell in his report were either established EMI recording artists, or had become contracted to the Company. At the conclusion of his artistic assessment of Italy, Bicknell observed – in what transpired to be an amusing and highly ironic comment concerning instrumentalists – "the best [are] violinist Gioconda de Vito, and cellist Enrico Mainardi. Neither are exceptional." Evidently, Gioconda de Vito impressed Bicknell more than he thought at the time, as they were married two years later. Within a few months of re-establishing EMI's presence in Italy, David Bicknell made the Company's first post-war recording of a complete Italian opera, Verdi's *Aida* (HMV DB 6392–411), featuring Gigli and Maria Caniglia and conducted by Tullio Serafin.

In 1948, the brilliant young Italian conductor Guido Cantelli, a figure seen by many as the natural successor to Toscanini, began his EMI recording career – a career that ended tragically in 1956, when he was killed in an air-crash. The 1950 release of Cantelli's recording of Tchaikovsky's Fifth Symphony with the Orchestra of La Scala (HMV DB 21187–91) was hailed as a triumph. The recording standards achieved created such demand for this record that EMI chose it as one of its first classical releases on LP (HMV ALP 1001). In the circumstances of the recording studio, Cantelli became a dedicated – if temperamental – perfectionist. Nonetheless, David Bicknell, who produced many of his recordings, said of his work: "I was usually enchanted … and never disappointed". [*Gramophone*, Vol.34, 1957] In his short recording career, Cantelli's partnership with the Philharmonia Orchestra yielded several great recordings, including Mozart's Symphony No.29 (HMV ALP 1461), Brahms's Third Symphony (HMV BLP 1083) and Ravel's *Daphnis et Chloé* Suite No.2 (HMV BLP 1089).

The Swedish tenor Jussi Björling (see box) the greatest lyric tenor of his generation, began his recording career in the 1920s as a child artist. His adult career began in the 1930s, when his recording activities encompassed Swedish ballads, folksongs and operatic arias. During the war, Björling remained in neutral Sweden, where he made a handful of operatic records. Shortly before his tragic death in 1960, at the age of only 49, Björling sang the role of Pinkerton in the famous stereo recording of Puccini's *Madama Butterfly* (HMV ALP 1795–7 and ASD 373–5). Recalling the singer and his final EMI recording, David Bicknell wrote in a tribute:

He had had a heart attack before he started and he had a small heart attack in the middle. I offered to suspend the recording but he would not hear of it. "Give me a few days and I shall be fine again" he said and

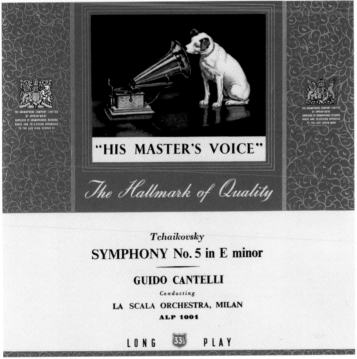

VICTORIA DE LOS ANGELES (BORN 1923)

★

Victoria de los Angeles' exceptional vocal talents have endeared her to millions during an illustrious career spanning more than 50 years. Victoria de los Angeles López García graduated at the astonishingly early age of 18 with full honours from the conservatory in her native Barcelona. Whilst still a student, she had begun to sing with the Spanish early music group Ars Musicae. She gave her first professional solo recital on 19 May 1944 in the Palay de la Música Catalana in Barcelona. Her operatic debut followed in January 1945, when she sang the Countess in *Le nozze di Figaro* at the Gran Teatro del Liceo, Barcelona. In 1947, she made her first recordings (of four Spanish songs) in Barcelona for EMI's Spanish branch, and she won the Geneva International Singing Competition. After this triumph, she was invited by the BBC to sing Salud in Falla's opera *La vida breve*. Her international career was soon established, and throughout the 1950s and 1960s she sang a wide range of roles in Italian, French and German opera in all the leading opera houses of the world. In 1948, she signed an exclusive contract with EMI: the relationship produced more than 21 complete operas and a large number of individual albums. Her warm personality and vibrant voice, capable of many different vocal colours, have made her exceptionally successful as a recitalist in a vast repertoire of French and German song as well as in the music of her native Spain, which is always included in her concerts and which she has recorded extensively. The American critic and composer Virgil Thomson wrote of her debut recital at Carnegie Hall in October 1950: "The voice is one of rare natural beauty, the schooling impeccable, the artistry first class. Here is vocal delight unique to our time".

so he proved to be, and he sang at the top of his form to the end. [*Gramophone*, Vol. 38, November 1960]

In 1948, HMV signed a contract with the talented young Spanish soprano Victoria de los Angeles (see box). The early recordings she made of Spanish songs established her reputation among the record-buying public across the world. She was easy to work with and very popular with recording executives. Victor Olof wrote of her: "Commercially, we have to consider that there is no artist on

Top Victoria de los Angeles recording *Cavalleria rusticana* with the tenor Franco Corelli in 1962.

Below Early LPs were issued in sleeves with standard designs based on the labels. This is ALP 1001, the first HMV 12" LP.

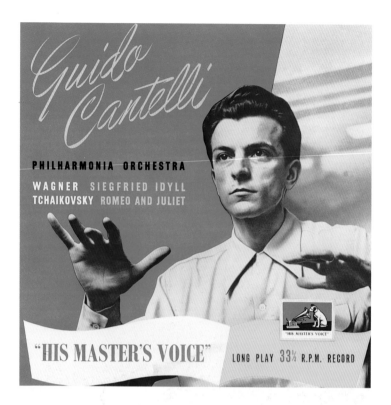

The Italian conductor Guido Cantelli (1920–1956) whose promising career was tragically cut short when he was killed in an air crash at the age of 36.

the horizon nor in the operatic field today who can be regarded on the same level as Victoria." During 1956, Victoria de los Angeles led the cast-list in what is regarded by many as the definitive recording of *La bohème* (HMV ALP 1409–10). David Bicknell wrote of this set:

I am very proud that I played a part in bringing Sir Thomas [Beecham], Jussi Björling and Victoria de los Angeles together for the recording of *La bohème* in New York in April 1956. A great success it turned out to be. Judging by the sales, one of the greatest, if not the greatest, success of its kind in the history of the gramophone industry. [*Gramophone*, Vol.38, November 1960]

Before the war, EMI's best-selling classical records were single discs of short pieces. In sharp contrast, EMI's post-war classical catalogues were dominated by recordings of complete works. However, many record buyers still preferred (or could only afford) single records, several of which became popular hits. One such record was "The Nuns' Chorus" from Johann Strauss II's *Casanova* (HMV C 3711); sung by the German soprano Anni Frind, it gained enormous popularity after it was broadcast on the BBC. Originally recorded in 1928, it was first released in Britain in 1932 (as HMV C 2435), but it achieved only moderate sales at the time

and did not survive the wartime deletions. Its success as a reissue in the late 1940s was notable and reflected both the growing demand for popular light classical music (see below and Chapter 6), and the power of broadcasting to generate interest in – and sales of – gramophone records.

WILHELM FURTWÄNGLER (1886–1954)

Wilhelm Furtwängler was one of the most charismatic conductors of the 20th century. Born in Berlin, Furtwängler showed great natural musical ability as a child. He originally intended to be a composer but first decided to take up conducting. In spite of a somewhat unconventional technique, he soon revealed special musical qualities which quickly took him to the top of his profession. When Nikisch died in 1922, the young Furtwängler succeeded him as conductor of the Berlin Philharmonic Orchestra, a post he was to retain until his death, apart from a short break at the end of the war. In addition to Berlin, Furtwängler frequently conducted the Vienna Philharmonic Orchestra, and his operatic engagements in London, Bayreuth and elsewhere were justly famous. His almost metaphysical approach to conducting resulted in deeply moving interpretations of the symphonic repertoire of Beethoven, Brahms and Bruckner, much of which he recorded for EMI. Of the many great musicians who paid tribute to his unique, quasi-mystical talents, Pablo Casals called him "the greatest conductor I have ever known" and Yehudi Menuhin said: "In listening to him, it is the impression of vast, pulsating space which is most overwhelming."

Rhapsody

REBIRTH THROUGH THE LP AND STEREO

By the early 1950s, EMI's classical record business was transformed by dramatic changes in technology, in particular the introduction of tape into the recording studio, and the advent of the LP (see Chapter 4). Although tape might have freed artists from the tyranny of the four-minute duration of a 78-rpm side, there was a counter-balancing change in the whole philosophy that had underpinned the art since 1898, when Fred Gaisberg made his first records at Maiden Lane. Yehudi Menuhin, who made recordings using both technologies, noted the nature of this change:

Victor Olof was the senior HMV classical
recording producer from 1957 until his
retirement in 1963.

[78 rpm recording] was like a performance, because there was the
knowledge that no correction was possible. With the advent of tape, the
opportunity to play half an hour or five seconds gave much more freedom.
Certainly one could give a performance of a whole movement if not a
whole concerto. There was something about the concentration of that
little wax disc. It was a remarkable feeling. I can see it now, the idea that
you are going to a given point. You are recording it, you are not playing it
for the public, you are not playing it for any other purpose than just to get
it on this little disc. [*Memoirs of a Musical Dog*, ibid.]

It became apparent that the new tape technology had to be handled
with care, or the consequences could be severe. A prime example of
this occurred in 1954, when it was revealed that, in the course of a
1952 recording of Wagner's *Tristan und Isolde*, featuring Kirsten
Flagstad and the Philharmonia Orchestra conducted by Wilhelm
Furtwängler (HMV ALP 1030–35), two top Cs were sung for the
then elderly Flagstad by the then young Elisabeth Schwarzkopf and
edited into the master tape. Although Flagstad had approved the
arrangement, she was outraged when the news leaked out. The
furore was so great that, despite healthy sales (in Britain more than
17,000 sets were sold during the six months after its release),
Flagstad refused ever to enter EMI's recording studios again.

David Bicknell said: "The LP was a major revolution, because it
enabled us to record works with very little interruption; and
consequently we were able to do justice to performers." [*Memoirs of a
Musical Dog*, ibid.] The creation of EMI's first LP catalogue helped
Legge and Bicknell define new roles for themselves as record
producers, a concept analogous to that of a film producer. In these
new conditions, they were able to forge relationships with artists
based on an equality of status and contribution to the art of record-
making. In his memoirs, Legge described this new role:

I was the first of what are called "Producers" of records. Before I
established myself and my ideas, the attitude of recording managers of all
companies was "we are here in the studio to record as well as we can on
wax what the artists habitually do in the opera house or on the concert
platform". My predecessor, Fred Gaisberg told me: "We are out to make
sound photographs of as many sides as we can get during each session".
My ideas were different. It was my aim to make records that would set
the standards by which public performances and the artist of the future
would be judged – to leave behind a large series of examples of the
best performances of my epoch. [*On and Off the Record*, p.16]

In 1954, EMI released the first ever LP recording of Mozart's
horn concertos (Columbia 33CX 1140). This record featured

DAVID OISTRAKH (1908–1974)

David Oistrakh, universally acknowledged as the greatest violinist of the Soviet Union, was born in Odessa, Russia. In 1930, he won the all-Ukrainian violin competition at Kharkov and, in 1935, he took first prize at Leningrad as the best violinist in Russia. International fame followed two years later when he won the Ysaÿe competition in Brussels. He appeared in Paris and elsewhere in the West before the outbreak of hostilities and the ensuing Cold War prevented his return to Western Europe until 1954. He was one of the first of the new generation of virtually unknown Soviet artists to emerge from behind the Iron Curtain and his success was enormous. Hailed as a master, he quickly became the world celebrity that he remained for the rest of his life. His technical mastery was complete, as was his musicianship, and, because he was always willing to perform new music, many Soviet composers, including Prokofiev, Khachaturian and Shostakovich, wrote works for him. He made a number of recordings for Melodiya (the Soviet record company), as well as for EMI. In a tribute written soon after his death from heart disease, the EMI producer Ronald Kinloch Anderson described David Oistrakh as: "a simple, warm-hearted man of great intelligence, charm, sincerity and integrity who had cultivated his tremendous gifts to their highest point of perfection at the cost of enormous work and concentration."

Dennis Brain and the Philharmonia Orchestra conducted by Herbert von Karajan. On its release, Brain received universal praise for the brilliance of his performance. However, only three years later he was killed in a motoring accident, leaving this recording as the jewel of his musical legacy. Although the record was originally made in mono, in the 1960s it was re-released in re-processed stereo. As such it remained in EMI's catalogue into the 1980s, when once again it was re-released, this time in the original mono on CD.

In the mid-1950s, further recording opportunities arose as Soviet artists began to visit and perform in the West. EMI obtained official permission to record them and as a result was able to release recordings by the violinist David Oistrakh (see box), the pianist Emil Gilels and the cellist Mstislav Rostropovich (see box, page 302), as well as discs of the composers Aram Khachaturian and Dmitri Shostakovich performing their own works.

The least successful aspect of EMI's International Artistes Department activities after the war was the management of relations between EMI and its American licensees, RCA Victor and Columbia Records. During the war, and for several years afterwards, the Company had become almost totally dependent on American-made classical recordings, some of which were unsuited to British or European tastes. However, post-war demand for classical music was so great that EMI was able to persuade the American companies to make records of the best American-based artists specifically for EMI's British and European markets. Recordings made a consequence of these agreements included Jascha Heifetz playing Vieuxtemps' Fifth Violin Concerto, with the London Symphony Orchestra conducted by Sir Malcolm

OTTO KLEMPERER
(1885–1973)

Otto Klemperer benefited in his early musical career from the support of Gustav Mahler. After working in a number of German opera houses, he was eventually appointed in 1927 to the Kroll Opera in Berlin, where his performances were highly acclaimed. The Kroll was forced to close in 1931, and in 1933 Klemperer moved to the United States, where he worked with a number of American orchestras, including the Los Angeles Philharmonic and the Pittsburgh Symphony. After 1939, he suffered a series of grave setbacks, including a brain tumour which left him partly paralysed. After the Second World War, he returned to Europe, working with the Budapest Opera from 1947 to 1954, but he made little impact on the international musical scene. An Indian summer came when Walter Legge invited him to London in the early 1950s for recordings and concerts with the Philharmonia Orchestra. His 1955 recordings of Beethoven's Third, Fifth and Seventh Symphonies (33CX 1346, 33C 1051 and 33CX 1379) caused a sensation and re-established his reputation as a giant among conductors. After Karajan left to take over the Berlin Philharmonic Orchestra, Klemperer became principal conductor of the Philharmonia (later New Philharmonia) Orchestra, with which he went on to make many outstanding recordings until his retirement in 1972. Famed for his caustic wit and brusque manner, Klemperer once said of himself during his time with the Philharmonia: "I am the last of the classical school – when Bruno Walter died, I put my fees up."

Sargent (HMV DB 6547–8), and Artur Rubinstein playing Rachmaninov's Rhapsody on a Theme of Paganini, with the Philharmonia Orchestra conducted by Walter Susskind (HMV DB 6556–8). Until the mid-1950s, despite the activities of Legge, Bicknell and others in Britain and elsewhere in Europe, American-made recordings dominated EMI's classical record catalogues. With the ending of the licensing agreements with RCA Victor and Columbia Records, EMI lost this repertoire.

It was bad luck that those agreements ended just at the time when EMI was desperately trying to recover from the debacle caused by its delay in introducing the LP (see Chapter 4). Furthermore, with new competitors springing up in Britain and Europe, and EMI's own American business – Angel Records – demanding new recordings, the International Artistes Department was forced to act swiftly to retain its existing roster of artists and at the same time enhance its classical catalogue with new recordings. To assist in this process, the Company hired two classical record producers in 1956. One was Victor Olof, and the other was a young Australian musician, Peter Andry, who subsequently succeeded David Bicknell as head of the International Artistes Department.

With the introduction of commercial stereo records in 1958, EMI took another technological leap, but was forced to begin once again to remake its classical record catalogue. Stereo technology, which had been developed by EMI during the 1930s, brought higher quality and definition to the art of recording, and proved a boon to the recording of classical music. However, not everyone saw it that way. Walter Legge had been an early enthusiast for the new process as a means of enhancing recordings, but others saw it rather differently. As Legge wrote:

I soon came into conflict with the technical and sales departments over this. They believed the public wanted the "gimmick" of stereo … It took a long time for me to induce these people that their ideas of stereo were the very opposite of what musicians and the musical public wanted. [*On and Off the Record*, p. 73]

Die Schöpfung

AN EXTRAORDINARY CATALOGUE

By 1961, with its newly expanded team of record producers, EMI had created a first-class classical record catalogue. To achieve this required a massive increase in resources and a vast increase in the number of recording sessions. Before the war, the Company's orchestral recording programme was easily encompassed within 50 or so recording sessions (that is, periods of three hours of recording) per annum. By 1958, 500 sessions were required. In the late 1950s, the demand for orchestral recording was so great that EMI found itself providing sufficient work to maintain, on a virtually full-time basis, two eminent British orchestras. As a consequence of this unprecedented demand for musicians, there was a corresponding increase in recording costs. Before the war, an orchestral session cost less than £100; in 1961, it cost £600. Recording costs for complete operas, which had been around £5,000 each before the war, had risen by 1961 to astronomical levels, with fees for the orchestra, chorus and minor singers alone accounting for £20,000. Notwithstanding these figures, during the four years after 1958, EMI released a total of 355 LPs. This figure includes 53 major works occupying more than one LP. To produce this extraordinary burst of creative activity required a total budget in excess of £1 million.

The soprano Maria Callas and the tenor Giuseppe di Stefano in Donizetti's *Lucia di Lammermoor*, the first opera Callas recorded for EMI, in 1953 in Florence.

The results were impressive. By 1961, the Company was able to boast a classical record catalogue with almost 2,000 LP records, around a quarter of which were in stereo, and was releasing on average 400 fresh classical titles per year. As a result of the brilliance of its team and the massive investment in recording programmes, EMI was able to recapture its leading role in the expanding British and overseas markets in classical records. This was no mean achievement, as the Company had lost the repertoire licensed from RCA Victor and Columbia Records also and faced growing competition. The quality of the Company's recordings was such that it had even been able to build a notable market position in the home territory of its erstwhile licensors: within five years of launching its Angel classical record label in the United States, EMI held 17 per cent of the domestic classical record market. Although sales of classical records accounted for only 16 per cent of EMI's total record turnover, their premium price ensured they were highly profitable: in 1961, classical records contributed almost half of the profits generated by EMI's record division. For EMI's International Artistes Department, the period 1931 to 1961 was a golden era that represented a most extraordinary marriage between art and commerce.

CHAPTER 6

Living Doll

EMI'S POPULAR MUSIC RECORDINGS, 1931–1961

The best thing EMI did for a long time was to strengthen its pop Artist and Repertoire departments. As a result, our own internally produced repertoire increased in volume and in stature, and when EMI Records was formed in 1957 we had the finest team of Artist and Repertoire managers the industry's ever known.
[Interview, L. G. Wood, managing director, EMI Records, 1959–1966]

Looking on the Bright Side of Life
SURVIVING THE DEPRESSION, 1931–1939

GEORGE FORMBY
(1904–1961)

In the 1930s and early 1940s, George Formby was Britain's foremost comic vocalist and a major film-star. George Hoy Booth was born in Wigan, Lancashire, the son of George Formby, a famous music hall comedian. After his father's death in 1921, George went on the halls to support the family. Using his mother's name of Hoy, he attempted without success to continue his father's old act. Beryl Ingham, another artist, rescued him, and encouraged him to find fresh material and develop his own personality. He started using his father's old stage name and introduced his ukelele into the act, to great effect. He and Beryl were married in 1924 and thereafter she managed his career with skill and determination. He starred in a number of touring revues and made his first full length film, *Boots, Boots*, in 1934, and signed his first EMI contract in 1935. His first big hit, "When I'm Cleaning Windows" (Regal-Zonophone MR 2199), was released in 1936, and many others followed. Formby's record sales were enormous. He became one of the most popular artists to broadcast and appear on the variety halls in Britain, whilst he continued to make a succession of hit comedy films until 1946. After the war, tastes changed and Formby's career declined. Formby's style was always simple and homespun, and he sang his saucy songs in a Lancashire accent with an irresistible grin. He said of his success: "I wasn't very good, but I had something the public seemed to want."

Just as the International Artistes Department was forced to reorganize and rationalize in response to the Depression (see Chapter 5), so, too, were the Company's various popular music labels. At the end of 1931, after price cuts across the whole product range failed to arrest the decline in sales, EMI merged the Regal and Zonophone budget labels and created a single Regal-Zonophone catalogue, priced at one shilling and six pence (7.5 pence). By the end of the decade, this label handled many important British popular artists, including Gracie (later Dame Gracie) Fields (see box, page 217), George Formby (see box), and the Joe Loss Dance Band. However, to survive the Depression and to get the full benefits of integration, it was necessary to implement more significant label and catalogue changes.

An important change was the transformation of the long-established HMV Plum label series (see Chapter 2) from a miscellaneous, mainly popular, music series into a vehicle for records of various kinds of classical music, including light classics featuring performers such as the Australian bass-baritone Peter Dawson. His three pages of recordings in the HMV catalogue, consisting of songs such as "The Floral Dance" (HMV C 2698) and "On the road to Mandalay" (HMV C 1770), achieved total sales in excess of one million copies in the decade to 1938 and were a mainstay of the pre-war HMV catalogue. Furthermore, after 1931, the bulk of releases in the Plum label series were of British classical music (see Chapter 5). However, some popular performers – such as Noël (later Sir Noël) Coward (see box, page 215) – continued to be released on this label, as were certain other non-classical records.

In February 1935, as part of the popular record catalogue reorganization, HMV created the one shilling and six pence (7.5 pence) 10-inch Magenta label to release dance band, jazz and swing music records, together with light vocal music by the singers Al Bowlly (see box, page 216), Elsie Carlisle, Monte Rey, Sam Browne, Leslie Hutchinson ("Hutch") (see box, page 219) and others. In addition, this catalogue contained records of light orchestral and organ music, together with live recordings of such variety artists as Max Miller, Arthur Askey and Richard Murdoch. Records of popular children's stories, songs and hymns introduced by the BBC children's radio performer Derek McCulloch ("Uncle Mac") were also to be found in the series. Among the other children's records listed were a number of special recordings taken from the soundtracks of Walt Disney cartoon films. These came complete with brightly coloured labels and covers featuring Disney characters.

Columbia's popular record catalogues, including the popular-classical hybrid Parlophone-Odeon label, were also rationalized, and two new Columbia dance and swing music labels were introduced. Despite these efforts to stimulate the record business, it continued to decline, and with it investment in recordings and

"BERYLDENE".
MAINS ROAD.
LITTLE SINGLETON,
Nr. BLACKPOOL.
PHONE: POULTON-LE-FYLDE 400.

NEW HIPPODROME.
COVENTRY.
19th. February.1938.

Sir Louis Sterling,
Electric and Musical Industries Ltd.
Blyth Road.
Hayes.
Middlesex.

Dear Sir,

May I take this opportunity of thanking you very much indeed for the beautiful gift I so kindly received on my last visit to the Recording Studios. It was a marvellous idea to have the matrix of the Window Cleaner Record done, and it is something I shall value more than words can express.

Thank you very much for your kind remarks contained in your letter and there is nobody more delighted than I am that the particular song has been such a success, and I sincerely trust it will not be long before we get another song as successful as that one.

With all good wishes,

Yours sincerely,

George Formby

George Formby letter
Formby thanking Sir Louis Sterling for presenting him with a metal matrix of one of his hits.

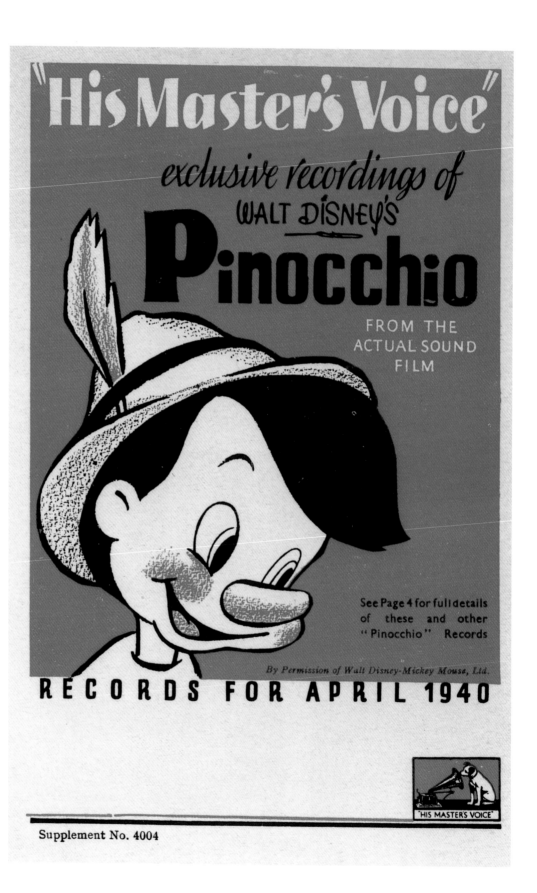

Supplement No. 4004

The records of songs and music from Walt Disney's cartoon films were and remain among the most popular of all children's releases.

PAUL ROBESON
(1898–1976)

Paul Robeson's commanding presence and superb bass voice made him the best-known black actor and singer of his time. Born in Princeton, New Jersey, the son of a former slave, Robeson abandoned a law career to take up acting. After several straight plays in New York and London, he had his first big success in *All God's Chillun Got Wings* in 1924 and the controversial *Emperor Jones* in 1925. That year he gave his first recital of Negro spirituals, revealing a depth of sincerity and musicality that greatly appealed to a wide audience. He returned to Britain in 1928 to star in *Show Boat*, in which he sang "Ol' Man River", a song with which he became indelibly associated. During an extended stay in Britain in the 1930s, he made a series of films. Many of his most successful HMV records were songs from his films. He returned to the United States in 1939, where he appeared in theatrical productions, including Shakespeare's *Othello*, the title role of which he had previously performed in London in 1930. An enthusiastic proponent of civil rights for black Americans, Robeson's career was halted when he embraced communism. He became involved in the McCarthy trials in the 1950s and, as a result, had his passport confiscated for a time. In 1959 he gave his final performance of *Othello* and in 1963 ill-health forced his retirement. After his first New York recital, Alexander Woolcott described Robeson's voice as: "the best musical instrument wrought by nature in our time."

marketing. The monthly record supplements bear witness to this decline. At the beginning of the 1930s, they were printed on high-quality art paper; by 1939, they were reduced to the cheapest paper, and often consisted of just a single sheet.

This calamitous collapse was caused by various factors. The Great Depression killed much of the demand, particularly among working-class consumers, who during the 1920s had been the backbone of the record business. With unemployment reaching more than 20 per cent of the insured workforce, the purchase of items like gramophone records seemed a luxury easily dispensed with. Collapsing record sales were a reflection of other important changes taking place in the leisure market which, in the 1930s, began to work against the record industry, and particularly against the sale of popular music records. EMI's chairman, Alfred Clark, identified one of these changes:

There is still a large public interest in the best recordings, but not as large as it formerly was and we have no doubt that this is due to the competition of broadcasting. We find, for instance, that in foreign countries where radio broadcasting is less efficient and less interesting, its detrimental effect upon the sale of records is less marked. [Chairman's Statement, Annual Meeting, EMI, 1935]

Competition from broadcasting was compounded by the BBC ban on advertising. Quite simply, EMI was unable to plug its records via the BBC. Paradoxically, however, technology came to the rescue. During the 1930s, radios capable of receiving medium- and short-wave transmissions from Europe and further afield were developed by EMI and other manufacturers. As a consequence of the rapid take-up of these new radios in Britain, mass audiences were created for English language programmes emanating from commercial continental radio stations. Programmes from these sources included several which were sponsored and produced by EMI's labels. An early example was the series of Sunday afternoon broadcasts of HMV records, begun in December 1931 from Radio Paris and introduced by Rex Palmer, formerly a BBC presenter and head of the International Artistes Department. The success of this new and novel way of advertising paved the way for other EMI-sponsored programmes, which, by the end of the decade, were being broadcast by all the major European English language commercial radio stations. Although EMI's association with commercial broadcasting opened up new methods of selling records, in the circumstances of the Depression, these programmes had a minimal effect on record sales, and, until the tide turned, they did little more than keep EMI's products before the public. In the longer term, they paved the way for EMI's post-war venture into broadcasting pop music on Radio Luxembourg.

The Blue Angel

MUSICALS AND TALKING PICTURES

Although the inter-war years saw the emergence of new artists, few had the impact, talent or versatility of Paul Robeson (see box, page 208). This great black American singer and actor began his recording career in 1925. His greatest musical triumph came with *Show Boat*, which opened in London in May 1928 at the Drury Lane Theatre. Over the next decade, the recording he made with Paul Whiteman and his Orchestra of "Vocal Gems from *Show Boat*", coupled with "Ol' Man River" (HMV C 1505), sold nearly 200,000 copies, and cemented his reputation with British audiences. Robeson spent much of the 1930s in Britain, where he starred in films and stage productions; he also made many records, which together sold more than one million copies. Robeson's enormous talent was readily acknowledged by the Company, who, at the time of his 1929 debut in Germany, told Electrola:

Paul Robeson is an exceptionally talented artist, with great dramatic powers, and a poignant appeal that is responsible for a large measure of the success which has attended his efforts in this country and the United States. His singing has drawn appreciation from the most unlikely quarters, and his records are deservedly popular.
[Robeson Artist File, EMI Music Archive]

Another major development in technology – talking pictures – began to affect the market for popular records. It became clear that the British public was turning away from popular records and looking to the cinema, and specifically to Hollywood musicals, for light entertainment. EMI recognized this change and began releasing records of hit songs from the movies. Among the earliest examples of this new musical genre were the recordings of Maurice Chevalier, particularly the 1929 HMV release that became associated with his name for the rest of his life, "Louise" coupled with "On Top of the World" (HMV B 3073), from his Hollywood musical *Innocents of Paris*.

Marlene Dietrich's recording of "Falling in Love Again" from the film *The Blue Angel*, coupled with "Blond Women"

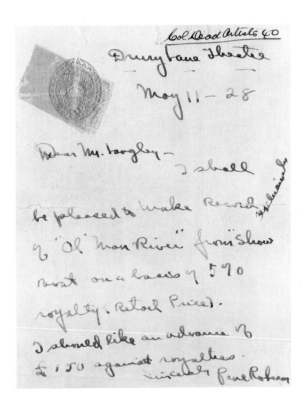

In 1928, Paul Robeson recorded "Ol' man river" from the musical *Show Boat*. It was his greatest success. This letter contract, written by Robeson, in which he agrees to record "Ol' man river" reveals the still informal nature of such agreements.

RAY NOBLE
(1903–1978)

The composer and arranger Ray Noble led
one of the best recording bands in Britain in
the 1930s, and was the first British bandleader
to become popular in America. Born in
Brighton, Sussex, Noble began writing songs
whilst still at school, but achieved his early
success as an arranger and recording artist.
From 1929 to 1934, he was employed as
director of light music by The Gramophone
Company, and all records made by the "house"
band of HMV during that period were directed
by him. The band was originally called the New
Mayfair Dance Orchestra but later went under
Ray Noble's name. Noble produced polished
and tasteful recordings of smooth-sounding
dance music, frequently with distinctive vocals
by the crooner Al Bowlly, which were
universally acclaimed and sold in vast quantities,
not only in Britain but also in America. Once
established on HMV, Ray Noble began to
record more and more of his own
compositions. These proved to be his greatest
successes, especially "Goodnight, sweetheart",
which became his signature tune. In 1934,
Noble went to New York and quickly
established himself there in a long residency at
the Rainbow Room, leading an all-star band
assembled by Glen Miller, with Al Bowlly as
vocalist. In a feature article in April 1934,
Melody Maker summed him up as "an
unbeatable combination of smash-song-writer,
ultra-modern commercial orchestrator, and
disciplinarian band leader."

Right Marlene Dietrich as Lola in the film
The Blue Angel.

(HMV B 3525), made in Germany during 1930, remains a raw,
haunting and timeless reminder of her art and times. Through a
licensing deal with Brunswick, another American record
company, Columbia brought the records of other film stars to
British audiences. Among the best-known of Fred Astaire's film
hits were "Let's face the music and dance" and "Let yourself go"
(Columbia DB 1633), and "Top Hat, White Tie and Tails",
coupled with "Cheek to Cheek" (Columbia DB 1825). By
contemporary standards, these records sold very well, as the
head of Columbia's British Sales Department told Louis Sterling
in 1936: "Although *Follow the Fleet* has not been as great a success
as *Top Hat* we have sold of the three Fred Astaire records
approximately 25,000 records to date at two shillings and six
pence [12.5 pence], and they are still selling well." Among Bing
Crosby's early Columbia releases was "Brother, can you spare
a dime" (Columbia DB 1829), a melancholy anthem to
The Depression.

Record buyers and filmgoers in the mid- and late 1930s did
not go to the cinema to watch films of gritty reality. Instead, they
looked for escapism in lush musicals, where the hero always got
his girl. The most successful songs derived from such films were
the duets by Jeanette MacDonald and Nelson Eddy. Between
1936 and 1938, their recordings of "Ah! sweet mystery of life"
and "Indian Love Call" (HMV DA 1537), from the film *Rose
Marie*, and "Will you remember?", coupled with "Farewell to
Dreams" (HMV DA 1559), from the film *Maytime*, were best

sellers both in Britain and in EMI's overseas markets. Musical films sometimes produced a hit song that swept the country. Allan Jones's 1938 film *The Firefly* produced "Donkey Serenade" and "Giannina mia" (HMV B 8714), which achieved British sales of more than 50,000 copies in the year following its release.

Lovely to Look at

DANCE BAND MUSIC

Throughout the 1930s, new British dance band talent continued to emerge. The most important of these newcomers was the songwriter, arranger and conductor Ray Noble (see box, page 210). Noble had joined HMV in 1929 as director of light and dance music. At the time, he was already the conductor of HMV's house orchestra, the New Mayfair Dance Orchestra. The reputation of Noble and his orchestra was such that he was able to pick his band members from the best London players. Vocalists who recorded with this ensemble included Al Bowlly, Cavan O'Connor, Stuart Richardson and Anona Winn. Nat Gonella, the great British jazz trumpeter, also featured in early recordings. During his time at HMV, Ray Noble composed and recorded hits such as "Goodnight, sweetheart' (HMV B 5984), "Love is the sweetest thing" (HMV B 6245) and "The very thought of you" (HMV B 6482). He was immensely valuable to HMV and was kept fully occupied as a result. In 1933, Rex Palmer tried to explain Noble's workload to RCA Victor (who wanted him to make records for their market):

THOMAS "FATS" WALLER (1904–1943)

Fats Waller, affectionately known as the "Harmful Little Armful", was a gifted composer, an outstanding jazz pianist, and an entertainer with an irrepressible sense of fun that endeared him to millions. Born Thomas Wright Waller in Waverley, New York, he spent his early career playing piano and organ in vaudeville theatres and silent-movie houses, but he soon established a reputation as a composer with songs like "Ain't misbehavin'" and "Honeysuckle Rose". His talent as a "stride" pianist was recognized when, in 1922, he became an Okeh "race" label artist; he also recorded for RCA Victor. His jazz records have always been prized, but it was his exuberant recordings (made from 1934 onwards for RCA Victor and EMI) of the popular songs of the day, often interspersed with comments and irreverent asides, that became huge hits. Waller made a number of recordings for EMI in 1938, including a version of "Ain't misbehavin'" (HMV BD 5415) in which he played the Compton Organ which was then a feature of Abbey Road Studios. He returned again in 1939, when he recorded more titles for EMI, including one of his most imaginative solo piano works, the *London Suite* (HMV B 10059–61). When Waller left London for the last time on 14 June 1939, *Melody Maker* said "One of the most brilliant true jazz artists ever to come from America to Britain, he returns a more popular idol than ever, and will long be remembered with great affection." Fats Waller was a huge man who lived life to the full, working hard and drinking hard.

Thomas "Fats" Waller recording at the Compton organ in Abbey Road Studios in 1938.

Above Duke Ellington was one of the most influential figures in the development of jazz in America.

***Opposite page* Columbia hot rhythm supplement**
During the 1930s records of increasingly diverse forms of American dance music appeared in Britain. This 1931 Columbia dance supplement draws on two such forms, "Hot rhythm dance music", as exemplified in the records of Duke Ellington, and the "Sweet dance music" of artists such as Rudy Vallee.

Ray Noble's time is already very fully occupied, both in orchestration, which naturally cannot be hurried, and in conducting at the studio, particularly now that he is making so many more dance titles, as well as arranging and conducting accompaniments, Vocal Gems, selections etc. and it is virtually impossible to guarantee that every month he would be free to do a complete session of four titles for you, with the prospect that the titles in question might not be required at all for our territory. [Noble Artist File, EMI Music Archive]

Between 1929 and 1933, Ray Noble and the New Mayfair Dance Orchestra sold 1.5 million records in Britain and, in 1932, even in the depths of the Depression, sales of their records amounted to 250,000. Besides Jack Hylton and Ray Noble, HMV dance bands included Ambrose and his Mayfair Orchestra (who appeared on the budget Zonophone label as the Blue Lyres) and Roy Fox and his Orchestra.

Columbia's list of dance bands included Henry Hall and the New BBC Dance Orchestra. BBC engineers used Hall's technically outstanding 1932 recording of "The Teddy Bears' Picnic" (Columbia DB 955) for many years after to test transmission lines. Carroll Gibbons and the Savoy Hotel Orpheans made records for Columbia, which included "Dancing in the dark", coupled with "Have you forgotten" (Columbia CB 407), and "The way you look to-night", coupled with "Never gonna dance" (Columbia FB 1529). In 1929, Jack Payne and his Orchestra recorded his two greatest hits: "The Stein Song", coupled with "Moonshine is better than sunshine" (Columbia CB 62), which sold almost 100,000 copies in that year, and "When it's springtime in the Rockies", coupled with "I'm falling in love again" (Columbia CB 106), sales of which exceeded 70,000. Other long-serving dance bands included Harry Roy and his Orchestra, and Billy Cotton; Cotton started his recording career in 1930, and was still making records and broadcasting in the 1960s.

Nat Gonella and his Orchestra were the most conspicuous imitators of the American style of playing, and the most successful. His scintillating 1935 recording of "Tiger Rag" (Parlophone-Odeon F 161) demonstrated that it was still possible to make and sell popular records. In 1935, 26 recordings by Nat Gonella were listed in the Parlophone catalogue and, by 1938, that figure had risen to 106. British and overseas sales of these records over the same period amounted to 500,000 copies.

STÉPHANE GRAPPELLI
(BORN 1908)

In a career spanning more than 70 years, the Franco-Italian violinist Stéphane Grappelli has raised the art of jazz violin playing to the highest level. Born in Paris, Grappelli began playing the violin at the age of 12. In 1934, he met the gypsy guitarist Django Reinhardt, and they formed a jazz group known as the Quintette of the Hot Club of France. Until the start of the Second World War, they recorded prolifically for EMI's French HMV and Swing labels, starting with titles such as "I'se a muggin" and "Oriental Shuffle" (French HMV K 7704) and "I can't give you anything but love" coupled with "Limehouse Blues" (French HMV K 7706). During the war, Grappelli came to Britain, where he appeared with the pianist George Shearing. When he returned to France in 1946, he teamed up again with Reinhardt until the guitarist's death in 1953, after which he pursued a solo career with many appearances at festivals and on television throughout Europe. In June 1972, following a television appearance together, Grappelli and Yehudi Menuhin made an album for EMI of popular songs in improvisatory-style jazz arrangements with the overall title of *Jealousy* (EMI EMD 5504). Its enormous success prompted a number of further albums. Recalling their work together, Lord Menuhin said of Grappelli: "Stéphane's gift for improvisation is absolutely unique and his sheer musicality never fails to move me."

Stéphane Grappelli (left) and Django Reinhardt, founder members of the Quintette of the Hot Club of France.

Ain't Misbehavin

JAZZ

Although dance band records dominated EMI's popular music record catalogues throughout the inter-war years, jazz records were also prominently represented. The release of such records in the circumstances of the 1930s was something of an act of faith on the part of the Company, and a testimony to the enduring popularity and dynamism of jazz music. The vast majority of these jazz records were derived from American recordings supplied under the RCA Victor and Columbia Records licensing agreements. These provided a treasurehouse of material. By 1939, the Parlophone-Odeon, Columbia and HMV labels each had their own Jazz, Blues, Hot Rhythm and Swing catalogues, which included records featuring artists such as Benny Goodman, Tommy Dorsey, Duke Ellington, Louis Armstrong, Bix Beiderbecke, the Boswell Sisters, Cab Calloway, Artie Shaw, Thomas "Fats" Waller (see box, page 211) and Joe Venuti.

Furthermore, during the mid-1930s, sales of records by Louis Armstrong and Fats Waller were boosted by their London and provincial tours. Waller's inimitable style made him an important recording artist on both sides of the Atlantic. This point was noted by RCA Victor when, in 1934, they wrote advising EMI that: "Fats

Above Prior to 1939, records by the great American jazz trumpeter Louis Armstrong featured in several of EMI's jazz and swing catalogues.

Right By the outbreak of war in 1939, Parlophone had assembled an impressive catalogue of swing records derived from British and American sources.

Waller ... has within the past three months become one of our most popular dance artists, outselling both Duke Ellington and Cab Calloway." However, surviving correspondence at the EMI Music Archive suggests that, in a number of HMV territories, the Fats Waller style was not appreciated. In a 1936 letter to RCA Victor, HMV noted: "many of Fats Waller's recordings would have much larger sales in a number of our territories provided there was no vocal refrain, or that it were more subdued." Fortunately for posterity, this advice was ignored, and, as a consequence, a unique legacy of recordings by this most spontaneous of artists continues to entertain us today.

Duke Ellington was another great American jazz musician to tour pre-war Britain with his orchestra, and during his 1934 British tour he introduced audiences to jazz classics such as "Mood Indigo" and "When a black man's blue" (HMV B 4842),

"Jubilee Stomp" (Parlophone R 144) and "Black and Tan Fantasy" (Parlophone R 3492). Such tours gave a tremendous boost to the sales of jazz records; without them, sales quickly declined. This downward trend can be seen in sales of Louis Armstrong's Parlophone-Odeon records. In 1935, British and overseas sales of eight Armstrong records were around 6,000 copies. Nine records were listed the following year, yet sales had fallen to 4,600, and in 1939, only 44 copies of the one remaining record were sold.

Although the bulk of 1930s classic jazz records came from the United States, some highly important records were made in Europe. Among the best were those made in France by the Quintette of the Hot Club of France, a group whose founding members were the violinist Stéphane Grappelli (see box, page 213), the guitarists Django and Joseph Reinhardt and Roger Chaput, and bass Louis Vola. The Quintette's distinctive sound was exemplified in a 1936 recording of "After you've gone" and "Oriental Shuffle" (HMV B 8479). For Grappelli, these recordings initiated a long and distinguished EMI recording career, one that, in the 1970s, included recordings of jazz duets with his equally famous contemporary, the classical violinist Yehudi Menuhin (see Chapter 9).

Poor Little Rich Girl
BRITISH STARS

In 1928, Britain's then greatest living playwright and performer, Noël Coward, began his recording career as an HMV artist. Three years earlier, his first encounter with the HMV recording studio had been an unmitigated disaster. On that occasion, he made test recordings of "Poor little rich girl" from his show *On with the Dance*, but the Artistes Department rejected them with the comment "voice too weak". However, between 1928 and 1953, Coward made more than 80 HMV recordings; evidently the Artistes Department had changed its opinion of the artist's voice. In 1930, Coward and Gertrude Lawrence recorded two scenes from his play *Private Lives* (HMV C 2043); the disc was an immediate success. In all, 120,000 copies of Coward's recordings were sold during the first six years of his association with HMV. Among the best sellers were "Mad Dogs and Englishmen" (HMV B 4269) and "The Stately Homes of England" (HMV B 8722). Coward wrote of the latter: "I have recorded and sung it all over the world, and it has been popular with everyone except a Mayoress in New Zealand, who thought it let down the British Empire."

SIR NOËL COWARD (1899–1973)

Noël Coward displayed a wide range of talents as composer, playwright, actor, director and performer. Coward began his professional career in 1910 as a child actor. His first major success came in 1923, with the revue *London Calling*, which he wrote and starred in, and the following year he caused a sensation with his serious play *The Vortex*, which dealt with drugs and sex. Over 40 plays, revues and operettas followed, all starring Coward himself. The most successful of his plays were *Hay Fever* and *Private Lives*, and his musicals included *Bitter Sweet*, *Conversation Piece*, *Sail Away* and the spectacular *Cavalcade*, a patriotic pageant that used the full resources of the huge Drury Lane Theatre. Throughout the 1930s, he recorded extensively for HMV; his song, "London Pride" (HMV B 9198), which he recorded in 1941, held a special poignancy for Londoners after the Blitz. Coward also appeared in a number of films, some of which he wrote and directed himself, including the much-praised wartime naval drama, *In Which We Serve*. In 1953, he began to appear in cabaret in London and Las Vegas and a whole new generation discovered his music and his polished and amusing performing style. Throughout his life, Coward saw his work go in and out of fashion: it was often dismissed by the critics as "ephemeral" and "brittle", but he managed to console himself with, in his own words, "the bitter palliative of commercial success." Coward was belatedly knighted in 1969.

Noël Coward and Gertrude Lawrence in a scene from *Private Lives*.

AL BOWLLY
(1899–1941)

★

During the 1930s, Al Bowlly was one of the most popular band singers in Britain, and appeared on hundreds of recordings. Albert Alick Bowlly was born of Greek descent in Maputo (Lourenço Marques) in Mozambique. In 1928, after playing and singing with bands in South Africa, Calcutta, Singapore and Berlin, he came to London to join Fred Elizalde's band at the Savoy. He then moved to the Monseigneur Restaurant with the bands of Roy Fox and, later, Lew Stone. Bowlly's work came to the attention of Ray Noble, at that time director of HMV's dance-band recordings. Noble used him as a vocalist in his recordings, and this resulted in big sales on both sides of the Atlantic, and made Bowlly a star. His rich, dark voice complemented his handsome appearance, making his performances of romantic ballads of the time, like "Time on my hands" (HMV B 5983) and "Please" (HMV B 6283), especially appealing to his female fans. Ray Noble said: "When he sang a love lyric it really got him. The sincerity came through. I have seen him sing at the mike in front of the band and there've been tears in his eyes as he turned away after finishing." In 1934, Bowlly went with Ray Noble to New York where he achieved a huge success, but he soon grew homesick and returned to Britain. He toured the variety theatres and after the outbreak of war, he spent much of his time entertaining British troops. In 1941, he was killed by a bomb whilst sleeping in his London flat.

The need for escapism during this dark period created demand for some rather exotic fare. For a while, recordings of Hawaiian and South American music had a vogue, but for much of the late 1930s, cowboy songs (perhaps stimulated by the Western movies of the time) dominated the monthly release supplements – records such as Al Bowlly's "South of the Border" (HMV BD 706), Les Allen's "Empty Saddles" (Columbia FB 1495), and "Where is my wandering boy tonight?", coupled with "What a friend we have in mother" (Regal-Zonophone MR 3086), by Montana Slim (described as the Yodelling Cowboy).

British light entertainers were also available on various other EMI labels. Among the most accomplished were Kenneth and George Western (known as the Western Brothers). Their dry and polished humour was exemplified in the 1934 recording "The Old School Tie" and "Ain't it gorgeous" (Columbia DX 586), which poked gentle fun at the British class system. But perhaps the most famous male entertainer of the time was George Formby, a Regal-Zonophone artist. The son of a famous earlier Zonophone artist of the same name, he created through his films and such records as "The Window Cleaner" (Regal-Zonophone MR 2199) and "Leanin' on a Lamp Post" (Regal-Zonophone MR 2490) the persona of a not very bright working-class man who eventually wins through: perhaps an ironic image given the state of Britain's eve-of-war military preparedness.

The most important female popular talent of the interwar period was Gracie Fields. With her beguilingly brassy voice, she was the personification of a Northern working-class woman – optimistic, yet at the same time enduring – in her records and films. One of her most successful records was "Looking on the bright side of life" (HMV B 4258). In February 1933,

DAME GRACIE FIELDS
(1898–1979)

★

In the 1930s, Gracie Fields, known as "Our Gracie", was Britain's best-known comedienne and most successful female film star. Born Grace Stansfield in Rochdale, Lancashire, she first appeared in London in 1915 in *Yes I Think So*, which starred her future husband, the comedian Archie Pitt. Pitt's revue *Mr Tower of London* (which ran for over nine years) came to the London Alhambra in 1922 and made Gracie a West End star. She made her first records for HMV in May 1928, including "My blue heaven" and "Because I love you" (HMV B 2733). They were an immediate success and thereafter she recorded regularly. Gracie Fields's first talking picture, *Sally in our Alley*, was released in 1932 and featured one of her most famous songs, "Sally" (HMV B 3879). On 14 February 1933, she visited the Hayes factory to press her four millionth record – "Play, fiddle, play" and "So long lads, we're off" (HMV B 4368). In 1940, she married the Italian director Monty Banks and they moved to America. She soon returned to Britain, however, and spent the war entertaining Allied troops all over the world. Her great hit from that period, "Wish me luck", sold over 150,000 copies. After the war, she went to live in Capri, returning to Britain occasionally for recordings, tours, television appearances and charity shows. Gracie Fields was made a Dame Commander of the British Empire in 1979, and died later that year.

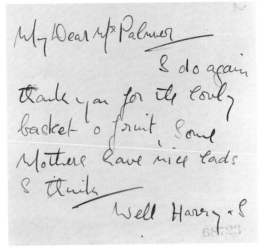

Above Gracie fields pressing her four millionth record, a copy of her hit "Play fiddle play".

Gracie Fields letter
A 1938 letter suggesting that she might record "Land of Hope and Glory", a record which later became one of her most enduring successes.

217

WINSTON CHURCHILL'S EMI WARTIME RECORDINGS

Already a regular BBC broadcaster, Winston Churchill was an experienced microphone speaker when he became prime minister in May 1940. Nor was he unused to the process of making records, having cut his first HMV disc as early as 1909. For many, Churchill's wartime broadcasts on the BBC provided inspiration and the will to go on during a time of great hardship. Early in his premiership, he had expressed the wish that his House of Commons speeches should be broadcast and recorded as they were being delivered in the Chamber. Unfortunately, permission for this was not forthcoming. Instead, after speaking to the House, he broadcast the same speech to the nation. These and other speeches were simultaneously recorded at Abbey Road Studios, and subsequently released as sets of records with special labels bearing the prime minister's image. The titles of Churchill's speeches – such as "This was their finest hour" – were devised at the suggestion of EMI's chairman, Alfred Clark. Although these recordings lack the polish of the late-1940s re-recordings he made for Decca, they provide a contemporary account, and reveal the man's deep emotions and extraordinary spontaneity, as well as the stress under which he was working. Furthermore, they have a remarkable intimacy, surprising in someone whose political experience had taught him how to speak at large gatherings rather than to the silent audience of the gramophone record and the airwaves.

Gracie Fields came to the Hayes record factory to press her four millionth record. At the time, it was reckoned that this prodigious output had given several years' continuous employment to over 120 people at the record factory. In 1935, Gracie Fields's HMV contract expired but, three years later, she returned to the Company, this time as a Regal-Zonophone artist. She specifically asked to be listed on this one shilling and six pence (7.5 pence) label, in order to give her public "which is so largely provincial and poor an opportunity to buy her records" (as Louis Sterling put it). It was coincidental but highly appropriate that, in September 1939 (the month war was declared) HMV released her recording of "Wish me luck", coupled with "Danny Boy" (Regal-Zonophone MR 3118). The first line, "Wish me luck as you wave me goodbye", summed up for many the hopes and fears of a country that, for the second time in just over a generation, was entering a war.

Wish me luck

POPULAR RECORDS DURING THE SECOND WORLD WAR

When war was declared in Britain, the adult population was mobilized and all of the nation's resources were devoted to the cause of defeating the enemy. In what quickly became a struggle for national survival, the government took complete control of the economy and other aspects of daily life, introducing rationing and the evacuation of major population centres. These measures, together with the effects of the blitz, fundamentally altered the aspirations, expectations and lives of the British people. In circumstances similar to those in the First World War (see Chapters 2 and 3), civilians and military personnel alike turned to gramophone records as a means of entertainment during the long hours of boredom and fear. From the start, the war provided a stimulus for popular record sales, a point noted by Alfred Clark, EMI's chairman, when he told shareholders in November 1939:

The war has further stimulated the sales of records and the public seems to realize more and more the need for brighter entertainment in the home itself during the blackened nights when public entertainment is curtailed and movement out of doors dangerous. There can be nothing more satisfying than a gramophone with one's own personal selection of records. [Chairman's Statement, Annual Meeting, EMI, 1939]

LESLIE "HUTCH" HUTCHINSON (1900–1969)

★

An accomplished pianist and stylish vocalist with a voice described as "milk chocolate", Hutch was the epitome of sophisticated cabaret entertainment in London during the 1930s. Born in the West Indies, Hutch went to Paris where he studied the piano and became a protégé of Cole Porter. Porter approved of Hutch's interpretations of his songs (many of which he later recorded), such as "Let's do it" (Parlophone R 342) and "Begin the Beguine" (Parlophone F 1443). The British impresario C. B. Cochran heard him performing in a Parisian bar and invited him to London, where he starred in several of Cochran's revues. Throughout the 1930s, he performed regularly at London's most fashionable night-spots, including the Café de Paris and Quaglino's, becoming the darling of high society. He recorded prolifically for Parlophone, switching to the HMV label in 1940, for which he recorded until 1948. Through his many broadcasts and recordings, he became known to a wide audience who had never seen him in cabaret or in the theatre, but who responded to the charm of his warm voice and inimitable singing style. During the war, he entertained British troops and topped the bill in variety theatres. He returned to the night club circuit after the war. Recalling Hutch, the jazz singer Beryl Bryden said: "He was always charming, always elegant, self-assured, sophisticated and immaculately turned out in full evening dress with a carnation in his buttonhole. Every night he enraptured an often young and well-dressed audience."

The wartime growth in sales of popular music records – despite price increases and the introduction of Purchase Tax – was such that, by 1945, sales were over one third higher than in 1938, although still a fraction of those in the late 1920s. This boom provided EMI with a platform for its post-war investment in popular records (see below). Furthermore, increased sales were all the more remarkable as they had been achieved in the face of the conscription, death or departure of EMI's Artist and Repertoire managers, technical staff and artists.

During the six years of war, the number of new HMV and Columbia record releases was halved. As an example, only 400 records were released on the popular HMV 10-inch Magenta label, compared to the more than 700 released during the four years before 1939. In an attempt to stabilize record releases, several popular Regal-Zonophone and Parlophone artists were transferred to the premium-priced Columbia and HMV labels. As a consequence, by the war's end, the Regal-Zonophone and Parlophone labels had declined to a shadow of their former selves.

Although wartime restrictions reduced opportunities for record-making, popular British artists continued to make records whenever possible. The dominant position played by the BBC in the nation's daily lives resulted in several important records by BBC light entertainment stars. Among these were Arthur Askey and Richard Murdoch, whose off-the-air recording of their BBC show, *Band Waggon*, was released in 1939 (HMV BD 693–5), and Gert and Daisy (Elsie and Doris Waters), whose recording "Food Talk" (HMV Private Recording JH 30), made for the Ministry of

Above A wartime visit to the Hayes factories by King George VI and Queen Elizabeth.

Inset One of the specially made microphones used for royal broadcasts and recordings.

JOE LOSS
(1909–1990)

★

Joe Loss was one of Britain's foremost ballroom bandleaders. Born in the East End of London, Loss led his own band for the first time at London's Astoria ballroom in 1930. During the early 1930s, he alternated between playing in ballrooms, theatrical touring and broadcasting. He began his record career in 1934 on Regal-Zonophone. His first big record hit came in 1939 with Cole Porter's "Begin the Beguine" (MR 3098), with vocal by Chick Henderson. This was quickly followed by "At the Woodchoppers' Ball", coupled with "In the Mood" (MR 3243). Loss later adopted "In the Mood" as his theme tune. The band continued to achieve record hits even after the coming of rock 'n' roll, including "Wheels Cha Cha" (HMV POP 880) in 1961 and "March of the Mods" (HMV POP 1351) in 1964. The Joe Loss Band achieved greater fame when it began to appear on the BBC television series Come Dancing, and it maintained its position as the country's most prestigious strict-tempo and society dance orchestra right up to the time of Loss's reluctant retirement in December 1989, 60 years on from his professional debut. On the occasion of the 50th anniversary of his entry into the business, Joe Loss said of himself: "I love my work. I have always tried to keep abreast of the times and give the public my all. Whether I am playing at Buckingham Palace, Windsor Palace, aboard the QE2 or in any establishment in the world, every night is a premiere for me."

The Joe Loss Orchestra recording at Abbey Road Studios.

Food, managed to combine the right blend of good humour with pertinent propaganda. In addition, HMV released recordings of Winston Churchill's wartime broadcasts (see *Winston Churchill's EMI Wartime Recordings*, page 218) and others made by members of the Royal Family. Other BBC-inspired wartime recordings included two 1941 broadcasts by Quentin Reynolds, the London-based American war correspondent. Reynolds's brilliant use of scathing irony was chillingly applied in broadcasts personally addressed to the Nazi propaganda chief Josef Goebbels, "Dear Doctor …" (HMV BD 940–1), and to Hitler, "Dear Mr S …" (HMV BD 947–8).

However, the mass of the British population at war, whether at home or abroad, needed records of the latest popular escapist romantic music. Until his death in 1941, the singer Al Bowlly filled this demand. His many wartime recordings included a 1940 cover version of "Over the Rainbow" (HMV BD 808), a quintessential song of romance, fantasy and escape from the film *The Wizard of Oz*. Leslie Hutchinson was EMI's most prolific popular romantic singer. In all, 87 "Hutch" records were released between 1939 and 1945. Among them were: "Fools rush in" and "I'll never fail you" (HMV BD 849) and "You're in my arms" and "That Lovely Weekend" (HMV BD 892). The two surviving EMI dance bands, led by Joe Loss (see box) and Victor Silvester (see box, page 223), remained mainstays of the popular record catalogues throughout the war and for years after. Loss made his first records in 1934 for the Regal-Zonophone label, and his last for EMI in 1980, whilst Victor Silvester originally

In 1960, EMI chairman Sir Joseph Lockwood (left) presented Victor Silvester with gold and platinum discs to mark the 25th anniversary of his association with the company.

recorded for Parlophone. In the course of the war, the prolific and versatile Joe Loss released 156 records on the HMV 10-inch Magenta label.

In 1960, Victor Silvester and EMI celebrated the 25th anniversary of their association. During those years, his releases appeared at the extraordinary average of two per month. His 78- and 45-rpm records over this period achieved world sales in excess of 30 million, and, by 1960, sales of his many LP records had reached more than 250,000. In recognition of this remarkable achievement, EMI presented Victor Silvester with Britain's first platinum disc (for singles sales) and a silver LP (for album sales).

Much dance band talent was lost to the forces. This led to the formation of military dance bands such as the RAOC Blue Rockets and the Squadronaires. Their HMV records, originally made for military use, found a market among the civilian record-buying public. To fill the gap, American-made recordings of bands led by artists such as Glenn Miller, Tommy Dorsey, Benny Goodman and Duke Ellington became widely available. Together with the presence in Britain of millions of American servicemen, this helped re-define British popular music, moving it towards big band music, swing, be-bop and jive music. By the end of the war, EMI's popular record catalogues had, in the same way as the classical catalogue, become dominated by American rather than British recordings. This unavoidable dependence had a profound impact on the way post-war recording of popular music developed at EMI.

Edith Piaf's unforgettable post-war recording "La vie en rose".

Hear My Song

THE BRITISH BUSINESS, 1945–1957

L. G. Wood, who later became the head of EMI Records, was conscious of the need to rebuild EMI's popular music business, despite the fact that there seemed to be an endless supply of American artists who sold well:

After the war Columbia America produced a first class roster of popular artists … we didn't have to worry too much about whether we could produce our own records or not. We'd got a first class source of income … from America, with artists like Frankie Laine, Johnny Ray, Doris Day, Dinah Shore, Percy Faith and his Orchestra, Mitch Miller and his Orchestra and Guy Mitchell. [Interview, L. G. Wood, 1994]

Matt Monro and George Martin
The ballad singer Matt Monro was one of George Martin's early successes as head of the Parlophone label.

Another American artist who struck a chord with British audiences was Frank Sinatra, "now selling better than ever over here. He is undoubtedly taking the place of Crosby, at least, as far as this country is concerned." [Mittell Papers, EMI Music Archive] The public was also interested in European performers, including the French artists Charles Trenet and Jean Sablon, and the great French Columbia artist Edith Piaf, who recorded "La Vie en rose" (Columbia DF 3152) in 1946; the record would forever be associated with her brilliant, elemental talent.

The key figures in the Company's efforts to regain its position in British popular music were Charles H. Thomas and L. G. Wood. They recruited four new Artist and Repertoire

NORMAN NEWELL
(BORN 1919)

★

Norman Newell began his musical career in his native London with the Cinephonic Music Company at the end of the Second World War. His song-writing talent was such that he was taken on in 1949 as an A & R manager for EMI's Columbia label, recording established artists like Josef Locke, Steve Conway, Petula Clark and Victor Silvester, and discovering new talent like Ronnie Ronalde and the Beverley Sisters. In 1952 he left EMI and went to America to concentrate on composing, but he was persuaded a few years later by EMI's chairman, Sir Joseph Lockwood, to return to the Company. Working for both HMV and Columbia, he recorded many stars, including Marlene Dietrich, Gracie Fields, Dorothy Squires, Shirley Bassey, Russ Conway, Ken Dodd, Alma Cogan, Joyce Grenfell, John Barry, Vera Lynn, Geoff Love, Paul Robeson and Noël Coward. He also produced a number of original cast albums of West End shows, made a series of opera and operetta highlights in English with the Sadler's Wells Opera Company and produced an enormous catalogue of records for EMI's Music for Pleasure budget label. He became a freelance in the mid-1960s but maintained his association with EMI until he finally retired as a record producer in 1990. A talented songwriter, Newell had many hits, including "More", "A portrait of my love" and "This is my life". He has won an Emmy, a Grammy, three Ivor Novello Awards, six British Music Industry Awards, plus many platinum, gold and silver discs.

Above For many years the Scottish dance band leader Jimmy Shand was Parlophone's most prolific recording star. His records of Scottish dance music enjoyed a popularity beyond his native Scotland.

Above, top The pianist Russ Conway's number one hit "Roulette".

Humphrey Lyttelton

During the early 1950s, EMI released records of a new generation of highly talented jazz musicians. The best of these was the trumpeter Humphrey Lyttelton who did much to re-establish British jazz as a potent force.

(A & R) managers to run the Company's pop music business. Their brief was to select the best available American recordings for release in the British record catalogues, and, crucially, to find and develop fresh British artistic talent to make hit records. They were: George (later Sir George) Martin (see box, page 316), a young musician trained at the Guildhall School of Music, who joined Oscar Preuss at Parlophone; Norman Newell (see box, page 225), who went to Columbia; Norrie Paramor (see box, page 228), a highly accomplished composer, arranger and conductor, who managed Columbia's popular music catalogue; and Walter Ridley (see box, page 232), composer and arranger, whose job it was to revitalize the HMV popular list. Wood's recollections reveal how the hands-on role of the A & R managers developed:

We would discuss the artists that we had on the list and what we were going to do with them for the next three to six months, what artists we hadn't already contracted we should endeavour to secure. Then how we would handle the promotion. [Interview, Wood]

George Martin, who had become head of Parlophone in 1956, summed up the frenetic activity that made up his working day as an A & R manager:

Where else would you be working with Albert Finney and Shirley Anne Field one day, Jimmy Shand the next, auditioning a "rock" group between dubbing on sound effects for a "Toytown" children's record, or perhaps supervising the editing of a new revue? [Martin, *Record Mail*]

Norman Newell at Columbia had a different task. He was described by L. G. Wood as:

[someone] who knew everybody, and everybody knew him inside the business, and he was very close to music publishers, particularly to Chappell's. So that we had first option on original cast recording rights of musicals that came in from America on to the London stage. [Interview, Wood]

In the 1950s, music publishers were both a powerful and a defining force in the popular music business, and their strong commercial links with American publishers meant they had a strong vested interest in promoting American rather than British pop songs. As a consequence they were regarded as something of

JOSEF LOCKE
(BORN 1917)

The tenor Josef Locke was born Joseph McLaughlin in Londonderry, Northern Ireland. After an early career in the Irish police force and war service with the Irish Guards, he decided to become a professional singer. His distinctive tenor voice was ideal for the romantic songs, operetta favourites and Irish ballads that he chose to perform and his career took off immediately. Engagements quickly followed, as exemplified by 19 summer seasons at the holiday resort of Blackpool. EMI signed him to its Columbia label in 1947 and one of his first releases was the hit "Hear my song, Violetta" (Columbia DB 2351), which became Locke's signature tune. Many other hits followed, including "If I can help somebody" (Columbia DB 2784) and "Cara mia" (Columbia DB 3503). Josef Locke's career continued throughout the 1950s until, while still at the peak of his powers, problems with the tax authorities caused him to disappear from the scene.

Above Josef Locke recording for Columbia in 1949.

Left Willie Kavanagh, managing director of EMI Ireland presenting Josef Locke with an award for his 1992 best selling CD *Hear My Song*.

a hindrance to the development of the British pop music industry. As Norman Newell pointed out in a highly critical 1951 report:

Most publishers seem to be of the opinion that the only worthwhile British songs are the type commonly known as the 'corny' variety. Were they to use a little more imagination in their choice of British material, we could bring about a great change in the business. We have the artists, the arrangers, people with ideas, and the promise of support from the BBC. A little more support from publishers and less dollars would leave the country and British artists and material would undoubtedly be on top. [Mittell Papers, EMI Music Archive]

NORRIE PARAMOR
(1914–1979)

★

London-born Norrie Paramor's early interest in music led to his working as pianist and arranger with dance bands led by Jack Harris and Maurice Winnick. After joining the RAF in 1941, he was sent to Blackpool to entertain the forces; he then became musical director for the Ralph Reader Gang Show, and arranged scores for artists like Noël Coward and Mantovani. With the end of the war he toured as pianist with Harry Gold's Pieces of Eight jazz band but left after five years to concentrate on musical arranging. In 1950 he joined EMI as a recording artist, leading his own orchestra, and in 1952 he began producing records for the Columbia label. His first big hit came at the end of 1953 with Eddie Calvert's "Oh mein papa" (Columbia DB 3337); this was soon followed by Ruby Murray's "Softly, softly" (Columbia DB 3558) and many others. During the 1950s he also created the Big Ben Banjo Band and the Big Ben Hawaiian Band, both of which were significant record sellers. In 1958 Paramor was responsible for signing Cliff Richard and the Shadows to EMI, and, in the early 1960s, he produced major hits with Helen Shapiro and Frank Ifield. Among the many other singers he recorded were Judy Garland, Michael Holliday, Gene Vincent and Al Martino. He left EMI in February 1968 to set up his own company, immediately scoring a number one hit with "Lily the Pink" by The Scaffold (Parlophone R 5734). From 1972 until 1978 he was director of the BBC Midland Radio Orchestra. He also wrote many successful songs and several film scores.

One of Norman Newell's most successful artists was the lush-toned tenor Josef Locke (see box, page 227). His greatest hits included "Hear my song, Violetta", coupled with "I'll take you home again Kathleen" (Columbia DB 2351), and "Goodbye", from Stolz's operetta *White Horse Inn*, coupled with "My heart and I" (Columbia DB 2336). The enormous success Locke's records achieved epitomized the then broad cross-generational appeal of popular records. Few popular singers survive in the collective memory beyond their moment of glory. However, following the 1990 film about Locke, *Hear My Song*, EMI released a series of successful CDs of his best-known records, *Hear My Song… Best of Josef Locke* (EMI CDP 7 98844 2), *A Tear, a Kiss, a Smile* (EMI CDP 7 99938 2) and *Take a Pair of Sparkling Eyes* (EMI CDP 7 99640 2).

With LPs of London musicals such as The Sound of Music (HMV CLP 1453 & CSD 1365), Norman Newell created an important and dynamic new market for popular music LPs. In addition to these London produced recordings, EMI also released – in conjunction with Capitol and MGM – LP records of American film soundtracks of musicals like *Oklahoma!* (Capitol SLCT/LCT 6100), *Carousel* (Capitol SLCT/LCT 6105), *Kiss me, Kate* (MGM C 753) and *Gigi* (MGM C 770). With these records EMI gained an important foothold in a development that in the 1960s became known as the "middle-of-the-road" (MOR) LP market (see Chapter 9).

Columbia's Norrie Paramor enjoyed a string of successes with British popular artists like Ruby Murray, who in the mid-1950s

SHIRLEY BASSEY
(BORN 1937)

Shirley Bassey's powerful voice and striking personality have made her one of Britain's greatest popular singers. She was born in Tiger Bay, Cardiff, Wales, the daughter of a West Indian seaman. She began singing in working men's clubs and toured in a show called *A Tribute to Al Jolson* before being spotted by Jack Hylton, who cast her in his 1955 West End revue *Such is Life*. She began recording for EMI in 1959 and scored major hits with "As long as he needs me" (Columbia DB 4490) and "Climb ev'ry mountain" (Columbia DB 4685). During the years that followed, she appeared with great success in Europe and America in cabaret and on concert tours, wearing spectacular costumes and giving super-charged performances, and sustained her career with a continued presence in the record charts throughout the 1970s and 80s. She also provided the theme songs for three James Bond films: *Diamonds Are Forever*, *Moonraker* and the biggest record hit of the group, *Goldfinger* (Columbia DB 7360). In 1981, she went into semi-retirement in Switzerland, but, since then, she has continued to make occasional television appearances and concert tours in even more lavish gowns, and given even bigger bravura vocal performances. A particularly successful tour in 1993 demonstrated that her popularity remains as great as ever.

Opposite page, left Donald Peers: "Powder your face with sunshine" was his first and greatest hit.

Opposite page, right Judy Garland When EMI bought Capitol Records in 1955 it acquired a whole stable of established American stars, including the extraordinary Judy Garland. Before her tragic death, she made many EMI recordings both in Britain and America.

Opposite page, inset The trumpeter Eddie Calvert was one of Columbia's most popular artists of the early 1950s.

had five records in the charts at the same time (a record not even achieved by the Beatles). Paramor made the early EMI recordings of the young Shirley Bassey (see box) who, in the two years before 1961, had five records in the charts, one of which "Climb ev'ry mountain" and "Reach for the sky" (Columbia DB 4685) achieved the top position. Of all Paramor's signings, none proved more successful and enduring than Cliff (later Sir Cliff) Richard (see box, page 238).

Walter Ridley transformed the HMV popular catalogue. He also changed the public image of HMV from one associated with classical music into a major pop music label. Among his early performers were the entertainer Max Bygraves and the singer Donald Peers. Later, he recorded Eartha Kitt, Ronnie Hilton and others. The many orchestral successes attributable to Ridley included his recording of "The Dam Busters March" (HMV B 10877) with the Central Band of the Royal Air Force conducted by Eric Coates, which achieved British sales in excess of 200,000 copies. Reviewing those days, Ridley recalled why popular artists made records in the 1950s, and the changing nature of the post-war popular record business:

Everyone wanted to record. Not so much for the money that they got from it, because they didn't make a lot. What they got was enormous publicity … the minute you had a hit record, it was played every day [on the radio], two, three times, five times a day.
[Interview, Walter Ridley, 1994]

Ruby Murray was one of Norrie Paramor's most important discoveries, and a major British pop star of the mid-1950s. In 1955 she scored a major hit with "Softly Softly".

Dreamboat

THE HIT PARADE

The most important change in the way pop records were promoted was the creation in 1952 by the popular music paper *New Musical Express* of the first British chart listing top-selling records: the "Hit Parade". The invention of the chart had a dramatic effect on the business and soon became the pop music industry's most influential barometer of success. During the ensuing decade, many EMI artists topped the Hit Parade. However, although pop records by rock'n'roll artists eventually came to dominate the charts, records of other more traditional forms of popular music sold in sufficient numbers to find their place in the charts. Among EMI's non-rock 'n' roll British artists to have number one hits during this time were the trumpeter Eddie Calvert with his 1953 record "Oh mein papa" (Columbia DB 3337); Alma Cogan in 1955 with "Dreamboat" (HMV B 10872), Ruby Murray also in 1955 with her record "Softly, Softly" (Columbia DB 3558); Michael Holliday's 1958 record "The Story of My Life" (Columbia DB 4058), and the pianist Russ Conway's two 1959 hit records, "Side Saddle" (Columbia DB 4256) and "Roulette" (Columbia DB 4298).

In the 1950s, broadcasts of pop records aimed specifically at teenagers, notably by Radio Luxembourg, became one of EMI's most important marketing tools. Programmes of popular music records had been a feature of pre-war broadcasting, particularly from European English-language stations. The surge in the 1950s was due to the growth, availability and range of pop music on record, in particular rock 'n' roll. In addition, television became an increasingly important medium for the marketing

Above "Powder your face with sunshine" by Donald Peers.

Left Alma Cogan's 1955 hit "Dreamboat".

of pop records, and, by 1961 – with television in more than 80 per cent of households – a whole range of programmes featuring the latest records and pop musicians fed the insatiable thirst of teenage record consumers eager for the latest music news and views of their favourite artists.

From the mid-1950s, the main growth sector within the popular record market became increasingly occupied by a new and distinct social group: teenagers. Teenagers acquired and asserted an economic independence denied their parents by the Depression and war. Without commitments, mortgages, or families to support, they became an important consumer group in the leisure market, and specifically in the record market. EMI recognized the importance of this segment to their plans for the pop record business both in terms of marketing and in the acquisition of talent.

Diana

NEW DEALS

The ending of its American licensing agreements loomed over EMI throughout the 1950s. It had to come up with ways of retaining its position as a major player in the rapidly expanding and increasingly competitive popular record market. As well as putting significant

WALTER RIDLEY
(BORN 1913)

★

Born in London, Walter Ridley won a scholarship to the Northern Polytechnic to study piano manufacture at the age of 13. In 1928 he joined the music publisher Feldman as a song plugger; he moved in 1935 to a rival publisher, Peter Maurice, as professional manager. During the Second World War he organized Vera Lynn's programmes and produced several top radio shows, including *Educating Archie*. In 1949 he was engaged by EMI to create a popular British catalogue for the HMV label, which at the time was perceived mainly as classical, although it also released American licensed popular product. His first hit record was with Donald Peers singing "Powder your face with sunshine" (HMV B 9764), quickly followed by many others by artists such as Max Bygraves, Ronnie Hilton, George Melachrino, Joe Loss, Semprini, Malcolm Vaughan, Alma Cogan and Andy Stewart, all helping to strengthen EMI's position in the British pop market throughout the 1950s. In the 1960s and 1970s Ridley's artists included Danny Williams, Johnny Kidd, the George Mitchell Minstrels, the Swinging Blue Jeans, Don Estelle and Windsor Davis, Benny Hill, and Iris Williams. He also recorded a number of West End shows, including *The Pajama Game* (HMV CLP 1062), *The Boy Friend* (HMV DLP 1078) and Harold Fielding's 1971 production of *Show Boat* (Columbia SCX 6480). A talented accompanist, arranger and composer, he wrote over 200 songs during his career and won two Ivor Novello Awards. He retired from EMI in 1977.

emphasis on new British talent, it needed to replace its American repertoire sources. The Company's solution was to develop a policy of obtaining licensing agreements with a host of small and medium-sized American record companies. It also acquired Capitol in 1955 as a major source of repertoire.

The policy was initiated in 1948 when EMI first released records licensed from the American film and record company MGM. Throughout the 1950s and beyond, L. G. Wood, on behalf of EMI, negotiated other such licensing agreements, notably with the American Paramount Record Corporation (ABC Paramount), which gave artists such as Paul Anka to Columbia – his record "Diana" (Columbia 45-DB 3980) achieved sales in excess of one million copies; and Verve Records, under which many excellent jazz records produced by Norman Granz were released, especially the famous series of Ella Fitzgerald "Songbook" albums; Mercury Record Corporation (including EM Arcy Records) provided many important popular and jazz performers, including Sarah Vaughan, Billy Eckstine, Dinah Washington, Patti Paige and Clifford Brown.

After 1957, when EMI finally lost RCA Victor's American repertoire, sales of EMI pop records suffered badly, though curiously not the number of "hits". As C. H. Thomas observed in 1959:

… in 1957 we had 22 records in the Top Ten that produced a total sale of nearly 8 million records, we had no less than 27 in the Top Ten in 1958 but they only produced a total of 6 million records. Out of the 27 in the Top Ten in 1958 no less than 12 were our own British artists, 5 MGM and 5 Capitol, the balance being miscellaneous small independent records from other sources. [Memorandum by C. H. Thomas to L. G. Wood, EMI Music Archive]

Heartbreak Hotel

THE BEGINNINGS OF ROCK'N'ROLL

Rock'n'roll was the single most important influence on the development of popular music in the 1950s. An American hybrid of dance band, be-bop and country blues, it had its greatest exponent in Elvis Presley. In the final years of the RCA Victor licensing agreement, HMV was able to release in Britain a total of twelve Presley singles, three extended-play and three LP records. Curiously, none of those early records became best-sellers. Walter Ridley, who issued them on the HMV POP label, said of them: "'Heartbreak Hotel'" (HMV POP 182) "had the worst reviews on record in the papers we'd had since I'd joined the Company." Nonetheless, as soon as he had listened to them, Ridley recognized that the Presley records were a watershed in the pop music industry. He observed: "[the Presley records] used echo chamber and guitar-playing (Chet Atkins) the like of which I hadn't heard in this country, we didn't have anybody who could play like that." When the RCA Victor licensing agreement ended, Presley's HMV records were withdrawn from sale.

Despite the boom in sales eventually caused by rock'n'roll, not everybody appreciated the new music. Dave Dexter,

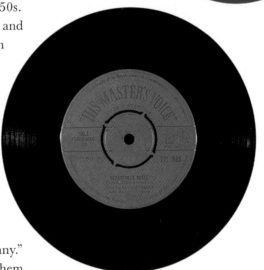

Above In 1956, HMV released "Heartbreak Hotel", the first British Elvis Presley record in both 78- and 45-rpm formats.

Opposite page, top In the mid-1950s, Gene Vincent was Capitol's hottest rock'n'roll star.

Opposite page, below Ronnie Hilton was one of the most successful of Walter Ridley's 1950s British pop stars.

The early records Elvis Presley made for RCA
Victor were released in Britain on the HMV label.

A & R manager at Capitol Records, wrote somewhat
despairingly to L. G. Wood:

We are in a most discouraging revolution in the pop singles field.
A great majority of singles are bought not by college students
but by mere children, youngsters as young as 11, 12 and 13 years
old. They buy strictly for "the beat" and as you can tell by the
Elvis Presley and Guy Mitchell hits over there, the lyrics are
juvenile and maddeningly repetitious.
[Presley Artist File, EMI Music Archive]

 **BEST SELLERS**
already issued on

"HIS MASTER'S VOICE"

(The number in brackets indicates the playing speed of the record)

America's Wonder Boy of Song
ELVIS PRESLEY

> BLUE SUEDE SHOES
> TUTTI FRUTTI........................POP213(78) or 7M405(45)

> HEARTBREAK HOTEL
> I WAS THE ONE......................POP182(78) or 7M385(45)

PERRY COMO

Hot Diggity (Dog Ziggity Boom)
My Funny Valentine .... POP212(78) or 7M404(45)

Wonderful recordings by
MARIO LANZA
from his latest film ' SERENADE '

> SERENADE
> MY DESTINY
> (Both recorded from the sound-track of the Warner
> Bros. film ' Serenade ')   DA2085(78)

MARION KEENE

Fortune Teller
A dangerous age...............................POP203(78) or 7M395(45)

MAX BYGRAVES

> TRY ANOTHER CHERRY TREE
> With Children's Chorus
> SEVENTEEN TONS.................POP208(78) or 7M400(45)

STUART HAMBLEN

singing his own compositions
  Hell Train
  A few things to remember...............POP202(78) or 7M394(45)

15

Marketing Elvis Presley
HMV simply did not know how to market the phenomenon that was Elvis Presley, promoting him with ballad singers like Perry Como and Mario Lanza.

ADAM FAITH
(BORN 1940)

Adam Faith was Cliff Richard's only serious rival in the British pop scene of the late 1950s and early 1960s. Born Terence Nelhams in London, Adam Faith adopted his new name at the beginning of his solo career away from the skiffle group, the Worried Men, which he had formed in 1956. In 1959, after two unsuccessful HMV singles the previous year, he became a regular on the television pop series *Drumbeat* and made a series of hit recordings, including "What do you want" (Parlophone R 4591) and "Poor me" (Parlophone R 4623), which both went to the top of the British charts. He appeared in several films, including *Beat Girl*, *Never Let Go* and *Mix Me a Person*, and, by giving an unexpectedly intelligent television interview on *Face to Face* and later discussing serious social and moral issues with the Archbishop of York on *Meeting Point*, became something of a spokesman for his generation. During the next seven years, Faith was in the charts 24 times with a succession of songs specially tailored to his somewhat melancholy style and mannered delivery. He left the pop music scene in the mid-1960s, and later became a financial consultant, record producer, artist manager, singer and actor.

Opposite page By the time Adam Faith made his hit "What do you want", EMI had successfully created attractive labels and packaging for the Company's singles.

Rock'n'roll threw the British pop record industry into turmoil. It seemed – for a while at any rate – that only American artists were able to succeed in this new and highly individual popular art form. In the short term, EMI with its American licensing deals was better insulated than most from this cold draught. Eventually, EMI succeeded in laying the foundations that led directly to the 1960s explosion in British pop and rock talent. That success was already beginning to show in 1960, when EMI artists at one point held the top six places in the British charts.

Walkin' Back to Happiness
BRITISH REVIVAL

In the four years between 1958 and 1961, three British pop artists, Adam Faith (see box), Helen Shapiro (see box, page 237) and Cliff Richard dominated both the EMI pop music labels and the British charts. Their success was based on a combination of raw talent, well-chosen songs and an ability to articulate the aspirations of Britain's increasingly affluent teenagers. Adam Faith had number one hits with "What do you want" (Parlophone R 4591) and "Poor me" (Parlophone R 4623). In 1961, the 14-year-old Helen Shapiro had the first of a string of hits, including "Walkin' back to happiness" (Columbia DB 4715). The disc jockey and writer Ray Orchard observed of her:

It's wonderful to hear someone with lung-power who's not afraid to use it. She belts out the numbers in a great way with drive and authority you seldom find in much older, more experienced performers. It's the most exciting thing I've heard in a long time. [*Record Mail*, March 1961]

The most enduring of all EMI's 1950s British pop artists was and is Cliff Richard. His first record, "Move it" (Columbia DB 4178), was released in 1958 and remained in the charts for 17 weeks. It did not take EMI very long to realize that it had a rare talent in Cliff Richard and his backing group, the Shadows (originally known as the Drifters; the name was changed in 1959 to avoid confusion with an American group). In 1959, "Living Doll" (Columbia DB 4306) from the film *Serious Charge* was released. This record, which became Cliff Richard's musical signature, was described at the time as "a slow, haunting ballad, with the essential beat ever predominant ... he will bring in an even wider public with "Living Doll", a factor always useful to a

HELEN SHAPIRO
(BORN 1946)

★

Helen Shapiro was born in the East End of London. Whilst still at school, she began attending weekly vocal classes in pop singing with Maurice Berman who, in 1961, arranged for her to do a test for Norrie Paramor. Paramor, at first unable to believe that he was listening to a 14-year-old schoolgirl, was impressed with her deep, mature voice and confident phrasing and signed her to EMI; she quickly produced a string of hit records, mostly songs written by Paramor's assistant John Schroeder, including "Don't treat me like a child" (Columbia DB 4589), "You don't know" (Columbia DB 4670) and "Walkin' back to happiness" (Columbia DB 4715). She began a series of concert dates, including a short season at the London Palladium, becoming the youngest performer ever to achieve such success before the age of 15. She was voted Top UK Female Singer in the 1961 *New Musical Express* readers' poll. In February 1963, while topping the bill at the Bradford Gaumont Theatre, she had the Beatles as one of her supporting acts. Her last chart entry was in January 1964 with "Fever" (Columbia DB 7190), and in 1967 she began straight acting, although she still continued to sing in cabaret from time to time and make the occasional album. She teamed up with jazzman Humphrey Lyttelton in 1985 and has continued to work successfully with him in jazz concerts ever since, as well as continuing her theatre work in plays, musicals and pantomimes.

Helen Shapiro receiving a Silver Disc from her producer Norrie Paramor.

rising star." [Gerry Wilmot, *Record Mail*, August 1959]. Wilmot was right in his prediction: by the end of 1959, more than one million copies of "Living Doll" had been sold.

Despite the record sales and the adulation of his fans, Cliff Richard's talent was not universally appreciated. In 1959, John Oakland, reviewing two of his extended-play records in the *Gramophone*, caustically observed:

I found myself musing, when listening to Cliff Richard (Col SEG 7903 and 7910) recording before a teenage audience in the Abbey Road Studios, that when the Beat Generation grows up, it will be heartily ashamed of itself, and that records such as these will provide irrefutable evidence of the temper of our times; the unintelligible and unintelligent mouthing to a twangy guitar, the pile-driver rhythm, the shrieks of rapture coming in smack on cue, and the lesson in mass hysteria that is given. [*Gramophone*, Vol.47, September 1959]

Between 1958 and 1961, a total of 13 Cliff Richard records reached the top five chart positions and, by the end of 1960, 5.5 million copies of his 45-rpm single records had been sold. Thirty years later, world sales of Richard's singles had reached the phenomenal figure of 80 million.

Cliff Richard's success was just one of the factors which contributed to the extraordinary revival in EMI's British business. By the early 1960s – in what had become a highly competitive market in pop records – EMI held around 40 per cent of the British market in pop records and was at the cutting edge of popular culture.

SIR CLIFF RICHARD
(BORN 1940)

★

Sir Cliff Richard is one of the most successful and popular figures in British pop music. He was born Harry Roger Webb in Lucknow, India, where his father worked for a catering firm. The family returned to England in 1948 and settled in Cheshunt. As a teenager, he was greatly impressed by Elvis Presley and the other rock'n'roll performers, and he decided to follow suit, forming a group called the Drifters with drummer Terry Smart and guitarist Norman Mitham. At the famous 2Is coffee bar in Soho, they teamed up with lead guitarist Ian Samwell and developed their act as a quartet. After performing in a Saturday morning talent show, they came to the attention of EMI's Norrie Paramor. He originally intended to record Cliff as a solo singer backed by an orchestra, but was persuaded to keep the whole group. Their first single was "Schoolboy crush" with Ian Samwell's "Move it" as the B side. An advance acetate was heard by TV producer Jack Good, who raved over "Move it". He immediately began promoting Cliff even before the record was released and featured him on his influential television show, *Oh Boy!* The single (Columbia DB 4178) swiftly rose to number two in the British charts and Cliff soon became a rock'n'roll star. *The New Musical Express* disapproved of his "violent hip-swinging and crude exhibitionism" but his ever-increasing legions of female fans plainly disagreed. Meanwhile, Ian Samwell, dissatisfied with the supporting role given to the Drifters, left the group and a new line-up emerged with Hank Marvin and Bruce Welch on guitars, Jet Harris on bass and Terry Smart still on drums (although soon to be replaced by Tony Meehan). To avoid confusion with an American group, they changed their name to the Shadows.

In 1959 Cliff starred in two completely different films – the non-musical drama *Serious Charge* and the comedy *Expresso Bongo*. Cliff had his most enduring hit with Lionel Bart's "Living Doll" (Columbia DB 4306), a reworking of a song he sang in *Serious Charge*, and another hit immediately afterwards with

"Travellin' Light" (Columbia DB 4351); both reached number one in the charts. As the 1960s progressed, Cliff became more of a middle-of-the-road entertainer, undertaking concert tours, appearing in variety shows and doing pantomime.

He further consolidated his position with several lively and attractive films, including *The Young Ones* and *Summer Holiday*, both of which produced number one singles of the title songs (Columbia DB 4761 and Columbia DB 4977). In 1968 Cliff sang Britain's entry in the Eurovision Song Contest, and, although placed only second, the song "Congratulations" (Columbia DB 8376) gave him one of the biggest-selling singles of the year. After a lull at the beginning of the 1970s, Cliff saw a resurgence of his record sales with the album *I'm Nearly Famous* (EMI EMC 3122), produced by his musical colleague Hank Marvin (who produced his next few albums as well). In 1979, his album *Rock'n'Roll Juvenile* (EMI EMC 3307), jointly produced by Cliff himself and Terry Britten, presented Cliff in a more contemporary setting; it heralded the start of another run of record successes throughout the 1980s. Cliff revealed yet another aspect of his talent in a number of highly effective duet records with stars like Olivia Newton-John, Phil Everley, Sarah Brightman, Elton John and Van Morrison. He celebrated his 50th birthday in October 1990 with the anti-war song "From a distance" (EMI EM 155) and followed it almost immediately with another number one hit, "Saviour's Day" (EMI XMAS 90). In recent years, Cliff has undertaken a number of major tours in which he has drawn capacity crowds to venues like Wembley Stadium and given polished performances of his many hit songs to highly appreciative audiences of all ages. Throughout his career, Cliff has been unstinting in his support of good causes and he has often sung to raise money for charity. He has received several special British music industry lifetime achievement awards, including a BRIT award in 1989 and an Ivor Novello award in 1990. He was honoured by the Queen with an OBE in January 1980 and knighted in June 1995. In 1993, the *Guinness Who's Who of Fifties Music* summed up Cliff Richard's achievement as follows: "Richard has outlasted every musical trend of the past four decades with a sincerity and commitment that may well be unmatched in his field. He is British pop's most celebrated survivor."

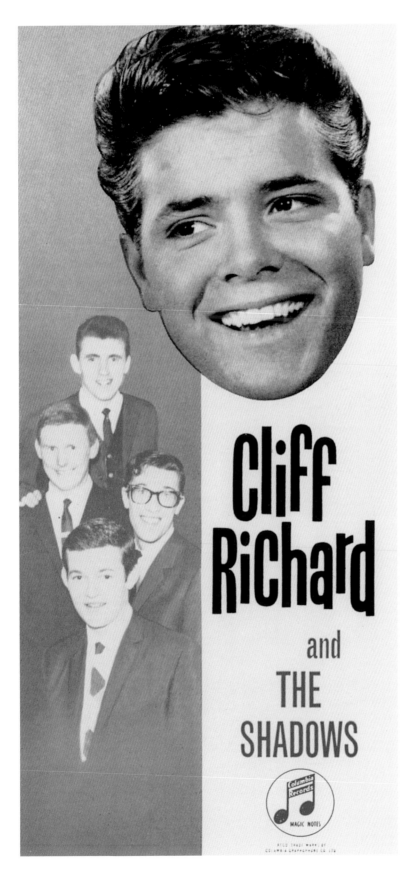

Above "Move it", Cliff Richard's first recording.

Top In 1959, Columbia released Cliff Richard's most successful hit record "Living Doll".

One of EMI's first classical CD's.

CHAPTER 7

A Kind of Magic

THE BUSINESS, 1962–1997

The music business is not a champagne-swilling, cork-popping, hippy business; it is very professional. I found this out even before I joined the payroll. I went to some of their meetings and got on to a wavelength with their music people far faster than with the people running any other part of the business.
[Sir Colin Southgate, chairman, THORN EMI plc, 1992]

The **EMI** *Group*

I Want To Hold Your Hand

THE SIXTIES

Sir John Read was chairman of EMI from 1974 to 1979.

In 1962, Sir Joseph Lockwood, EMI's chairman and chief executive, presided over a highly successful multinational business encompassing domestic electrical appliances, defence equipment, electronic goods – including computers – a music business and a growing retail trade. EMI's Central Research Laboratories (CRL) supplied the Company with its next generation of ideas and products. EMI also had extensive overseas operations, with factories, marketing facilities and representation in more than 30 countries. The United States provided the Company with its largest single overseas market and was its most consistent profit earner.

The 1960s were a period of exceptional growth for EMI. In 1962, sales and pre-tax profits stood at £82.5 million and £4.4 million respectively; and by 1970 – the year Lockwood ceased to be chief executive – these figures had increased (with relatively little price inflation to boost them) to almost £225 million and £21 million. In short, the business had grown dramatically and its profitability had doubled to almost ten per cent of earnings. A notable feature was the contribution made by the Company's record business, which throughout the decade accounted for more than half the turnover and profits. EMI's performance was partly due to the worldwide boom in its industry and partly due to huge interest in its British artists. The international record business – particularly in the wake of the Beatles phenomenon (see below and Chapter 9) – began to generate enormous earnings from the sales worldwide of pop records. In 1965, £1 million, or half the profits of EMI's British record company, was earned from overseas sales of British-made recordings, a three-fold increase on the level in 1964. By the mid-1960s, the Company's strength in British-made pop and rock records had turned it into the world market leader.

Happiness

EMI'S ENTERTAINMENT BUSINESS

The Company soon found itself sitting on a large and growing cash surplus, and Lockwood, joined after 1966 by John (later Sir John) Read as managing director, sought ways to invest the Company's new-found wealth. Following the fashion of the time, they focused on areas entirely unconnected to music. For example, the Grade Organization was purchased in 1966. Then one of

Britain's largest entertainment and leisure groups, and the country's most important artists' agency, it owned major theatrical, film and music publishing interests, and a substantial cinema chain. With the deal came Grade's formidable head, Bernard (later Lord) Delfont, who joined the board of EMI and became the chief executive of the Company's new Leisure Division. Delfont later wrote of EMI's purchase of the Grade Organization:

[Lockwood and Read told me] if I joined EMI I would enjoy unrivalled opportunities to build up the Leisure Division into a major company in its own right. There was no shortage of investment money and I would have virtually a free hand on how to spend it. It was an offer I could not resist. [Bernard Delfont, *East End, West End* (London 1990), p.174]

In the decade to 1976, Bernard (later Lord) Delfont masterminded EMI's leisure-based expansion.

After joining EMI, Delfont did indeed embark on a massive programme of acquisitions. These included the Blackpool Tower Company, owners of the famous seaside resort tower and leisure complex, and Associated British Picture Corporation Ltd (ABPC), owners of the Elstree film studios and one of Britain's largest film makers and distributors, cinema chains, bowling alleys and squash courts. One of ABPC's most important assets was a controlling interest in Thames Television, which operated the commercial television weekday franchise for the London area.

In 1972, the Golden Egg restaurant chain was purchased. During the 1970s, other deals followed, including an expansion of restaurant interests, hotels and pubs, sports centres, bingo halls and dance halls, together with the purchase of the New London Theatre. By 1979, Delfont's Leisure Division was one of EMI's largest and most profitable businesses and EMI itself was the largest entertainment company in Britain.

From me to you

THE BRITISH RECORD BUSINESS

The ten years which ended in 1971 saw a dramatic increase in the size of the British record market, from £20 million in 1962 to almost £70 million in 1971. Within the market, growth was most keenly felt in the LP sector, where sales rose from 17 million units in 1962 to 84.5 million units ten years later. In sharp

1

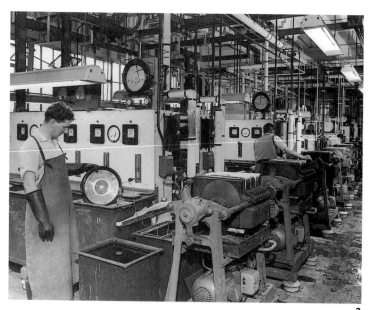

2

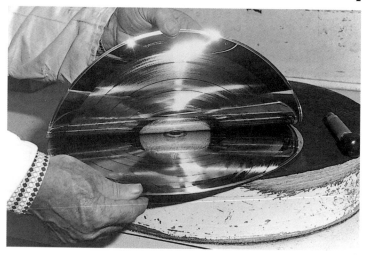

3

1. Disc-cutting engineer Chris Blair examines a master laquer disc at Abbey Road Studios in 1974.

2. The electrotyping process used to create metal masters and negatives for pressing records has changed remarkably little during the past 100 years.

3. Separating the stamper from the metal positive.

4. A record press mounted with two metal stampers, labels and blob of vinyl plastic.

5. The Beatles record "I want to hold your hand" on a 45-rpm automatic press in November 1963.

6. By the mid-1980s, LP manufacture involved automatic machinery fed by skips filled with the vinyl plastic resins.

7. To meet the one million advance orders for "I want to hold your hand", automatic bagging of the record was an essential feature of the manufacturing process.

contrast, over the same period sales of 45-rpm records remained static at around 52 million units. The premium market for full-price pop and rock LPs expanded rapidly (see Chapter 9), mimicking the growth in the premium market for full-price classical LPs.

The dramatic increase in record sales was in part stimulated by price reductions, themselves a consequence of cuts in Purchase Tax on records and of rising living standards. The price of a 45-rpm single pop record in 1962, including tax, was six shillings and six pence (33 pence), whilst a decade later that price had risen only to 50 pence, an increase well below the rate of inflation. Similarly, in 1962, the average cost of an EMI full-price classical LP was one pound, 19 shillings and 11 pence (£1.99), whilst a decade later it was only £2.29.

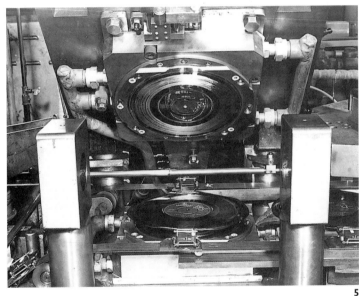

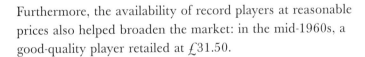

Furthermore, the availability of record players at reasonable prices also helped broaden the market: in the mid-1960s, a good-quality player retailed at £31.50.

Music for Pleasure

Among other changes in the British record market in the 1960s was the development of a budget and mail order trade. This presented EMI with great opportunities. By 1965, the year the budget market really began to grow, the Company had accumulated a large number of deleted former full-price LP recordings. The creation of a budget catalogue provided an

Music For Pleasure

The Complete Catalogue 1995

ideal opportunity to re-use these and in parallel develop a low-cost recording programme of new releases.

EMI's most enduring venture into the budget record market was Music for Pleasure (MFP). Originally a joint venture with the Paul Hamlyn Publishing Group, it became a wholly-owned subsidiary in 1971. MFP records retailed at 12 shillings and 6 pence (62 pence), and were sold in racks, principally by non-traditional retail outlets such as supermarkets and booksellers. This transformed and extended the record market and made records available to new types of consumers. Recordings released on budget labels were aimed at the middle-of-the-road market, and included film soundtracks, original-cast musicals, light classics, jazz, rhythm and blues, and country and western music. In addition to back catalogue, it used "soundalike" cover versions of pop hits and material licensed from other record companies. Once established, MFP also initiated its own recording programme. By 1972, the combined sales of budget records accounted for almost 15 per cent of the value of EMI's British record sales. Although these records brought new consumers into the record market, and, with low recording costs, provided the Company with dependable profits, the profits remained small by comparison with those from the mainstream business. As a result, although unit sales of EMI's LP records rose dramatically during the five years before 1972, their value remained static at £9 million.

In the 1970s, other MFP derivative labels were launched, including Surprise Surprise (a children's series), Classics for Pleasure (see Chapter 8), Listen for Pleasure (audio books on cassette), and, in 1983, the Fame label, which featured pop and rock artists like The Stranglers (see box, page 340), Whitesnake, ELP, T. Rex (see box, page 338), Cliff Richard and Deep Purple (see box, page 335). MFP's introduction of a CD range in 1987 enabled the Company to scour its archive for material worthy of transfer to the new medium, and, at the same time to continue to commission and acquire fresh repertoire. In 1996, MFP changed its name to EMI Gold.

Freedom come, freedom go

NEW COMPETITION

The 1960s saw other important structural changes in the British record market. The most significant was the decision by a number of large American record companies, known as "majors", to establish their own British and European businesses; previously they had relied on licensing agreements with companies like EMI to press and distribute their repertoire outside the United States. They were attracted by the growth in the British and European record markets, the seemingly endless supply of British pop and rock talent, and the allure of good profits. Another trend in the 1960s was the appearance of significant numbers of small businesses catering for specialist music interests and markets. The competition from American majors and the "independents" (as they became known) began to eat into EMI's market share. To some degree, however, EMI was able to absorb and profit from the independents' activities, by selling studio time at Abbey Road Studios, and by offering pressing, marketing and distribution facilities.

These structural changes forced long-established British record companies like EMI to adopt a whole range of new ideas and organizational forms. One was the ending in the latter part of the 1960s of the system of staff record producers. As a consequence, producers (including some EMI producers like George Martin) left and established themselves as independents. Working on a royalty basis, they provided EMI (and other record companies) with a complete package – artist, musical arrangement, accompaniment and recording – with EMI pressing, promoting and distributing the finished product. Although this system seemed at first sight attractive, it resulted in significantly lower profits for the Company. Also, as the ownership of the master tape often remained with the producer or artist, re-issues became more costly and less attractive. The emergence of keener competition also pushed up artists' costs, which in turn forced many record companies, including EMI, to cut back on their investment in new artists.

Another brick in the wall

TECHNOLOGY

By 1972, alongside the existing vinyl 45-rpm and LP discs, consumers had two additional recording formats to choose from.

ABBEY ROAD STUDIOS

★

In the 1960s Abbey Road Studios in St John's Wood, London, became famous because of their association with the Beatles. Today, decades after their final recordings sessions, fans still visit Number Two Studio (where the Beatles made their records) and walk across the zebra crossing featured on the cover of their 1969 album *Abbey Road*.

Abbey Road Studios were already more than 30 years old when the Beatles made their first EMI record. In 1929, recognizing the inadequacies of existing studio facilities and the growing demands for recording time, The Gramophone Company conceived the idea of creating purpose-built recording facilities in London. The site chosen for the project was a large house in Abbey Road. The cost of building and converting the site and equipping the studios was in excess of £100,000. At the time they were opened by Sir Edward Elgar in 1931, the Studios boasted the best recording and studio technology then available in the world.

Abbey Road proved a highly suitable location for recording a wide range of classical repertoire and, until recently, almost all varieties of popular music. The large Number One Studio has been used for the most complex works involving up to several

Abbey Road Studios, St John's Wood, London.

hundred musicians and singers to solo piano pieces. The second studio has catered for popular songs, dance bands and, latterly, pop and rock music, whilst the smaller third studio has been used mostly for classical chamber and piano music. Over the years, individual studios have been upgraded to meet the needs of the day, and in 1980 a fourth studio was added to the complex; as a result of its location and size, this studio was dubbed "The Penthouse". Today, Abbey Road boasts the latest computer-based technology including Sonic Solutions and CEDAR (a system designed to remove noise in the remastering of 78-rpm records). To artists, engineers and record producers alike, the enduring appeal of Abbey Road goes far beyond its technical expertise. Many artists would agree with Paul McCartney when he wrote: "I love Abbey Road because it has depth, back up, tradition, and all those things."

The 16-year-old Yehudi Menuhin recording Elgar's Violin Concerto with the London Symphony Orchestra conducted by the composer in Number One Studio, Abbey Road, 14 July 1932.

The Beatles recording in Number Two Studio, February 1964.

RECORDING TECHNIQUES

★

Abbey Road bought its first four-track stereo machine in 1959 – a Telefunken which used one-inch tape. At first, the idea was to use it for opera and choral recordings, where it was quite difficult to get the right balance between the orchestra, chorus and soloists. Splitting the various elements in tracks provided the opportunity to get the right sound at the remix stage, long after the artists had departed. It was not envisaged that pop recordings would be done in four-track since radio broadcasting was monaural. As pop bands discovered the possibilities of recording in four-track, Abbey Road purchased eight superb Studer J37 machines from Switzerland.

The Beatles were not, however, the first pop group to use four-track; that distinction went to Cliff Richard and the Shadows. But the Beatles did adopt four-track fairly early on in their career, before their historic American tour, first of all in the single "I want to hold your hand" (Parlophone R 5084). Four-track allowed the basic rhythm to be laid down on two tracks, a process which could require many takes; the best take was then used as the master for the overdubbing. It was possible to record over and over again the other parts of the track – vocals for instance – and then drop into the master the most satisfactory. The flexibility offered by four-track soon made it the standard in pop recording technology.

In their constant quest for new sounds the most famous pop groups spent many hours experimenting in the studio. This led to innovative approaches, with four-track machines being used in tandem, and inventions such as ADT and phasing, an adaptation of which enabled two four-track machines to be locked in parallel for the final track of the Beatles *Sgt. Pepper* album, "A Day in the Life". As eight-track machines became available, so in 1968 EMI Central Research Laboratories introduced a 24-input eight-track console to accommodate them. Whereas eight-track was used extensively on classical recording, it was soon superseded on pop by sixteen-track, as the new rock innovators such as Pink Floyd demanded more tracks for their synthesizers and electronic keyboards.

By 1974, equipment manufacturers satisfied the likes of bands such as Pink Floyd, Emerson, Lake and Palmer, the

Electric Light Orchestra, and countless others by introducing 24-track machines as standard together with noise reduction systems such as Dolby. It was not long before two 24-track machines were being locked together to provide 48-track. SSL were soon to come up with their remarkable computerized mixing console with total recall.

By 1979, the Central Research Laboratories had come up with a prototype stereo digital tape recorder. However, it was not possible to edit on this system; it was left to Japanese manufacturers to develop the industry's first digital standard by using converted video machines and computer-based technology to incorporate editing. Later on, digital 49-track machines on the DASH format were to become standard studio equipment. Digital recording created the modern revolution in recording and duplication technology: it eliminated tape hiss and provided the ability to make almost infinite numbers of copies-of-copies without degradation.

At Abbey Road, the advent of the compact disc (CD) in the early 1980s required a new generation of post-production facilities, including the PQ editing rooms, which supply encoded tapes to EMI's manufacturing facilities in Britain and elsewhere. In addition, parts of Abbey Road are now dedicated to the digital remastering of analogue tapes to enable the public to enjoy the Company's unparalleled back catalogue newly refurbished for CD.

In the 1990s, Abbey Road remains at the forefront of industry innovations. A technology venture with Apple Computer has lead to the installation at the studios of a state-of-the-art multimedia studio which combines recording and multimedia technology. This provides artists with the most comprehensive facilities for their multimedia projects. It is hoped that the venture will speed the introduction of the new enhanced CD format, which carries digital sound recordings alongside visual and interactive features relating to the artists and the recordings.

Above Number Three Studio in the 1970s.

***Opposite page* Otto Klemperer and EMI producers**

A playback in the control room at Abbey Road during the 1966 recording of *Don Giovanni* illustrates the concentration on artist and producer alike: (left to right) Peter Andry (EMI), Nicolai Gedda, Paolo Montarsolo, Otto Klemperer, Ronald Kinloch Anderson (EMI), Nicolai Ghiaurov, Suvi Raj Grubb (EMI), Walter Berry (foreground), Claire Watson, Mrs Gedda, Mirella Freni, Christa Ludwig, Mrs Ghiaurov and Henry Smith (EMI).

These were the pre-recorded eight-track tape cartridge, a format that lasted until the late 1970s, and the more successful cassette. These new formats opened up important markets in pre-recorded music; particularly in the burgeoning in-car stereo market. (There had been a market in pre-recorded reel-to-reel tape since the 1950s, but it had always remained small.) In the eyes of many consumers, the pre-recorded cassette tape quickly established itself as a more durable and more convenient format than vinyl records; by 1990, cassette sales accounted for almost half of all EMI's album sales.

Hello Goodbye

THE SLOW DECLINE OF EMI

Well before the 1970s, EMI had recognized that it needed to rationalize what had become an increasingly disparate and uncoordinated international organization. As early as 1966, Sir Joseph Lockwood, EMI's chairman and chief executive, told shareholders:

Our record business, particularly in recent years, has become completely international. Our classical recordings have always had good world sales, but now in every field, not least in the "pops", our records sell right across the free world. We have therefore felt that we need a top "records man" to coordinate our record business internationally. [Chairman's Statement, Annual Meeting, EMI Ltd, 1966]

L. G. Wood, the managing director of EMI's British business, was appointed to this task, with a seat on the main board.

The problems Wood faced were immense, particularly in the highly lucrative but volatile British and overseas pop market. Quite simply, EMI was unable to replicate its previous spectacular achievements in pop and rock music. In a business based on a regular supply of new artists, the extraordinary talent of those years was not easily replaced, and there was intense competition between record companies. Also, from the mid-1960s onwards, the Company had to respond to the emerging consumer trend away from singles to LPs, and a broadening of the popular end of the record market from pop and rock to other types of music, particularly the budget middle-of-the-road market (see above). Nonetheless, as pop singles and albums remained EMI's largest and most profitable sector, its continued success depended on sustaining the creative achievements of the early and mid-1960s. In a note to the EMI board in 1965, Wood had warned of its vulnerability:

Number Two Studio in April 1996, following a £500,000 refit which included the installation of a VRP 60 channel-mixing console.

We must be constantly on our toes in the pop field since approximately 70 per cent of our total singles business is attributable to records which get into the Charts, that is to say the Top 30. Albums show 36 per cent of business comes from the Top 20, and EP's 18 per cent from the Top 20. [Board Papers, EMI Music Archive]

During the 1960s, a single reaching the number one position in the singles charts might expect to have to achieve sales exceeding 750,000. However, by the mid-1970s, to achieve the same position, fewer than 150,000 copies were necessary (this decline continued throughout the 1980s, when sales of 50,000 or less for a single could result in a number one position). Declining unit sales were compounded by the fall in the number of EMI artists achieving hit records (both singles and albums). By 1970, EMI had lost 18 percentage points of the British market share it held in 1960.

Its problems in Britain were compounded by a sudden downturn in its American business. In the United States, the British pop invasion provided EMI's American business, Capitol Records, with substantial profits. Yet, in 1971, poor management, combined with changes in the American record market and a slowdown in the economy, turned a profit of £7.6 million in the previous year into a loss of £6.2 million – a staggering £13.8 million downturn. Lockwood acted quickly, installing a new management team headed by Bhaskar Menon, the former head of The Gramophone Company of India Ltd. Menon reorganized the business and within a short time returned it to profit. He was subsequently to take over as chief executive of EMI Music, a position he held until 1988.

EMI's internal difficulties coincided with the end of the post-war boom. In the wake of this, there emerged a worldwide inflationary spiral of unprecedented proportions, of a kind unseen in Britain since the First World War. Its force was such that prices increased two and a half times between 1970 and 1980. With the end of economic stability came rising unemployment, uncertainty in world markets and collapsing currency values. These were not ideal circumstances to manage a major international business, particularly one that relied heavily on the highly volatile music and leisure industry as a source of sales and profits.

By 1977, it was clear that the Company simultaneously faced profound problems in its American and British record businesses. As L. G. Wood told the EMI board that year:

"The competition facing the EMI Group throughout the world, but principally in the United States of America and in the United Kingdom, is now becoming intense and extremely serious." [Report by L. G. Wood to the Board of EMI, 1977, EMI Music Archive]

These problems arose as a result of the Company's failure to invest in the development of new artists, and its inability to cope with changing patterns of competition which squeezed EMI's record business hard for an increased share of lucrative markets. The Company experienced a period of stagnation, with an effective nil growth in unit sales. Because of strength in other sectors of repertoire, the impact on EMI's market share was less pronounced than might have been expected: for instance, the Company's 1980 share of the British record market was 19 per cent, only 2 per cent down on the 1970 figure. However, EMI was unable to develop a strong roster of pop and rock artists capable of reaching international markets. It was increasingly marginalized, particularly in the pop singles market, a sector of great importance as a vehicle for introducing new pop artists to the public, and for promoting new full-price pop and rock albums.

These problems were aggravated by changes in the broader pop music business. Pop music was becoming fragmented, with each

genre appealing to diverse tastes, so that EMI was catering for
smaller and smaller niche markets that, by their nature, could not
generate the same level of sales that artists such as The Beatles had
done a decade earlier (see Chapter 9). The then dominant British
pop music genres – Punk and New Wave (see Chapter 9) – appealed
to domestic pop music consumers, but failed to sell abroad, especially
in the United States. For EMI, the decline in the international
popularity of British artists reduced pressing-fee income and, at the
same time, increased the costs borne by British sales. Capitol
Records' market share was reduced significantly and its profits were
squeezed. From the mid-1970s, a reassertion of American pop and
rock repertoire further reduced the popularity of EMI artists in
Britain. However, American pop and rock had also fragmented.

To sustain its market share EMI increasingly turned towards its
established performers and the existing back catalogue of LP album
recordings. Whilst these measures satisfied and even helped
develop the middle market – and maintained stable unit sales – the
return on sales of these usually mid- or budget-priced LP records
proved insufficient to maintain profit at the level of earlier years.
After 1977, with inflationary pressures and rising unemployment
pricing the product beyond the pockets of the key impulse
consumer, even this market began to decline.

A significant decline in its position in the classical market added
to the Company's misfortunes. The full-price classical record market
was a sector of the business that had appeared immune from market
changes and movements in the economy. However, as in the other
parts of its record business, EMI seemed unable to develop new
talent. Its classical market share slumped precipitously, from 26 per
cent in 1972 to 20 per cent in 1975. In an attempt to rescue the
deteriorating situation, the Company developed a business licensing
its own repertoire to third parties, usually small specialist re-issue
companies. Costs were further cut by a reorganization of the existing
British catalogue. In 1978, 67 per cent of all sales were derived from
23 titles in this catalogue, whilst a further 452 titles sold less than 500
copies each. As a consequence, many titles and artists were dropped.

Compounding these problems were several new ones, including
piracy (the copying, manufacture and sale of recordings without the
permission of the owners of the copyright, often in single or multi-
album compilation records). Other illicit activities included
counterfeiting – where the artwork and trademarks were illegally
copied, as well as the recording – and bootlegging (selling
recordings made illegally at live concerts). In a small way, piracy
and counterfeiting in one form or another had been with the
industry since its foundation. In the 1970s, however, a shadow
industry and a worldwide distribution network appeared (centred

in the Far East) which specialized in making illegal records. It took a decade of industry and governmental activity to begin to bring this situation under control. Furthermore, from the mid-1970s, home taping of records became widespread, the direct result of low-cost blank cassette tape and a new generation of integrated hi-fi equipment. By the end of the 1970s, these problems had become so widespread and alarming that, together with the severe economic down-turn in 1979, they threatened the industry's very existence.

We don't talk anymore

THE CAT SCANNER

Problems in the music business coincided with severe difficulties in EMI's other activities. In the crisis year of 1979, despite sales of £870 million, pre-tax profits collapsed to £28.5 million (post-tax to a mere £2 million). Much of the losses arose as a result of the way that the Company handled the most important technical

CAT Scanner developed by EMI in the early 1970s.

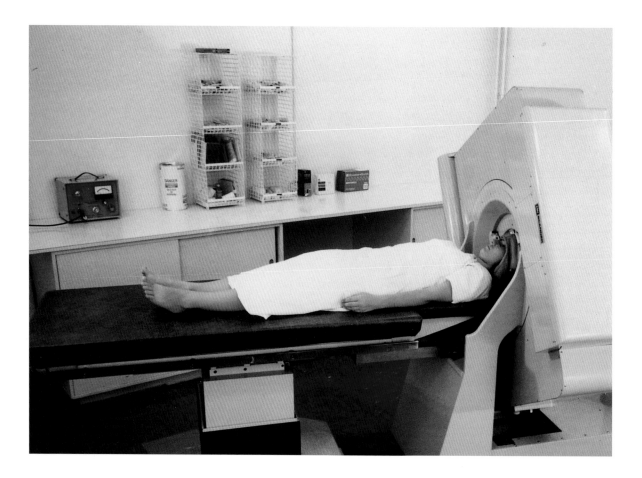

development it ever achieved: the CAT scanner. In 1971, Godfrey (later Sir Godfrey) Hounsfield, a senior engineer at EMI's Central Research Laboratories, developed the Computerized Axial Tomography (CAT) scanner. His work followed the CRL's tradition, developed in the 1930s by Sir Isaac Shoenberg and Alan Blumlein, of finding practical solutions to electrical engineering problems. With the CAT scanner, EMI believed that it had a winner. It was right in terms of the technology; however, as a business venture the scanner quickly became a disaster. Despite heavy investment in the project (using profits derived largely from the record business), by 1979 the project had run into deep trouble. As Lord Delfont later wrote:

We made the mistake of rejecting an American franchise deal on the grounds that we wanted a British invention to stay British. This prompted our [American] competitors to lobby Washington for import restrictions to give them time to produce a superior scanner. Before we knew where we were, the barriers were up on the American market, which up to then had been one of our strongest markets.
[Delfont, ibid., p.202]

I want to hold your hand

THE ACQUISITION AND AFTER

In May 1979, EMI faced a second-half loss and appointed Lord Delfont as its chief executive. Delfont pursued a number of avenues to shore up the rapidly deteriorating financial situation, including an attempt to sell the by then loss-making music business. In his memoirs, Lord Delfont summed up the disastrous situation:

The Music Division, once assumed to be a licence to print money, was going through a difficult period. In this respect, at least, EMI was not alone. The record business is notoriously volatile. Other record companies were experiencing a sales dive that was the equivalent of a free-fall parachute jump. The causes of the disaster were many and various – a failure to cope with home piracy (for every LP sold three were taped), the flood of cheap imported discs from the Far East, rising production and marketing costs and, top of the list, the dearth of talent to follow in the wake of the Beatles and the Rolling Stones and all the other trailblazers of the Sixties and early Seventies.
[Delfont, ibid., p.202]

THE COMPACT DISC

★

By 1982, Philips and Sony had developed a major new record format: the digital audio compact disc (CD). The CD produced a quality of sound thought significantly better than the finest digital-mastered LP, and proved to be an innovation of seminal importance – on a par with the introduction of electrical recording in 1925, the launch of the LP and 45-rpm singles in the late 1940s, and the advent of stereo recording in the late 1950s. Furthermore, the use of a laser to scan the CD – as opposed to a stylus tracking through a groove – marked a vital break with existing recording technology, the principles of which had been laid down during the 1880s in the Bell Tainter graphophone and Berliner gramophone patents.

The CD revolution came at a time when EMI (and the rest of the record industry) was desperately trying to break out of a cycle of stagnation and decline. However, in what was almost a re-run of the LP debacle of 1950 (see Chapter 4), EMI agonized over whether or not to adopt the CD format. There were a number of reasons for this hesitation. Philips wanted a royalty payment for every CD record sold (just as Western Electric had in 1925). Also, at this early stage, and in a way reminiscent of the production problems experienced in the early days of LP manufacture, the manufacture of CDs, with an initial rejection rate of almost 50 per cent was proving to be both technically difficult and costly. The project also required major capital expenditure, which would have been lost had the new format failed (as quadraphonic records and 8-track cartridge tape had done earlier). The Company was also concerned about the retail cost of CDs, which – because of significantly higher manufacturing and processing costs – was appreciably greater than that of LPs, at a time when the economic cycle was just beginning to recover from the worst recession since the 1930s.

Balancing these concerns was a whole range of reasons why EMI simply had to adopt the CD. The most important was the decision of EMI's major competitors to embrace the new format and pay the Philips royalty. Furthermore, the premium retail price enabled EMI to cover the Philips royalty payments and, after years of squeezed margins, obtain a more realistic return on its investment. The coming of CDs also helped the Company to achieve its goal of a truly integrated international business. The manufacture of records had from the earliest days of the business been

dispersed across the Company's major markets. With CDs, it finally became possible to locate factories in a few strategic places around the world and develop a regional distribution network capable of supplying all EMI's international markets. Initially, CD manufacture was undertaken by EMI's Japanese joint venture, Toshiba–EMI; then EMI opened its own British and American facilities at Swindon and in Jacksonville, Illinois (later, a Dutch factory was also opened). The use of international manufacturing facilities had also permitted the creation of a worldwide standard packaging for CD products, and, with standard packaging and products, the Company finally adopted a worldwide logo on all its records.

In November 1982 – a year before the simultaneous launch of EMI's first CDs in Britain, Europe and the United States – Toshiba–EMI released EMI's first ever CD records to test the product in the Japanese

market. The releases included Paul McCartney's *Tug of War* (Toshiba–EMI CP 35-3001), and Sibelius's Symphony No.2 (Toshiba–EMI CC 38-3005), with the Berlin Philharmonic Orchestra conducted by Herbert von Karajan. The Japanese trial, and the subsequent launch in Europe and America, was an enormous success, and sparked a revival in the fortunes of the record industry in general and EMI in particular. In the 18 months following the launch, EMI sold nearly 2.5 million CDs, with Pink Floyd's *Dark Side of the Moon* (EMI CDP 7 46002 2) achieving sales in excess of 140,000. The first classical best-seller was Beethoven's Violin Concerto (EMI Angel CDC 7 47002 2), with Itzhak Perlman and Carlo Maria Giulini, which achieved initial sales of 25,000 units. EMI's release policy at this early stage – with rising demand for CDs restricted by limited manufacturing facilities – was to seek catalogue titles with the greatest common interest to all the Company's sales territories, either from outstanding new releases, or from the best recordings of the past.

The CD technology was quickly accepted by artists, manufacturers, retailers and consumers. Furthermore, as the cost of CD players fell to little more than the price of a conventional record player, the CD market mushroomed. By 1988, world sales of CDs had overtaken those of vinyl LPs, and, by the early 1990s, the LP (just like the 78-rpm disc 30 years earlier) was pushed to the margins of the business, leaving the CD and tape as the industry's two dominant formats.

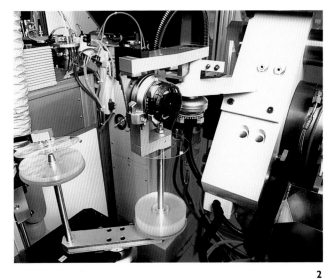

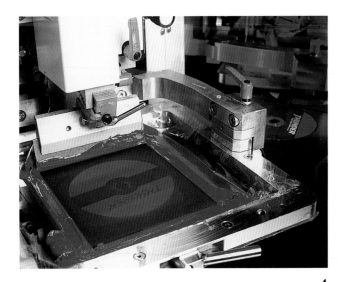

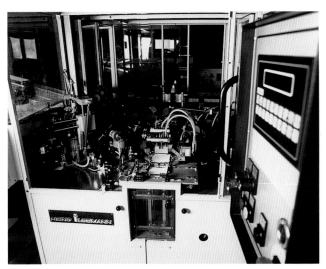

Compact disc manufacturing

1. The CD master disc.
2. Clear discs are stamped from the master.
3. They are given a thin aluminium coating.
4. The label is screen printed on the disc.
5. The discs are automatically packed into their cases.

During 1979, there was a 22 per cent fall in world sales of records manufactured by EMI. As Sir John Read told his shareholders: "The record industry worldwide suffered a severe setback from January 1979, with a marked reduction of sales of recorded music". [Chairman's Statement, Annual Meeting, EMI, 1979] Because of EMI's reliance on its record business to deliver a substantial proportion of the Company's profits and working capital, this disaster caused a sudden and immediate cash flow crisis. In July, EMI recorded a net loss of £14 million, the majority of which arose in the Medical Electronics Division.

It was not until the autumn of 1979 that a bid from Thorn Electrical Industries Ltd – the lighting, consumer electronics, domestic appliances and engineering conglomerate – rescued the Company from impending bankruptcy. The Thorn offer valued EMI at £165 million. Describing the rationale and background to the Thorn bid, Delfont said:

It was not the first time that Thorn had been mooted as a likely partner for EMI. That Company was heavily involved in television manufacture and rentals. With the uncertainties of a market coming to terms with video players and compact discs, it made sense to link with a software manufacture like EMI. When Sir Jules Thorn had been in charge, talks had foundered on his worries of losing control of the business he had built from nothing, but his successor, Sir Richard Cave, was not deterred by tradition. [Delfont, ibid., p.208]

Delfont and Read joined the new THORN EMI board, as did Bhaskar Menon, by now the head of EMI's music division. Under the chairmanship of Sir Richard Cave, the new board set about rationalizing and rebuilding the business. The first casualty was the loss-making Medical Electronics Division. THORN EMI subsequently sold the Hotels and Restaurant Division, and then the Leisure Division, which was acquired by a team headed by Lord Delfont.

Saviour's Day

THE REBIRTH OF EMI

In 1985, THORN EMI appointed a fresh management team, with Sir Graham Wilkins as chairman and Colin (later Sir Colin) Southgate as managing director. The Company abandoned its strategy of diversification and focused on its three core and potentially most profitable businesses: music, rental and retailing. In the wake of this strategy, peripheral activities were disposed of and

Manchester Square and Brook Green
In July 1995, EMI left its Manchester Square home of 35 years for new offices in Brook Green, West London. In the move, the Company took the landing railings made famous in cover photographs of the Beatles.

the money used to reduce indebtedness. In 1985, for instance, EMI's film-making activities were sold. The new team recognized the need for a significant change in direction at EMI which was, by then, barely profitable. EMI operated in an international marketplace and, in order to prosper, it needed new, often novel, organizational and management forms. One of the most important decisions of the time was the recruitment of Jim Fifield as successor to Menon. He spearheaded a major revival in the business, investing heavily in new talent whilst rationalizing and streamlining operations.

EMI's rationalization – reminiscent of Sir Louis Sterling's restructuring in the 1930s (see Chapter 4) – involved the closure of factories in many countries, including the United States, Argentina, Sweden and Ireland, and a complete overhaul of the Company's distribution network. Inevitably, this led to substantial reductions in

THE MUSIC PUBLISHING BUSINESS

★

EMI MUSIC PUBLISHING

Music publishing was the first commercial music business, born when cheap industrialized print production caused an explosion in demand for sheet music. The concept of copyright in music and lyrics subsequently evolved and transformed music publishing into a substantial business. Music publishers are often mistakenly confused with record companies. Most of them operate on an arm's length basis with record companies, and sometimes their interests conflict. Music publishers are the owners or licensees and the protectors of these copyrights and earn their income by marketing them. Copyrights can be bought and sold outright, or "leased". Many successful writers retain ownership of their copyrights but assign their management and administration to a larger organization, usually for a fixed term. In return, the larger publisher pays a recoupable advance and receives a share of the writer's royalties. This is known as sub-publishing.

There are several sources of publishing income, of which sheet music sales are still one. Today, the most important is the so-called mechanical royalty, which arises from the reproduction of the music and lyrics in any mechanical form, such as CD, tape or video. This royalty is paid to the copyright owner by the producer (usually a record company). Next comes the performing fee, paid when a song is broadcast on radio or television, or played in public. The third main source of income is derived from licensing "synchronization" rights. These are licences granted to film, television, video, computer game or advertisement producers for the use of songs in soundtracks.

Like the record companies, music publishers have artist and repertoire managers, whose task it is to find talented songwriters and composers. Often, the music publisher nurtures that talent until finished compositions are ready. Sometimes, the music publisher represents established songwriters, whilst other songwriters are also recording artists of their own and others' compositions.

EMI Music Publishing, the largest music publisher in the world with over one million copyrights owned or administered, has an impressive history stretching back to 1793. The multinational company began to take shape in Britain in 1958 around EMI's small local music publishing subsidiary, Ardmore and Beechwood. In 1969 Keith Prowse Music, Peter Maurice Music and the KPM Background Music Library were purchased. Three years later, the Affiliated Music Publishers group was acquired; it included three renowned publishing firms, Francis, Day & Hunter, B. Feldman & Co and Robbins Music Corporation. This, together with KPM, meant that EMI had brought the cream of British music publishing under its banner. A year later, these companies were grouped under the designation of EMI Music Publishing as an independent entity within EMI. Over the years, EMI Music Publishing has made further important catalogue acquisitions, such as Screen Gems and Colgems Music Publishing from Columbia Pictures in 1976, SBK Entertainment in 1989, Filmtrax in 1990 and Virgin Music Publishers in 1992.

Copyrights published or sub-published by EMI Music Publishing range from turn-of-the-century music hall favourites such as "Don't dilly dally on the way", through wartime morale builders like "We'll meet again", "Pack up your troubles in your old kit bag" and "It's a long way to Tipperary". Examples of later successes include "Blue Moon", "A nightingale sang in Berkeley Square", "New York, New York", "From coming to town". Pop classics include "Wild Thing", "On Broadway", "Will you still love me tomorrow", "Back for Good" and "Bohemian Rhapsody". The artists and composers represented by EMI Music Publishing are as diverse as Rachmaninov, Elgar, Rodgers and Hammerstein, Simply Red, Queen, Enya, Rod Stewart, the Pet Shop Boys and Hootie & the Blowfish.

EMI Music Publishing also administers many exceptional catalogues, amongst which are ATV Music (the Beatles), Jobete (Classic Motown), Flyte Tyme (Jam & Lewis and Janet Jackson) and 20th Century Fox. It owns the rights to music featured in film classics of the calibre of *Meet Me in St. Louis*, *Singing in the Rain* and *The Wizard of Oz*, and has songs represented on numerous feature film soundtracks, including the James Bond, Pink Panther and Rocky series, plus major successes like *Pretty Woman*, *Sleepless in Seattle*, *Forrest Gump*, *Pulp Fiction*, *The Bodyguard*, *Batman Forever*, *Bridges of Madison County*, *Richard III*, *Independence Day* and the much acclaimed *Trainspotting*.

EMI Music Publishing's British subsidiary won the prestigious Queen's Award for Export Achievement in 1995 and is the country's leading music publisher. The American company has also won numerous awards over the years.

**The Queen's Award
for Export Achievement**

VIRGIN MUSIC GROUP

★

Virgin Music was established in 1972 by Richard Branson and Nik Powell. The company came into being after Branson had bought a 17th-century manor house, Shipton Manor, in Oxfordshire and installed in it a recording studio.

Virgin's first major success was in 1973 with Mike Oldfield's *Tubular Bells* (Virgin V 2001). Rejected by all the other British labels, it was recorded entirely at the Manor studio. The album was hailed by underground guru John Peel as "a record of such strength, energy and real beauty that to me it represents the first breakthrough into history that any musician primarily regarded as a rock musician has made." This album is still among Virgin's best-selling albums ever.

Unlike EMI, Virgin courted controversy and made it seem fun. After the Sex Pistols were dropped by EMI in 1976, they were signed by Virgin. Virgin's first promotional gambit was to organize a boat trip on the Thames to mark the release of "God Save the Queen" (Virgin VS 181) in the week of the official Jubilee celebrations. The boat, aptly called the *Elizabethan*, was finally stormed by the police outside the House of Commons, and Malcolm McLaren and other members of the band's entourage arrested. One of the Sex Pistols' subsequent albums, *Never Mind the Bollocks* (Virgin V 2086) was also prosecuted under the Indecent Advertisement Act of 1899. The case

turned on the appropriate – or otherwise – usage of the 18th-century word in the title; it was dismissed, and the album was extremely successful.

With a reputation within the industry for creativity and flair, Virgin had no difficulty in attracting artists who became very successful, and by the early 1990s had become the world's leading independent record company and a force in music publishing. At the time it was acquired by THORN EMI in 1992 it had built up an impressive roster of artists, including Paula Abdul, Belinda Carlisle, Neneh Cherry, Phil Collins, Bryan Ferry, Peter Gabriel, Genesis, Simple Minds, Gary Moore and UB40 and had recently signed new contracts with Janet Jackson and the Rolling Stones. Virgin had established operations in North America, France, Germany, Italy, Canada, Australia, Scandinavia, the Benelux countries, Spain and Hong Kong.

At the time of the acquisition, many inside and outside the record industry questioned whether the purchase price of £560 million was not excessive, given that Virgin's operating profit had been a mere £21 million in its previous financial year. There was also a fear that the Virgin spirit would suffer from culture clash with the "suits" at EMI, leading to unhappy artists and demoralised staff. But the savings achieved by rationalizing the administrative functions of the labels and other benefits proved to be considerable. Virgin's creativity was safeguarded by allowing the Virgin labels across the world to maintain their independence.

Virgin's continuing success speaks for itself: in Britain, its profitability is just short of EMI's, whilst Virgin as a whole made a contribution exceeding £100 million to EMI's profits in the 1995 financial year. Many of the company's earlier signings, such as Phil Collins and Genesis, Peter Gabriel, Bryan Ferry, Gary Moore, Janet Jackson and Meat Loaf, have continued to produce successful albums. Virgin has also been able to develop exciting artists like Lenny Kravitz and Shaggy, and bands such as Spice Girls, Everything but the Girl, Smashing Pumpkins and Massive Attack, whilst revitalizing the careers of industry legends such as George Michael and Iggy Pop.

the workforce. Other features of the reorganization involved the full integration of the Liberty/United Artist business (acquired in 1979) into the EMI organization. Critical to the success of the new management's plans for growth was a large-scale programme of investment in new artists.

At the same time, EMI began a substantial programme of acquisitions which continued through the 1980s and into the early 1990s. Among its major acquisitions were the music publishing business SBK (see *The Music Publishing Business*) and the record label Chrysalis. By 1991, EMI's situation had been transformed, with sales exceeding £1,000 million for the first time, and profits of

£109 million; and EMI's share of the world market hovered around the 12 per cent mark. From the low point of 1985, operating profits had risen at a compound growth rate of 120 per cent per annum. Profitability, as measured by the ratio of operating profits to sales, had risen from 1 per cent to 10.7 per cent. In the circumstances, it is possible to understand the pride Sir Colin Southgate felt in 1992 when he said:

I have saved the jewel in the crown and brought it back to its former glory. It's totally global, has a product that travels globally to a lot of people. I think it is a wonderful business. [Sir Colin Southgate, Interview, *The Times*, 18 April 1992]

That comment was made following the announcement of the acquisition of the Virgin Music Group (see Virgin Music Group, page 263) for £560 million. This was the largest acquisition made after 1985 and turned out to be one of Sir Colin's greatest coups. Virgin's continuing creativity (safeguarded by its independence from other EMI labels) has produced a string of successes.

Record retailing in the 1950s
Until the coming of LPs in the 1950s, retailing was a largely utilitarian affair. The rear wall of this 1950s record shop is covered with brightly illustrated LP sleeves, whilst in the foreground 78-rpm records are displayed still in their cardboard transit packaging.

Virgin's profitability has more than quadrupled in the five years since its acquisition by EMI, and it now contributes over a quarter of EMI's profits. The effect on EMI's overall financial performance has been dramatic: since 1991, sales have more than doubled, from £1.1 billion to over £2.7 billion; operating profits have risen by a compound annual growth rate of 31 per cent; and worldwide market share is estimated at around the 15 per cent level.

In some ways, the rebirth of EMI is due to the return to its earliest strengths at the beginning of the century: investment in the core music business and a focus on national repertoire on successful international operations in the most diverse of the world's markets. For over 40 years following the Second World War, the world music market was dominated by Anglo-American repertoire. In addition, the record industry's fortunes were entirely dependent on sales in the United States, Europe and Japan. During this period, EMI focused its A & R activities on EMI in Britain and Capitol Records in the United States, and on its international classical

When it opened in 1921, HMV's Oxford Street record store in London featured an all-electric illuminated advertising sign.

labels. During the prosperous 1960s and early 1970s, cash flow from the music business was used to bankroll the Company's diversifications into a host of unrelated areas. Paradoxically, the diversification was undertaken to shelter the Company from a downturn in the core business. The collapse of EMI in 1979 demonstrated the weaknesses of this strategy, when all three sources of repertoire suffered simultaneously from creative shortcomings and severe problems in unrelated businesses emerged.

Today, EMI has a network of companies around the world: it operates directly in 42 countries and through licensees in another 36. In over half of the markets in which it has its own operating company, it is estimated that it has achieved the number one or two position (in terms of sales value). It is now one of the most international of record companies. Whilst the record industry's traditional markets are still extremely important, rapid growth is occurring in South East Asia, Latin America and Eastern Europe. Consumers everywhere are increasingly responding to music which

HMV GROUP

★

Before 1920, the Columbia and Gramophone Companies each had retail outlets, but they formed a marginal part of their businesses: records, gramophones and graphophones were sold primarily through a network of dealerships and wholesalers. After the First World War, The Gramophone Company decided that it needed a high-profile flagship shop in London which would appeal to connoisseurs. Sir Edward Elgar opened HMV's first shop, in Oxford Street, in 1921, in the presence of, amongst others, the artist Francis Barraud. A contemporary account described the store as occupying "handsome premises … something beyond an ordinary merchandise emporium … an effort to clothe commerce in a new light, to apply science to the ordinary routine of salesmanship." The new store offered for sale a selection of 200 records, which was considered very broad for the time, whilst a very early electric motion sign on the shopfront displayed both the Nipper trademark and the names of ten of the period's leading HMV artists. To attract potential customers into the store, HMV provided concerts of the latest releases and personal appearances by artists. Another attraction was the staff, who from the store's earliest days were renowned for their musical knowledge.

Until the mid-1950s, the HMV Oxford Street store only stocked musical offerings from EMI labels. Customers were

served at a counter, where they had to ask for a specific title; this they could then listen to in one of 25 sound-proof audition rooms before deciding whether to purchase. When Sir Joseph Lockwood took over as EMI chairman in 1954, he made sweeping changes to the store, including the introduction of self service and a range of inexpensive record players. Lockwood also ended EMI's policy of allowing only one store in each major British town or city to distribute HMV's titles. This change encouraged many new retailers to go into the business of selling records. By 1960, the HMV store itself had begun offering other labels' titles. The Oxford Street store remained HMV's sole outlet until the mid-1960s, when the revolution in music and youth culture created the opportunity for the company's expansion. By the end of the 1960s, HMV had opened some 15 stores in London.

In the early 1970s, HMV expanded its operations beyond London. Whilst the small stores in London were gradually closed, new and larger stores were opened in Manchester, Glasgow and elsewhere in Britain. By the end of the decade, HMV had become one of the country's leading specialist music retailers. By the mid-1980s, HMV had 40 stores in Britain. In 1986, it was established as a stand-alone business in its own right and began expanding overseas. Today, HMV has 241 music stores worldwide and has substantial music retailing operations in seven other countries – the United States, Australia, Japan, Australia, Canada, Hong Kong and Germany. It is now one of the world's largest international music retailing groups.

From the start, HMV's aim has been to appeal to the committed music buyer. Today, its stores offer one of the widest ranges of product, across all genres of popular and classical music, supported by skilled, knowledgeable staff, in exciting and stimulating retail environments.

In 1995, HMV added another major retail brand to its portfolio with the acquisition of the book chain Dillons and its historic flagship store, Hatchards, which by happy coincidence celebrates its bicentenary in 1997.

HMV logo Nipper updated as the current British HMV store signage.

Opposite page, top Sir Edward speaking at the opening of the first HMV shop.

Opposite page, below The first HMV shop was opened in 1921 in Oxford Street, London. The opening ceremony was performed by Sir Edward Elgar, then The Gramophone Company's most distinguished artist. Seated next to Elgar at the inaugural lunch is Alfred Clark, who was then managing director, and next to him is Francis Barraud, who created the famous HMV trademark.

develops out of their own culture and language. More than half of EMI's worldwide sales now come from the repertoire of artists sold in their home country. Its top ten releases typically account for less than 15 per cent of its total sales.

Since 1985, EMI has been transformed into a truly global organization and many of its vulnerabilities have been overcome to create a much more robust company. During this period, Sir Colin also presided over one of the most far-reaching corporate restructurings of the 1980s, entailing the sale of over 100 businesses. In the pursuit of the objective to focus only on globally competitive

Above HMV's store in Terminal 1, Heathrow Airport.

Opposite page HMV's Sands Building superstore, Hong Kong.

In the pursuit of the objective to focus only on globally competitive businesses, THORN EMI reduced itself to EMI, the Thorn rental group and HMV. This strategy proved to be remarkably successful: by 1996, THORN EMI's operating profit was four times higher than a decade earlier, whilst the return on sales had more than doubled. With EMI and Thorn well established and strong in their own right, it was now possible to take the logic of business focus to its ultimate conclusion: THORN EMI demerged into two independent companies, the EMI Group and Thorn plc. Appropriately, a portrait of Alfred Clark, EMI's first chairman, now hangs next to that of Sir Colin Southgate, the chairman of the EMI Group, and the man who oversaw EMI's rebirth and who restored its independence.

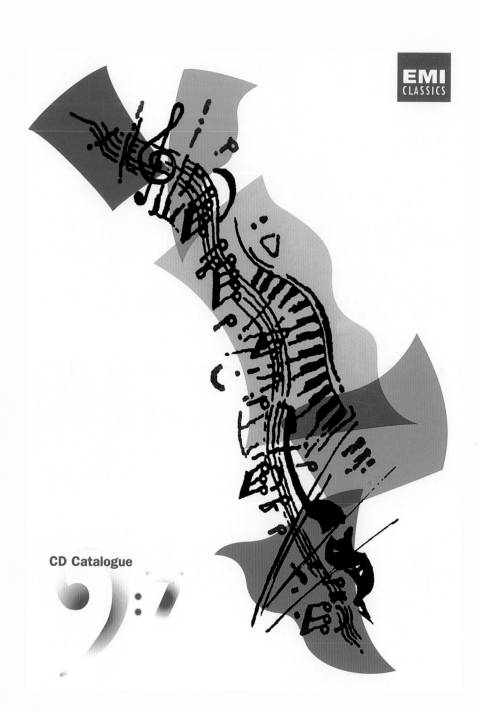

EMI
CLASSICS

CD Catalogue

CHAPTER 8

The Art
of the Recorder

EMI'S CLASSICAL MUSIC RECORDINGS, 1962–1997

When I first joined the department the Classical business was not only the most glamorous but also the most profitable line which the Company possessed and it continued that way for many years.
[David Bicknell, manager, International Artistes Department, 1957–1969]

100 YEARS OF GREAT MUSIC

The Art of the Recorder

EMI'S CLASSICAL RECORDINGS, 1962–1997

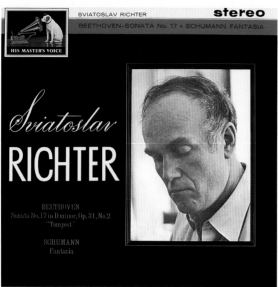

The idea of using LP covers to promote artists was well established by the end of the 1960s.

Although sales and profits from classical music have always accounted for a small percentage of the total, it remains a good and profitable trade. As an additional bonus, it conferred a great deal of prestige on the Company, and this helped attract the greatest classical performers of the modern era. As a result, EMI retained and developed its role as a custodian of an amazing range of recordings, and thus as a major force in the world's art and culture. In its centenary year, the Company remains one of the world's leading producers of classical records.

Sea Pictures

CHANGES IN THE CLASSICAL BUSINESS

The introduction of stereophonic recording in the 1950s dramatically improved the sound quality and spaciousness of LP sound, but its introduction ultimately rendered obsolete EMI's existing catalogues of monophonic LP recordings. This was a bitter blow to the Company, whose heavy investment in the 1950s had been aimed at retrieving the leadership it had ceded following its late adoption of the LP and the loss of American licensed repertoire (see Chapter 5). However, to remain competitive and to retain the confidence and services of performers, EMI had little choice but to remake its LP catalogue, this time using stereo technology. There were some positive aspects to the advent of stereo recording: the Company persuaded existing consumers that it was an improvement of sufficient magnitude for them to re-build their collections of records, and, at the same time, new consumers were attracted into the marketplace. However, to create new stereo catalogues, an even heavier investment was required than had been necessary to build the first LP catalogue. By 1964, this investment was beginning to pay off, with a catalogue of around 500 stereo titles. A large number of these new recordings are considered among the finest EMI ever made and can still be found in the current EMI Classics catalogue.

The other new feature in the classical record business was the start of effective and sustained competition. Although not blind to this pressure, the Company was not panicked either: it could rely to some extent on its relationships with many of Europe's

EMI Classics The worldwide trademark of EMI Classics recordings, together with the Angel and His Master's voice trademarks which are now restricted to local releases.

greatest artists, orchestras, conductors and record producers. However, the evolving environment convinced EMI's senior executives that the organization and marketing strategy of its own classical record business had to change.

The heart of EMI's classical record business was still the International Artistes Department (see Chapter 5). Despite the passage of time, the department's responsibilities had remained remarkably unchanged. The head of the department between 1957 and 1969 was David Bicknell, an enormously able and cultured man who had begun his career at The Gramophone Company in 1927 (see Chapters 2 and 5). Bicknell took on the task of reforming what had become an increasingly unstable organization. To start with, the main HMV and Columbia labels, although officially within his department, were, in practice, distinct semi-autonomous bodies, complete with their own staffs, special interests and rivalries. EMI's senior producers, Victor Olof (who had succeeded Bicknell as the head of the HMV label) and Walter Legge (the head of Columbia), enjoyed unprecedented autonomy and independence. They competed against each other for artists, who were under contract to their

High quality reproduction of attractive paintings were often used to enhance the appearance of LP sleeves.

labels rather than to EMI. They were also entirely responsible for those artists, the development of their repertoire and the marketing and release of their records. In those circumstances, it was by no means unusual for each label to release simultaneously recordings of the same work, with different artists.

This extraordinary and, by the 1960s, indefensible duplication dated back to the formation of EMI in 1931. At the time, the existence of two separate organizations within a single department was seen as an essential prerequisite to retaining the important RCA Victor and Columbia Records licensing agreements (see Chapter 4). It may have been possible to justify this in the circumstances of the 1930s and 1940s, but, by the 1950s, and especially after the agreements with RCA Victor and Columbia were terminated, it had become irrelevant and an obstacle to the proper management of the business. Furthermore, by the early 1960s, the competition between the HMV and Columbia labels made the organization inward-looking, and unable to focus on what was becoming a strongly competitive international environment. Sir Joseph Lockwood, EMI's chairman, recognized this and was clearly irritated by the apparent arrogance of the classical music side and its inability to sort itself out. He said:

It was a conscious decision of mine to support pop music and play down the importance of the classical people a bit – not to discourage them but not to let them think they owned the bloody place … We would never have been anything in the music business without pop music, we couldn't just go on relying on classical. [Southall, *Abbey Road*, p.56]

Internal resistance to integration between the labels and to tighter management of the Company's staff producers was partly resolved when the mercurial Walter Legge left in 1964. Moves were also made to rationalize artist management, and, for the first time since the merger, artists came under contract to EMI rather than to HMV or Columbia.

The first attempts were also made to create a common corporate identity for EMI's products. Until that time, for a range of historical and licensing reasons, EMI's premium-priced classical recordings had been marketed by the various local EMI companies (such as EMI Records in Britain and Electrola in Germany) on an assortment of record labels, using an extraordinary variety of trademarks. Part of the problem centred on the Company's inability, because of deals done with Emile Berliner and the Victor Company at the turn of the century, to use its premier HMV trademark throughout the world. Some steps were nevertheless taken to limit the variety of record labels used and to define their repertoire. For instance, in Britain, classical artists who had previously appeared on the Columbia label were transferred to HMV; Columbia was exclusively given over to popular music. Despite these actions, the lack of uniform labelling and trademarks on EMI products proved to be a crucial and enduring weakness in EMI's international marketing organization, and added significantly to costs. Unfortunately for the Company, this issue remained unresolved until the coming of the CD.

Bicknell and Lockwood also had to find a way to tame EMI's powerful local companies so as to improve disparate international classical record marketing. These companies enjoyed a great deal of independence. For instance, they commissioned and made their own classical recordings to meet the particular needs of their domestic markets. Unfortunately, many of these recordings duplicated those already in the catalogue or competed with the premium-priced big-name recordings made by the International Artistes Department, and some had no sales potential in any other market.

In 1958, Lockwood attempted to resolve these problems by creating the International Classical Repertoire Committee to determine and manage the Company's classical recording

The career of pianist and Tchaikovsky prize winner John Ogdon was destroyed by illness. Fortunately for posterity he recorded a representative sample of his exceptional repertoire.

programmes. The Committee combined the talents of creative, sales and financial staff from the local EMI companies in Britain, Germany, France, Italy and the United States (and later Japan) together with members of the International Artistes Department. The department and local record producers proposed works they

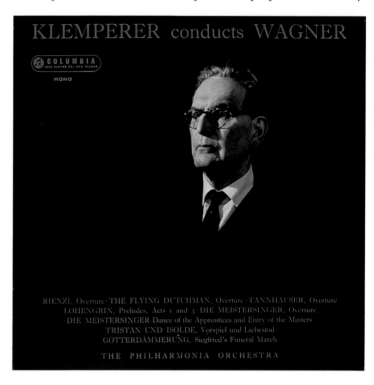

One of Otto Klemperer's best-selling records.

wished to record, whilst the commercial representatives indicated their sales potential. Armed with this information – and estimates for recording and other costs – it was possible for the first time to try to identify those recordings which might show a profit.

There were understandable fears that the existence of the Committee would destroy the intimate relationship between the producers and performers. Previously, the producers had been the sole judge of artistic talent, and had been allowed to assess performers' repertoire and to initiate recording commitments. However, in the event, these fears proved to be unfounded. Another concern was that popular best-selling works would dominate the Company's recording programmes. Fortunately, Lockwood had built into the budget a sum dedicated to making records of works failing to meet his strict financial criteria. Within a few years, the Committee had achieved significant reductions in costs and overheads, and had almost doubled the profits of the classical division. There is no better proof of its continuing effectiveness than the fact that the Committee has remained in place for 40 years.

Salome

THE GROWING POWER OF ARTISTS

Throughout its history, the Company had had long-term exclusive contracts with most of its artists. However, from the late 1950s onwards, the number of wholly exclusive artists was drastically reduced, and other artists were signed on long-term but non-exclusive agreements. This gave EMI more flexibility to seek out the best available performers on a project-by-project basis, while still keeping a small number of major names like Menuhin and Klemperer as flag-bearers.

One of the main reasons why the Company reorganized its classical roster was the spiralling cost of making recordings. In the early 1960s, the average cost of making classical LP records grew from £4,200 to £6,000. The costs involved in recording complete operas and some orchestral works increased by even greater amounts: the three-LP recording of *Carmen* (HMV Angel SAN 140–42), featuring Maria Callas and made in 1964, cost almost £30,000 to make – or £10,000 per LP. These sharp rises were mainly attributable to demands for larger session payments by performers, conductors and orchestras.

Peter Andry joined the International Artistes Department in 1956 as an HMV producer. When he became manager of the Department in 1969, he consolidated EMI's worldwide classical recording and marketing activities by forming the International Classical Division, which he headed until he left the Company in 1989.

A Mass of Life

THE EMERGENCE OF EMI CLASSICS

EMI's great post-war record producers – Walter Legge, David Bicknell and Victor Olof, all of whom had made the transition from the 78-rpm format to complete recordings using stereo technology – ended their association with the Company during the 1960s. Their successors, Peter Andry, Ronald Kinloch Anderson, Christopher Bishop, Suvi Raj Grubb, David Mottley, John Willan, John Mordler, John Fraser and Michel Glotz, proved just as effective in developing the art of record-making. Between them, they made many distinguished classical recordings for EMI which continue to find appreciative audiences throughout the world.

Peter Andry, who succeeded David Bicknell in 1969, restructured the business. He formed the International Classical Division, merging the creative and recording responsibilities of the International Artists Department (when he took over, Andry dropped the archaic "e" in "artistes") with the marketing arm of EMI's international classical record business. As a consequence of this change, there was greater uniformity in record sleeves, sleeve notes and booklets, and,

DAME JANET BAKER
(BORN 1933)

★

The mezzo-soprano Dame Janet Baker, one of the finest singers Britain has produced this century, was born at Hatfield, Yorkshire. She began singing with the Ambrosian Singers in 1955, and a year later she joined the Glyndebourne Festival Chorus and made her operatic debut as Roza in Smetana's *The Secret* with the Oxford University Club. She began to perform regularly in concerts and increasingly took on important operatic roles, singing for the first time with the Handel Opera Society in 1959, and with the English Opera Group in 1962. In 1966 she made her debut at Covent Garden as Hermia in Britten's *Midsummer Night's Dream*. American engagements followed, beginning with New York in 1966 when she took part in a concert performance of Donizetti's *Anna Bolena* and a particularly memorable song recital in Town Hall. Throughout her career she divided her time between the operatic stage and the recital platform, where audiences responded to her strong personality and highly expressive voice in deeply penetrating performances of songs from the French, German and English repertoire, much of which she recorded for EMI. She continued to appear at Covent Garden, Glyndebourne and with the English and Scottish Opera until 1982 when she gave her final performances as Orfeo in Gluck's *Orfeo ed Euridice* at Glyndebourne and the Royal Albert Hall. She was honoured with the title of Dame Commander of the British Empire (DBE) in 1976. Ronald Kinloch Anderson, who produced many of her recordings, once said of Janet Baker: "she has the ability of making each individual member of the audience feel that she is singing just for them."

although local companies continued to make specialist classical recordings for their domestic markets, they found their activities severely curtailed.

It was not until 1990 that the task of consolidating all EMI's worldwide classical record activities started by Joseph Lockwood in 1959 was completed. At that time, the organization was rechristened EMI Classics, and, for the first time ever, virtually all the Company's classical records were marketed under the same trademark. Another feature of this consolidation was the creation of a single international catalogue, printed in three languages. Thus, almost 60 years after EMI's formation, the Company presented consumers throughout the world with a single classical catalogue, using a uniform record numbering system, and trilingual sleeve notes.

Song of the High Hills
THE CLASSICAL MARKET TAKES OFF AGAIN

In Britain, during the mid-1960s, EMI Records sold on average 800,000 classical LP records, and around 300,000 classical singles and extended-play records (the 45-rpm format was phased out of the classical market in the late 1960s) each year. However, after 1969, as the Company developed new mid-price and budget-range products, the classical record sector grew rapidly (see below). Other changes spurred its growth, including a growing worldwide interest in classical music, increasing competition (which multiplied the range and diversity of releases), and significant improvements in the marketing of artists and releases.

One consequence of this rapid growth after 1970 was a radical change in the Company's and the broader industry's methods of doing business (see Chapter 7). The growth in the classical market attracted many new competitors – some with very deep pockets – who offered serious competition. As a result of this, the Company experienced a steady diminution in its share of the international market, which fell from 26 per cent to 16 per cent in the 15 years to 1987. By way of contrast, British sales remained significantly ahead throughout this period and, by the late 1980s, it held steady at a 28 per cent share of the market. At this time, about one fifth of its sales were derived from recordings made by British performers such as the violinist Nigel Kennedy and the singer Dame Janet Baker (see box, page 278), the New Philharmonia Orchestra, and the Choir of King's College, Cambridge, in music by Elgar, Vaughan Williams, Walton and Britten.

Also sprach Zarathustra
CONDUCTORS

From the start, EMI's repertoire strategy has been to create and maintain a large and representative catalogue of classical recordings from the orchestral repertoire. At the heart of this strategy is the need to attract and retain the best available conductors, and to provide them with opportunities to record a wide range of repertoire.

During the 1930s and 1940s, EMI was remarkably successful at recruiting and retaining under contract a whole generation of renowned conductors – a number of whom had been mainstays of the classical record catalogues since the days of the old mechanical recording process – and their subsequent recordings dominated the Company's catalogues. However, during the course of the 1960s, a number of these celebrated figures ended their careers through retirement or death. Among the

The Australian conductor Charles Mackerras with producer Christopher Bishop in the control room at the Kingsway Hall, London, during the recording of Handel's *Messiah* in 1966.

losses through death were the British conductors Sir Malcolm Sargent, Sir John Barbirolli and Sir Thomas Beecham. Beecham's final operatic recording – Mozart's *Entführung aus dem Serail* (Columbia 33CX 1462–3 & SAX 2427–9) – was released posthumously in early 1962. As an affectionate tribute to this great man, EMI also released a recording called *Beecham in Rehearsal* (HMV ALP 1874). Using rehearsal and other out-takes, this remarkable and highly entertaining record eavesdropped on the preparations for the *Entführung* recording. It revealed Beecham's sheer professionalism, his leadership qualities, and his famed rapier wit and repartee.

As a contrast, there was the unexpected late flowering of Otto Klemperer, who had become the principal conductor of the Philharmonia (after 1964, the New Philharmonia), EMI's main house orchestra. From 1954 until 1971 (the year before his retirement), and despite failing health and growing infirmity, Klemperer created an extraordinary recorded legacy, including works by Haydn, Mozart, Beethoven, Brahms, Wagner and Mahler. Reviewing Klemperer's 1962 recording of Beethoven's opera *Fidelio* (Columbia 33CX 1804–6 & SAX 2451–3), with Christa Ludwig, Jon Vickers and the Philharmonia, the critic Harold Rosenthal observed:

And here now preserved for all time is this great conductor's conception and realization of what has been called "that noble faulty work, which makes most other operas seem shabby by comparison" – and no more so than when conducted and performed as it is in this magnificent new recording. [*Opera*, Vol.13, No.8, August 1962]

Klemperer's other complete opera recordings with the New Philharmonia Orchestra included Mozart's *Don Giovanni* (HMV SLS 923), *Le nozze di Figaro* (HMV SLS 955), *Così fan tutte* (HMV SLS 961) and *Die Zauberflöte* (HMV SLS 912), as well as Wagner's *Fliegende Holländer* (HMV SLS 934).

In addition to Klemperer and Karajan, EMI's roster of conductors in the 1950s contained several others whose names began with the same letter, including Paul Kletzki, Rafael Kubelik, Efrem Kurtz, Henry Krips and Rudolf Kempe. Of this group, only Kempe continued to record for EMI into the 1960s and 1970s, concentrating on the music of Wagner, Beethoven and especially Richard Strauss.

Herbert von Karajan, whose association with EMI as a non-exclusive artist continued until his death in 1989, made many outstanding recordings during this period. His appointment in 1964 as director of the Salzburg Festival led to extensive

Beethoven's Triple Concerto, featuring three Russian superstars and the Berlin Philharmonic Orchestra conducted by Herbert von Karajan, was one of EMI's best-selling classical albums of the 1970s.

ANDRÉ PREVIN
(BORN 1929)

In the 1970s, André Previn established himself in Britain and the United States as a leading conductor and popularizer of classical music. He was born Andreas Ludwig Priwin of Russian Jewish parents in Berlin. In 1938, the family left Nazi Germany for Paris, where Andreas studied at the Conservatoire. Then, in 1939, changing their name to Previn, the family emigrated to America where a relative, Charles Previn, was head of music at Universal Studios. While still at school, André started to work in Hollywood, orchestrating and arranging scores, and writing his first complete film score at the age of 18. During the mid-1940s, his interest in jazz developed and he made a number of successful recordings with his own trio. He continued to work on musical films, winning four Oscars between 1958 and 1964, but also developed a career as a concert pianist and classical conductor. He made his conducting debut in St Louis, and, in 1967, succeeded Sir John Barbirolli as music director of the Houston Symphony Orchestra. In 1969, he became principal conductor of the London Symphony Orchestra and began recording exclusively for EMI for whom he quickly produced an extensive catalogue of successful recordings. Among his first major projects were complete versions of the Tchaikovsky ballets: *Swan Lake* (HMV SLS 5070), *Sleeping Beauty* (HMV SLS 5001) and *The Nutcracker* (HMV SLS 834). In 1977, he became musical director of the Pittsburgh Symphony Orchestra and also appeared as guest conductor with the Vienna Philharmonic, recording a number of works with both orchestras for EMI.

recordings of festival productions. Among the greatest of these were Beethoven's *Fidelio* (HMV SLS 954), Wagner's *Tristan und Isolde* (HMV SLS 963), Richard Strauss's *Salome* (HMV SLS 5139), and a number of Verdi operas, including *Otello* (HMV SLS 975), *Aida* (HMV EX 29 0808 3) and *Don Carlos* (HMV SLS 5154). Karajan was at the time principal conductor of the Berlin Philharmonic Orchestra, with whom he explored Mozart, Schubert, Bruckner and Tchaikovsky, and recorded a famous version of Richard Strauss's *Don Quixote* (HMV ASD 3118), with the Russian cellist Mstislav Rostropovich. By the 1980s, Herbert von Karajan's position in the musical world was unassailable, and his enthusiastic espousal of the CD format proved decisive in the acceptance of it by the classical record-buying public.

In 1965, André Previn (see box), one of EMI's new generation of conductors, began to record for the Company. As principal conductor of the London Symphony Orchestra (LSO), he soon established his reputation as a leading interpreter of Romantic composers, recording much of the popular Russian and French repertoire. His LSO recording of Rachmaninov's Second Symphony (HMV ASD 2889) achieved British sales of 14,000 copies in the year following its release. Previn was also a great interpreter of English music, as is evident in the recordings he made of the music of Vaughan Williams, Walton and others. However, his greatest achievement was to popularize classical music through his many recordings, concerts and television appearances. His mass appeal was demonstrated by the success of the record series *André Previn's Music Night*. Despite Previn's popular appeal, he was not averse to taking chances, and explored

DANIEL BARENBOIM
(BORN 1942)

★

Daniel Barenboim was born in Buenos Aires of Russian Jewish descent, and made his first public appearance there as a pianist at the age of seven, having been taught to play by his parents. Barenboim moved to Israel with his family in 1952, and studied music with a number of distinguished teachers in Europe. His American debut was made at Carnegie Hall in January 1957, when he played Prokofiev's First Piano Concerto under Stokowski. His conducting debut took place in Israel in 1962 and, from 1964, he appeared regularly with the English Chamber Orchestra as conductor and sometimes soloist as well, directing from the keyboard. In 1966, he was signed by EMI and began recording at a prodigious rate, completing some 20 LPs in the first year alone, as both pianist and conductor. His very first album, of Beethoven's *Moonlight*, *Appassionata* and *Pathétique* Sonatas (HMV HQS 1076), was an immediate hit and helped establish him as a major artist. He married the cellist Jacqueline du Pré in Israel in June 1967, and they recorded a number of chamber works and concertos together. In 1973, he made his first appearance as an opera conductor at the Edinburgh Festival; he went on to develop this side of his career considerably. In recent years, he has made a number of important recordings for EMI with the Berlin Philharmonic Orchestra, including Beethoven's piano concertos once again (EMI Angel CDS 7 47974 8) and the Beethoven Triple Concerto with the violinist Itzhak Perlman and the cellist Yo-Yo Ma (EMI Classics CDC 5 55516 2).

some of the less frequented by-ways of the classical repertoire, for example, Messiaen's *Turangalîla* Symphony (HMV SLS 5117).

In 1979, EMI released its first digitally recorded classical record, of Debussy's haunting *Images* and *Prélude à l'après-midi d'un faune* (HMV ASD 3804), with the LSO conducted by Previn. Previn's interpretation and the quality of sound achieved made this a landmark record, an achievement made all the greater given the technological limitations of the very earliest digital recordings, which permitted neither editing nor remixing. The record was such a success that it was chosen to launch EMI's first classical CD series in 1983. Previn's contribution to the art of recording combined both creativity and control in the often difficult surroundings of the recording studio. As the writer Arthur Jacobs said of him:

From his earliest professional years he became a master of the problems of timing and tact in the recording studio, and under his direction the LSO fulfilled an extensive and profitable recording programme. [Ed. Stanley Sadie, *The New Grove Dictionary of Music and Musicians* (London 1980) Vol.15, p.223]

The versatility of the virtuoso pianist and conductor Daniel Barenboim (see box), whose first EMI records were released in the mid-1960s, also exemplified the Company's new generation of classical performers. By 1974, he had completed the mammoth task of recording all Mozart's piano concertos (HMV SLS 5031), as well as Beethoven's complete piano

DIETRICH FISCHER-DIESKAU (BORN 1925)

★

The baritone Dietrich Fischer-Dieskau, one of the world's leading exponents of Lieder, was born in Berlin. He made his concert debut in 1947 in Freiburg and his operatic debut a year later in Berlin. He was soon singing regularly in the main musical centres and at the most prestigious festivals, including Salzburg, Edinburgh, Bayreuth, Vienna and Berlin. His commanding stage presence and exceptional voice were well-suited to the operatic stage, but his greatest achievements have been in Lieder. With a repertoire of more than 1,000 songs and a vast catalogue of recordings covering almost every work suitable for a male singer, his accomplishment is unique. Walter Legge first recorded Fischer-Dieskau for EMI in October 1951 in Beethoven's *An die ferne Geliebte* (HMV DB 21347–8) and Schubert's cycle *Die schöne Müllerin* (HMV DB 21388–95), accompanied by Gerald Moore. In the following years he continued recording Lieder for EMI, as well as oratorios and operas such as Richard Strauss's *Capriccio* (Columbia 33CX 1600–602), Wagner's *Tannhäuser* (HMV ALP 1876–9 and ASD 445–8) and Hindemith's *Mathis der Maler* (HMV SLS 5182). At the end of his singing career, Fischer-Dieskau published several important books on Lieder. Fischer-Dieskau's long-standing accompanist Gerald Moore, in his autobiography *Am I Too Loud?*, said of the singer: "He understands what the composer felt, and is able to reveal and express it so piercingly that it goes to the heart."

sonatas (HMV SLS 794) and piano concertos (HMV SLS 5180). He also recorded works by Bartók, Brahms and Chopin. As conductor of the English Chamber Orchestra, Barenboim recorded several of Mozart's greatest works, including the *Requiem* (HMV ASD 2788), featuring Sheila Armstrong, Janet Baker, Nicolai Gedda (see box, page 289) and Dietrich Fischer-Dieskau (see box); several late symphonies; and the operas *Le nozze di Figaro* (HMV SLS 995) and *Don Giovanni* (HMV SLS 978).

Above Dietrich Fischer-Dieskau and Gerald Moore.

Left Janet Baker shares a joke with the pianist and conductor Daniel Barenboim (centre) and EMI producer Suvi Raj Grubb during a playback.

Opposite page André Previn with the original EMI digital recording equipment.

SIR CHARLES GROVES
(1915–1992)

★

Sir Charles Groves contributed considerably to music in Britain, both by his work in Bournemouth and Liverpool and also through his many recordings of music by British composers. Born in London on 10 March 1915, Groves was educated at the Choir School of St Paul's Cathedral and later at the Royal College of Music. He began professionally in music as a freelance accompanist; in 1938 he joined the BBC, where he worked until 1951, regularly conducting several of the corporation's orchestras. From 1951 to 1961 he was music director of the Bournemouth Symphony Orchestra, which he helped to found from the old Bournemouth Municipal Orchestra; then, after two years with the Welsh National Opera, he was musical director of the Royal Liverpool Philharmonic Orchestra from 1963 to 1977. In 1967 he was also appointed associate conductor of the Royal Philharmonic Orchestra. Groves made a substantial number of recordings for EMI, mainly with the Royal Liverpool Philharmonic Orchestra, including music by Delius and other British composers and also a group of popular titles for the Columbia Studio Two series, such as *Overture Spectacular!* (Columbia TWO 190), *Reverie* (Columbia TWO 199) and *The Best of Eric Coates* (Columbia TWO 226). His recordings with other orchestras included Malcolm Arnold's Second Symphony with the Bournemouth Symphony Orchestra (HMV ASD 3353), a programme of Holst choral pieces with the London Symphony Orchestra (HMV ASD 3435) and the first complete recording of Vaughan Williams's opera *Hugh the Drover* with the Royal Philharmonic Orchestra and a large cast of leading British singers (HMV SLS 5162). He was knighted in 1973.

Right The Italian conductor Riccardo Muti has recorded for EMI since 1973, producing an extensive catalogue of operas, orchestral works and concertos with the world's finest orchestras, singers and instrumentalists.

Riccardo Muti was another of the generation of conductors whose recording career began with EMI in the 1970s. As the relationship developed, Muti made significant contributions to EMI's classical catalogue, with recordings of sacred, operatic and symphonic music, at first mainly with the Philharmonia Orchestra, of which he was principal conductor at the time. His early operatic recordings included Verdi's *Aida* (HMV SLS 977), featuring Montserrat Caballé and Placido Domingo; *Un ballo in maschera* (HMV SLS 984), with Placido Domingo and Martina Arroyo; and *Macbeth* (HMV SLS 992), with Sherrill Milnes, Fiorenza Cossotto and José Carreras. Muti's later recordings included several with the Berlin Philharmonic Orchestra, as well as a series of orchestral works and Mozart operas with the Vienna Philharmonic Orchestra, some of these made "live" during performances at the Salzburg Festival. During his time as music director at La Scala, Milan, he recorded a series of Verdi operas, and he produced an extensive catalogue of recordings during his tenure as music director of the Philadelphia Orchestra in the United States.

The British conductor Sir Charles Groves (see box, page 284), came to prominence as an EMI artist during the 1970s and 1980s, and was also the genial successor to Sir Malcolm Sargent as conductor of the Last Night of the Proms. His affiliations with the Royal Liverpool Philharmonic Orchestra, the Royal Philharmonic Orchestra and other ensembles resulted in many important recordings of music by English composers. He was a great exponent of the music of Delius, and among his finest Delius recordings were *A Mass of Life* (HMV SLS 958), recorded in German with Heather Harper, Robert Tear, Benjamin Luxon and the London Philharmonic Orchestra; the choral-orchestral *Sea Drift* (HMV ASD 357), with the Royal Liverpool Philharmonic Orchestra; and *Song of the High Hills* (HMV ASD 2958), with Miriam Bowen and Peter Bingham, also with the Royal Liverpool Philharmonic Orchestra. In addition, Groves recorded several of Delius's orchestral works and made the first complete recording of his opera *Koanga* (HMV SLS 974), with Eugene Holmes, Raimund Herincx and the London Symphony Orchestra. Groves's EMI recordings also included works by Elgar, Frank Bridge, Havergal Brian, Eric Coates and Malcolm Williamson, and Sir Arthur Sullivan's rarely performed "Irish" Symphony (HMV ASD 2435).

Cello Concerto

JACQUELINE DU PRÉ AND PAUL TORTELIER

Perhaps the most remarkable British instrumentalist to emerge during the 1960s was the cellist Jacqueline du Pré (see box). In the course of her tragically short career, which ended in the early 1970s when she was struck down by multiple sclerosis, she made a series of justly famous recordings for EMI. Among these were Beethoven's Cello Sonata Nos. 3 and 5 (HMV ASD 2572), with Stephen Kovacevich (then known as Stephen Bishop), and Beethoven's piano trios (HMV SLS 789), with her husband Daniel Barenboim and the violinist Pinchas Zukerman. Jacqueline du Pré also recorded the Delius Cello Concerto (HMV ASD 2764) with Sir Malcolm Sargent and the Royal Philharmonic Orchestra, as well as other cello concertos by Haydn, Schumann, Boccherini, Saint-Saëns and Dvořák, with Barbirolli, Sargent and Barenboim. However, her most enduring legacy was the 1965 recording of the Elgar Cello Concerto,

JACQUELINE DU PRÉ
(1945–1987)

★

Jacqueline du Pré's intensely emotional and romantic style of cello playing helped transform popular perception and understanding of the cello literature. She was born in Oxford and made her London debut at the age of 16 with a sensational recital at the Wigmore Hall. Soon afterwards, she played to great acclaim the Elgar Cello Concerto at the Festival Hall with the BBC Symphony Orchestra and Rudolf Schwarz. She repeated the work at her American debut on a concert tour with the BBC Symphony Orchestra in early 1965. On her return to Britain, she made her classic recording of the concerts for EMI at Kingsway Hall, London, on 19 August 1965. During the early 1970s she began to display symptons of the debilitating disease multiple sclerosis, which forced her to retire from the public stage soon afterwards. She gave her last public performance in New York in 1973, playing the Brahms Double Concerto with the violinist Pinchas Zukerman with the New York Philharmonic Orchestra conducted by Leonard Bernstein.

PAUL TORTELIER
(1914–1990)

Paul Tortelier, one of France's most distinguished cellists, was born in Paris. He began to play the cello at the age of six and studied at the Paris Conservatoire, winning the Premier Prix in 1930 with a performance of the Elgar Cello Concerto. He made his debut at the Concerts Lamoureux in 1931, and in 1935 he became first cello of the Monte Carlo Orchestra, moving in 1937 to the Boston Symphony Orchestra, where he remained until 1939. He spent the war years in Paris and in 1946 joined the Paris Conservatoire Orchestra. In 1947 he was invited by Sir Thomas Beecham to make his British debut at the Richard Strauss Festival in London playing *Don Quixote*, a work he had previously played in Monte Carlo under the composer's direction. The performance was a great success, and the subsequent recording with Beecham (HMV DB 6796–800) set the seal on Tortelier's international solo career. Throughout his life, Tortelier continually studied and performed the solo cello suites of J. S. Bach; he published two separate editions of the suites and made two authoritative recordings of them for EMI. A striking performer on the concert platform, combining poetic phrasing and sensitivity with great strength and muscularity of playing, Tortelier found his reputation in Britain was further enhanced by a series of charismatic master classes on television beginning in 1964. The doyen of cellists, Pablo Casals, once praised Tortelier's mastery of his instrument thus: "When you play you make it talk."

with the London Symphony Orchestra conducted by Sir John Barbirolli (HMV ALP 2106 & ASD 655).

Barbirolli, a cellist himself, advised and guided Jacqueline du Pré throughout the recording. When it was all over, the old man mused: "I've accompanied a few of the great ones … in this in my time [including] Casals … This girl's remarkable though – she plays it from the heart." [*Jacqueline du Pré*, EMI, Eyewitness Report] As soon as the record was released, it acquired a status as one of the seminal recordings of the century. As the *Gramophone*'s reviewer noted: "Not only is every phrase eloquent – so is every note. It is a totally committed performance, to a degree that one all too rarely encounters." [*Gramophone*, Vol.43, December 1965]

In contrast to Jacqueline du Pré, Paul Tortelier (see box) enjoyed a long and fruitful recording career. He first came to the Company's attention as a result of a prescient letter written early in 1930 by his teacher, the great French violinist Eugène Ysaÿe, to Fred Gaisberg at HMV. He wrote: "Paul Tortelier, who at the age of sixteen has just obtained a brilliant first prize at the Paris Conservatoire, is a very interesting personality, and is destined for a magnificent career." [Tortelier Artist File, EMI Music Archive] By the 1970s, Tortelier was at the height of his career, with a string of successful EMI recordings behind him, including the Elgar and Dvořák cello concertos (HMV ASD 2906 & 3652). His love of chamber music resulted in several fine recordings and brought him into contact with other virtuoso performers, such as the violinists Yehudi Menuhin and Shuku Iwasaki and the pianist Eric Heidsieck. They variously recorded the Beethoven cello sonatas (HMV SLS 836), and the Delius and Brahms double concertos (HMV ASD 3343 and EG 27 0268 1).

Songs of the Auvergne

SINGERS

EMI's tradition of recording great singers reached one of its periodic peaks during the 1960s, when the Company's three great post-war sopranos, Maria Callas, Elisabeth Schwarzkopf and Victoria de los Angeles, made some of their most successful recordings. The enduring quality of EMI's recordings is best demonstrated by the number of Callas albums listed in EMI's current classical catalogues. Of these, her 1964 recording of Bizet's opera *Carmen* (HMV Angel SAN 140–42), which also featured Nicolai Gedda, Andréa Guiot and the Paris Opera Orchestra conducted by Georges Prêtre, was considered by many as near perfection. As the critic Philip Hope-Wallace wrote: "Hers is a Carmen to haunt you." The following year, EMI brought together Maria Callas, Tito Gobbi and the Paris Conservatoire Orchestra conducted by Georges Prêtre to record Puccini's *Tosca* (HMV Angel SAN 149–50), the opera in which Callas had made her triumphant return to the operatic stage in Zeffirelli's

The soprano Elisabeth Schwarzkopf (front) with (from left to right) the tenor Nicolai Gedda, the soprano Henny Steffek, the producer Walter Legge and the conductor Lovro von Matačić in the control room at the Kingsway Hall, London, during the recording of Lehár's operetta *The Merry Widow* in July 1962.

CARLO MARIA GIULINI
(BORN 1914)

★

Carlo Maria Giulini's deep musical sensitivity and total dedication to his work have singled him out as one of the greatest conductors of our time. Born in Barletta, Italy, Giulini began his musical career as an orchestral viola player in Rome. He soon graduated to conducting, particularly opera, and in 1953 succeeded Victor de Sabata as principal conductor of La Scala, Milan. His first recordings for EMI were the Cherubini Requiem in Rome (Columbia 33CX 1075) and Gluck's *Iphigénie en Tauride* at Aix-en-Provence (Pathé DTX 130–32). In the mid-1950s, Walter Legge began to invite Giulini to London for recordings and later concerts with the Philharmonia Orchestra, but it was his performance of Verdi's *Don Carlo* at the Royal Opera House in 1958 and the 1959 all-star recording of Mozart's *Don Giovanni* (Columbia 33CX 1717–20 and SAX 2369–72), in which Giulini replaced an indisposed Otto Klemperer, that set the seal on his reputation as an opera conductor of the very highest calibre. Giulini's deeply moving performances of the Verdi *Requiem* became a regular feature of the Philharmonia concert schedules for several years, and his EMI recording of this work, completed in 1964, remains justly famous (HMV Angel SAN 133–4). In the 1970s, Giulini withdrew from opera to concentrate on concert work, and EMI continued to record him with his orchestras in Vienna and Chicago. His digital recording of the Beethoven Violin Concerto with Itzhak Perlman (HMV ASD 4059) became one of EMI's first successes in the then new formats of both CD (CDC 7 47002 2) and video.

magnificent production at Covent Garden in 1964. The sessions at the Salle Wagram in Paris were a joy. Writing of the event, Nicholas Wortley left not just an account of a recording session, but also of the art of recording at the time:

The duet was recorded complete in a take of 18 minutes and was repeated thrice in full. In recording a complex work, to record in a three-hour session more than 12 minutes of music is accounted good; here the takes frequently lasted up to 18 minutes. Normally such lengths are a strain on both musicians and engineers, but here long takes were the rule and most repeats were of full length.
[Nicholas Wortley, *Record Times*, July 1965]

During the 1960s, Elisabeth Schwarzkopf also made many fine recordings for EMI. Among these were the first stereo recordings of Brahms's *German Requiem* (Columbia SAX 2430–31), and Handel's *Messiah* (HMV Angel SAN 146–8), both conducted by Otto Klemperer. She also featured in Verdi's *Requiem* (HMV Angel SAN 133–4), with the Philharmonia Orchestra and Chorus conducted by Carlo Maria Giulini (see box). Schwarzkopf's operas included *Così fan tutte* (HMV Angel SAN 103–6) conducted by Karl Böhm, and *Die Zauberflöte* (HMV Angel SAN 137–9) conducted by Otto Klemperer. Schwarzkopf also ventured into operetta, with a well-received version of Lehár's *Merry Widow* (HMV Angel SAN 101–2).

Likewise, the recordings of Victoria de los Angeles' professional maturity laid down fresh standards in both the arts of singing and of recorded performance. Among the most important was a series of song recitals from her native land: *Spanish Songs of the Renaissance* (HMV ASD 452); *Songs of Andalusia* (HMV Angel SAN 194); and the haunting *Songs of the Auvergne* (HMV ASD 2826). She also featured in several complete operas, including Mascagni's *Cavalleria rusticana* (HMV Angel SAN 108–9), and sang in a recording of the Glyndebourne production of *Il barbiere di Siviglia* (HMV Angel SAN 114–16). This great artist also featured in the first stereo recording of Purcell's *Dido and Aeneas* (HMV Angel SAN 169), with the English Chamber Orchestra conducted by Sir John Barbirolli. According to Ronald Kinloch Anderson (who produced the record), to create a more accurate interpretation of the opera, preparations included researching the various versions of the score. As he noted, Barbirolli studied the revised score in great detail:

It [the score] is now full of Sir John's pencilled marks giving the most minute details for performance. It also contains some splendidly

evocative remarks such as "To be sung with disgusting delight" for the last Witches' Chorus, and "Could we try a mixture of Ho, ho, ho, Ha, ha, ha, Hi, hi, hi — might sound a little more evil" for the theme in Act I!
[Ronald Kinloch Anderson, *Record Times*, October 1966]

In February 1967, Elisabeth Schwarzkopf and Victoria de los Angeles came together with the baritone Dietrich Fischer-Dieskau for a concert at the Royal Festival Hall in London to mark the retirement of the veteran accompanist and EMI artist Gerald Moore, who had collaborated with them throughout their careers. One of the highlights of this farewell concert, which was recorded and released as *Homage to Gerald Moore* (HMV Angel SAN 182–3), was the remarkable performance by Schwarzkopf and de los Angeles of the comic *Duetto buffo di due gatti* (the Cats' Duet, attributed to Rossini).

The recording coupled with Jacqueline du Pré's groundbreaking Elgar Cello Concerto was Elgar's song cycle *Sea Pictures*, and the soloist was another fresh young British artist, then on the threshold of a great career, the mezzo-soprano Janet Baker. Her long list of EMI recordings span early and contemporary English songs and works by a wide range of composers, including Bach, Schubert, Mahler and Richard Strauss. Janet Baker also featured in several fine oratorio recordings, including Bach's Cantata No.147 (HMV HQS 1254), Christmas Oratorio (HMV SLS 5098), and St Matthew Passion (HMV SLS 827). She also participated in recordings of operas such as Handel's *Julius Caesar* (HMV EX 27 0232 3), with Valerie Masterson and James Bowman, and Donizetti's *Mary Stuart* (HMV SLS 5277), with Rosalind Plowright, both conducted by Sir Charles Mackerras and based on English National Opera Company productions. The two recordings were sponsored by the Peter Moores Foundation.

EMI's principal male operatic stars throughout the 1960s were Nicolai Gedda and Franco Corelli, while Dietrich Fischer-Dieskau continued to be the outstanding interpreter of Lieder. Gedda's refined musicality, stylish singing and remarkable linguistic talents made him ideal for a great number of recordings of opera, oratorio, religious music and Lieder. He also moved effortlessly into the field of operetta, recording a number of popular titles, mainly works by Franz Lehár. Corelli's powerful tenor voice thrilled audiences in the world's opera houses, especially at the Metropolitan in New York, where he sang every season from 1961 to 1974. He recorded most of his roles for EMI, including Calaf in

NICOLAI GEDDA
(BORN 1925)

The musical versatility of the Swedish tenor Nicolai Gedda made him one of EMI's most valuable singers in the 1950s and 1960s. Gedda was born Nicolai Harry Gustaf Ustinov in Stockholm, the son of a Swedish mother, whose maiden name he adopted, and a Russian father, Mikhail Ustinov, who was a member of the celebrated Kuban Don Cossack Choir. He made his professional debut at the Royal Opera Stockholm on 8 April 1952, as Chapelou in Adam's *Postillon de Longjumeau*. Shortly afterwards, he was chosen by Walter Legge to sing the role of Dmitri the Pretender in EMI's first complete recording of Mussorgsky's *Boris Godunov* (HMV ALP 1044–7) with Boris Christoff in the title role. He was soon invited to appear at the world's leading opera houses and won great acclaim at Salzburg and other international festivals. Gedda excelled in a particularly wide range of repertoire, including sacred works, songs by French, German, Russian and Scandinavian composers, as well as many French, German, Italian and Russian operas. John Steane, in *The Grand Tradition*, said of Gedda: "Few singers are so readily at home with the whole body of European music."

Puccini's *Turandot* (HMV Angel SAN 159–61) and Radames in Verdi's *Aida* (HMV Angel SAN 189–91), both opposite the renowned Swedish soprano Birgit Nilsson.

En saga

SPECIALITY SERIES

To create new markets for classical records, EMI developed Classics for Pleasure (CFP) as a budget label aimed specifically at consumers who were interested in classical music, but who could not afford premium-priced records. CFP, a spin-off from the Company's Music for Pleasure (MFP) series (see Chapter 7), became the first British budget classical record label to achieve widespread acceptance. Following the pattern set by the MFP series (and earlier ventures), once CFP had established itself (sales doubled in the first five years of trading), it began to commission its own recordings. As a result, CFP was able to build its own impressive catalogue, at the heart of which was a series of important orchestral recordings. These included Sibelius's First and Second Symphonies (CFP 40055 and 40047), with the Scottish National Orchestra conducted by Alexander (later Sir Alexander) Gibson. Other important CFP recordings included Sibelius's Violin Concerto and *En saga* (CFP 40218), whilst Gibson and Norman Del Mar made recordings of the Tchaikovsky symphonies. During the 1970s and 1980s, recognizing the enormous potential of this market, EMI added other budget-priced classical labels to its product range. In 1987, CFP released its first CD recordings, transferring the best of its existing catalogue to the new medium and, at the same time, continuing its policy of releasing its own new recordings.

Another new idea developed by EMI in the 1970s was the HMV Treasury series. Launched in 1972, Treasury records were dedicated to re-releasing (often for the first time on LP) records from EMI's wealth of recordings from the past, including some from the earliest days of the business. Releases on this label included anthologies by some of the greatest singers of the 20th century, including *Richard Tauber* (HMV Treasury HLM 7010); Isobel Baillie's *Never Sing Louder than Lovely* (HMV Treasury RLS 7703); and *The Art of John McCormack* (HMV Treasury EX 29 0056 3) and *John McCormack: Popular Songs and Ballads* (HMV Treasury EX 29 0007 3). The most ambitious of all the HMV Treasury projects was the massive four-volume *Record of Singing* (HMV Treasury RLS 724,

RLS 743, EX 29 0169 3 and EX 7 69741 1), which provided a survey of the vocal arts and national styles throughout the entire 78-rpm period. The Treasury series was not simply confined to recordings of great singers of the past; it also encompassed works by the most important 20th-century instrumentalists. Among these were Pablo Casals's recordings of the six Bach cello suites (HMV Treasury RLS 712), together with his interpretation of the Dvořák Cello Concerto (which was coupled with Bruch's *Kol nidrei* on HMV Treasury HLM 7013), and the 1930s HMV Beethoven Society series of Beethoven piano sonatas (HMV Treasury RLS 753–5 & 758) played by Artur Schnabel.

In 1976, the mid-price reissue label HMV Greensleeves was launched. Its catalogue reflected the important market for records by British orchestras and composers. Greensleeves records included such titles as *The Lighter Elgar* (HMV Greensleeves ESD 7009), with the Northern Sinfonia Orchestra conducted by Neville (later Sir Neville) Marriner.

A unique survey of singers and singing up to 1914
12 LPs with Michael Scott's 256 page
fully illustrated book The Record of Singing

Presented with Michael Scott's fully illustrated book
The Record of Singing Volume Two
published by Duckworth

The Art of Courtly Love
THE EARLY MUSIC REVOLUTION

The late 1960s and early 1970s saw a flowering of interest in music composed during the Middle Ages, the Renaissance and the Baroque. EMI's interest in this music was by no means new. As far back as the 1930s, the Company had released pioneering recordings of early music by performers such as Wanda Landowska, the Dolmetsch family and Adolf Busch (see Chapter 5). Spurring the renewed interest in early music were young musicians and musicologists who sought a more authentic sound through the use of original or reproduction instruments, appropriate forces and period practices. At the same time, the accessible early repertoire broadened as scholars made performing editions of the fruits of their explorations among original sources and treatises and also collaborated as consultants to recording projects. As a result, EMI's efforts to record in this field were given fresh impetus and this helped to establish early music as an important part of the classical repertoire.

During this period, David Munrow (see box, page 292), the woodwind virtuoso, transformed the early music movement in Britain. In 1969, he cautiously wrote to Peter Andry proposing a number of recording projects with himself and his Early Music Consort of London. This group was formed in 1967 and

DAVID MUNROW
(1942–1976)

★

During the later 1960s and early 1970s, David Munrow did much to popularize music written before the time of Bach and Handel, most of which was then virtually unknown outside academic circles. After leaving school at 18 and spending a year doing voluntary teaching in South America, he joined the Royal Shakespeare Company Wind Band as a bassoonist but soon left to devote himself full time to the Early Music Consort of London, which he had co-founded in 1967. In 1971, he began a series of BBC children's radio programmes called *Pied Piper*. His intelligence and good judgement, coupled with his personal charm and wit, made the series so successful that, by the time of his death five years later, he had written and presented over 700 programmes for radio and television. As a solo recorder player, he featured in several EMI recordings, but it was with the Early Music Consort of London that he made his most important titles, including *The Art of the Recorder* (SLS 5022) and *Instruments of the Middle Ages and Renaissance* (SLS 988). His untimely death (by his own hand) at the age of 33 was an incalculable loss to the world of music. The BBC producer Arthur Johnson, who worked with Munrow on several series of *Pied Piper*, said in a tribute that Munrow's extraordinary career "shook the stuffing out of early music-making and left the reactionaries breathless and bemused; a career that re-established virtuosity on neglected instruments and a neglected era to a delighted public; a career which lasted, unbelievably, only ten years."

comprised Munrow, Christopher Hogwood (harpsichord), James Tyler (lute), Oliver Brookes (viol) and James Bowman (counter-tenor). He told Peter Andry:

Would you be prepared to see me sometime – or could you suggest someone else I might approach – if you think there would be a possibility of The Early Music Consort recording for EMI? We have, in fact, already taken part in "Anthems in Eden" with the folk singer Shirley Collins [see Chapter 9] to be issued on EMI's new Harvest label. I have many ideas around which records of early music could be sold: would it be possible to have an opportunity to put some forward, backed by tape recordings? [Munrow Artist File, EMI Music Archive]

Thus began a fruitful relationship between David Munrow, his colleagues, and EMI's record producers Christopher Bishop and John Willan. Munrow's infectious enthusiasm, together with his extraordinary skills as a musician, arranger and communicator, made him an ideal collaborator. His letters to Bishop and others reveal a genuine bond of friendship and affection, and also a respect all too rare between creative colleagues. They also show the intense pressures that bore down on him. Writing in 1973, Munrow noted:

First may I thank you for all your help and patience with the instruments record. It was a very complicated project for me and in the case of those last sessions very tiring too. I feel it all went really well, tho'

One of David Munrow's most significant contributions to the early music catalogue.

when the editing's done, you may argue that one or two pieces may have to be re-done. The trouble with the whole idea, is that there musn't be any omissions! [Munrow Artist File, EMI Music Archive]

As David Munrow's talents developed, he became a master performer, at home on the concert platform, broadcasting or in the recording studio. As a result, his high profile and attractive personality were important in boosting demand for the Consort's records. Their first EMI solo album, *Two Renaissance Dance Bands* (HMV HQS 1249), was released in 1971 and, by the end of 1972, had achieved sales in Britain of 7,000 units. Other recordings followed in quick succession. They included *Music for Ferdinand and Isabella of Spain* (HMV CSD 3738), *The Art of Courtly Love* (HMV SLS 863) and *The Art of the Netherlands* (HMV SLS 5049). In 1976, this remarkable period ended suddenly and tragically when David Munrow, regarded by then as one of the most influential musicians of his generation, took his own life.

Munrow's vital contribution to the recording of early music resulted in a dramatic increase in EMI's recording programme in this field. The Reflexe label was created and was dedicated entirely to recordings of early music, including music of the Baroque period, in "authentic" period performances. Reflexe opened up many opportunities for scholars and musicians to record interpretations that reflected

Above The choirmaster and conductor David Willcocks explains a point to the Choir of King's College, Cambridge, during the recording of Handel's *Dixit Dominus* (HMV ALP 2262 & ASD 2262) in the College Chapel in 1964.

Right David Willcocks conducting the English Chamber Orchestra during a recording session at King's College, Cambridge in 1964.

as nearly as possible the composers' intentions and that revealed the unvarnished beauty of the music.

Other opportunities presented themselves to broaden and develop the range of music available in EMI's classical catalogues. One of the most important, prestigious and enduring was the relationship formed in 1964 with the Choir of King's College, Cambridge, a relationship which continues to this day. It was not the first time the Company had recorded the choir: before and after the Second World War both the Columbia and Gramophone Companies made 78-rpm recordings of it. Under the successive leadership of Sir David Willcocks, Philip Ledger and Stephen Cleobury, the choir's recordings were made within the beautiful setting and ambience of King's College Chapel itself. The extraordinary vocal standards achieved by the choristers have resulted in some of the finest recordings of English choral music. In addition to recording the famous Christmas Eve *Festival of Lessons and Carols from King's* (HMV ASD 3778), the choir has recorded a wide repertoire from early music to Britten and Bernstein, Górecki and Pärt.

Another spin-off from developments in early music were the recordings EMI made in the 1970s and 1980s with the King's Singers. A group of classically trained singers, they

The Hilliard Ensemble, here joined by four guest singers, was one of the most prolific groups to record for EMI's specialist early music Reflexe label when it was launched in the 1980s.

One of the albums featuring carols sung by the Choir of King's College, Cambridge, at their annual service of Nine Lessons and Carols held on Christmas Eve and broadcast by the BBC.

Dame Kiri Te Kanawa with the King's Singers, EMI producer Simon Woods (seated left) and conductor Richard Hickox (seated, second right) during the recording of an album of Christmas songs.

successfully merged Renaissance consort and American close-harmony repertoire and, in the process, became among EMI's most popular classical artists. They achieved this by the sheer breadth of their repertoire and the extraordinary versatility of their combined talents, both as classical and popular artists. Few performers have felt able to release on a single CD music as diverse as that of the Beatles and Simon and Garfunkel, together with English and European madrigals. The King's Singers' CD series of Anthologies encompass all these and more.

British artists have been among EMI's most prominent performers of early music. For instance, the Hilliard Ensemble recorded Byrd's *Masses and Lamentations* (HMV Reflexe EX 27 0096 3); Dufay's *Missa 'L'Homme Armé'* (HMV Reflexe EL 27 0426 1); Josquin Desprez's *Motets and Chansons* (EMI Reflexe CDC 7 49209 2); and Palestrina's *Canticum canticorum* motets and *Madrigali spirituali* (HMV Reflexe EX 27 0319 3). Other important exponents of early music who have recorded for EMI include Andrew Parrott and his Taverner Consort, Choir and Players, the soprano Emma Kirkby, the tenor Rogers Covey-Crump and the bass David Thomas. These artists came together to record a highly successful version of Monteverdi's Vespers of 1610 (HMV Reflexe EX 27 0129 3).

Fascinating Rhythm

CROSS-OVER MUSIC AND MUSICIANS

Over the past 20 years, EMI has accommodated a number of unexpected changes of direction in the classical record market. One of the most surprising, and one that EMI has sought to exploit, has been the rapid growth in popularity of so-called cross-over recordings – recordings of popular music by classically trained performers. When cross-over records appeared in the 1980s they were hailed as an innovation, whereas in fact the most popular of the early HMV and Columbia Celebrity recordings were those of the popular music of the time by artists such as Melba, Caruso, McCormack, Kreisler and Tauber.

Possibly the most surprising and certainly among the most successful of EMI's modern cross-over recordings came about as a result of combining two of the most remarkable talents ever to make records for EMI: the great classical violinist Yehudi Menuhin with the legendary French jazz violinist Stéphane Grappelli. They made a number of albums together, including *Jealousy* (HMV EMD 5504), *Fascinating Rhythm* (HMV EMD 5523), *Tea for Two* (HMV EMD 5530), and *Strictly for the Birds* (HMV EMD 5533). In these records, Menuhin and Grappelli explored the works of such popular composers as Irving Berlin, George Gershwin, Jerome Kern and Cole Porter. The records were commercial successes: within four months of its British release, the first sold almost 10,000 copies, while the second sold nearly the same number in three weeks. Menuhin had already made records of Eastern music with the sitar player Ravi Shankar, including *West Meets East* (HMV ASD 2294), which broadened the public's interest in Indian classical music. These records had an importance beyond their commercial success: they demonstrated to classical performers that, by venturing into new fields of repertoire, they would enhance rather than endanger their reputations.

Another key EMI cross-over artist is Itzhak Perlman (see box, page 298), one of the greatest violinists of the century. His acclaimed performances of the great masterpieces of the violin repertoire are among EMI's best-selling classical recordings, whilst his recordings from the popular repertoire include an album of Scott Joplin rags he made with André Previn, *The Easy Winners* (HMV ASD 3075).

Andrew Parrott is both a scholar specializing in historical performance practice and an accomplished conductor who works in the field of early music with his Taverner Choir, Consort and Players, and also in later orchestral music and opera.

ITZHAK PERLMAN
(BORN 1945)

★

The renowned Israeli violinist Itzhak Perlman was born in Tel-Aviv. He moved to the United States in 1958 and, after completing his training at the Juilliard School in New York, made his American professional debut with the National Orchestra Association in Carnegie Hall in March 1963. His international career was launched when he won the prestigious Leventritt Memorial Competition in 1964, and he quickly established himself as one of the world's leading violinists. His first recording for EMI in July 1971 was an album of Bach violin concertos with the English Chamber Orchestra conducted by Daniel Barenboim (HMV ASD 2783) and he has gone on to record an enormous range of repertoire from the baroque to the contemporary, including all the great violin concertos. He has also made a substantial number of cross-over recordings of ragtime, jazz and salon music and several albums of traditional Jewish music, the most recent being the best-seller *In the Fiddler's House* (EMI Classics CDC 5 55555 2). Perlman's flawless technique and deep musicality, combined with a great deal of charm and charisma, have enabled him to establish a unique hold on the public imagination. His irrepressible joy in making music communicates itself vividly to his listeners at live concerts, on television and even on record. He has received many awards and honours, including a Medal of Liberty presented to him in 1986 by President Reagan in appreciation of his outstanding achievements and contribution to American life.

Right Yehudi Menuhin and the sitar player Ravi Shankar first came together in 1966 to produce their ground-breaking album, *West Meets East*, which fused Indian and Western classical music.

In Britain alone, the sales of this record reached an astonishing 100,000. He also recorded *Tradition* (EMI EL 27 0572 1), featuring arrangements of popular Jewish melodies; and an anthology of duets, *Together* (EMI CDC 7 54266 2), with Placido Domingo, as a tribute to the violinist Fritz Kreisler and the tenor John McCormack. Perlman also helped to revive another light classical musical form that had previously dominated the old 78-rpm record catalogues, but which had been discarded with the coming of LP records: the encore piece (as exemplified in the art of his distinguished predecessors, Fritz Kreisler and Pablo de Sarasate). His encore recordings included *Kreisler* (EMI EL 27 0477 1) and *Encores* (EMI Classics CDC 7 49514 2).

The cross-over idea proved very attractive to performers and consumers, and caught on rapidly. EMI continues to release CD records by artists such as opera singers Placido Domingo and Kiri (later Dame Kiri) Te Kanawa. Domingo's contribution to the EMI Classics catalogue has been rich and varied, ranging from Boito's opera *Mefistofele* (EMI Classics CDS 7 49522 2) to an album of Viennese operetta arias, *Vienna, City of My Dreams* (EMI CDC 7 47398 2) and, in 1990, a CD of popular songs, *Be My Love* (EMI CDP 7 95468 2). By the end of the 1980s, Domingo was gaining a reputation as a conductor, and during the present decade, his recording activities have extended further into this new field.

Kiri Te Kanawa's recordings for EMI Classics have followed a similar pattern. She featured in recordings of Strauss's *Rosenkavalier* (EMI Classics CDS 7 54259 2), with the Dresden Staatskapelle conducted by Bernard Haitink, and in the role of the Waldvogel in Wagner's *Siegfried* (EMI Classics CDS 7 54290 2), which forms a part of EMI Classics' recording of Wagner's *Ring*, also conducted by Haitink. In addition, from the late 1980s, her cross-over recordings have appeared at regular intervals and include an anthology of songs by George Gershwin, *Kiri Sings Gershwin* (EMI Classics CDC 7 47454 2), and a selection of popular songs, *Heart to Heart* (EMI CDC 7 54299 2).

In the late 1980s, the cross-over concept was further developed when the Company began making recordings of Broadway musicals. For these, EMI's producers utilized ideas derived from recording early music, including the use, wherever possible, of the composer's original scores and the finest available classically trained performers. EMI Classics began ambitiously with the first ever complete recording of Jerome Kern's *Show Boat* (EMI Angel CDS 7 49108 2). The cast featured Frederica von Stade, Jerry Hadley, Teresa Stratas, Bruce Hubbard and the London Sinfonietta conducted by John McGlinn. This pioneering three-CD set won the *Gramophone* magazine's 1989 Music Theatre Award, as well as the Belgian Grand Prix Caecilia, and received a coveted rosette in the *Penguin Guide to Compact Discs*. Its strong international sales encouraged EMI Classics to develop the idea and, at regular intervals, further releases of Broadway shows have appeared.

Cross-over is dominated by classical artists performing works outside their normal sphere. In 1991, however, former Beatle Paul (later Sir Paul) McCartney reversed the trend with the composition *Paul McCartney's Liverpool Oratorio*, which received its premiere, appropriately enough, in Liverpool. EMI Classics later recorded the work (EMI Classics CDS 7 54371 2), with Dame Kiri Te Kanawa, Sally Burgess, Jerry Hadley, Willard White and the Royal Liverpool Philharmonic Orchestra and Choir conducted by Carl Davis, who was also Paul McCartney's collaborator in the writing of the work. This remarkable piece was a triumph for an artist whose versatility and talent have been demonstrated in an unparalleled career that has extended over four decades.

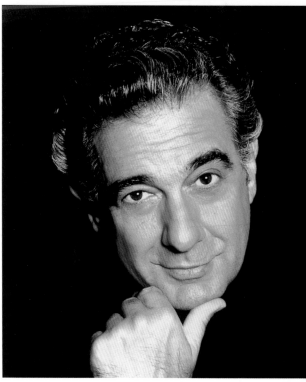

Above The Spanish tenor Placido Domingo is one of today's greatest opera stars.

Above, top The soprano Dame Kiri Te Kanawa is just as much at home in popular music and songs from classic Broadway shows as she is in the field of opera and classical music.

WORLD PREMIÈRE RECORDING OF THE COMPLETE MUSICAL

SHOWBOAT

FREDERICA VON STADE, JERRY HADLEY, BRUCE HUBBARD, PAIGE O'HARA, DAVID GARRISON, KARLA BURNS, ROBERT NICHOLS, NANCY KULP, LILLIAN GISH

AND TERESA STRATAS AS JULIE

MUSIC BY JEROME KERN
BOOK & LYRICS BY OSCAR HAMMERSTEIN 2nd
ADAPTED FROM THE NOVEL "SHOW BOAT" BY EDNA FERBER
AMBROSIAN CHORUS
LONDON SINFONIETTA
CONDUCTED BY JOHN McGLINN

FEATURING THE HIT NUMBERS:
OL' MAN RIVER • MAKE BELIEVE • BILL • CAN'T HELP LOVIN' DAT MAN

Above In 1987, 60 years on from its 1927 Broadway premiere, EMI made a pioneering recording of the complete musical score of *Show Boat*.

Right Frederica von Stade and Bruce Hubbard during the recording of *Show Boat* in the Number One Studio at Abbey Road.

Left Carla Burns, who sang the part of Queenie in *Show Boat*.

Below From left to right: Robert Nichols, Frederica von Stade, Jerry Hadley, Lillian Gish and conductor John McGlinn at the final recording session for Jerome Kern's *Show Boat* in 1987.

MSTISLAV ROSTROPOVICH (BORN 1927)

Mstislav Rostropovich was born in Baku in the former Soviet Union. He won an international competition in Prague in 1950 and when he first appeared in the West in 1956, his complete mastery of the cello was universally acclaimed. In 1955, he married the eminent Russian soprano Galina Vishnevskaya, for whom he has often acted as piano accompanist. He is also an accomplished conductor of both opera and symphonic repertoire, having made his conducting debut in 1968 with Tchaikovsky's opera *Eugene Onegin* at the Bolshoi in Moscow. As a cellist, he is noted for his commanding technique and the intensity of his playing, and he has inspired the world's finest composers to increase the cello repertoire with many works specially composed for him. Rostropovich is now considered one of the leading interpreters of the music of Shostakovich (with whom he studied), Britten and Prokofiev, all of whom dedicated major compositions to him. Although he was awarded the Lenin prize in 1963, disputes with the authorities over his views on cultural freedom and his support of the author Solzhenitsyn led to his departure from the Soviet Union in 1974. In 1977, he was appointed musical director of the National Symphony Orchestra of Washington, D.C., with whom he made a triumphant return to his homeland in 1990. Throughout his career, Rostropovich has continued to be outspoken in his defence of human and artistic freedoms and has been honoured with many awards, both musical and humanitarian.

Lady Macbeth of Mtsensk

MSTISLAV ROSTROPOVICH

In 1956, the great Russian cellist, conductor and accompanist Mstislav Rostropovich made his debut as an EMI artist with a recording of Miaskovsky's Cello Concerto (HMV ALP 1427). By 1974, he was considered one of the most important classical artists in the world. In April that year, EMI executives heard of his imminent departure into political exile from the Soviet Union. Once he was safely in the West, EMI secured a recording contract with him and began to exploit a unique and mature talent. By 1979, Rostropovich had recorded 14 major works for EMI, the world sales of which exceeded 500,000 copies. Conducting the London Philharmonic Orchestra, Rostropovich performed and later recorded the complete Tchaikovsky symphonies (HMV SLS 5099). These recordings were a stunning success, both artistically and commercially. By 1979, world sales of another Rostropovich recording, his 1976 Haydn cello concertos (HMV ASD 3255), with the Academy of St Martin-in-the-Fields, exceeded 90,000 copies, and won for the artist and EMI the prestigious French Grand Prix du Disque. In 1979, Rostropovich conducted the London Philharmonic Orchestra in the first recording

of Shostakovich's powerful opera *Lady Macbeth of Mtsensk* (HMV SLS 5157). The recording featured Rostropovich's wife, Galina Vishnevskaya, as well as Nicolai Gedda and Robert Tear. In 1995, after a gap of several years, Rostropovich renewed his association with EMI Classics with a milestone recording of the Bach cello suites (EMI CDS 5 55363 2).

The Four Seasons

THE CURRENT GENERATION

In 1977, the Company began its association with the young British conductor Simon (later Sir Simon) Rattle (see box), with a recording of Suites 1 and 2 from Stravinsky's *Pulcinella* with the Northern Sinfornia (HMV ASD 3604). He transformed the City of Birmingham Symphony Orchestra and then recorded many important works for EMI, including the first recording of Nicholas Maw's *Odyssey* (EMI Classics CDS 7 54277 2), and Mahler's Second Symphony (EMI Angel CDS 7 47962 8), which won two *Gramophone* awards and was named Record of the Year in 1988. The French

SIR SIMON RATTLE (BORN 1955)

★

Born in Liverpool, Simon Rattle won the John Player International Conducting Competition in 1974 and was soon working with most of the leading British orchestras. He made his American debut in 1977, the same year in which he first appeared at the Glyndebourne Festival, to which he has returned regularly ever since. In 1980 he became principal conductor and artistic director of the City of Birmingham Symphony Orchestra, with whom he remained for 16 years, turning them into a world-class ensemble. During his time at Birmingham he has continued to conduct elsewhere, appearing with many of the world's greatest orchestras. Rattle and the Birmingham Orchestra began recording for EMI in 1981 with works such as Janáček's *Glagolitic* Mass (HMV ASD 4066) and Britten's *War Requiem* (HMV SLS 1077573), and have built up a wide catalogue covering music by Sibelius, Stravinsky, Rachmaninov, Mahler and many other composers. Rattle recordings with other orchestras include his multi-award-winning version of Gershwin's *Porgy and Bess* (EMI Angel CDS 7 49568 2) with the London Philharmonic and Liszt's *Faust Symphony* (EMI Classics CDC 5 55220 2) with the Berlin Philharmonic Orchestra. Despite his youth, Rattle has consistently been compared with the greatest conductors of the past and present. *Gramophone* reviewer Michael Kennedy said of his recording of Mahler's "Resurrection" Symphony: "But where Simon Rattle's interpretation is concerned, we must go into the realm of such giant Mahlerians as Walter and Klemperer, dissimilar as they were. For we are dealing here with conducting akin to genius, with insights and instincts that cannot be measured with any old yardstick."

KLAUS TENNSTEDT
(BORN 1926)

The conductor Klaus Tennstedt, the natural successor to Furtwängler, was born in Merseburg, Germany, and studied music at the Leipzig Conservatory. His conducting career began in 1948 in Halle and he eventually joined the Dresden State Opera, making guest appearances with other leading German orchestras. In 1971, he defected from what was then East Germany and began to work in Scandinavia. In 1974, his first American appearances in Toronto and Boston caused a sensation and led to many other engagements, including his London debut with the London Symphony Orchestra in 1976. He first conducted the London Philharmonic in 1977 and soon established a special relationship with that orchestra, eventually becoming its principal conductor and music director in 1983 and later Conductor Laureate. Tennstedt has recorded exclusively for EMI since 1977. His recordings include works by Beethoven, Wagner, Dvořák and Richard Strauss, and an outstanding set of Mahler symphonies with the London Philharmonic (completed in 1986). More recently, he embarked on a new series of live recordings of Mahler symphonies, beginning with Symphony No.1 with the Chicago Symphony Orchestra (EMI Classics CDC 7 54217 2). In 1994, shortly before ill-health finally forced him to announce his retirement from public performance, Tennstedt was honoured with a *Gramophone* Lifetime Achievement Award.

Grand Prix du Disque and the Belgian Grand Prix Caecilia were awarded for his recording of Messiaen's *Turangalîla Symphony* (EMI Classics CDS 7 47463 8), with the pianist Peter Donohoe and the City of Birmingham Symphony Orchestra. Rattle's recording activities are not just confined to the classical repertoire: his cross-over anthology *The Jazz Album* (EMI Classics CDC 7 47991 2) had a remarkable line-up, including classical artists Peter Donohoe, Michael Collins and the London Sinfonietta, and the pop group Harvey and the Wallbangers. Simon Rattle's first complete opera recording of the Glyndebourne production of Gershwin's *Porgy and Bess* (EMI Classics CDS 7 49568 2) appeared in 1989, and won an astonishing seven industry awards, including the French Grand Prix in Honorem. The continuing association between EMI Classics and Sir Simon has resulted in a flow of recordings in the 1990s, consolidating his position as one of the world's most exciting and innovative conductors.

The conductor Klaus Tennstedt (see box) has recorded exclusively for EMI since the late 1970s. In 1983, after a period as the London Philharmonic Orchestra's principal guest conductor, he became the orchestra's principal conductor and music director. As a consequence of this important relationship, Tennstedt undertook a series of exceptional recordings for EMI, including his celebrated series of all Mahler's symphonies. Made between 1977 and 1986, these records were greeted with great acclaim, especially the Eighth Symphony, which won a *Gramophone* award in 1987. Other Tennstedt recordings with the London Philharmonic Orchestra include the Beethoven and Bruch (No.1) Violin Concertos with Kyung-Wha Chung (EMI Classics CDC 7 54072 2); the Brahms Violin Concerto with Nigel Kennedy (EMI Classics 7 54187 2); and Strauss's *Also sprach Zarathustra* (EMI Classics CDC 7 49951 2).

Wolfgang Sawallisch (see box, page 307) made his first recordings for EMI in the 1950s, when Walter Legge identified him as one of the most promising young conductors of the day. His early EMI recordings included Richard Strauss's opera *Capriccio* (Columbia 33CX 1600–602), starring Elisabeth Schwarzkopf; Carl Orff's *Carmina Burana* (Columbia 33CX 1480); and a number of orchestral recordings with the Philharmonia Orchestra. EMI is recording him extensively in a wide range of repertoire, including major works like Tchaikovsky's *Swan Lake* (EMI Classics CDS 5 55277 2) and Richard Strauss's opera *Elektra* (EMI Classics CDS 7 54067 2).

Roger Norrington (see box, page 305) and the London Classical Players have been among the most prolific recorders of "authentic" performances. Their EMI recordings include the complete Beethoven symphonies (EMI Classics CDS 7 49852 2), Berlioz's *Symphonie fantastique* (EMI Angel CDC 7 49541 2), Mendelssohn's "Scottish"

and "Italian" Symphonies (EMI Angel CDC 7 54000 2) and two of Mozart's operas, *Don Giovanni* (EMI Classics CDS 7 54859 2) and *Die Zauberflöte* (EMI Classics CDS 7 54287 2).

The spectacular and controversial career of Nigel Kennedy, a former pupil of one EMI's greatest violinists, Lord Menuhin, provides a musical and recording continuum that goes back to the famous recording Elgar made of his Violin Concerto with the young Menuhin (see Chapter 5). In the mid-1980s, Kennedy was awarded a gold disc and a *Gramophone* Record of the Year Award for his interpretation of that work with the London Philharmonic Orchestra conducted by Vernon Handley (EMI EMX 2058). This recording launched Kennedy's career. In 1989, EMI released Kennedy's version of Vivaldi's *The Four Seasons* (EMI Classics CDC 7 49557 2), with the English Chamber Orchestra. World sales of this disc have totalled more than 1 million copies, and the record had the unique distinction of achieving a place in the British Top 10 album charts, to become the best-selling classical record of 1989. Kennedy continues to record for EMI, and achieved great success with his recording of Bruch's (No.1) and Mendelssohn's violin concertos (EMI Classics CDC 7 49663 2). Although *The Four Seasons* brought classical music to the pop charts, Kennedy's own deep interest in the jazz and rock repertoire has resulted in several non-classical recordings, including *Mainly Black*, his own arrangement of Duke Ellington's *Black, Brown and Beige Suite* (EMI EL 27 0538 1), *Let Loose* (EMI SCX 6709) and, more recently, *Kafka* (EMI EMD 1095).

ROGER NORRINGTON
(BORN 1934)

★

The British conductor Roger Norrington is one of the foremost exponents of period performance on original instruments. He was born in Oxford and was a choral scholar at Cambridge. He later studied conducting with Sir Adrian Boult at the Royal College of Music. He began his musical career as a professional tenor in 1962, the same year in which he founded the amateur Heinrich Schütz Choir, which performed at a number of festivals, including Aldeburgh and Bath, and on record. In 1966, he became musical director of Kent Opera, substantially raising the company's standards in the years that followed. He began to conduct various orchestras in Britain and other countries and, in 1978, founded the London Classical Players, an ensemble of virtuoso players of original instruments. Norrington and his orchestra began by giving concerts of the music of Mozart, Schubert and Mendelssohn, recreating the style and sound of its first performances – a practice that had until then usually been applied only to the music of Bach, Handel and composers of earlier periods. His concerts, often preceded by illustrated talks, were a huge success and, in 1986, EMI began to record a series of Beethoven symphonies with him, starting with the Second and Eighth Symphonies (HMV EL 27 0563 1). These were followed by Beethoven's piano concertos (EMI Classics CDS 7 54063 2) with Melvyn Tan (fortepiano) and then music by other composers including Rossini, Berlioz, Mendelssohn, Schumann, Wagner and even Bruckner.

Left The violinist Nigel Kennedy.

Right Mariss Jansons is one of today's most charismatic conductors, renowned particularly for his brilliant performances of the colourful orchestral repertoire.

Opposite page Roberto Alagna has established himself in the world of opera as a new heir to the great tenor tradition.

Odyssey

THE FUTURE

The tenor Roberto Alagna is among the most outstanding of the new generation of EMI Classics artists. Since he came to international prominence when he won the Luciano Pavarotti International Competition in 1988, Alagna has earned critical and public acclaim for his accomplished performances at Covent Garden and other leading opera houses. His first recital album of French and Italian arias (EMI Classics CDC 5 55477 2) was released in 1995 and received high praise. It was followed in 1996 by a disc of arias and duets with his wife, the Romanian soprano Angela Gheorghiu (EMI Classics CDC 5 56117 2), and his first complete opera, *La bohème* (EMI Classics CDS 5 56120 2), with the Philharmonia Orchestra conducted by Antonio Pappano.

Other leading singers on EMI Classics include the American baritone Thomas Hampson, who is featured in an astonishingly wide range of repertoire, from French song through German, French and Italian opera to Broadway musicals; the German baritone Olaf Bär, who excels in Lieder; the French-based American soprano Barbara Hendricks; and the Swedish mezzo-soprano Anne Sofie von Otter.

WOLFGANG SAWALLISCH (BORN 1923)

Wolfgang Sawallisch, the leading German conductor, began his professional career in 1947 as a repetiteur in Augsberg after graduating from the Hochschule für Musik in Munich, the city of his birth. After working as musical director in Aachen, Wisebaden and Cologne he was general music director at Hamburg from 1960 to 1970 and had charge of the Suisse Romande Orchestra from 1972 to 1980. In 1971, he also became musical director of the Bavarian State Opera in Munich, and acquired complete artistic responsibility there in 1982. In September 1990 he was appointed music director of the Philadelphia Orchestra, beginning with the 1993–4 season. As well as being a conductor, Sawallisch is also an accomplished pianist and accompanist, and made his first appearance in London accompanying Elisabeth Schwarzkopf in a Hugo Wolf recital in 1957. He began his association with EMI in 1955 with a recording of Orff's *Carmina Burana* (Columbia 33CX 1480) in Cologne, followed by several important opera recordings in London including Richard Strauss's *Capriccio* (Columbia (33CX 1600–602) with a cast headed by Elisabeth Schwarzkopf and Dietrich Fischer-Dieskau. He continued to make occasional recordings for EMI until the Company signed him exclusively in 1988. He then began an extensive programme of recordings, amongst which was the first uncut version of Richard Strauss's *Frau ohne Schatten* (EMI Classics CDS 7 49074 2), which won several international awards, and Wagner's *Meistersinger von Nürnberg* (EMI Classics CDS 5 55142 2).

In 1990, EMI Classics entered into an exclusive contract with the pianist Stephen Kovacevich. This fine artist soon showed his mettle by winning the 1994 *Gramophone* Best Concerto Award for his recording of Brahms's First Piano Concerto with the London Philharmonic conducted by Wolfgang Sawallisch (EMI Classics CDC 7 54578 2). Kovacevich is renowned for his mature interpretations of the masterpieces of the piano literature and has embarked on an extensive series of recordings of solo works by Schubert and Beethoven. In February 1996, the critic Robert Layton wrote in the *Gramophone* of Kovacevich's recording of Beethoven's Op. 31 piano sonatas (EMI Classics CDC 5 55226 2): "I believe that if the series continues as it has begun, the Kovacevich cycle will occupy a standing not far short of that enjoyed by Schnabel in the heyday of 78s."

Another artist of the future is the brilliant young Korean cellist Han-Na Chang, who took first prize at the Fifth Rostropovich Cello Competition in Paris in 1994, having previously won major competitions in New York and her native Seoul. She made her London debut in November 1995

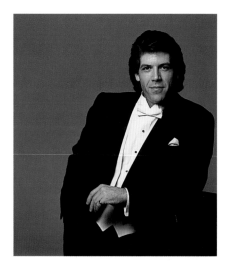

Above The young violinist Vanessa-Mae has become an international star with her exciting pop-style performances of new and old music. Over two million copies of her debut EMI album *The Violin Player* have been sold.

Above, top The American baritone Thomas Hampson is one of today's most versatile and successful singers.

Right The pianist Stephen Kovacevich now records exclusively for EMI Classics.

with the London Symphony Orchestra conducted by Mstislav Rostropovich, and immediately afterwards made her first recording at Abbey Road, of Tchaikovsky's "Rococo" Variations, Saint-Saëns's First Cello Concerto and other pieces (EMI Classics CDC 5 56126 2). This was the first time Rostropovich, very much Han-Na Chang's mentor and spiritual godfather, had made a recording with another cellist. After the London concert, one critic reported that "Chang's musical intelligence made it very difficult to believe that a child was responding to Tchaikovsky's rapidly changing moods with so much understanding." [Annette Morreau, *Independent*, 27 November 1995]

With exciting new artists like Roberto Alagna and Han-Na Chang joining the ranks of the many established stars on its roster, EMI Classics can today look forward to renewing its catalogue with recordings that will stand comparison with the finest made during the previous hundred years.

1897 1997
100 YEARS OF GREAT MUSIC

NEW PARLOPHONE & MERCURY SINGLES
ORDER NOW FROM YOUR LOCAL E.M.I DEPOT OR FACTOR

 **PARLOPHONE** | Weekly releases for **OCTOBER 5th 1962** (Release No. 448)

THE KING BROTHERS

Nicola
Way down the mountain   45-R4947

JOHNNY ANGEL

Better luck next time
The power of you   45-R4948

THE BEATLES

Love me do
PS I love you   45-R4949

 **MERCURY** | Weekly release for **OCTOBER 5th 1962** (Release No. 448)

LITTLE RICHARD

He got what he wanted (but he lost what he had)
Why don't you change your ways?   45-AMT1189

The only occasion a Beatles record ever received a minor billing was on this Parlophone release sheet for October 1962, which featured their first single.

CHAPTER 9

Strawberry Fields

EMI'S POPULAR MUSIC RECORDINGS, 1962–1997

Anyone who's been EMI trained really knows what their doing.
[Paul McCartney, musician, composer and EMI artist since 1962]

Imagine

An essential feature of EMI's success over the past 100 years has been its willingness to stay at the forefront of popular music. In this volatile and ephemeral market, EMI has continued to seek out fresh talent and new popular musical forms. Sometimes, these policies have resulted in stupendous hits – as in the case of the Beatles – and, on other occasions, equally stupendous misses. But as this chapter shows, creative risk-taking is the foundation of success in the popular music business.

The record industry, and popular music generally, underwent a rapid and remarkable transformation in the early 1960s. In 1961, most British pop musicians still relied on tours of Britain for the bulk of their income, and they made singles (from which they earned very little money) rather than albums. By the 1990s, the CD album provided the core pop and rock statement, and the single (now also available on CD) had been reduced to the role of a sampler. EMI's pop business in 1961 was British and very parochial, whereas by the 1990s it had become truly international. The Company's top pop and rock musicians had meanwhile become major international performers, deriving huge incomes from international sales of their records, and rather less from touring.

All you need is love

THE BEATLES

In the 1960s, EMI seized the opportunity to define and mould popular culture for a generation. In June 1962 a leading Liverpool record retailer and manager of Merseyside pop musicians called Brian Epstein met with George Martin, then head of EMI's Parlophone label. The meeting had been arranged so that Martin could hear a tape of a rock'n'roll group called the Beatles. At the time, Martin was unaware that Epstein had previously hawked his Beatles tape around to every other EMI record producer, and just about every other record company, and been rejected by them all. Later, Martin wrote of that first encounter with the music of the group that transformed his life and career, the fortunes of EMI, and those of the broader record and musical world:

THE BEATLES

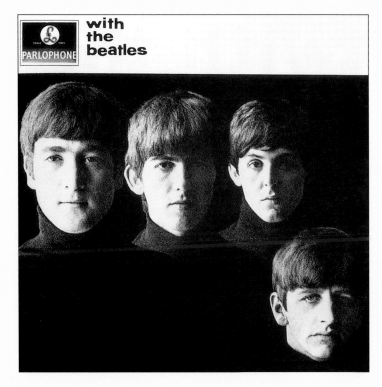

"Yeah the Beatles were a pretty good group …" (Paul McCartney)

In 1957, the 16-year-old John Lennon formed the Quarry Men, a skiffle band which initially comprised him and a number of other boys from Quarry Bank Grammar School in Liverpool. By 1960, the group consisted of Lennon with Paul (later Sir Paul) McCartney, George Harrison and Stuart Sutcliffe, and had finally settled on the name the Beatles. The band began to acquire their distinctive sound and look in Hamburg: with Pete Best on drums, the fivesome's cathartic six-hour sets at clubs such as the Indra set the frantic pace of their early career.

The influence of Brian Epstein and George Martin upon the Beatles' fortunes needs little elaboration. Minus Sutcliffe (who died in 1962) and Best (who was replaced by Ringo Starr, born Richard Starkey),

the group scored a succession of British chart-toppers, starting with their debut album *Please, Please Me* (Parlophone PMC 1202) in 1963. Helped by merchandising mania, the Beatles' popularity spread abroad to North America in 1964. By April of that year, the band held the top five positions in the American *Billboard* singles chart and nine out of the Canadian top ten.

The Beatles' achievement extends beyond the simple equations of commercial success. In an era when recording technicians still wore white coats, their assertive behaviour in the studio bridged the unspoken divide between band and producer, setting a precedent for future generations. As McCartney recalled, "we figured that if anyone's going to know how much bass there should be on a record, or how loud the guitar solo should be … it ought to be us."

The producer/arranger George Martin's involvement diminished as the Beatles increasingly controlled the production of their own material, "always", as McCartney put it, "pushing ahead; louder, further, longer, more, different".

The musical experimentation at Abbey Road Studios reflected the maturing ability of Lennon and McCartney as songwriters. The 1965 album *Rubber Soul* (Parlophone PMC 1267), the fruit of this relationship, was far more than a simple collection of hits. Although 1966 proved a difficult year on tour, the trend continued, including the hits "Eleanor Rigby" coupled with "Yellow Submarine" (Parlophone R 5493) from their seventh album, *Revolver* (Parlophone PMC/PCS 7009).

The *Sgt. Pepper* album (Parlophone PMC/PCS 7027) is considered the Beatles' finest achievement. Although the figures on the sleeve evoked the band's past, the fantastic context of their presentation heralded the psychedelic future. It spawned perhaps their greatest single, "Strawberry Fields" coupled with "Penny Lane" (Parlophone R 5570). The release of *The Beatles* (known as the "White Album"; Parlophone PMC/PCS 7067–8) in 1968 marked another milestone, yet relations within the band were disintegrating. "Get Back" (Parlophone R 5777) provided yet another number one, but the same year the Beatles gave their last "public" performance. The albums *Abbey Road* (Parlophone PCS 7088) and *Let it Be* (Parlophone PCS 7096), although highly successful, proved a shadow of past glories. The Beatles split in 1970. The multi-platinum *Anthology* series (released in 1996 and featuring Lennon's "posthumous" single "Free as a Bird" (R CDR 6422), however, proved a massively successful reprise and showed that Beatlemania was alive and well.

The Beatles: Ringo Starr, George Harrison, Paul McCartney and John Lennon.

There was an unusual quality of sound, a certain roughness that I had not encountered before. There was also the fact that more than one person was singing, which in itself was unusual. There was something tangible that made me want to hear more, meet and see what they could do. [George Martin, *All You Need Is Ears* (London 1979), p.121]

Later that month, George Martin met the Beatles for the first time at a test recording session in what later became their creative home: Abbey Road Studios. On the strength of that test, Martin signed them to EMI, on a standard one-year contract (with options to extend) paying a royalty of one penny per single sold. On 11 September 1962, the group – now in its final form of John Lennon, Paul McCartney, George Harrison and Ringo

In 1963, EMI released the Beatles' first album, *Please, Please Me*.

Starr – returned to Abbey Road, where they made their first commercial record for EMI: "Love me do", coupled with "P.S. I love you" (Parlophone R 4949). The record was released in Britain during October 1962, and enjoyed modest success: it had sold 17,000 copies by Christmas. Royalties from these initial sales would have earned each Beatle £17.70 (before Epstein took his share). On its first release the record eventually reached the number 17 spot in the British singles charts. The enormous popularity of the Beatles' subsequent records caused a reawakening of interest and curiosity in this first recording (just as, generations earlier, Enrico Caruso's later recordings stimulated music lovers to buy his first discs). By October 1965, three years after its original release, British sales stood at almost 120,000. At a time when few artists earned large sums from their singles, the £125 in royalties each Beatle earned was considered good money.

The sessions which resulted in the Beatles' second record began on 26 November 1962. Again, the group and George Martin assembled at Abbey Road Studios. There they made "Please, Please Me" (Parlophone R 4983). The creative power and genius revealed during that session was extraordinary, as George Martin later recalled: "When it was all over I pressed the intercom button in the control room and said 'Gentlemen, you've just recorded your first number one record'. From that moment,

In October 1962 EMI released "Love me do", the Beatles first single.

SIR GEORGE MARTIN (BORN 1926)

★

George Martin was born in London. After war service with the RAF, he studied at the Guildhall School of Music for three years before working as a freelance oboist. In 1950 he was offered a job at EMI as assistant to Oscar Preuss, then in charge of the Parlophone label. Martin assisted with all types of recordings, from light orchestral through Victor Silvester to the pop music of the day, while his Guildhall training enabled him to produce classical sessions as well. When Preuss retired in 1955, George Martin took over as head of Parlophone.

Among the first recordings he produced as Parlophone manager were several with the London Baroque Ensemble under Karl Haas, performing music by composers such as Haydn, Bach, Handel and Mozart. However, his big break came when he spotted a gap in the market for comedy records. His first experiment was

"Phoney Folk Lore" and "Mock Mozart" with Peter Ustinov (Parlophone R 3612). He continued with singles and albums by The Goons, Peter Sellers, Spike Milligan, Michael Bentine and Bernard Cribbins, all of which made use of new, innovative recording techniques. Amongst these unusual records were a number that got into the charts, including "Goodness gracious me" (Parlophone R 4702), in which Peter Sellers was joined by Sophia Loren, and "Hole in the ground" (Parlophone R 4869) by Bernard Cribbins. He also recorded the witty Flanders and Swan revue *At the Drop of a Hat* (Parlophone PMC 1033 and PCS 3001) at the Fortune Theatre, London, and cashed in on the boom in satire with live recordings of *Beyond the Fringe* (PMC 1145), *That Was the Week That Was* (Parlophone PMC 1197) and *The Establishment* (Parlophone PMC 1198). He had big chart

hits with singles from the Temperance Seven, Matt Monro, Shirley Bassey and Rolf Harris, and produced such diverse items as Jimmy Shand's Scottish country dance records and jazz recordings by Humphrey Lyttelton and Johnny Dankworth.

In June 1962, he signed the Beatles to EMI. Their first album, *Please, Please Me* (Parlophone PMC 1202) was recorded and mixed in 13 hours, but, in later recordings, under Martin's guidance, they experimented with musical and technical ideas to create new kinds of sounds. The release of *Sgt. Pepper's Lonely Hearts Club Band* (Parlophone PMC/PCS 7027) in June 1967 marked the culmination of his inventiveness with recording technology and production techniques. In addition to the Beatles, Martin recorded a number of other Merseybeat acts, including Gerry and the Pacemakers, Billy J. Kramer, Cilla Black and the Fourmost.

In 1965, taking three other EMI producers with him, Martin left EMI to set up the independent production company AIR (Associated Independent Recording). A few years later, he opened AIR Studios in London and also on the Caribbean island of Montserrat. As a producer, he worked with acts like America, Neil Sedaka, Jimmy Webb and Jeff Beck and, after the break-up of the Beatles, Paul McCartney continued to work with him on projects like the albums *Tug of War* (Parlophone PCTC 259) and *Pipes of Peace* (Parlophone PCTC 1652301) and the theme for the James Bond film *Live and Let Die*. After Martin sold his AIR Studios to Chrysalis (which was itself later acquired by EMI), he occasionally produced new artists such as Andy Leek. He was knighted in 1996.

Summing up his work with the Beatles in his 1994 book *Summer of Love*, George Martin wrote: "I've been privileged to work with some of the best composers and writers, musicians and arrangers, singers and actors in the world. But of them all, none even begins to match up to the genius of those teenagers I met over thirty years ago."

we simply never stood still." [Martin, *All You Need is Ears*, p.130]
That turned out to be something of an understatement:
the record ignited the most extraordinary popular musical
phenomenon the world had ever known. Sales of Beatles records
rapidly reached astronomical proportions. During the first three
years of the group's association with EMI, British sales of their
ten singles totalled 9 million copies, whilst 2.5 million copies of
their extended-play records, and 3.5 million copies of their first
five albums, were sold – and that was just the beginning. By the
standard of the times, the figures were staggering. From the

Paul McCartney and George Martin
in the early days: apprentice and master.

The entertainer Peter Sellers with George Martin at Abbey Road Studios.

foundation of EMI in 1931 until the arrival of the Beatles, no performer or group had ever achieved sales on this scale. By 1969 (the year the Beatles made their final recording together), sales of their records in Britain accounted for almost 20 per cent of all EMI's British sales. The Company had not had an act of this magnitude since the days of Jack Hylton in the late 1920s (see Chapter 2). Similarly, in the decade to 1973, sales of Beatles albums in the United States reached 35 million copies. Such a mass phenomenon, sustained over such a length of time, helped transform the record industry into a truly international business with significant earnings potential (see Chapter 7).

Despite their creative and financial success, it was some time before EMI recognized that the Beatles were the key to the Company's future success. L. G. Wood, who was managing director of EMI Records at the time, readily confessed that he never conceived how important they would become. In the summer of 1963, he noticed unusually large orders being placed with the factory to manufacture the group's next record:

In those days, the record factory used to close down automatically for two weeks at the beginning of August. So, if you wanted to be sure of the records you were going to sell, you put in advance manufacturing orders. We'd released "From me to you" in April, and it sold very well indeed. In July, I saw that there was a Beatles record coming out towards the end of August called "She loves you" for which the marketing men had put in a manufacturing order of 350,000. I couldn't believe it. I mean we're talking 350,000, extraordinary in those days!
[L. G. Wood, Interview, 1994]

The marketing men told Wood that, in the three months following its April release, 200,000 copies of "From me to you" (Parlophone R 5015) had been sold. They argued that even greater sales could be expected from "She loves you" (Parlophone R 5055). After a major row, Wood consented to the manufacture of 250,000 records. At the end of 1963, sales of "She loves you" exceeded 1.3 million copies, earning the Beatles the first of their gold discs (for sales in excess of one million copies), together with the prestigious Ivor Novello Award. After the April 1963 release of "From me to you", the Beatles experienced 15 successive British number one single hits, all with standard advance orders in excess of one million copies, their most successful being their 1968 recording "Hey Jude" (Parlophone R 5722).

The Beatles' relationship with their producer was pivotal. Martin described his role "as making sure that they made a concise commercial statement. I would make sure that the song

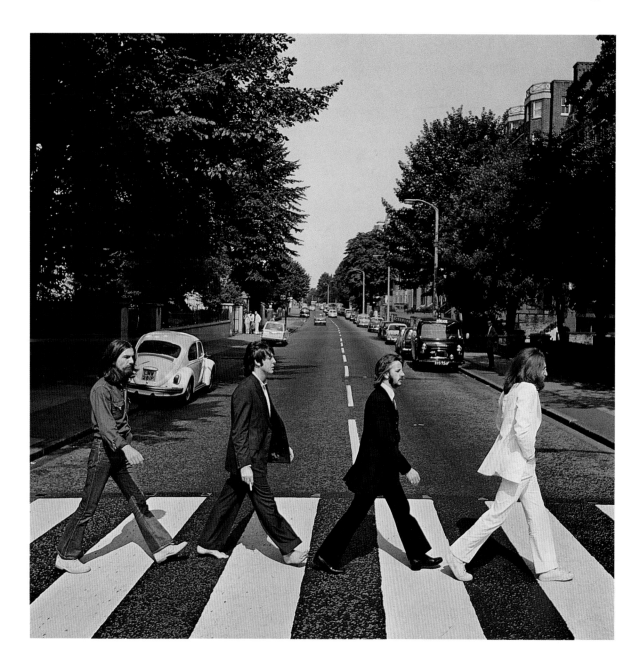

ran for approximately two and a half minutes, that it was in the right key, and that it was tidy, with the right position and form." [Martin, ibid., p.132] In the beginning, George Martin was very much in charge but, as time went on, the balance in the relationship shifted, as Paul McCartney observed:

George [Martin] was very helpful in the early days, he was the mastermind then. But as it went on the workers took over the tools more, and we started to say "we're coming in late, and we might not need you, George. If you can't make it, we'll go in on our own". [Mark Lewisohn, *The Complete Beatles Recording Sessions* (London 1988), p.6]

Honouring their artistic home, the Beatles' *Abbey Road* album gave the building and its locality a cult status it retains to the present. It also persuaded EMI to officially name the complex Abbey Road Studios.

CILLA BLACK
(BORN 1943)

★

Cilla Black's distinctive vocal sound launched her highly successful career as a singer. Born Priscilla White, she came to the attention of Brian Epstein whilst appearing as a guest vocalist at the Cavern Club. The Beatles' manager promptly changed her name and EMI released her first single, a reworking of the Fab Four's "Love of the Loved" (Parlophone R 5065), which reached the top thirty in late 1963. Yet it was the songstress's emotional ballads "Anyone who had a Heart" (Parlophone R 5101) and "You're my world" (Parlophone R 5133), both of which reached number one, that established her as one of the most commercially successful female singers of the era. Other lucrative covers followed, including Randy Newman's "I've been wrong before" (Parlophone R 5269) and the Righteous Brothers' "You've lost that lovin' feelin'" (Parlophone R 5225). After Epstein's death in 1967, Cilla Black's recording career continued apace. With the aid of her manager husband, Bobby Willis, the singer's involvement in film and television increased her popularity. Further top ten hits, including "Surround yourself with sorrow" (Parlophone R 5759), "Conversations" (Parlophone R 5785) and "Something tells me" (Parlophone R 5924), capped a glittering career for the Merseyside entertainer during the 1960s. Cilla's recording career slowed in the 1970s as she concentrated on television appearances and live performances. She is now best known as the presenter of *Blind Date* and *Surprise Surprise*.

John Lennon recognized that recording provided the group with a golden opportunity to extend their creativity beyond the traditional bounds of performance and into production. He said of this change:

We were just getting better technically and musically that's all. Finally we took over the studio. In the early days we had to take what we were given, we didn't know how you could get more bass. We were learning the technique on *Rubber Soul*. We were more precise about making the album that's all and we took over the cover and everything. [Brian Southall, *Abbey Road* (London 1982), p.101]

The Beatles began to use Abbey Road as a creative sanctuary from the pressures of the outside world, which included the relentless adulation of their fans. By 1969, when they recorded for the last time together at Abbey Road, it had become their second home, and the centre of both their creative and recording activities. As the Beatles and George Martin experimented with new ideas, they created new and substantive recording techniques, many of which became adopted as studio standards. Furthermore, the studios were forced to adapt to their unorthodox timetable, including late-night recording sessions. George Martin remembered:

The studio became a workshop, a permanent experimental thing. The Beatles were an example of how well artists could adapt to the technical side but not many other people did. It worked well with them and tracks became things that everybody got involved with. [Southall, ibid., p.120]

The Beatles were seen by many as outsiders, as they were in 1960s Britain. As such, they represented a challenge to the existing order of things. Because of this, both they and EMI attracted much criticism from the establishment. Even Sir Joseph Lockwood, chairman of EMI at the time, had problems with them: "In many ways they were a bloody nuisance. When they became famous they often came to see me when they were in trouble." [Southall, ibid.] Predictably, the British establishment used the group's success to emphasize their view that standards among the young were collapsing. In his 1964 article "The Menace of Beatlism", the writer Paul Johnson noted:

If the Beatles and their like were what the youth of Britain wanted, one might well despair. I refuse to believe it. Those who like the Beatles are the least fortunate of the generation, the dull, the idle, the failures, while those who will be the real leaders and creators of society tomorrow never go near a pop concert. [*New Statesman*, Vol.LXVII, 28 February 1964, pp.326–7]

In spite of such polemical attacks, the Beatles succeeded in creating a broad popular base for their art. In 1965, Queen Elizabeth II bestowed MBEs on the group for services to exports.

Sgt. Pepper

THE TURNING POINT

By the mid-1960s, The Beatles had stopped being a singles band who made albums and become the creators of what would be known as the concept album, in which themes and ideas were explored through music. In 1967, *Sgt. Pepper's Lonely Hearts Club Band* (Parlophone PMC/PCS 7027) marked a transformation in the musical content of the pop album. George Martin said of it:

Sgt. Pepper turned the Beatles from being just an ordinary rock-and-roll group into being significant contributors to the history of artistic performance. It was a turning point – the turning point. It was the watershed which changed the recording art from something that merely made amazing sounds into something which will stand the test of time as a valid art form. [Martin, *All You Need is Ears*, p.214]

As an interesting footnote, the recording of the first Beatles album, *Please, Please Me*, was made in a single day and cost a mere £400, whilst *Sgt. Pepper* took four months to make and cost £25,000. Furthermore, the Beatles' considerable involvement in the design of the *Sgt. Pepper* album cover (a design that used the images of leading figures of the century) marked an historic extension of artists' power.

In 1968, the Beatles formed their own record company, Apple, which recorded such artists as Mary Hopkins, James Taylor and Badfinger. From that date on, Parlophone used the distinctive Apple label for all the Beatles recordings it released. In 1969, the party ended and the Beatles went their separate ways. Each maintained his association with EMI and each experienced considerable success as a solo performer.

The enduring image of the *Sgt Pepper* album in picture disc form.

In 1972, George Harrison became the first to achieve a solo number one single, with "My Sweet Lord" (Parlophone R 5884). Between 1971 and 1974 Ringo Starr achieved four top ten singles, "Back off Boogaloo" (Parlophone R 5944) reaching number two. Paul McCartney had to wait until 1977 for his first number one single, "Mull of Kintyre" (Parlophone R 6018). However, it was worth waiting for: this record became Britain's most successful single ever, with sales in excess of two million. McCartney's album *Band on the Run* (Parlophone PAS 10007) also achieved dramatic sales both in Britain and abroad. John Lennon developed his own musical career, initially as a solo composer, writer and performer, and, later, with his wife Yoko Ono. Between them they made many records, including "The Ballad of John and Yoko" (Parlophone R 5786) in 1969, which stayed at the top of the charts for 14 weeks. His best-selling album and musical testament was *Imagine* (Parlophone PAS 10004). "Imagine" was also released as a single in 1975 (Parlophone R 6009) and reached the number one spot in the British charts five years later following the shocking tragedy of Lennon's murder in New York.

How do you do it

MERSEYBEAT

Had Brian Epstein brought only the Beatles to EMI, his place in musical history would have been assured. That he also brought a whole stable of Mersey-based talent, who – with the Beatles – gave that exciting decade the distinctive Merseybeat sound, marks him out as one of the most extraordinary managers of all time. Among these other artists were Gerry and the Pacemakers. After signing an EMI contract in February 1963, they released their first record, "How do you do it" (Columbia DB 4987) – a song the Beatles had turned down. It made them the first Merseybeat artists to reach the number one spot in the British singles charts. "How do you do it" was followed by "I like it" (Columbia DB 7041) and "You'll never walk alone" (Columbia DB 7126), both of which went to the top of the charts. "You'll never walk alone", a ballad from the Rodgers and Hammerstein musical *Carousel*, sold nearly 750,000 copies in Britain, and in the process became a Liverpool anthem. Billy J. Kramer and the

Gerry and the Pacemakers, Cilla Black, Billy J. Kramer and the Dakotas
A select early 1960s gathering of EMI's top Merseybeat acts at the Company's Manchester Square offices. Left to right: Billy J. Kramer, Cilla Black and Gerry Marsden.

323

Opposite page, top With vocalist Paul Jones, Manfred Mann was a blues-based band that quickly became teenage heartthrobs.

Opposite page, below The Dave Clark Five, seen here recording at Abbey Road Studios in the early 1960s, were billed as London's answer to the Beatles.

Swinging Blue Jeans HMV's contribution to the Mersey boom, the Swinging Blue Jeans enjoyed five major hit singles in the early Sixties.

Dakotas was another of Epstein's groups to record for EMI. Although they never achieved the same degree of success as Gerry and the Pacemakers, they did secure several hit records by using songs written by Lennon and McCartney. Epstein's most important female artist was Cilla Black (see box, page 320), described by George Martin as a "rock and roll screecher in the true Cavern tradition, with a piercing nasal sound." [Martin, *All You Need is Ears*, p. 135] She began her recording career in 1964 with records such as "Anyone who had a heart" (Parlophone R 5101) and "You're my world" (Parlophone R 5133). The success of these transformed Cilla Black into a ballad singer, and laid the foundations for her subsequent career as a middle-of-the-road recording artist and television entertainer.

The Beatles and the Merseybeat sound were not the only new musical ideas or performers to emerge in the 1960s, although they were the most important. As George Martin's time was increasingly taken up by his work with the Beatles and other Epstein artists, EMI's other A & R managers went on the road in search of fresh talent. Their task was made easier because EMI, by virtue of being the Beatles' record company, had acquired a reputation for creative innovation. One of A & R manager Ron Richards' discoveries was the Manchester-based group The Hollies. They became immensely popular and, between 1963 and 1966, had six top ten hits, although the competition by then was so intense that only one of their records – "I'm alive" (Parlophone R 5287) – made it to number one. The Hollies continued to make records and tour on into the 1990s; in 1988, 25 years after the release of their first EMI record, they achieved a number one hit with "He ain't heavy, he's my brother" (EMI EM 74) following its use on a television commercial for Miller Lite beer. For a while, it appeared that every budding or established pop and rock artist wanted to join the Company's extraordinary roster. Among them were Peter and Gordon, Georgie Fame, Manfred Mann, the Swinging Blue Jeans, the Dave Clark Five, Freddie and the Dreamers, and the rhythm and blues group the Yardbirds. With this unprecedented array of talent available on EMI labels, the Company became so strong that, in 1963, by shrewdly managing release dates, it was able to achieve 15 out of that year's 19 number one hit single records.

The House of the Rising Sun

THE SIXTIES AND SEVENTIES

Although the Beatles and the Merseybeat sound transformed EMI's popular music activities in the 1960s, the Company's previous roster of artists flourished simultaneously with the new music and musicians. In 1962, the year of the first Beatles record, EMI dominated the British record charts. The Columbia record "Stranger on the Shore" (Columbia DB 4750), by the jazz clarinettist Acker Bilk, became the year's number one best-selling record on both sides of the Atlantic, remaining in the British charts for 55 weeks, with total sales of more than 1 million copies. In the same year, Shirley Bassey's remarkable career as a singer and entertainer was further enhanced with her hit single "What now my love" (Columbia DB 4882) and the album *The Fabulous Shirley Bassey* (Columbia 33SX 1178). Her continued association with EMI has resulted in regular new releases of highly successful albums. In 1962, another vocalist, the Australian Frank Ifield, sold more than one million copies of "I remember you" (Columbia DB 4896), the first of his many number one hit singles, whilst the American blues singer

THE ANIMALS

The Animals' enormous popularity spanned the Atlantic, at times challenging that of the Beatles and the Rolling Stones. Formed in Newcastle-upon-Tyne in 1963, the Animals comprised Eric Burdon (vocals), Alan Price (piano), Hilton Valentine (guitar), John Steel (drums) and Chas Chandler (bass). Their exciting live performances quickly attracted attention and the group became stars at the Club a-Go-Go in Newcastle. By 1963, the Animals had moved to the London club circuit and swiftly debuted with the pacy hit single "Baby let me take you home" (Columbia DB 7247). Yet it was their next release, Josh White's tale of a New Orleans brothel, "The House of the Rising Sun" (Columbia DB 7301), which topped the charts across the world. Over the next two years the Animals had seven major hits on both sides of the Atlantic, including the tortured "I'm crying" (Columbia DB 7354) and the despairing chorus of Weill/Mann's "We gotta get out of this place" (Columbia DB 7639). The mid-1960s saw Steel and Price's replacement by Dave Rowberry and Barry Jenkins; the new line-up enjoyed success with the single "It's my life" (Columbia DB 7741). However, Burdon and Valentine's increasing fascination with psychedelia alienated the rest of the group and, in 1967, the group finally disbanded. Burdon, however, retained the name and went on to enjoy considerable success in America with the New Animals. Although they also split up at the end of 1968, the original Animals line-up regrouped twice, in 1977 and 1983, before Chas Chandler's death in 1996.

Ray Charles scored a major success with "I can't stop loving you" (HMV POP 134). Cliff Richard also continued to flourish in the changing musical climate, with such hits as "Summer Holiday" (Columbia DB 4977).

As the 1960s progressed, the extraordinary success of EMI created a ripple effect throughout the British and broader world record industry, and it experienced a rapid expansion. New independent recording studios opened in London, reinforcing the capital's position as a world centre for recorded music. Rapid structural changes, particularly competition from new players such as independents and American majors, had important consequences for large established companies like EMI (see Chapter 7).

First in the field was Mickie Most, who had formed RAK in the early 1960s. RAK licensed several important artists to EMI. The first of these was The Animals (see box), a Newcastle rhythm and blues group. Their second single, released in June 1964, was an adaptation of the American blues song "The House of the Rising Sun" (Columbia DB 7301). This dramatic record, which played for four and a half minutes (extraordinary for the time), had taken a mere fifteen minutes to record. The haunting

sound and raw emotions expressed revealed Eric Burdon's exceptional talent as a blues singer. In the summer of 1964, "The House of the Rising Sun" became a British number one hit, and it eventually achieved sales in excess of one million copies, then still a rare distinction for a pop record. Later, one of the group's albums, *Most of the Animals* (Columbia SX 6035), achieved a gold disc for sales of more than 500,000. Between 1964 and 1969, many other Mickie Most artists appeared on EMI, including Herman's Hermits with Peter Noone, whose combined sales from 20 hit singles in the United States and Britain was more than 50 million units, and the Scottish entertainer Lulu.

Above Scotland's Lulu had her first hit single in 1964 and has remained steadfast to her music for nearly 35 years.

Left More than 30 years after the release of their first record, The Hollies, one of the most enduring pop music groups of all time, are still recording and touring. Left to right: Terry Sylvester, Bernie Calvert, Allan Clarke, Tony Hicks, Bobby Elliott.

Good Vibrations

EMI'S AMERICAN CONNECTIONS IN THE SIXTIES

In a historic shift, the Beatles, followed by other British pop and rock artists, reversed the post-war domination of the British popular music scene by American music and musicians. This change did not mean that new American artists or fresh musical genres ceased to interest the British or American record-buying public: in fact during the 1960s several important new American artists came to the fore.

To give more prominence to such artists, EMI created the Stateside label in 1962. The range of repertoire released on this label embraced American pop, jazz, country and western, and rhythm and blues records. EMI also continued to license recordings from other American sources for distribution in Britain and Europe. EMI supplemented its existing deals with United Artists, Liberty and MGM by entering into licensing

One of Motown's leading acts, Diana Ross and the Supremes released their first recordings in the British record market on EMI's Stateside label.

agreements with other American labels, such as Verve, Bell, Impulse and Probe. During the late 1960s and into the 1970s, as certain artists and their American record companies became increasingly important, EMI began releasing their records on their own rather than on the Company's British labels. As a consequence, Stateside experienced a precipitous decline, and was phased out completely in 1973. The label's remaining artists were

THE BEACH BOYS

★

The most successful American pop group ever was formed on America's West Coast in 1961. The "classic" Beach Boys line-up comprised brothers Brian, Carl and Dennis Wilson, cousin Al Jardine and schoolfriend Mike Love. After the moderate local success of Brian's independently released "Surfin'" the band signed to Capitol Records in 1962. Over the next year-and-a-half, the Beach Boys went on to enjoy ten American hit singles and also released four albums. In 1963, they eventually broke the Merseybeat domination of the British charts with the single "Surfin' USA" (Capitol CL 15305). In a rally against the Beatles' American invasion, the Beach Boys' musical output over the following years was prolific. Yet 1966's *Pet Sounds* album (Capitol T 2458), undoubtedly the group's masterpiece, sold poorly in America; this devastated Brian, whose deteriorating mental state had led to drug-dependency. Bruce Johnston eventually filled his public role and, in 1966, the band scored a colossal hit with "Good Vibrations" (Capitol CL 15475). Yet Brian's worsening condition, Love's devotion to the Maharishi Mahesh Yogi and Dennis's dubious involvement with Charles Manson brought an end to their success, and in 1969 the Beach Boys finally left Capitol. After the addition of Ricky Fataar, Blondie Chaplain and Daryl Dragon, the group recovered their worldwide popularity with the hugely selling *Endless Summer* compilation (1974). Dennis Wilson died in 1983 and his brother Brian, the group's creative genius, finally severed his links with the Beach Boys in 1990.

transferred to the then new EMI label, the first time in its history that the Company had used its own name on a British record. Subsequently, the EMI label absorbed many of the Company's own, long-established British and overseas record labels, including Columbia and HMV.

The most successful licensing agreement of this period was the one entered into in 1963 with a small Detroit-based record company, Motown. Motown specialized in a new black American beat-driven sound derived from soul music (itself a derivative of gospel music) which quickly became one of EMI's most important growth sectors. Motown's roster of artists included Stevie Wonder, Marvin Gaye, Diana Ross and the Supremes, The Temptations and the Jackson Five. Surprisingly, the Company failed to recognize Motown's value. In 1965, it was offered the entire Motown business for $17 million and turned it down as too expensive. However, four years later, the Company did recognize the increasing importance of this highly individualistic musical genre and gave the Tamla Motown label its own separate organization within EMI. During the 1970s, the Company could rely on two out of every three Motown record releases becoming hits.

Alongside its American licensors, EMI relied on Capitol Records for fresh American talent. Capitol provided it with many fine recordings by American pop and rock artists, including the Beach Boys (see box). The Beach Boys were a close harmony

Anne Murray, possibly Canada's most successful music export, enjoying a career with Capitol Records that has lasted over 25 years.

pop group whose fans perceived them as the epitome of the West Coast, that fantasy land of permanent sunshine, wealth and hedonism. They were also highly professional artists and perfectionists: it took them six months to record their most successful single, "Good Vibrations" (Capitol CL 15475), which became that group's first British million-selling single. Twenty-five years after its first release, this seminal record was described as "a glorious collage of musical pattern with its changes in tempo, unusual lyrics and incredible dynamics." [(Ed.) Colin Larkin, *Guinness Who's Who of Sixties Music* (London 1992), p.22] The Beach Boys' output of records was prolific and, by the early 1990s, their recorded legacy had achieved cumulative world sales of 65 million copies.

During the 1960s, Capitol's other major exports to Britain included Grand Funk Railroad, Anne Murray, Helen Reddy, Andy Kim and Dr Hook. However, its most important solo artist was the country singer Glen Campbell. His reputation was cemented by a regular output of albums – 37 by 1980 – and retrospective anthologies which, combined with his highly individual performance style and regular British and European tours, built up and retained a loyal and dedicated band of followers.

Happiness

MIDDLE-OF-THE-ROAD POPULAR MUSIC IN THE SIXTIES AND SEVENTIES

One of the most important changes in the buying habits of pop record consumers was the growth of the so-called middle of the road record market ("MOR"), defined as records that were neither classical nor contemporary pop or rock. Middle-of-the-road consumers, with an age profile of between 25 and 60, formed a large, affluent and rather neglected group. In a concerted effort to woo this middle sector, EMI released singles and albums by a host of British-based performers, such as the entertainer Ken Dodd, whose most successful single was "Tears" (Columbia DB 7659); Rolf Harris, whose 1971 record "Two Little Boys" (Columbia DB 8630) sold more than 850,000

copies; Des O'Connor, who had a number one hit in 1968 with "I pretend" (Columbia DB 8397); and The Seekers, an Australian group, who had enormous success with two singles, "I'll never find another you" (Columbia DB 7431) and "The carnival is over" (Columbia DB 7711), each of which sold more than one million copies.

EMI released other MOR singles and albums. Some of these drew on the Company's rich tradition of records of music hall and variety artists such as Stanley Holloway and Charles Penrose, and of revue artists like Noël Coward. Among these were several by television performers such as Clive Dunn, who recorded "Grandad" (Columbia DB 8726) in 1971, and Benny Hill, whose 1971 recording of "Ernie (the fastest milkman in the west)" (Columbia DB 8853) became one of the most unusual novelty songs ever to reach the top of the British singles charts. EMI also released a highly successful album by entertainers Windsor Davies and Don Estelle, *Sing Lofty* (EMI EMC 3102),

The entertainer Ken Dodd, self-styled King of Knotty Ash, receiving a silver disc from EMI chairman Sir Joseph Lockwood.

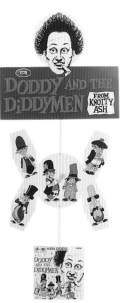

With their distinctive style, the Australian folk group the Seekers enjoyed a string of popular hits in the 1960s.

as a spin-off from their television series *It Ain't Half hot, Mum*. Many other comic performers made records for EMI, including Peter Sellers and Spike Milligan, satirists Peter Cook, Dudley Moore, Jonathan Miller and Alan Bennett (*Beyond the Fringe* (Parlophone PMC 1145), The Scaffold, Max Boyce and Bernard Cribbins. The considerable success of these and other MOR records confirmed the fact that the charts were not the exclusive domain of any specific musical form.

In the decades following 1970, the teenage pop and rock fans of the 1960s grew up and became a new generation of record purchasers. By recognizing that the passage of time had not dimmed the appeal of the recording artists and the music of their youth, EMI redefined the term middle of the road to encompass a much wider range of music, including earlier pop and rock. As a result, several 1960s pop and rock musicians, including the Beach Boys and Cliff Richard, were transformed into best-selling middle of the road entertainers.

Piper at the Gates of Dawn

PINK FLOYD AND PROGRESSIVE ROCK

When George Martin left EMI in 1965, his job as head of Parlophone was taken by Norman Smith, the man who had engineered the Beatles' June 1962 test recording session. For several years after his appointment, Smith trawled aggressively through a new generation of British pop and rock artists then emerging from the cauldron of talent and new musical forms that had developed in the wake of the Beatles-Merseybeat revolution. EMI's existing record labels – particularly the Parlophone label – had become synonymous with the Beatles and other Merseybeat artists in the minds of the British public. To give a fresh identity to the so-called "progressive" or "underground" rock music then emerging, the Company created the Harvest label.

In 1967, Norman Smith first heard the group whose fortunes

PINK FLOYD

★

As the *Financial Times* commented on the *Meddle* album in 1971, Pink Floyd had "the furthest frontiers of pop music to themselves". In 1965, architecture students Roger Waters, Nick Mason and Rick Wright linked up with a restive Camberwell Art College kid called "Syd" (b. Roger) Barrett. Pink Floyd were formed as a rhythm and blues outfit whose name paid living homage to Syd's heroes Pink Anderson and Floyd Council. Syd's passion for free-form improvization and ambitious audio-visual displays made the group the darlings of London's psychedelic counter-culture. By 1966, they had had two top 20 singles and the top ten album, *Piper at the Gates of Dawn* (Columbia SCX 6157). However, by 1968, Barrett had become increasingly unstable and was replaced by David Gilmour, his one-time classmate. In 1973, Pink Floyd scored a massive worldwide success with the enormously popular *Dark Side of the Moon* (Harvest SHVL 804). Floyd's spectacular live performances increasingly reflected the band's desire to redefine the group as an experience. The *Wall* (Harvest SHDW 411) concerts of 1980 embodied just such an aspiration although, unhappily, Floyd was now an association of solo artists rather than a group. In 1985, Waters left amid a legal tangle over the band's name. However, Pink Floyd continued to record, releasing *A Momentary Lapse of Reason* (EMI CDP 7480682) in 1987. The group's 1994 album *The Division Bell* (EMI CDEMD 1055) entered the British and American charts at number one.

were to be so intimately tied into those of EMI for the next three decades: Pink Floyd (see box). Smith recalled:

What I saw absolutely amazed me. I was still into creating and developing new electronic sounds in the control room, and Pink Floyd, I could see, were into exactly the same thing; it was a perfect marriage. [Southall, *Abbey Road*, p.114]

Pink Floyd began their recording career in 1967 and quickly established themselves as the successors to the Beatles as creators

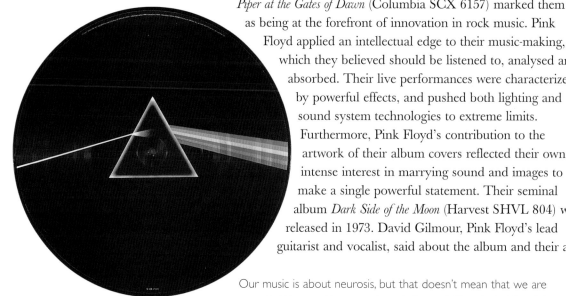

of concept albums. During their initial 11 years as EMI artists they released virtually no singles, whilst the first of their many albums was released less than six months after their debut single. *Piper at the Gates of Dawn* (Columbia SCX 6157) marked them out as being at the forefront of innovation in rock music. Pink Floyd applied an intellectual edge to their music-making, which they believed should be listened to, analysed and absorbed. Their live performances were characterized by powerful effects, and pushed both lighting and sound system technologies to extreme limits. Furthermore, Pink Floyd's contribution to the artwork of their album covers reflected their own intense interest in marrying sound and images to make a single powerful statement. Their seminal album *Dark Side of the Moon* (Harvest SHVL 804) was released in 1973. David Gilmour, Pink Floyd's lead guitarist and vocalist, said about the album and their art:

Our music is about neurosis, but that doesn't mean that we are neurotic. We are able to see it, and discuss it. The dark side of the moon itself is an allusion to the moon and lunacy. The dark side is generally related to what goes on inside people's heads – the subconscious and the unknown. [Chris Welch, *The Giants of Rock: Pink Floyd* (London 1974)]

The seminal image of Pink Floyd's album *Dark Side of the Moon* in picture-disc form.

Since its original release, *Dark Side of the Moon* has become one of EMI's most celebrated rock albums. It remained in the British album charts for an astonishing six years, and was awarded a platinum disc in 1977 for sales in excess of one million copies. By 1990, world sales of this record exceeded 35 million copies. Twenty-five years after its original release, *Dark Side of the Moon* – now in CD format – still achieves significant annual sales.

The Harvest label also became the vehicle for "underground" rock musicians such as Deep Purple (see box, page 335). Although many underground rock music fans considered it to be a non-commercial form of rock music, its finest exponents actually commanded enormous worldwide sales. In the case of Deep Purple, their most successful album, *Fireball* (Harvest SHVL 793), released in 1971, reached the top of the British album charts. By 1974, the group had earned a total of 25 gold discs for world sales of their albums. Deep Purple's eclectic musical style and experiments with different sounds, musical forms and instruments led them to perform and record the *Concerto for Group and Orchestra* with the Royal Philharmonic Orchestra, conducted by Malcolm Arnold (Harvest SHVL 767).

Other Harvest label stars included the Edgar Broughton Band, Roy Harper, the Electric Light Orchestra, the Move and the Pretty Things.

Dirty Old Town

FOLK MUSIC

The 1960s saw a major revival of interest in folk music in Britain. To exploit this, EMI developed a roster of folk artists, including Roger Whittaker. His album *This is Roger Whittaker* (Columbia SCX 6341) contained his most popular songs, such as "Dirty Old Town" and "The Leavin (Durham Town)". In 1975, Whittaker's single "The Last Farewell" (EMI 2294) became a best-seller and reached the top ten in the singles charts. Another important folk singer and writer was the American Tom Paxton. He featured on the MAM label – at that time licensed to EMI – and made his best-remembered recording, "Last thing on my mind" (MAM 153), in 1976 at Abbey Road.

DEEP PURPLE

★

While on a brief tour of Scandinavia in 1968, Rod Evans (vocals), Jon Lord (keyboards), Ritchie Blackmore (guitar), Nick Simper (bass) and Ian Paice (drums) adopted the name Deep Purple. Their debut album, *Shades of Deep Purple* (Parlophone PCS 7055), was released in the same year and included a number of cover versions such as "Hush" and "Hey Joe". "Hush" eventually reached the American top five. Although the group was still largely unknown in its native country, consistent touring in America and the originality of its material soon brought popularity. In 1969, Evans and Simper were replaced by Ian Gillan and Roger Glover to create the "classic" Deep Purple line-up. After the ambitious *Concerto for Group and Orchestra* album, *Deep Purple in Rock* (Harvest SHVL 777) cast the group as a heavy metal outfit and established their popularity in Britain. The single "Black Night" (Harvest HAR 5020) reached number two, whilst "Strange Kind of Woman" (Harvest HAR 5033) followed it into the British top ten. The band's next two albums, *Fireball* (1971, Harvest SHVL 793) and *Machine Head* (1972, Purple TPSA 7504), both topped the charts. The latter album contained the seminal "Smoke on the Water" (Purple PUR 132). *Who do we think we are?* (1973, Purple TPSA 7508) marked the end of the "classic" line-up, with Gillan and Glover replaced by David Coverdale and Glenn Hughes. Later albums made the British top ten, but Blackmore's departure in 1975 led to Deep Purple's break-up a year later. The "classic" line-up reformed again in 1984, although various personnel changes have since taken place including Blackmore's second departure in 1993.

Using authentic instruments, Shirley and Dolly Collins revitalised the playing of folk music.

Among EMI's many other folk musicians were the sisters Shirley and Dolly Collins. Released on the Harvest label (in the unlikely company of Deep Purple and Pink Floyd), their records attempted to recreate the true spirit of folk music. They used a flue organ modelled on a medieval original, and enlisted the support of the early music specialist David Munrow (see Chapter 8). Their best-known albums were *Anthems in Eden* (Harvest SHVL 754) and *Love, Death and the Lady* (Harvest SHVL 771).

Bohemian Rhapsody

QUEEN

Queen (see box, page 337) signed their first EMI record contract in 1972 and the following year released their debut album, which established them among the leaders of the British rock scene. With the flamboyant showman Freddie Mercury as lead singer, Queen soon became known as an outstanding and visually exciting live performance act. They also developed a highly individual recording style and, in 1975, broke fresh ground with "Bohemian Rhapsody" (EMI 2375). Lasting an extraordinary six minutes, this record became the best-selling single of the year, with British sales in the year of its release totalling one million

John Deacon, Freddie Mercury, Roger Taylor (obscured) and Brian May of Queen.

QUEEN

★

Following the demise of their band Smile in 1970, students Brian May (guitar) and Roger Taylor (drums) joined up with one of their keenest fans, Freddie Bulsara (vocals). Bulsara promptly changed his name to Mercury and the band's name to Queen, and a year later John Deacon (bass) successfully auditioned as its fourth member. It was the massive success of Queen's third album, *Sheer Heart Attack* (1974, EMI EMC 3061), that truly established their popularity on both sides of the Atlantic. Hits such as "Bohemian Rhapsody" (EMI 2375), "We are the champions" (EMI 2708), "Radio Ga Ga" (EMI QUEEN 1) and "Innuendo" (Parlophone QUEEN 16), among many others, ensured huge record sales. During 1986, Queen sold 1,750,000 albums in Britain alone. Their success was also fuelled by spectacular live performances. In 1981, 131,000 people watched Queen play at the Morumbi Stadium in São Paulo (the largest paying audience for a single band anywhere in the world). Queen's energy on stage was equally mirrored by their flamboyant lifestyle off it. Despite their huge success, the musical innovation which Queen consistently strove to achieve should not be overlooked: the groundbreaking video for "Bohemian Rhapsody"; the use of synthezisers on *The Game* (1980, EMI EMA 795); and their collaboration with the British Film Institute for *Made in Heaven* (Parlophone CDPCSD 167) in 1995, the band's twentieth album, which concluded an astonishing recording career.

copies. Throughout the 1970s and 1980s, Queen retained the rare talent of translating the raw energy of their live performances into electrifying recordings. In the course of the first decade of their association with EMI, they released ten albums, which between them achieved world sales in excess of 40 million copies. Their output remained prolific into the 1980s, and, during this final decade together, they produced a further 11 albums. Numerous gold discs were awarded as a result of British and international sales of their records. It was a testimony to their enduring popularity that their 1981 compilation album *Greatest Hits* (EMTV 30) remained in the British album charts for six years. Freddie Mercury's diversity and range were such that he performed with ease and confidence the signature tune for the 1990 Barcelona Olympics with the opera singer Montserrat Caballé. In 1991, the fusion of genius that was Queen tragically ended with Mercury's death from Aids. The subsequent re-release of their greatest recording, "Bohemian Rhapsody", raised large sums for Aids charities.

Live after Death

THE BIRTH OF THE MUSIC VIDEO

Although the music video was originally conceived as an important new tool for promoting music, it quickly took on a life of its own and fed new methods of consuming music, particularly after the start of the music video channel Music Television (MTV) in the early 1980s, initially in the United States and then on a worldwide basis. As a consequence, the format developed

T. REX (MARC BOLAN)

Tyrannosaurus Rex began as a six-piece band, but upon the repossession of their musical equipment they were reduced in 1967 to an acoustic twosome. Guided by Radio 1's John Peel, Marc Bolan (vocals/guitar) and Steve Took (percussion) debuted with the British top forty single "Deborah" (Regal Zonophone RZ 3008). The duo were to find great adulation for their early albums, such as *My people were fair* (1968, Regal Zonophone SLRZ 1003). After 1969's "Unicorn" (Regal Zonophone SLRZ 1007), Took was replaced by Mickey Finn and, with Tony Visconti as producer, the band's musical direction changed. Now simply T. Rex, and aided by new recruits Bill Legend (drums) and Steve Currie (bass), they achieved number one British hits with the singles "Hot Love" (Fly BUG 6) and "Get It On" (Fly BUG 10). The 1971 album, *Electric Warrior* (Fly HIFLY 6) similarly topped the charts, but the ensuing release of the single "Jeepster" (Fly BUG 16) without Bolan's permission caused the singer to leave the Fly label. On their own T. Rex label, Bolan's group enjoyed further success in 1972 with a number of top five releases, including the chart-toppers "Telegram Sam" (T Rex 101) and "Metal Guru" (EMI MARC 1). "20th Century Boy" (EMI MARC 4) and "The Groover" (EMI MARC 5), both 1973, proved to be the group's last major hits. The addition of soul diva Gloria Jones did little to improve T. Rex's flagging fortunes and Currie, Legend and Finn eventually departed. On 16 September 1977, Marc Bolan was killed in a car crash.

Steve Took and Marc Bolan.

into a new art form and became as essential a statement as the recording itself to many performers. This coming together of the arts of sound recording and video production proved a crucially important addition to the richness of the musical experience. EMI launched its new product range with Queen's video of "Bohemian Rhapsody". The particular combination of Queen's music and performance with film-making was seen at the time as ground-breaking and created a benchmark against which subsequent music videos have been judged. Music videos soon became so important that the Company developed its own in-house video production company, Picture Music International (PMI). As a result, the cream of EMI's artists appeared in PMI videos. Among these were *Queen's Magic Years* (MVB 99 1157 2), Iron Maiden's *Live after Death* (MVN 99 1094 2), Pink Floyd's *Delicate Sound of Thunder* (MVN 99 1186 3) and Cliff Richard's *From a Distance "The Event"* (MVB 99 1247 3).

Electric Warrior

PUNK AND NEW WAVE

By the early 1970s, the British pop and rock industry had begun to run out of steam. Consumers reacted against the attitudes and lifestyles of established artists and the increasingly rarefied intellectualism of their concept albums. This reaction was exacerbated by Britain's deteriorating economic situation, with rising unemployment and unprecedented inflation pushing many would-be consumers out of the market (see Chapter 7). Punk music emerged as the *cri de coeur* of an angry generation. Intent on shocking the wider public, punk – with its torn clothes, safety pins, wild hairstyles, make-up and outrageous, anarchic music – was a movement that attracted many young people who felt marginalized and alienated from society. In the climate of the mid-1970s, it was perfectly natural for EMI to develop punk music as a new musical genre. One of its early successes in the new genre was a musician who successfully made the transition from pop to punk, Marc Bolan. Between 1970 and 1973, Bolan (see box) enjoyed ten successive pop single hits, and was such a successful and gifted talent that EMI gave him his own label. His early death in a car crash deprived popular music of a rare and largely unfulfilled talent.

Later on, EMI found itself in an unprecedented and widely publicized row with one of its own acts. The Sex Pistols had been signed in October 1976. At the time, they were seen as having the same kind of energy, excitement, raw talent and potential as the

Above The Sex Pistols, at the cutting edge of 1970s British punk: their image as much as their music defined the times.

Left Marc Bolan, an icon of his times, at a 1976 *Top of the Pops* reception.

THE STRANGLERS

★

Band rehearsals for the Stranglers began in 1974 and two years later the full line-up of Hugh Cornwell (vocals/guitar), Jean Jacques Burnel (vocals/bass), Jet Black (born Brian Duffy; drums) and Dave Greenfield (keyboards) was signed to United Artist Records. "Get a grip (on yourself)" (United Artists UP 36211) was released in 1977 but only reached number 44 in the British charts (apparently because of an error by the chart compilers). In the same year, the Stranglers' gritty first album *Stranglers IV (Rattus Norvegicus)* (United Artists UAG 30045) sold extremely well despite criticism from the press for songs such as "Hanging Around" and "Down in the Sewer". Their next single, the women-baiting "Peaches" (United Artists UP 36248), similarly caused outrage. If anything, the band's increasing alienation from the press and frequent clashes with the law served to promote its cult popularity: the singles "Something better change" (United Artists UP 36277) and "No More Heroes" (United Artists UP 36300), both reached the British top ten. The album *La Folie* (1981, Liberty LBG 30342) spawned their greatest hit, the heroin-tinged "Golden Brown" (Liberty BP 407), which reached number two in the British charts. Further hits followed, including a cover of the Kinks' "All day and all of the night" (Epic VICE 1), which reached the British top ten. Despite these successes, the Stranglers' later albums failed to replicate earlier successes. The departure of Cornwell in 1990 heralded the end of an era and the break-up of the group.

top 1960s rock groups. After an infamous television appearance EMI sustained a wave of highly embarrassing and damaging publicity, and immediately dropped the group. The incident itself proved no more than a storm in a tea cup (the band were in fact signed to the Company for only three months), but their behaviour and the manner of their departure were seen at the time – both by the Company and the wider public – as a watershed in defining the limits of good taste in public behaviour. Rather ironically, the Sex Pistols went on to sign with Virgin Records, which was subsequently acquired by THORN EMI in the early 1990s.

In the late 1970s, the Stranglers (see box) – released on the United Artists/Liberty label – were able to make the transition from punk to new wave music. Combining, punk, new wave and old fashioned rock, the Stranglers had a whole string of hits, including their album (and single) *No More Heroes* (United Artists UAG 30200). Their commercial success was all the more remarkable in that they were banned from the BBC airwaves and were engaged in a continual war of attrition with journalists and made headlines with their drugs convictions. Their talent to move with the times was such that, by the mid-1980s, they were among the few remaining EMI artists from the short-lived punk era still performing and making records.

Exodus

DISCO AND REGGAE

In the late 1970s, the elemental beat of disco music had become widespread. The United States, and particularly EMI's Capitol catalogue, was the dominant source of disco repertoire. Among

EMI's most popular American disco artists were Tavares, who had a string of successful albums including *The Best of Tavares* (Capitol E-ST 11701) and *Supercharged* (Capitol E-ST 12026), and bands such as Taste of Honey and Maze.

Other forms of music which appealed to teenagers also emerged as distinct musical forms. Reggae was derived largely from West Indian culture, although two-thirds of EMI's reggae records were made by British artists. In an attempt to give reggae its own clear identity, EMI acquired access to a specialist reggae label, Safari Records. Among the artists to appear on this label were Matumbi, Jennifer Gray and the Doyley Brothers. However, the greatest exponent of reggae was Bob Marley. His recordings were distributed in Britain by EMI through a licensing deal with Island Records. They included *Wailers Live* (Island ILPS 9376), *Exodus* (Island ILPS 9498) and *Survival* (Island ILPS 9542).

By 1979, disco, soul and reggae between them accounted for almost half the singles and almost one third of all popular albums EMI sold in Britain. To meet the needs of the increasingly important disco market, EMI introduced a new product, the 12-inch single, which lasted up to 15 minutes, and contained several different versions (or mixes) of a song or piece of music. When CD singles appeared in the 1980s, the concept of presenting different mixes on a single disc had become well established and a standard method of release: effectively, the record industry had re-invented the extended-play (EP) record.

Hot Chocolate, RAK Records' most successful hit makers.

Miss You

LICENCES

As it had at other moments of relative weakness in its popular music business, the Company developed and extended its American licensing deals. The new deals negotiated included a 1974 agreement with MCA covering labels such as MCA, Brunswick, Coral and Ace of Hearts. The top MCA artists at that time included Cher, Rick Nelson, Brenda Lee and Buffy St Marie. In addition to this roster of current talent, the deal gave EMI access to MCA's impressive back catalogue, which included recordings by Buddy Holly, Neil Diamond, Al Jolson, Jack Jones, Louis Armstrong, Bing Crosby and Judy Garland. Also in 1974, EMI concluded a licensing deal with Elektra which brought Judy Collins, Carly Simon and Bread to the catalogue. Among the other important licensing deals concluded during the 1970s were ones with labels such as Bell, Stax and Fantasy.

The mid-1960s group Davy Jones and the Lower Third: David Bowie's first incarnation.

In 1977, EMI pulled off a coup when it signed a recording and distribution deal with the Rolling Stones for their next six albums which included the records they had previously released on their own label. The Rolling Stones' first recording session under the new deal took place at the Company's studios in Paris. Bob Mercer, one of EMI's senior executives, recalled how they worked:

In October 1977 they started to work – usually from two or four in the morning for around nine hours. They set up as though they were doing a live show, recording straight off with no over-dubbing at that stage. Within eight weeks they had finished – and they had enough for two albums, not one. [David Lewin, "Personal View", *EMI News*, October 1978]

Some of the songs they recorded were written by Mick Jagger actually during the course of the recording sessions. Jagger had been working on others such as "Far away eyes", for years. The album which contained that song and another classic Stones single, "Miss You", was *Some Girls* (Rolling Stones, CUN 39108), which was released in 1978. Subsequent new albums released by EMI included *Emotional Rescue* (Rolling Stones, CUN 39111) in July 1980, *Tattoo You* (Rolling Stones, CUN 39114) in September 1981 and *Still Life* (Rolling Stones, CUN 39115) in June 1982. In April 1980 EMI also re-released five earlier albums, including *Black and Blue* (Rolling Stones, CUN 59106). The Rolling Stones eventually disbanded their record label and signed with another record company; however, they later resumed their association with EMI through their contract with Virgin Records.

In the 1980s, EMI achieved another artistic coup with the signing of David Bowie, and the acquisition of a substantial interest in his existing catalogue of recordings. This material arrived just as EMI was beginning a major expansion of its CD rock and pop catalogues. These new format recordings gave fresh life to the Bowie material (and to many other pop and rock recordings), with several achieving sales exceeding those of the original vinyl albums. The signing coincided with Bowie's return to more commercial sounds. His highly successful EMI hits include 1983's album and single *Let's Dance* (EMI America EA

152), "China Girl" (EMI America EA 157), "Modern Love" (EMI America EA 158) and the Live Aid contribution "Dancing in the Street" (EMI America EA 204).

Break Every Rule

COMPILATIONS

The Music for Pleasure phenomenon convinced the Company that an important market existed for the re-issue of deleted repertoire. This idea evolved into re-releases of previously released material, either in the form of singles, or collections by a group or solo performer – like *The Beach Boys' Greatest Hits* (World Records ST 21628); or a variety of recordings reflecting a theme – such as dance or disco music. In 1976, the compilation idea was extended when recordings began being marketed through television advertising. That year, EMI launched the so-called "TV Concept Album" as a premium-priced product, with a £100,000 advertising campaign and high expectations of volume sales. Once again, the ever popular Beach Boys led the way, with *The Beach Boys' 20 Golden Greats* (EMI EMTV 1). This album went to the number one spot in the album charts, remained there for 10 weeks and earned a platinum disc. Following on from this success, EMI released Glen Campbell's *Twenty Golden Greats* (EMI EMTV 2), which also obtained a platinum disc. EMI continued to release compilations assembled from material by its most popular artists. Later, the classical repertoire was exploited in the same way, particularly in the *Classic Experience* series.

IRON MAIDEN

★

Formed in London in 1976, Iron Maiden made their debut at the Cart & Horses pub in Stratford the following year. It was not until 1980 that the band's talent translated into record sales, with the single "Running Free" (EMI 5032) reaching number 34 in the British charts. This resulted in Maiden's first live appearance on *Top of the Pops*, the line-up then consisted of Paul Di'anno (vocals), Steve Harris (bass), Dave Murray (guitar), Dennis Straton (guitar) and Clive Burr (drums). Maiden's eponymous first album was even more successful, reaching number four in the British charts. Their 1982 release, *Number of the Beast* (EMI EMC 3357), pushed the band to the forefront of the new wave of British heavy metal; with Di'anno replaced by Bruce Dickinson and Straton by Adrian Smith, the album's title-track (EMI 5287) and "Run to the Hills" (EMI 5263) proved major British hits. Backed by further success (and their mascot "Eddie"), Iron Maiden now devoted much of their time to world tours. After a slight musical departure with *Somewhere in Time* (1986, EMI EMC 3512) and *Seventh Son of a Seventh Son* (1988, EMI EMD 1006), the band returned to their old formula with *No Prayer for the Dying* (1990, EMI EMD 1017) and *Fear of the Dark* (1992, EMI EDEMD 1032). Both albums spawned massive hit singles, the former's "Bring Your Daughter to the Slaughter" (EMI EMPD 171) being Iron Maiden's only British number one. Dickinson's replacement by Blaze Bayley in 1995 has so far led to one album, *The X-Factor* (EMI CD EMD 1087).

In 1983, the concept was further expanded with the *Now That's What I Call Music* series of records, which was conceived as a joint venture with Virgin Records and PolyGram. These collaborations gave the record-buying public access to anthologies of recent and current hit singles by the best of the three companies' artists, as well as tracks licensed from elsewhere. By the end of 1996, the series had reached Volume 35 and had achieved unprecedented success. Each of these compilations was awarded a platinum disc and, by 1995, cumulative sales of the whole series were approaching 30 million copies.

Private Dancer

THE EIGHTIES

At the beginning of the 1980s, Cliff Richard was still EMI's best-selling popular artist. He was closely followed by other established performers, such as the Beatles, Paul McCartney and Wings, Queen, Diana Ross and Pink Floyd. Between them, these artists accounted for almost half of all EMI's sales of popular music. Once again, the Company had to struggle to reassert its creative potential and stay at the cutting edge of British popular music. One of the new waves in the industry was heavy metal, which EMI was able to plug into with the group Iron Maiden (see box, page 343). Their first album, *Iron Maiden* (EMI EMC 3330), released in 1980, marked the start of a long and fruitful association with the Company. Iron Maiden's creativity was so great that, for much of the 1980s, they were able to release an album every year, together with several PMI-produced videos.

The Company also benefited from its American Capitol and Liberty-United catalogues. New American performers emerging from these sources were Bob Seger and the Silver Bullet Band, Kim Carnes, Kenny Rogers, the Knack and, most impressively, Tina Turner (see box, page 345). EMI's two most important British female pop artists during the period were Kate Bush (see box, page 346) and Sheena Easton. The singer-songwriter Kate Bush was spotted at the age of 15 by David Gilmour of Pink Floyd and, after being nurtured by EMI for several years, she began her recording career aged 19 in 1977. Her first single, "Wuthering Heights" (EMI 2719), was released in 1978, and was an immediate number one hit. This was followed by the first of her many albums, *The Kick Inside* (EMI EMC 3223), which launched her successful international career. Uniquely, Sheena Easton's climb to the top as a pop artist was chronicled by BBC television, who charted her progress from audition to first hit

TINA TURNER
(BORN 1939)

Tina Turner has pursued a remarkable career over the past four decades, and is still going strong. Just like the song says, Anna Mae Bullock was born in Brownsville, Tennessee, and raised in the "li'l ol town" of Nutbush. Relocating to St Louis in 1956, Anna got her first break four years later when a session singer booked to record Ike Turner's "A Fool in Love" didn't show. She stepped in, a rhythm and blues hit and American top thirty pop crossover ensued, and the Ike and Tina Turner Revue was born. The duo's recording activity in the 1960s and 1970s was prolific, the seminal "River Deep, Mountain High" being a case in point. However, the violent disintegration of the Turners' marriage ended their collaboration and in the summer of 1976 Tina went solo. With the help of the young Australian manager Roger Davies, whom she met in 1979, Tina Turner rediscovered the form of her best recordings. The 1984 album *Private Dancer* (Capitol TINA 1), with its lead-off single "What's love got to do with it" (Capitol CL 334), sold over 11 million copies worldwide. Tina's 1989 release "Foreign Affair" (Capitol ESTU 2103) also proved to be massively successful, debuting in the British charts at number one and going multi-platinum in 14 countries. Her more recent collaboration with Bono and the Edge to record the "Goldeneye" theme (Capitol CDR 007) produced yet another hit single in the British and foreign charts. Tina's continuing success is best explained by her own maxim in her 1996 *Wildest Dreams* album (Capitol CD EST 2279): "What you want, work towards it, that's my attitude".

record. She launched her international career with her 1981 album *Take My Time* (EMI EMC 3354), which had world sales totalling one million within a year of its release. International sales of Sheena Easton's single "When he shines" (EMI 5166) exceeded two million copies.

Duran Duran (see box, page 348) formed part of a fresh wave of talent that took Britain and the United States by storm. They became so popular that, in the early years of the decade, their records accounted for almost 12 per cent of EMI's British record sales. Of their many hit records, the single "Is there something I should know" (EMI 5371) and album *Seven and the Ragged Tiger* (EMI CDP 7 46015 2) reached number one in the singles and album charts. Other successful British artists recording for EMI at

KATE BUSH
(BORN 1958)

★

Kate Bush's ethereal voice and conspicuous song-writing ability established her as one of the most successful British female artists of the 1980s. Born in Bexleyheath, Kent, in 1958, Kate had violin lessons and studied mime and dance under Lindsey Kemp. Her first single, "Wuthering Heights" (EMI 2719), was released in January 1978, became a number one hit and catapulted her to overnight fame. A European tour in 1979 was followed by the release of her third album, *Never Forever* (EMI EMA 7964), which similarly entered the charts at number one. Its follow-up, *The Dreaming* (EMI EMC 3419), saw Kate move into production. Her self-produced 1985 album *The Hounds of Love* (EMI KAB 1) cemented her reputation as an international star. Containing the enormous hit singles "Running up that Hill" (EMI KB 1) and "Cloudbursting" (EMI KB 2), it demonstrated the musical experimentation that is the core of her art. It also paved the way for a memorable duet with Peter Gabriel on the top ten hit "Don't Give Up" (1986, Virgin PGS 2). Like much of Kate's work, the 1989 album *The Sensual World* (EMI EMD 1010), was inspired by literature (this time James Joyce's *Ulysses*); it became her seventh top ten album. A career-encompassing boxed set *This Woman's Work* (EMI CDS 7 95237 2) was released the following year. *The Red Shoes* (1993, EMI CDEMD 1047), written in conjunction with a 50-minute film *The Line, the Curve and the Cross*, testifies to her continuing musical output; Kate's latest venture encapsulates the experimentalism which has characterized her recording career.

this time included Thomas Dolby, New Model Army, Whitesnake, Jaki Graham, Eddy Grant, Morrissey and Marillion.

During the 1980s Kraftwerk, a German experimental group, created a new musical form by marrying new computer-based technology with a unique robotic style. As a *MixMag* article noted in 1991: "Here is a sparse electric groove that will show up a lot of today's techno records for what they really are – poor imitations of the original." In 1982, their single "The Model" (EMI 5207) became a number one hit in Britain, making Kraftwerk the first German band ever to reach the top of the British singles charts, and their album *Man Machine* sold 100,000 copies in Britain, and twice that number in France.

After 1985, The Pet Shop Boys – Neil Tennant and Chris Lowe (see box, page 349) – became the brightest British pop act in the EMI firmament with an innovative style based on computer-derived musical orchestrations. They combined hardware such as synthesizers, sequencers and samplers with traditional pop vocals. The Pet Shop Boys enjoyed a string of successful albums and singles, including *Actually* (Parlophone PCSD 104) and *Disco* (EMI PRG 1001), and by 1987, were EMI's top-selling artists. This talented duo has continued to develop with regular releases.

Above The British singer Sheena Easton was launched on her international career after Esther Rantsen's *That's Life* TV series featured her arrival at EMI.

Above, left Former Smiths singer Morrissey revived the HMV label for his solo recordings.

Left The 1980s British rock group Whitesnake developed a softer kind of rock music centred on ballads and anthems.

DURAN DURAN

★

Formed in Birmingham during 1978 by
Nick Rhodes (born Nick Bates; keyboards)
and John Taylor (guitar), the pop quintet
finally settled in 1980 with the addition of
Roger Taylor (drums), Andy Taylor (guitar)
and Birmingham University drama student
Simon Le Bon (vocals). They took their
name from a character in the 1967 movie
Barbarella, and their debut single, "Planet
Earth" (EMI 5137), reached the British top
twenty. The vanguard of the "new romantic"
movement, Duran Duran's eclectic mix
of guitar and dance music was also ideally
suited to the then new music video format.
In 1981, they secured three more hit singles,
and their eponymous debut album (EMI
EMC 3372) became the first of five to reach
the top ten in Britain and the United States.
The band's massive teen popularity spanned
the Atlantic for much of the 1980s, when
they scored a total of 16 British and 10
American top 20 singles, including "Is there
something I should know" (EMI 5371), "The
Reflex" (EMI DURAN 2) (in 1984 number
one on both sides of the Atlantic) and "View
to a Kill" (Parlophone DURAN 007). In 1986
Andy and Roger Taylor departed, but the
remaining trio continued with the *Notorious*
album (EMI DDN 331), whose title-track
(EMI DDN 45) and "I don't want your love"
(EMI YOUR 1) became hits. Warren
Cuccurullo and Sterling Campbell later joined
and in 1990, the group's album *Liberty*
(Parlophone PCSD 112) became a top ten
album hit. In 1993, their more reflective
album *Duran Duran* (*The Wedding Album*)
(Parlophone CDDB 34) finally stifled the
critics who had dismissed the band as a
transient pop sensation.

Right The German group Kraftwerk
pioneered computer-generated electronic
music in the 1970s and early 1980s.

The Great Escape

THE BRITISH COMPANY IN THE 1990S

The 1990s has witnessed the arrival of prodigious new talent on
the EMI roster. After the exceptional success of 1994 in which
Blur (see box, page 351) and Eternal each sold in excess of two
million copies worldwide, 1995 ushered in further advances.
Radiohead followed up their debut album, *Pablo Honey*
(Parlophone CDP 7 81409 2), with the critically acclaimed *The
Bends* (Parlophone CDPCS 7372), and Oxford's other aspiring
stars, Supergrass, released an inspired debut album, *I should Coco*
(Parlophone CDPCS 7373) which contained a series of smash
hits. Supergrass's parallel achievements in the British singles
chart were mirrored by the success of other EMI groups, such as
Reel 2 Reel, Terrorvision and Shampoo, whose "bubblegum"
popularity in Japan has reached remarkable proportions.

PET SHOP BOYS

★

On 19 August 1981 disco fanatic Chris Lowe
met *Smash Hits* journalist Neil Tennant in an
electronics shop on the King's Road,
London. The duo adopted the name Pet
Shop Boys because they "thought it sounded
like an English rap group". A subsequent
meeting with prolific New York dance
producer Bobby Orlando in 1983 spawned
"West End Girls", an instant club hit.
The group were signed to Parlophone and
re-recorded the track (Parlophone R 6115),
which became a British and American
number one, selling 1.5 million copies and
scooping an armful of awards. A string of
successes followed, which included the
singles "It's a Sin" (Parlophone R 6158) and
the Elvis Presley remake "Always on my
Mind" (Parlophone R 6171), both of which
topped the British charts. Collaborations
with Dusty Springfield and Liza Minelli also
proved highly fruitful. In 1989 the duo finally
went on tour, working with film-maker
Derek Jarman to produce what they termed
a "theatrical concert". Then, after the 1990
album *Behaviour* (Parlophone PCSD 113),
the Pet Shop Boys spent the following year
launching their own record label Spaghetti.
Returning in 1993 with the number one
studio album *Very* (Parlophone CD PSD
143), they scored another massive hit
with the anthemic single "Go West"
(CD R 6356). The long-awaited *Bilingual*
album (CD PCSD 170) was released in
1996 and has added to the Pet Shop Boys'
cumulative sales of 24 million albums
worldwide. They are the most successful
pop duo of all time, with four British number
ones and 25 top thirty singles.

Left Radiohead, currently one of EMI's top acts,
achieved their initial fame on the United States
college circuit in the early 1990s.

Above Sir Cliff Richard today.

Above, right 1990s soul singers Eternal meeting with Pope John Paul II.

Right Garth Brooks, Capitol Records' biggest selling artist of the 1990s.

In 1996, Babylon Zoo dominated the British singles charts with its number one hit "Spaceman". This highly individualistic brand of dance was showcased in the album *Disgraceful* (EMI CD 7243 8 35216 2 3). EMI's centenary year starts with promising new and talented performers, including Mansun, Phil Campbell, Kaydee, Murray Lachlan Young and a host of others on the brink of stardom.

Notwithstanding EMI's many new artists and the increasing diversity of popular music, established artists continue to attract record consumers in large numbers. In 1993, Cliff Richard released a new album called simply *The Album* (EMI CDP 7 89114 2), it immediately went to the number one spot in the British album charts. Almost 32 years earlier, EMI had released Cliff Richard's fifth album *21 Today*, his first album to go to the top of the then newly created album charts.

BLUR

Formed in London at the end of the 1980s, Seymour (as they were then known) comprised Damon Albarn (vocals), Alex James (bass), Graham Coxon (guitar) and Dave Rowntree (drums). Renamed Blur in 1989, the group drew its influences from Manchester and the burgeoning Indie "shoegazing" scene. After a top ten hit with their second single, "There's no other way", (CD FOOD 29), Blur's debut album *Leisure* (FOOD CD 6) entered the British charts at number two in 1991. A miserable US tour and the failure of the subsequent single "Popscene" (CD FOOD 37) caused some to write off the band as a one-album wonder. However, 1993's *Modern Life is Rubbish* (FOOD CD 9), with its attendant singles "For Tomorrow" (CD FOOD 40) and "Chemical World" (CD FOOD 45), proved them wrong. Demonstrating a quality of songwriting absent from *Leisure*, this album pushed Blur's "shoegazing" phase was pushed aside to reveal a more experimental and individual sound. Blur's diversity of talent was revealed in their 1994 album *Parklife* (FOOD CD 10). A considerable commercial success, *Parklife* featured the disco-beat of "Girls and Boys" (CD FOOD 47), the Cockney swagger of "Parklife" (with Phil Daniels) and the romance of "To the End" (CD FOOD 50). Their follow-up the next year was *The Great Escape* (FOOD CD 14), in which Blur continued to mine this rich musical vein, scoring yet another hit with the number one single "Country House". In 1997 Blur's eponymously titled fifth album (FOOD CD 19) topped the charts.

Notable famous names which also continue to sell extremely well include the Beatles, Pink Floyd and Queen. The combination of successful new and established artists has proved a powerful one: EMI's British subsidiary was awarded the Queen's Award for Export Achievement in 1994, an award it had last won in 1978.

This extraordinary continuity amid great change, remarkable even among established performers, can also be discerned in the work of artists such as Blur, EMI's most successful British pop group of the mid-1990s. Blur's music and performance style have wide appeal across age and generation barriers. Consciously or unconsciously, they have mined a much older musical tradition – music hall. One hundred years on, their albums – *Parklife* (FOOD CD 10) and *The Great Escape* (FOOD CD 14) – contain discernible echoes of the earliest popular music records, as well as of the group which created modern British popular music, the Beatles. It would clearly be impossible for the shades of great music hall performers and other popular artists of the past to appreciate the revolution in the art of sound recording that has taken place since their day. However, they would have little difficulty in identifying something of their own art in Blur's music. Although the technology of the messenger may have moved on, the message remains the same.

Select Bibliography and Suggested Further Reading

Journals and Magazines

Gramophone (published monthly by *Gramophone* Publications).
International Classical Record Collector (published quarterly by *Gramophone* Publications).
International Opera Collector (published quarterly by *Gramophone* Publications).
Hillandale News (published six times a year by the City of London Phonograph and Gramophone Society).

Books

John Culshaw *Putting the Record Straight* (London 1981).
Ed. Colin Larkin *The Guinness Encyclopedia of Popular Music*, 6 volumes (London 1995).
Mark Lewisohn *The Complete Beatles Recording Sessions* (London 1988).
George Martin *All You Need Is Ears* (London 1978).
George Martin *Summer of Love* (London 1994).
S. A. Pandit *From Making to Music: the History of THORN EMI* (London 1996).
Christopher Proudfoot *Collecting Phonographs and Gramophones* (London 1980).
Mike Read, Nigel Goodall and Peter Lewry *Cliff Richard – The Complete Chronicle* (London 1993).
Tim Rice, Paul Gambaccini and Jonathan Rice *The Guinness Book of British Hit Singles* (London 1995).
Ed. Stanley Sadie *The New Grove Dictionary of Music and Musicians*, 20 volumes (London 1980).
Elisabeth Schwarzkopf *On and Off the Record* (London 1982).
Michael Scott *The Record of Singing*, 2 volumes (London 1977 & 1979).
Brian Southall, Allan Rouse and Peter Vince *Abbey Road* (London 1997).
J. B. Steane *The Grand Tradition: Seventy Years of Singing on Record* (London 1974).

Annual Publications

Gramophone Classical Catalogue Master Edition (Entertainment Data Publishing Ltd).
The Penguin Guide to Compact Discs (Penguin Books).
The Gramophone Classical Good CD Guide (*Gramophone* Publications).

Index

Figures followed by asterisks refer to illustrations

Index

Index